Collections for Young Scholars®

FRAMEWORK FOR EFFECTIVE TEACHING®

Kindergarten: Sounds and Letters
Teacher's Guide

Collections for young Scholars®

FRAMEWORK FOR EFFECTIVE TEACHING®

Kindergarten: Sounds and Letters
Teacher's Guide

PROGRAM AUTHORS
Marilyn Jager Adams
Carl Bereiter
Jan Hirshberg
Valerie Anderson
Robbie Case

CONSULTING AUTHORS
Michael Pressley
Marsha Roit
Iva Carruthers
Bill Pinkney

**Open Court
Publishing
Company**
Chicago and Peru, Illinois

CHAIRMAN
M. Blouke Carus

PRESIDENT
André W. Carus

EDUCATION DIRECTOR
Carl Bereiter

SENIOR EXECUTIVE EDITOR
Sheelagh McGurn

EDITORIAL DEVELOPMENT
Learning in Motion

SUPERVISOR, EDITORIAL SERVICES
Rebecca Blankenhorn

PROJECT EDITOR
Fran Lehr

ART DIRECTOR
John Grandits

VICE-PRESIDENT, PRODUCTION
AND MANUFACTURING
Chris Vancalbergh

PERMISSIONS COORDINATOR
Diane Sikora

COVER ARTIST
Nelle Davis

DESIGN
Diane Hutchinson

ISBN 0-8126-0343-5   4 5 6 7 8 9 10

Contents

Using Open Court's *Collections for Young Scholars*®

A Program for the 21st Century

Open Court's *Collections for Young Scholars*® represents a profound departure from mainstream reading programs. Its completely new approach to the teaching of reading demands more of students. Yet if a reading program is to prepare students to lead productive lives in twenty-first century society, it must be demanding. Basic literacy skills are not enough. Traditional approaches are not adequate.

Students who experience *Collections for Young Scholars*

- learn how to read and respond to a variety of text
- acquire strategies for accessing information and for exploring concepts from many areas of knowledge—including some that do not even exist today
- learn how to communicate effectively in both oral and written language
- learn how to work both independently and collaboratively
- give sustained effort to thinking and problem solving

THE PRINCIPLES

Collections for Young Scholars is built upon principles that reflect the consensus of leading literacy researchers and practitioners on what is essential for reading success.

No Assumptions

In *Collections for Young Scholars,* initial reading instruction relies on the explicit teaching of sounds, on the blending of sounds into words, and on the leverage of using this knowledge for reading and writing.

For phonics instruction to work, it has to be systematic. It cannot start somewhere in the middle. It cannot assume that children will "pick it up somehow." *Collections for Young Scholars* does not assume that children already know the letters or can distinguish individual sounds. It systematically teaches letter knowledge and phonemic awareness before and during the introduction of sound/letter associations. The introduction of sounds and letters is also systematic. And, because young students find it difficult to analyze the phonemic structure of words, the program offers direct instruction in blending. The teaching of writing begins with interactive dictation. All of these techniques are used together in predictable and recurring activities that teach the children how to think about the sound/letter associations and about their connections with word meanings.

Authentic Literacy Experiences

Along with systematic instruction in the sound/letter associations, children participate daily in reading-aloud activities with authentic, high-quality literature in Big Books and student anthologies. Beginning in kindergarten, the children experience a range of text genres, including nonfiction. There are also many opportunities for writing, allowing the children to understand the uses of writing even as they are learning to write. These experiences help to reinforce children's print awareness and their understanding of the structure and conventions of written language.

Throughout the program, the children are encouraged to construct meaning by interacting with and responding to outstanding literature. They read widely, write frequently, and listen and speak effectively. The focus is always on building knowledge rather than on routinized performance.

Integrated Instruction

The use of learning frameworks, or predictable teaching techniques, ensures substantive integration of instruction. Lessons in which learning is presented as isolated, unrelated bits and pieces are replaced with learning units tied to important concepts that call on students to make connections across all areas of the curriculum and to acquire knowledge that can be used beyond a single lesson. Activities within a unit are integrated through reading, writing, discussion, and exploration activities that become increasingly complex and demanding.

Intentional Learning

Learning to read empowers children. Learning to learn enables them to use that power intelligently and to take charge of their own lives and their own learning process as soon as possible. In *Collections for Young Scholars,* learning is the goal of instruction, rather than an incidental outcome. The children explore critical areas for depth and understanding rather than march through large amounts of material for superficial learning. The intent of instruction is to engage the children in the kinds of activities that will prepare them for the reading, thinking, and problem-solving typical of real-world situations.

Support and Challenge for *All* Students

Collections for Young Scholars is designed so that every child is able to participate fully in class. No child gets bogged down in repetitive practice. Grouping is flexible and based on interest, not ability. The top priority of the program is to give all children important insights into the vast amount of knowledge available so that they can set learning goals for themselves.

Diverse and individual needs are met by varying the time and intensity of instruction, not by using watered down content or by having the children read simplified and pointless texts or complete boring, repetitive skill sheets. In addition, the children have access to a variety of activities that provide for differing language proficiencies and abilities.

Multicultural activities are a natural part of the curriculum, not an add-on, and these activities enable students to appreciate the contributions to society of all cultural and ethnic groups. Children for whom English is the primary language work with and learn from their classmates who are learning English as a second language. Conversely, English Language Learners have opportunities to practice their new language in an environment in which their ideas and contributions are sought and valued by their classmates and teacher.

Plentiful and Relevant Practice Opportunities

It is important to give children time during the day in which to practice what they are learning. Time for practice, called Workshop, is an integral part of *Collections for Young Scholars.* In Workshop, the children work independently, collaboratively, or with the teacher to practice and review material taught in their lessons. Practice materials are also important, and the program contains a number of such materials that can be used by individual children or small groups as needed.

The goal is to use all class time as efficiently and productively as possible. No time is wasted on mindless repetition and seatwork.

Teacher Leadership, Collaborative Learning

In *Collections for Young Scholars* classrooms, the learning environment is established by the teacher. The powerful learning frameworks in the program help you to focus the children's attention on real learning and away from busywork. The program encourages you to model how to pursue both personal and collaborative learning and how to communicate that learning to others. Equally important, the program provides children with ample opportunities to learn from and work with classmates in collaborative learning groups. These groups allow children to work on topics of mutual interest, to share ideas, and to help each other gain understanding of complex concepts. Learning groups composed of both English-proficient students and English Language Learners encourage the children to learn more about each other's languages and backgrounds and make it possible for those learning English to ask questions they might be reluctant to raise in a whole-class setting. Carefully structured activities involve special-needs children in learning groups in ways that make their ideas and efforts crucial to the group's success.

Home/School Connections

Families are kept informed of their children's classroom activities and are consulted on matters of importance to their children. Homework assignments are extended in ways that invite family members to become closely involved in their children's learning. In turn, families are expected to participate actively in helping their children attain full literacy.

High Expectations, Positive Assessment

Children perform to the level of expectations set by their surroundings. It is unfair to them not to expect their best. Open Court has a long tradition of respecting the intelligence of children and of teachers. *Collections for Young Scholars* continues that tradition by providing high-quality literature and meaning-based, relevant activities that honor the abilities of the program's users.

Although expectations are high, assessment is positive. It focuses on what the children do right, not on what they do wrong. Above all, it helps them to move continuously up the learning ladder.

THE LEARNING FRAMEWORKS

In *Collections for Young Scholars,* principles are translated into instruction by means of powerful learning frameworks, or teaching techniques that recur frequently. The use of learning frameworks frees the children to focus on the content of a lesson without the distraction of learning a new format for its presentation. The framework used to introduce key skills and concepts is also used to present increasingly complex or expanded versions of the skills and concepts as the children progress through the curriculum. For you, this means that the time spent setting up a lesson is minimized.

In each teacher's guide, the learning frameworks are noted by an asterisk (✱). The learning frameworks for kindergarten through grade 6 are shown in the following chart, with the kindergarten frameworks highlighted. The kindergarten learning frameworks are discussed in detail on pages 28F–33F.

The Learning Frameworks

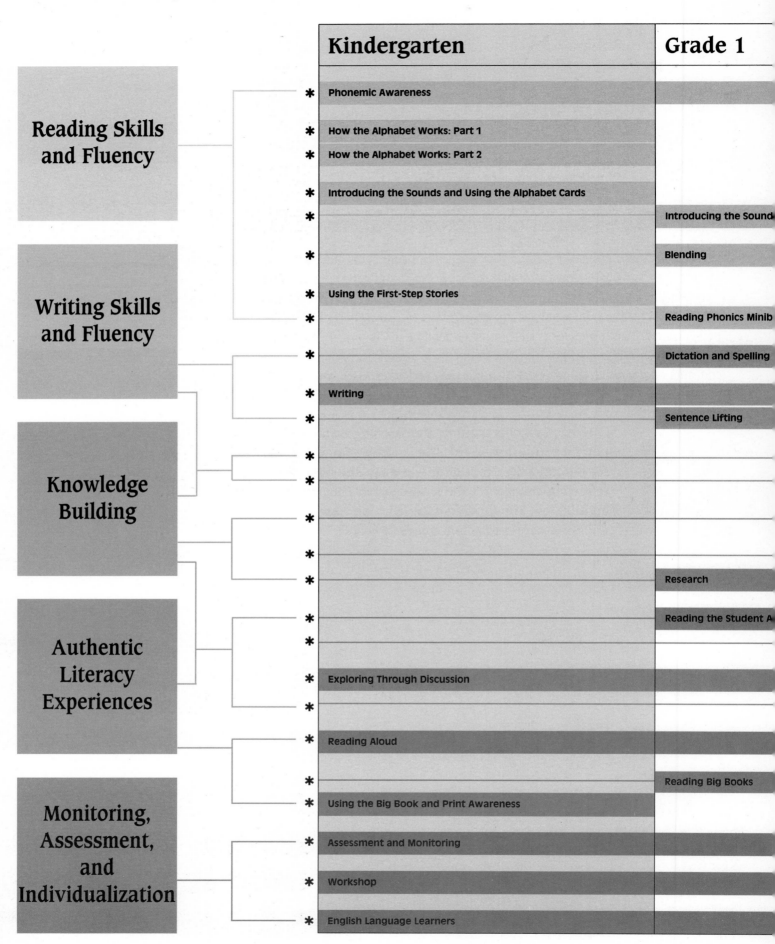

	Kindergarten	Grade 1
	Reading Skills and Fluency	
*	Phonemic Awareness	
*	How the Alphabet Works: Part 1	
*	How the Alphabet Works: Part 2	
*	Introducing the Sounds and Using the Alphabet Cards	
*		Introducing the Sound
*		Blending
*	Using the First-Step Stories	
*		Reading Phonics Minib
*	**Writing Skills and Fluency**	Dictation and Spelling
*	Writing	
*		Sentence Lifting
*		
*	**Knowledge Building**	
*		
*		
*		Research
*		Reading the Student A
*	**Authentic Literacy Experiences**	
*	Exploring Through Discussion	
*		
*	Reading Aloud	
*		Reading Big Books
*	Using the Big Book and Print Awareness	
*	**Monitoring, Assessment, and Individualization**	
*	Assessment and Monitoring	
*	Workshop	
*	English Language Learners	

	Grade 2	Grades 3–6	
the Sound/Spelling Cards			
tep-by-Step Practice Stories			
	Writing Process		
	Writing Seminar		
	Exploring Through Reflective Activities		
	Exploring Through Research		
	Cognitive and Responsive Reading		
	Reading Roundtable		
	Formative Assessment (Separate Teacher's Guide)		

Senior Author Team

The goal is to let children in on the excitement of literacy—not just doing things they couldn't do before, but knowing things they never knew before, thinking about things they never thought about before, and understanding things they never understood before.

—Marilyn Jager Adams

Marilyn Jager Adams is a Senior Scientist in the Psychology Department at Bolt Beranek and Newman, Inc., a research and development laboratory in Cambridge, Massachusetts. She is also a Senior Research Scientist at Brown University and has been affiliated with the Center for the Study of Reading at the University of Illinois since 1975. She is the author of *Beginning to Read: Thinking and Learning About Print* (MIT Press, 1990), written on behalf of the U.S. Secretary of Education as mandated by Congress. The book, the most comprehensive study of beginning reading undertaken to date, examines instructional practices from a historical perspective and critiques them in terms of theoretical and empirical research in education, psychology, and linguistics.

Carl Bereiter is Professor at the Center for Applied Cognitive Science at the Ontario Institute for Studies in Education in Toronto and a member of the National Academy of Education. He has coauthored many curriculum projects, including Open Court's reading and mathematics programs. He is coauthor with Marlene Scardamalia of *The Psychology of Written Composition* (1987) and *Surpassing Ourselves: The Nature and Implications of Expertise* (1993); and he has published extensively on the nature of teaching and learning. Computer-supported intentional learning environments and collaborative knowledge building have been the subjects of his most recent classroom investigations and publications.

Beginning readers have a lot to learn about how written language works. But at the same time, they are fully formed human beings who wonder, think, get absorbed by a good story, and enjoy and make jokes. A good reading program will honor all these facts. This program, when taught in the right spirit, will do that.

—Carl Bereiter

In order for children to learn how to read, they have got to break the code. And by teaching them about how the sound structure of their language works, you're only making it that much easier for them to break the code.
—Jan Hirshberg

Jan Hirshberg holds an Ed.D. in reading, language, and learning disabilities from Harvard University. She has taught in elementary school classrooms and has also served as a school district reading consultant. At Harvard she was a teaching fellow, research assistant, instructor, and lecturer at the Graduate School of Education. Her reading specialties are in linguistics and early literacy. Her work has focused on how children learn to read and write and on the logistics of teaching reading and writing in the early elementary grades. She is an author of the kindergarten and grade-1 levels of Open Court's 1989 reading and writing program as well as *Collections for Young Scholars.*

Robbie Case is Professor of Education at Stanford University and Director of the Laidlaw Centre at the Institute of Child Study, University of Toronto. He received his Ph.D. from the Ontario Institute for Studies in Education. He has conducted research on the relationship between children's learning and their cognitive development during the elementary school years. His books and scholarly articles on that topic have been translated into many languages, and he has received many awards, including a Guggenheim Fellowship. His current work focuses on the special instructional needs of children from low socioeconomic status homes during their first two years of schooling.

For too long we have had to choose between education that is child centered and education that is teacher centered. What we need is a new generation of curricula: one which honors children's natural way of understanding the world—but which also does justice to their thirst for learning, and the responsiveness to direct instruction by caring adults.
—Robbie Case

Young children need to learn to do more than simply go through the motions of reading and writing. They need to learn to take an active role in the wondering, problem solving, and responsiveness that literate people engage in as they read and write.
—Valerie Anderson

Valerie Anderson is Research Associate at the Centre for Applied Cognitive Science at the Ontario Institute for Studies in Education and is on the editorial advisory boards of *The Reading Teacher* and *The Journal of Reading Behavior.* Anderson has extensive experience both in designing curricula and in training teachers. She has been coauthor of a number of curriculum projects, including *Thinking Games* (with Carl Bereiter), *The Reading Connection,* and *Catching On.* Her main professional focus is on training teachers how to apply the latest educational theories in their classrooms. Her most recent work with children has centered on helping them learn to use thinking strategies to become independent readers.

Consulting Authors

You've got to have a dream. And when you have a dream, you've got to find out what it takes to make that dream come true. Everything takes something. There's no free lunch. It's not just going to happen. You're going to have to do something. And, if you're willing to pay that price, you can make the dream a reality. —Bill Pinkney

Michael Pressley is Professor of Educational Psychology and Statistics at the State University of New York at Albany, as well as Principal Investigator for the National Reading Research Center, centralized at the Universities of Maryland and Georgia. He does both basic laboratory research on cognition and learning and applied work in educational settings. Memory development and reading comprehension strategies have received much of his attention.

Marsha Roit spends considerable time in classrooms working with children to develop and demonstrate reading and writing activities and training teachers and administrators. Her work has been published in a variety of education journals, including *Exceptional Children, Journal of Learning Disabilities, Educational Leadership,* and *The Elementary School Journal.* She has presented her work at national and international conferences.

Iva E. Carruthers is Professor and former Chairperson of the Sociology Department of Northeastern Illinois University. She is also President of Nexus Unlimited, Inc., a human resources development and computer services consulting firm, and of Ed Tech, a computer software development company. In addition to developing educational software aids for teaching history and interdisciplinary subjects, she has produced fourteen study guides on African-American and African history.

Bill Pinkney is the first African American to sail solo around the world, traveling around the five great capes in his sailboat named *Commitment.* Only forty-one individuals have accomplished this feat. More than 30,000 students across the United States were able to share in his legendary voyage, thanks to advanced satellite and computer technologies. Not only did he give these students lessons in math, science, geography, and social studies, but Captain Pinkney also modeled for them the courage, perseverance, skill, and commitment required to realize one's dreams.

Instructional Consultants

Mary Fritz
Director, Prekindergarten
Park Street School
Westbury, New York

Amy Koenning
Principal
Shallert Elementary
Alice, Texas

Ann Mintz
Language Supervisor
Howard County PSD
Ellicott City, Maryland

Ernestine Riggs
North Central Regional Educational Laboratory
Oak Brook, Illinois

Barbara Schweiger
Director, Reading
Omaha Public School District
Omaha, Nebraska

Jody Steele
Primary Principal
Gulliver Academy
Miami, Florida

Teacher Reviewers

Barbara Appleberry, *Grade 1*
Mollison Elementary School
Chicago, Illinois

Marie Beacham, *Grade 1*
Ephraim Elementary School
Ephraim, Utah

Joyce Bell, *Grade 1*
Brown School
Newburyport, Massachusetts

Peggy Clelland, *Grade 1*
Washington Terrace Elementary
   School
Ogden, Utah

Joanne Daly, *Kindergarten*
St. Mary's Academy
Glens Falls, New York

Emmy Daniel, *Grade 1*
South Shores School
Decatur, Illinois

Tony Dillon, *Grade 1*
John Foster Dulles School
Chicago, Illinois

Diane DiNicola, *Kindergarten*
Park-Dryden Early Childhood
   Center
Westbury, New York

Eileen Eagan, *Kindergarten*
Bancroft Elementary School
Omaha, Nebraska

Sr. Susan Faist, *Grade 2*
Christ the King School
Toledo, Ohio

Mary Fatsi, *Grade 1*
Brooklyn Elementary School
Brooklyn, Connecticut

Susan Fowler, *Grade 2*
Yaquina View Elementary
Newport, Oregon

Pat Garcia, *Kindergarten*
Shallert Elementary
Alice, Texas

Lena Gates, *Grade 1*
Crispus Attucks School, P.S. 21
Brooklyn, New York

Norma Gehr, *Kindergarten*
Cockranton Elementary
Cockranton, Pennsylvania

Janice Green, *Grade 1*
Francis T. Bresnahan School
Newburyport, Massachusetts

Joyce Green, *Kindergarten*
George Pullman Elementary
Chicago, Illinois

Dorothy Hines, *Grade 2*
Benefield Elementary School
Lawrenceville, Georgia

Hurtice Howard, *Grade 1*
Julia L. Armstrong Elementary
   School
Greenville, Mississippi

Nancy Hughes, *Grade 2*
Eleanor Roosevelt School
Vancouver, Washington

Celeste James, *Grade 1*
John Foster Dulles School
Chicago, Illinois

Ann Johnson, *Kindergarten*
West Friendship Elementary
   School
West Friendship, Maryland

Christine Johnson, *Grade 1*
Kelley School
Newburyport, Massachusetts

Brenda Jolly, *Kindergarten*
Stewart Elementary
Petersburg, Virginia

Carol Komperda, *Kindergarten*
Albany Avenue School
Massapequa, New York

Carole Langan, *Kindergarten*
Walnut Elementary School
Omaha, Nebraska

Charlotte Lewis, *Grade 1*
L. B. Weemes Elementary School
Los Angeles, California

Sandra Loose, *Grade 1*
Indian Lane Elementary School
Media, Pennsylvania

Kathryn Lopez, *Grade 1*
Millville Elementary School
Panama City, Florida

Pam Martin, *Grade 1*
L. B. Weemes Elementary School
Los Angeles, California

Melony Maughan, *Grade 1*
Grantswood Community School
Birmingham, Alabama

Mary McElroy, *Kindergarten*
Avalon Park Elementary School
Chicago, Illinois

Sue Miller, *Grade 1*
The Valwood School
Valdosta, Georgia

Trudy Mockert, *Grade 1*
Nicolaus Copernicus School,
    P.S. 25
Jersey City, New Jersey

Anna Molina, *Grade 1*
Ezra Nolan School, P.S. 40
Jersey City, New Jersey

Patti Neidig, *Kindergarten*
Centennial Lane Elementary
    School
Ellicott City, Maryland

Margaret Nichols, *Grade 1*
Brown School
Newburyport, Massachusetts

Cindy Noland, *Grade 2*
Jefferson Elementary School
Parkersburg, West Virginia

Bettye Nunnery, *Grade 2*
Otken Elementary School
McComb, Mississippi

Judith Palermo, *Grade 1*
St. Helen's School
Chicago, Illinois

Becky Philips, *Grade 2*
Sunderland Elementary School
Sunderland, Maryland

Stacey Phillips, *Kindergarten*
Gulliver Academy
Miami, Florida

Donna Powell, *Grade 2*
Melville School
Portsmouth, Rhode Island

Sharon Robinson, *Grade 2*
Flournoy Elementary School
Los Angeles, California

Judith Roy, *Grade 1*
Grantswood Community School
Birmingham, Alabama

Renee Rubin, *Kindergarten*
Chickering Elementary School
Dover, Massachusetts

Agnes Schutz, *Grade 1*
Alamosa Elementary School
Albuquerque, New Mexico

Ruth Seiger, *Grade 1*
Francis T. Bresnahan School
Newburyport, Massachusetts

Cheryl Sheehan, *Grade 1*
Nicolaus Copernicus School,
    P.S. 25
Jersey City, New Jersey

Cindy Silva, *Kindergarten*
Shallert Elementary
Alice, Texas

Renee Singer, *Grade 1*
Grantswood Community School
Birmingham, Alabama

Susan Sitek, *Kindergarten*
Bollman Bridge Elementary
    School
Jessup, Maryland

Jacqueline Smith, *Grade 1*
John Foster Dulles School
Chicago, Illinois

Mary Lou Strauss, *Kindergarten*
Saratoga School
Omaha, Nebraska

Inez Taylor, *Kindergarten*
Gulliver Academy
Miami, Florida

Barbara Uhrin, *Grade 2*
Amos Hutchinson Elementary
    School
Greensburg, Pennsylvania

Jimmie Walis, *Kindergarten*
Oak Hall Elementary
Ardmore, Oklahoma

Laurie Walters, *Grade 1*
L. B. Weemes Elementary School
Los Angeles, California

Maria Wentworth, *Kindergarten*
Boulevard School
Gloversville, New York

The Kindergarten Program of
Collections for Young Scholars®

The transition from oral to written communication is a milestone in the history of humankind. It is also a critical turning point in the development of an individual human being. Literacy does not displace oral communication; it supplements it and extends the range of human communication and inquiry. As it changes the nature of our thought, literacy also greatly extends the range of an individual person's ability to find things out. It makes the world much larger and richer.

Open Court's approach to this momentous transformation in the lives of students reflects the long and valuable experience of many teachers in classrooms across the country. It also reflects a generation of intense empirical research into the factors that lead to success in early reading. This research has been summarized in documents such as *Beginning to Read: Thinking and Learning About Print.*

The Open Court approach brings this research and practice together in a way that you can pick up and use. This approach has been successful in thousands of classrooms for three decades. *Collections for Young Scholars®,* while retaining the basic core of the approach that has worked so well for long, incorporates the experiences of a new generation of teachers and the wisdom of highly respected reading researchers, including Marilyn Jager Adams, the author of *Beginning to Read* and a leading proponent of balanced reading instruction.

The Open Court approach makes it clear that phonics and whole-language instruction are not mutually exclusive but complementary. To find their way into the world of written language, students need both systematic instruction in phonics *and* rich experience with authentic literature.

The kindergarten program of Open Court's *Collections for Young Scholars* offers a variety of instructional options and activities that are designed to

- introduce the children to the new role of student and to the new learning community they have become part of
- introduce the children to the alphabet and how it works
- provide the children with essential exposure to how the sounds of the language work together
- provide the children with early reading experiences at which they can be successful
- help the children focus not only on the importance of learning but also on the joy learning can bring to their lives

The kindergarten program of *Collections for Young Scholars* is designed as a group of self-contained modules. These modules can be combined in any number of ways to suit your particular requirements and to meet the needs of your students—however wide-ranging those needs may be. The modules can also be combined with other high-quality, commercially available kindergarten materials.

- The **Sounds and Letters** module focuses on giving children a strong foundation in phonemic awareness and on helping them to understand how the alphabet works. It is accompanied by the Big Book, *Pickled Peppers.* **You are reading the teacher's guide for the Sounds and Letters module.**

- The **Discovery**, or learning modules, cover a variety of important content area and universal concepts: School, The Wind, Shadows, Finding Friends, Stick To It, and Pictures Tell Stories. Each module is developed around Big Book and Read-Aloud selections. The teacher's guide for each module contains a variety of activities to help you develop these concepts.

- The **Story Thinking** module consists of two components: Story Crafting, a series of activities that encourage the children to think about stories and to become aware of how they work, and Willy the Wisher, which is built around *Willy the Wisher and Other Thinking Stories,* a collection of humorous interactive Read-Alouds designed to help the children recognize faulty and clear thinking. The Story Thinking module teacher's guide contains the Story Crafting activities and follow-up activities for Willy the Wisher.

The teacher's guide that accompanies each individual component contains detailed information about the materials and activities specific to each. Suggestions for ways to integrate the components and activities of the kindergarten modules are found in the program overview, *Frameworks for Effective Teaching and Learning: Kindergarten.*

The Sounds and Letters Module

Faced with an alphabetic script, children's levels of phonemic awareness on entering school may be the single most powerful determinant of their success—or failure—in learning to read.
—Marilyn Jager Adams

The Sounds and Letters module of the kindergarten program focuses on helping children learn to distinguish individual sounds, as a prerequisite for associating those sounds with letters.

THE MATERIALS

The teacher and student materials for the Sounds and Letters module give all children the foundation necessary to become enthusiastic, proficient readers and learners.

Framework for Effective Teaching®: Sounds and Letters

The teacher's guide for the Sounds and Letters module contains one hundred lessons. These lessons provide a solid foundation in phonemic awareness and print awareness and introduce sound/letter associations. The guide accompanies the Big Book *Pickled Peppers*.

Pickled Peppers

The companion Big Book for *Framework for Effective Teaching: Sounds and Letters* supports the children's developing phonemic and print awareness and invites them into the world of good literature, even before they are reading on their own. *Pickled Peppers* features selections by award-winning authors and illustrators and selections representative of various cultures. The selections include traditional songs and rhymes such as "Hickory, Dickory, Dock" (illustrated by Nadine Bernard Westcott), "Sing a Song of Sixpence" (illustrated by Barbara Garrison), "Bluebird, Bluebird" (a version of a traditional African-American ring game prepared by Cheryl Warren Mattox, illustrated by Gershom Griffith), and "Peter Piper" (illustrated by Victor Ambrus), and more contemporary works such as "There Was Once a Fish" (illustrated by Arnold Lobel), "One Hungry Monster" (written by Susan Heyboer O'Keefe, illustrated by Lynn Munsinger), and "The Top and the Tip" (written by Charlotte Zolotow, illustrated by Roz Schanzer). Multicultural selections such as "Los Pollitos" ("The Baby Chicks") (written by José-Luis Orozco, illustrated by Juana Caminos) focus on topics that every child can relate to and expand upon.

Exploring Sounds and Letters

The workbook for the Sounds and Letters module provides activities that allow the children to practice what they are learning about letter formation and sound/letter associations.

First-Step Stories

First-Step Stories are used in Sounds and Letters to provide the children with meaningful "reading" experiences before they are actually reading on their own and to increase their print awareness. There are three kinds of First-Step Stories: reprints of selections from the Sounds and Letters Big Book, *Pickled Peppers;* poems not contained in the Big Book; and wordless stories. Some First-Step Stories contain only pictures and some contain only text.

Sounds and Letters Kindergarten Kit

The lessons in the teacher's guide are supported by resources contained in the Sounds and Letters Kindergarten Kit. These resources are as follows:

- **Alphabet Cards**—brightly colored wall cards, each of which contains a picture of something that begins with the sound of the letter on the card.
- **Alphabet Flash Cards**—a set of cards for use in whole-group and small-group lessons to reinforce letter recognition.
- **Individual Alphabet-Sound Cards**—sets of cards for the children to use in sound/letter matching activities. Each card contains an Alphabet Card picture on one side and its corresponding letter on the other side.

- **Uppercase and Lowercase Letter Cards**—sets of uppercase and lowercase cards for use by the children in various activities.
- **Lion Puppet**—for use with phonemic awareness activities.
- **Game Mats**—plasticized maps for use with alphabet and sound recognition games.
- **Pickled Peppers Poster**—a colorful and fun wall-poster rendition of the characters on the Alphabet Cards.
- **Listening Collections Audiocassette**—a tape that contains the music and words to songs from the Big Book, *Pickled Peppers*.

The Sounds and Letters Kindergarten Kit also contains a Teacher Toolbox that can be removed from the larger box and kept on your desk for easy reference. The Teacher Toolbox contains:

- *Frameworks for Effective Teaching and Learning: Kindergarten*—an overview of the kindergarten program that provides you with help in deciding how to arrange your day, week, and year and how to incorporate the various components and activities of the kindergarten modules.
- **Learning Framework Cards**—reference tools in convenient card format that contain descriptions and discussions of the key learning frameworks used throughout Sounds and Letters (see pages 28F–33F). The cards also contain suggestions for applying the learning framework to other areas of the curriculum and for working with English Language Learners.
- **Teacher Tool Cards**—cards that provide words and music to songs used in Sounds and Letters lessons, as well as suggestions for using the songs; instructions for playing the games used in the module; and classroom support activities for letter formation, using the Pocket Chart, teacher conferencing, and alphabet activities.
- **Reproducible Masters: Activity Sheets**—masters of activities for use in Workshop.
- **Reproducible Masters: Sounds and Letters**—masters that contain figures and pieces of games to be cut out and used with various activities.
- **Home/School Connection: Sounds and Letters**—reproducible masters of materials, in both English and Spanish, to help you keep the children's families informed of class lessons and activities.
- **Cumulative Class Folder**—a convenient folder for your use in recording the children's progress in phonemic awareness, print awareness, and writing.

Pocket Chart Kit

The Pocket Chart Kit serves as an invaluable tool to help you and your students get the most out of the print awareness and rhyming activities in Sounds and Letters. Each Pocket Chart Kit includes:

- **A Pocket Chart**—a large canvas chart with pockets in which Letter Cards, Picture Cards, and Word Cards can be manipulated by you and the children.
- **Pocket Chart Letter Cards**—a set of large-sized Letter Cards, more suitable for use on the chart than are the smaller individual sets of Letter Cards.
- **Picture Cards**—cards that contain brightly colored pictures that tie into many of the selections in *Pickled Peppers,* but can also be used in activities of your own making.
- **Word Cards**—cards that also tie into many of the selections from *Pickled Peppers.* They can be used by you and the children to recreate lines from the selection or to make up sentences.

Getting Started

Instruction in the kindergarten program of *Collections for Young Scholars®* is organized by way of key techniques, or learning frameworks that recur frequently. The key learning frameworks for Sounds and Letters are:

1. Phonemic Awareness
   1A. Oral Blending
2. Reading Aloud
3. Using the Big Book and Print Awareness
4. Introducing the Sounds and Using the Alphabet Cards
5. How the Alphabet Works: Part 1
6. How the Alphabet Works: Part 2
7. Writing
8. Using the First-Step Stories
9. Exploring Through Discussion
10. Workshop
11. Assessment and Monitoring
12. English Language Learners

Organizing instruction by learning frameworks means that by varying the time and intensity of instruction, individual and special needs can be addressed without ability grouping. All children in the classroom receive the same high-quality learning experiences. However, because children learning English occasionally require extra help, the teacher's guide provides **Teaching Tips for English Language Learners** whenever the tips are appropriate for a specific lesson.

Throughout the *Framework for Effective Teaching®: Sounds and Letters* teacher's guide, the learning frameworks are noted with an asterisk (✱). In addition, Learning Framework Cards found in the Teacher Toolbox of the Sounds and Letters Kindergarten Kit contain detailed discussions of each learning framework.

The learning frameworks incorporate and develop all key areas of instruction in Sounds and Letters. Although the learning frameworks are each clearly identifiable, as the chart on pages 12F–13F shows, they often overlap to reinforce learning of key skills and concepts:

Reading Skills and Fluency

Reading skills are taught explicitly and systematically. Instruction is sequenced, attentive to individual needs, and includes a great deal of relevant practice with engaging yet predictable reading materials.

There are five key reading skills and fluency learning frameworks: Phonemic Awareness/Oral Blending; Introducing the Sounds and Using the Alphabet Cards; How the Alphabet Works: Part 1; How the Alphabet Works: Part 2; and Using the First-Step Stories.

✳ Phonemic Awareness/Oral Blending

Phonemic awareness lessons provide the children with practice in discriminating the sounds that make up words. Phonemic awareness is taught by means of two techniques: oral blending and segmentation. These two techniques complement each other. Oral blending puts sounds together to make words, while segmentation separates words into sounds. Lessons are brief and engaging. They often involve a puppet who leads the children in word games. The lessons are carefully sequenced, and each series begins with a great deal of teacher support for every child. As the children advance, this support is gradually removed. The lessons in Sounds and Letters are reinforced through activities in Exploring Sounds and Letters, the workbook that accompanies the module, and in games the children play as they read selections from the module's Big Book, *Pickled Peppers.*

Because the phonemic awareness lessons are purely oral and do not involve the teaching of any sound/letter associations, they work equally well with all children. The easy-to-harder sequence of the lessons provides ample support for both English Language Learners and special-needs children, and the gamelike nature of the activities encourages all children to participate readily.

✳ Introducing the Sounds and Using the Alphabet Cards

Large Alphabet Cards are used to remind the children of the sounds of the English language and their letter correspondences. The name of the picture on each card contains the target sound at the beginning of words for the consonants and in the middle for most of the vowels. In addition, the picture associates a sound with an action. This action-sound association is introduced through a short, interactive story in which the pictured object or character "makes" the sound of the letter.

This procedure for introducing sounds and letters is especially beneficial for English Language Learners, even for sounds that are not found in their primary languages. Because the Alphabet Cards are language independent, it is unnecessary for the children to know the English name for the picture on the card in order to associate the action with a sound.

✳ How the Alphabet Works: Parts 1 and 2

How the Alphabet Works lessons engage the children in experiences that develop their awareness of key concepts that are important to a thorough understanding of the alphabetic principle. How the Alphabet Works: Part 1 introduces the children to the idea that letters and their associated sounds work together in a systematic way to create words. The lessons help the children to gain insight into this system of associations. In these lessons, the children are not expected to master sound/letter associations, nor are they expected to blend sounds into words. Instead, each child is asked to become an "expert" on a special letter as the entire class learns how the alphabet works.

How the Alphabet Works: Part 2 introduces the children to specific sound/letter associations for a small set of consonants and for two short vowels. The children listen for sounds in specified positions in words and link sounds to their corresponding letters. With this information and with a carefully structured set of lessons, the children begin to explore and understand the alphabetic principle.

How the Alphabet Works activities are of special benefit to English Language Learners. Looking closely at how English sounds and letters work together helps them to make the transition from their primary languages to English.

✳ Using the First-Step Stories

For those First-Step Stories with pictures only, the children are encouraged to comment on what is shown and to connect it to previous reading or to the theme they are currently studying. For those stories with text only, the children are asked to follow along as the teacher reads and to comment or fill in missing information when necessary. For all the stories, the children can illustrate, color, or "write" text on their own. During class time and in Workshop, the children "read" and enjoy the stories they have created, sharing them with partners, the teacher, or with a small group.

Because artwork is language independent, illustrating First-Step Stories is an excellent opportunity for English Language Learners to experience success. Discussing the illustrations with the children is also a good way to assess an individual child's understanding of a reading selection.

Writing Skills and Fluency

Early explorations with writing help children to construct valuable insights about how written language works. For this reason, writing is developed alongside reading. The writing skills and fluency learning frameworks stimulate the children to think about writing and how it is used and stress the importance of communicating in print.

The writing skills and fluency learning framework is Writing.

* Writing

Early writing activities direct the children's attention to the kinds of print they encounter daily and stress the importance of communicating in print. In Sounds and Letters, these activities recognize the children's differing developmental levels and involve labeling pictures, using scribbles to tell stories, forming letters, printing, and making individual and class books. Children are encouraged to use invented spelling as a transition to standard spelling. Independent and collaborative writing projects allow the children to experience the pride of being authors and illustrators and to share their work with others.

Language difficulties may prevent some English Language Learners from capturing their ideas in written language. However, dictation allows these children to participate fully in all writing activities. In addition, conferences with the teacher along with small-group and individual work give the children many opportunities to practice and develop their English language writing.

Authentic Literacy Experiences

Throughout Sounds and Letters, children receive constant reminders of the goal and purpose of their learning: real reading.

There are two authentic literacy experiences learning frameworks: Reading Aloud and Using the Big Book and Print Awareness.

* Reading Aloud

In conducting reading-aloud sessions, the teacher

- introduces the selection by telling its title and by commenting briefly on the topic, but does not summarize the story
- activates the children's prior knowledge quickly and simply
- reminds the children to interrupt the reading to clear up anything they do not understand
- reads the selection expressively, modeling reactions and questions
- points out illustrations and invites the children to comment on them
- calls on volunteers to retell the story
- discusses the selection with the children, encouraging their responses and questions

Reading aloud serves multiple purposes: It provokes the children's curiosity about text, conveys to them an awareness that text has meaning, and demonstrates to them the joys and pleasures that reading brings to life. For maximum effectiveness, reading-aloud sessions involve the children's active attention, prompting them to wonder and to ask questions about the meaning of the text and to think about how the ideas in the text fit into their own prior knowledge.

For English Language Learners in particular, reading-aloud sessions provide needed opportunities to observe and practice the behaviors and strategies they need for reading in English. In addition, hearing their classmates discuss problems they may have had with a reading selection allows English Language Learners and special-needs children to see that even skilled English readers sometimes need help.

✳ Using the Big Book and Print Awareness

The shared reading of the Big Book *Pickled Peppers* engages the children in listening to a reader and provides exposure to written language, which is especially crucial for children who have not been read to frequently in the home. Shared-reading experiences invite the children to participate in reading behaviors and to use the strategies of expert readers: responding to the illustrations, wondering about the content and predicting what might happen, and commenting on events and characters.

Sharing the Big Book with the children also helps them to develop an awareness of the nature of print—how words look on a page, the spaces between words, the connection between pictures and words, the left-to-right and top-to-bottom progression of reading and writing, the clues that announce the beginnings and ends of sentences, and so forth—and the conventions of books—title pages, tables of contents, page numbers, and much, much more.

The nature of Big-Book reading—sharing and experiencing written language—lends itself well to learning English. Repetitive passages and illustrated text help English Language Learners with vocabulary development. Big Book reading is doubly valuable as an introduction to the print conventions of English.

Knowledge Building

Although young children are fascinated with the world around them, most have little awareness of how much there is to know about the world. They have limited experiences with the cognitive strategies they must apply if they are to become full participants in the literate world. The goal of knowledge building is to help the children enter that world by increasing their ability to think about, appreciate, and contribute to the vast richness of human knowledge.

All learning frameworks contribute to knowledge building. However, the key learning framework is Exploring Through Discussion.

✳ Exploring Through Discussion

Exploring Through Discussion activities are a principal means of helping children tie together all of the things they are learning and to examine the edges of their knowledge and understanding. These activities also help children learn the conventions of conversation, of give-and-take, and of expressing opinions, all of which prepare them for success in school and beyond.

The children develop and use important cognitive strategies through whole-class and small-group discussions that allow them to ask questions, confirm their understandings, predict outcomes, and compare their ideas with those of others.

Setting aside time for children to share experiences, particularly in classrooms where several cultures are represented, can open new worlds to all the children. In addition, class discussions are excellent occasions to elaborate on content-specific vocabulary, to emphasize proper vocabulary, and to provide the children with more information about a selection, all of which are important to English Language Learners and special-needs children.

Monitoring, Assessment, and Individualization

Collections for Young Scholars provides for multidimensional, continuous monitoring and assessment to ensure that all children are progressing toward clearly established goals and benchmarks. Individualization is accomplished through Workshop. When necessary, instruction is individualized for those English Language Learners who need additional help.

The learning frameworks for monitoring, assessment, and individualization are Assessment and Monitoring, Workshop, and English Language Learners.

✳ Assessment and Monitoring

Assessment is aligned with the goals of the curriculum and with what students are expected to learn. It is a tool that measures change in students' performance, checks their progress, and detects their strengths and weaknesses in each area of the literacy curriculum. The assessment and monitoring components of each module apply equally well to all students, regardless of their specific individual needs.

✳ Workshop

Workshop gives the children an early experience of managing their own learning process. Workshop time is a crucial aspect of the kindergarten day. In Workshop, the children work independently or collaboratively to practice and review material taught in the lessons or to complete projects of their own choosing. As the children gradually take more and more responsibility during Workshop, they learn to set learning goals, to make decisions about the use of time and materials, and to collaborate with their classmates. Of equal importance, Workshop gives you a designated time to work with individuals or with groups to reinforce learning, to provide extra help to those who need it, and to assess and monitor the progress of individuals or of the whole class.

Workshop can be a supportive but open forum in which special-needs and gifted children express themselves freely and experiment with different approaches to learning. It is also a good way for children to help each other over hard spots. Placing English Language Learners in pairs and in small groups takes away an emphasis on individual performance, something that can interfere with learning a second language in the initial stages.

✳ English Language Learners

In *Collections for Young Scholars,* English Language Learners receive the same high-quality instruction as do all other students. Instruction across the modules respects and builds on English Language Learners' existing knowledge and competencies. A wide range of oral language activities gives them opportunities to hear and to use English for valid communicative purposes— to learn new things from and with their classmates. Frequent reading and writing experiences help the children acquire English vocabulary, learn English spellings, and become familiar with the mechanics of writing and the writing process.

Preparing to Use Sounds and Letters

Before you begin to use Sounds and Letters you should do the following:

GET ACQUAINTED WITH THE INSTRUCTIONAL GOALS

The goals and ideas that motivate the instructional design of the *Collections for Young Scholars* kindergarten program are found in *Beginning to Read: Thinking and Learning About Print—A Summary* by Marilyn Jager Adams (University of Illinois at Urbana-Champaign, Center for the Study of Reading, 1990). We recommend that you read this book before you begin instruction.

CHECK YOUR MATERIALS

Check to see that you have the following materials for each student:
- Exploring Sounds and Letters
- Uppercase and Lowercase Letter Cards
- First-Step Stories 1-6

In addition to this teacher's guide, you should also have the following teacher resources:
- *Pickled Peppers* (Big Book)
- Sounds and Letters Kindergarten Kit
- Pocket Chart Kit

ORGANIZE YOUR MATERIALS AND SET UP YOUR CLASSROOM

- The **Sounds and Letters Kindergarten Kit** serves as easily accessible storage for your instructional materials. Unpack the materials (see pages 24F–26F) and use the dividers to organize the box.
- Remove the first twenty-six **Alphabet Cards** from the Sounds and Letters Kindergarten Kit and place them above the chalkboard or along a wall, with only the back of each card visible. These cards form a model alphabet for the children to use during the first lessons. In lessons in which sound/spellings are introduced, you will be told to turn a particular card to display the picture side.

  The remaining Sound/Spelling Cards will be introduced one at a time. You should display each card as it is introduced.

- Select an area of the classroom for **Workshop** and a place for keeping Workshop materials. Choose an area with enough space to expand as the year progresses. **Learning Framework Card 10** contains more information about establishing Workshop.

GET ACQUAINTED WITH THE LESSON FORMAT

There are one hundred lessons in *Framework for Effective Teaching: Sounds and Letters.* A lesson can either be completed in a day or across several days. The instructional activities within a lesson need not be done in a single block of time but rather spread out across the kindergarten day.

Each lesson opens with Lesson Overview that contains a listing of new learning that appears in the lesson, the materials needed, and any special preparation to be done in advance of a class.

Activities in a lesson are arranged under these heads:

- **Reading the Big Book** Shared-reading activities tied to the Big Book *Pickled Peppers* help the children develop an awareness of print and how it works.

- **Phonemic Awareness** These activities are presented in two main formats—oral blending and segmentation—and are purely oral. They do not involve the teaching of any sound/letter associations.

    The activities are intended to be presented in a quick and snappy manner. You should not let them drag, and you should not require or expect mastery before moving on to the next lesson's activities.

- **Letter Names and Shapes** (Lessons 1-30) Songs, games, and Alphabet-Card activities help the children learn and remember the names and shapes of the letters of the alphabet.

- **How the Alphabet Works: Part 1** (Lessons 21-30) These activities engage the children in experiences to ensure that they have a basic understanding of how letters and sounds are associated.

- **How the Alphabet Works: Part 2** (Lessons 31-50) These lessons introduce the alphabetic principle by taking the children through the alphabet letter by letter and by attaching sounds to each letter. The convention that vowels each have a short sound as well as a long one is introduced in Lesson 45.

- **Letter Names, Shapes, and Sounds** (Lessons 51-100) Games, songs, and review activities are used to reinforce what the children have learned about the alphabet and how it works.

- **Using First-Step Stories** (Lessons 45-48, 83-90, 97-100) Activities related to the First-Step Stories prepared by the children reinforce their awareness of print and give them early writing practice.
- **Phonics** (Lessons 96-100) In this brief introduction to phonics, the children have their first experiences in linking written letters to sounds on their own.
- **Workshop** This is the time during the day when children work individually or collaboratively in small groups, with or without your guidance. This gives them a first experience of managing their own learning process and working on their own. For you, it is a time for giving individual attention to students and for monitoring their progress.

Using Open Court's *Framework for Effective Teaching*® : *Sounds and Letters*

LESSON 1

●●● Lesson Overview

New Learning

- Print awareness
- Phonemic awareness: listening; rhythm
- Letter names and shapes: letter names, Alphabet Song
- Letter formation: straight lines
- Introduction to Workshop

Materials

- "I'm a Little Teapot," page 5 of *Pickled Peppers*
- Materials for environmental sounds such as whistle, hand bell, harmonica, drum, or tambourine
- Listening Collections Audiocassette
- Learning Framework Card 10
- Songs Teacher Tool Cards 1, 2
- Classroom Support Teacher Tool Card 1
- Activity Sheet 1
- Home/School Connection 1

✱ READING THE BIG BOOK

"I'm a Little Teapot"
page 5 of *Pickled Peppers*

Pickled Peppers is the Big Book for the Sounds and Letters Module. Sharing the Big Book with children will help them develop an awareness of the nature of print—how words look on a page, the existence of spaces between words, the connection between pictures and words, the left-to-right progression of reading and writing, and much more. Whole-class reading of the selections, encouraging children to illustrate Big Book selections in their own First-Step Stories, and using other extensions of the Big Book will help children develop this fundamental print awareness.

- Have children gather around you so that they can all see the Big Book, *Pickled Peppers*. Before you begin, tell the children you have a book that the class will be able to read together. Explain briefly that people read books both for pleasure and to get information. You might mention quickly other things that people read: newspapers, magazines, road or store signs, shopping lists, and food packages.
- Show *Pickled Peppers* and talk about its size. Explain that it is an extra-large book so that everyone in the class can see it. Point out

the front and back covers, explaining that the title, or "name" of the book, is on the front cover. Point to the title, running your hand under each word and saying it again. Open the book and note that the pages between the covers have words and pictures.

- Turn to the selection "I'm a Little Teapot." Point to the title and read it aloud. If some children already know the song, let them sing it for the class. Some children may automatically perform the motions in the song as well. Tell these children that they can be your "helpers" when the whole class learns the motions tomorrow, but that for now you want to read the words to "I'm a Little Teapot." Read the song slowly, accentuating the rhyming words and moving your finger from line to line. Explain that you are going to read the song once more and that you will point to each word as you read it. Read the song once more, pointing word by word.

- Now sing the song, or you may prefer to use the Listening Collections Audiocassette. Refer to **Songs Teacher Tool Card 2** for the music. Sing the song several times, pointing to each line as the children sing along. Clarify unfamiliar words such as *stout, shout, steam.*

- Point to the pictures and explain that pictures are different from words but that they also help give meaning to the song. Name and point to the word *handle,* and then to the girl making the handle with her arm. Name and point to the word *spout,* and ask a child to point to the boy making the spout. Point to the words *tip me over*, one by one, and say each word. Ask a child to find the picture that illustrates *tip me over.*

- Help children focus on the way words look in print. Tell them you are going to point to words. Point to the words *pour me out* one by one, and say each word slowly. Explain that the words are separated from each other by blank spaces and point to those spaces.

TEACHING TIP

You might want to show the children some real teapots or pictures of teapots. Ask the children if they have a teapot at home that makes a loud noise when the water boils. You might ask the children what kinds of sounds their teapots make. Explain that when the water boils, the rising steam comes through a small hole and makes a sound. Talk about the song and why the teapot "shouts" when it gets "all steamed up."

TIP FOR ENGLISH LANGUAGE LEARNERS

English Language Learners might be unfamiliar with the song. Practice the song with them before singing with the whole group. Read each sentence and ask them to repeat it after you, using rhythm and actions to help them memorize the song.

✳ PHONEMIC AWARENESS

Listening

Listening games help children learn to listen for sounds in general. This, in turn, sharpens their ability to attend selectively to single sounds. In later lessons, the children will transfer this skill to listening for separate words in sentences, parts of words, and individual phonemes in words.

Along with learning how to listen for and isolate single sounds, children need to learn how to describe and analyze these sounds. You can model this by having the children listen for a sound, then saying, "We heard the sound of a _____," and then encouraging them to describe what they heard in the same way. When you move on to listening to two or more sounds, say, "First we heard _____, in the middle we heard _____, and last we heard _____." Do not expect children to name the order of sounds at first, but do take the opportunity to model the use of the terms *first, middle,* and *last.*

Listening for Sounds   Assemble your materials to make sounds, or play recordings of familiar environmental sounds that the children will be able to identify.

- Prepare the children for this listening game by first asking them to be very quiet. Then ask them to close their eyes and listen carefully to all the sounds around them. Then have them open their eyes and name some of the sounds they heard. Note any sounds they might have left out: "Did you hear the sound of the car horn honking? the sound of the bird chirping?"
- Now have the children close their eyes again. Make (or play) one sound you have selected. Model the response you will be asking for: "I heard the sound of a _____."
- Now make (or play) another sound. Ask the children, "What sound did you hear?" Call on individual children and encourage them to answer in complete sentences: "I heard the sound of a _____."
- Continue with other sounds, one by one, always encouraging the children to answer, "I heard the sound of a _____."
- Once again have the children close their eyes. Make or play two sounds. Ask, "How many sounds did you hear?" When they answer "two," review the sounds: "Yes. First we heard a _____, and last we heard a _____."
- If you feel your students are ready, repeat with a series of three sounds and ask for the number, not the names, of the sounds. When they answer "three," review the sounds: "First we heard a _____, in the middle we heard a _____, and last we heard a _____." Repeat the activity with three more sounds.

Rhythm

Children naturally play with language. Their repetitive playground songs and rhymes attest to this. Extending children's natural love of rhythm into classroom instruction will allow you to help them focus on the form of language. Clapping, singing, and "feeling" the pattern of language are fun, but more importantly, they provide a learning framework. Through familiar poems and "ditties," children will learn to attend to the sound structure of language and to distinguish meaning and form. Following a natural progression, children will be able to see that sentences are made up of words, words are made up of separate parts, and that these parts are made up of individual sounds.

Feeling the Rhythm   Tell the children that they are going to learn a new poem.

- Teach the children the classic nursery rhyme, "Polly Put the Kettle On."

Polly put the kettle on.
Polly put the kettle on.
Polly put the kettle on.
We'll all have tea!

Sukey, take it off again.
Sukey, take it off again.
Sukey, take it off again.
They've all gone away!

Repeat the poem with the children several times until everyone can say the words correctly. Clap each time you say the names *Polly* and *Sukey.* Take the lead on the fourth and eighth lines, and have the children focus on the repeating lines.

- When the children are comfortable with the poem, substitute a child's name for *Polly* in the first three lines. Point to the child and say, for example, "Patrick put the kettle on. Patrick put the kettle on. Patrick put the kettle on. We'll all have tea!" Remember to clap when you say the name. Encourage the children to join in. Then point to another child and say, "Mark, take it off again. Mark, take it off again. Mark, take it off again. They've all gone away!" Repeat the poem using other children's names. Each time, encourage the children to recite and clap with you.

LETTER NAMES AND SHAPES

Letter Names

Throughout the lessons, you will find a variety of songs to help children remember the letters of the alphabet. The traditional Alphabet Song, with a slight variation, is used first. Some children may be familiar with the Alphabet Song, but they may not have heard this version. (The music can be found on **Songs Teacher Tool Card 1.**) In this version of the Alphabet Song, all letters except *W* are sung very slowly. This allows the children to focus on the name of each individual letter. The best way to teach this version, particularly if the children already know another version, is to teach it through the letter *G*, then through *N*, through *Q*, through *T*, and finally through *Z* and the ending. For this introduction, the children will only sing. In the next lesson, you will make the connection between the names for the letters and their written symbols by pointing to the letters on the Alphabet Cards.

Alphabet Song Tell the children that this version of the Alphabet Song is a little different from other versions they may already know.
- Have the children listen as you sing the song or play it on the Listening Collections Audiocassette. Sing each letter slowly, so that they will learn to enunciate each.
- Sing the song together several times, clapping as you say the letters *G, N, Q, T, W,* and *Z.* These letters each come just before a pause in the song. Clapping to emphasize the letters reinforces the rhythm of the song and helps children keep their place and say each letter.

ABCDEFG

HIJKLMN

OPQ

RST

UVW

XYZ

Now I never will forget

How to say the alphabet.

Letter Formation Overview

This lesson and the next three provide children with an introduction to the basic strokes needed to form complete letters: straight lines, slanting lines, curves, and circles. Working on these strokes gives children valuable practice with the components of letter formation before tackling the more difficult task of printing the complete letter.

Using either an overhead projector or the chalkboard, make the strokes so that everyone can see them. Talk the children through the strokes you are making, encouraging them to follow along. It is important that you and the children form strokes and letters in unison. For the strokes in this and the following three lessons, use the oral descriptions that are provided. **Classroom Support Teacher Tool Card 1** contains more information on presenting strokes and letters on an overhead projector or at the chalkboard.

Straight Lines Direct children's attention to the overhead projector or chalkboard and tell them that they are going to practice first making straight "up-and-down" lines, and then making "across" lines.

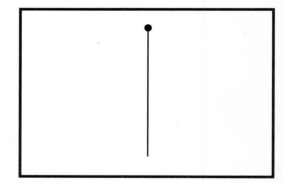

- As you make strokes on the overhead, have the children mimic your strokes by making their own strokes in the air with their fingers. Make a small starting point, then place your pen or chalk "here, on this starting point." Have the children place their fingers in the air. Say, "Start at the top and move straight down." Make the stroke. Repeat the stroke several times, watching to see that the children are moving their fingers from top to bottom.

- Now ask the children to pick up their pencils and place their blank sheets of paper in front of them. On the overhead projector or the chalkboard, make a starting point. Place your pen or chalk on the point and ask children to place their pencils at the top of their blank sheets. Now make a line and ask them to do what you have done. Say, "Start at the top and move straight down."

- Repeat the procedure for horizontal lines. Tell the children they are now going to make "across" lines. Say, "Start here and move across."

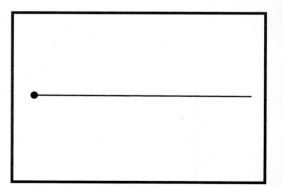

Introduction to Workshop

Workshop will become an important part of your students' day. During this time, you will be able to work with individuals or groups to review the day's instruction, offer individual assistance, or assess children's progress. It is also a time when children learn to work independently, eventually becoming responsible for their own learning.

Use the early lessons to establish your classroom procedures for Workshop, to become acquainted with the children, and to help them work with each other. In the beginning lessons, there is only one activity in Workshop. This allows children to become familiar with your class organization. As children become more independent, you can offer them more activities.

It is wise to designate a shelf or area of the classroom where Workshop materials will be kept. You may want to integrate Workshop with the Learning Centers you already have. Children should be responsible for the area and the care of the materials. Allow them to collect and return their materials to the Workshop area daily, reminding them that it is important to keep their workplace in order. You may want to establish distinct Workshop areas for writing, reading, and other activities. **Learning Framework Card 10, Workshop,** contains more information about establishing and conducting Workshop.

- Explain that every day there will be Workshop time, a time when they can work on projects and activities on their own, or sometimes with partners. Explain that you will go over the Workshop activities each day before they begin to work. Stress that they will need to pay attention to the directions so that they will know what to do. Show children where the materials will be kept for each day's activity.

- Tell the children that they are going to practice making straight lines because many letters have straight lines in them. Hold up **Activity Sheet 1.** Point to the complete *E*. Then point to the incomplete *E* and note its missing line. Tell the children that by placing their pencils at the dot and following the dotted line, they will be able to complete the letter. Trace the line with your finger. Have the children trace the line on their paper, first with their finger, then with a pencil. Repeat the procedure with the remaining letters.

- Circulate during Workshop, offering assistance. If children are able to, have them write their names at the top of their Activity Sheets. If they are not able to write their names, have them try to write the first letter. If you need to write children's names for them, encourage them to trace their names with their pencils. Or you might suggest they practice making the first letter in their name on the back of the Activity Sheet.

Home/School Connection Home/School Connection 1 explains to adults the importance of reading aloud to children and of discussing what they read. Distribute copies for the children to take home.

LESSON 2

••• Lesson Overview

New Learning

- Rhyming words
- Phonemic awareness: listening for first, middle, and last sounds; rhythm
- Letter formation: slanting lines
- Introduction to Workshop

Materials

- "I'm a Little Teapot," page 5 of *Pickled Peppers*
- Alphabet Cards
- Materials for environmental sounds: same used in Lesson 1
- Learning Framework Card 1
- Classroom Support Teacher Tool Card 1
- Activity Sheet 2

✱ READING THE BIG BOOK

"I'm a Little Teapot"
page 5 of *Pickled Peppers*

The rhythm and cadences of poems and songs can help children become familiar with print. Poems and songs are fun, and children naturally repeat them again and again. Because children need to hear patterns over and over until they become familiar, do not hesitate to repeat songs and poems many times. Anytime there is a break in the class or the children need to stand and move, songs such as "I'm a Little Teapot" can be used. You will find other songs and clapping and motion poems sprinkled throughout the lessons. Children will gain confidence in their oral language by engaging in these activities; thus, they will feel more secure when they approach print.

- Bring out the Big Book and review its title, pointing to the words on the front cover and saying: "*Pickled Peppers.*"
- Review "I'm a Little Teapot" in *Pickled Peppers* by singing it through once and pointing to each line of the text.
- Ask the children to stand up. Tell them you want them to pretend they are short, stout teapots. Make sure the children have enough elbow room. Teach them the motions for the song, standing with your back to the children so that they can mimic you. Have your

student "helpers" who are familiar with the motions in the song take part in leading the other children through them.

- Sing the song several more times, performing the motions with the children.

- Have the children gather around you and the Big Book again. Explain to them that there are some rhyming words in the song. Name and point to the word *stout.* Name and point to the word *spout.* Explain that when words sound alike, like *stout* and *spout,* we say that they rhyme. Ask the children if they can hear the rhyme, and ask them to repeat after you: *stout, spout.* Explain that *stout* and *spout* sound alike because they both end in *out.* Read the song through again. Ask if anyone hears more words that sound like or rhyme with *stout* and *spout.* If anyone suggests a nonrhyming word, such as *teapot,* say the two words together: *teapot, stout.* Say, "I don't hear the same sound, *out,* in these two words." Say the rhyming words again and ask the children to listen for the rhyme and to stop you when you come to a rhyming word. Recite the song slowly, emphasizing *stout, spout, shout,* and *out.*

- Remind the children that yesterday you pointed to separate words in the song and that a moment ago you pointed to all the rhyming words in the song. Explain that words are *groups of letters* separated by spaces. Say that the spaces make words easier to read. Point to the words *pour me out* again, and say them one by one. Have the children notice that there are many more words in the song "I'm a Little Teapot"; some that are shorter than others because they have fewer letters, some that are longer than others because they have more letters. Point to the words *my handle,* and say them. Point to *my.* Say, "*My* is short. It only has two letters." Point to *handle.* Say, "*Handle* is longer than *my* because *handle* has more letters than *my.*"

- Choose a line from the song and point to words and spaces, saying, "Here is a word, here is a space," and so on. If they are ready, ask children to point to words and spaces. Encourage them to say, "Here is a word" or "Here is a space." Say the words they point to.

Listening

Listening for the First, Middle, or Last Sounds Along with learning to listen for and isolate single sounds, children need to learn how to describe and analyze these sounds. Listening for the first, middle, and last sounds in a series; learning to identify those sounds; and using the words *first, middle,* and *last* (or *beginning, middle,* and *end*) will help them to do this.

The ability to recall and name an entire sequence of sounds in order is not the aim of this activity. Rather, it is intended to help children learn to listen to your question; to understand that the *first* position is very different from the *middle* or *last* positions; and then, to be able to identify a sound in one of these positions by using the correct positional term.

TIP FOR ENGLISH LANGUAGE LEARNERS

Reinforce the meanings of the terms *first, middle,* and *last* (or *beginning, middle,* and *end*) for English Language Learners by using a book, a list, or a group of people or objects in a row to physically demonstrate the concepts. Point to the first object as you say the word *first.* Have the children repeat the word. Then continue with the words *middle* and *last.* Repeat the procedure with other objects, pointing to the beginning, middle, and end as you say the terms aloud.

Understanding that sounds have position in relation to one another will prepare students to listen for individual phonemes in words. **Learning Framework Card 1, Phonemic Awareness** contains more information about phonemic awareness.

- Tell the children that you will again make (or play a recording of) some familiar sounds and that, for now, they should just listen. Make two familiar sounds. Say, "The first sound was a ____, and the last sound was a ____." Now make the sounds again. Have the children supply the answers as you say once more, "The first sound was a ____, and the last sound was a ____." Next make three familiar sounds. Say, "The first sound was a ____, the middle sound was a ____, and the last sound was a ____." Make the sounds again and have the children supply the answers.

- Tell the children to listen closely as you make two more sounds. Ask a child, "What was the first sound you heard?" Encourage the child to respond in a complete sentence: "The first sound was a ____." Make two more sounds. Ask another child, "What was the last sound you heard?" Encourage the child to respond in a complete sentence: "The last sound was a ____."

- Now make a series of three familiar sounds. Remember, it is not important that the children be able to repeat the entire sequence of sounds. They just need to be able to identify a single sound in a specific position and identify it using the correct positional word. Ask the children, "What was the first sound you heard?" Encourage them to answer in a full sentence, using the positional word: "The first sound was a ____."

- Make three new, though familiar, sounds. Say, "What was the middle sound you heard?" Again, the children should answer in a complete sentence using the positional word: "The middle sound was a ____."

- Make another three sounds. Say, "What was the last sound?" Encourage children to answer in a complete sentence, using the positional word: "The last sound was a ____."

- You may want to extend this activity into a second day so that all children have a chance to respond and so that you are able to verify that the children understand and can articulate the idea of first, middle, and last.

Rhythm

Feeling the Rhythm Gather the children around you in a circle and review "Polly Put the Kettle On," emphasizing the names *Polly* and *Sukey.*

Polly put the kettle on.
Polly put the kettle on.
Polly put the kettle on.
We'll all have tea!

Sukey, take it off again.
Sukey, take it off again.
Sukey, take it off again.
They've all gone away!

TEACHING TIP

To ensure that every child is responding fully, institute a wait time that is tied to something you do, such as tapping your pencil or snapping your fingers twice. Then children should listen to your question, wait for your movement, and then respond together. Their initial efforts may be a bit ragged, but they will catch on quickly if you remember to use wait time whenever it is appropriate.

- The children should be quite familiar with the poem by now. Tell them that you are all going to say the poem together, and that each of them will take a part. Remind them to use the names, *Polly* and *Sukey*. Tell them that when you point to a child, that child should repeat the next line of the poem.
- Say the first line: "Polly put the kettle on." Point to a child. If the child needs it, provide help in saying the line. Point to another child to say the third line. Then hold your arms out wide, nod your head, and say, "We'll all have tea!"
- Begin again, saying the fifth line: "Sukey, take it off again." Point to a child, helping him or her with the line, if necessary. Point to another child to say the seventh line. Then hold your arms out wide, nod, and say, "They've all gone away!"

LETTER NAMES AND SHAPES

Letter Names

Alphabet Song Position the Alphabet Cards in the room so that the children can point to them or touch them. You may want to lean them against the eraser shelf on the chalkboard or along a low windowsill. Make sure that the cards are arranged to show the letter side and not the picture side. All future lessons assume that the Alphabet Cards are in place.

- Remind the children that the Alphabet Song is a great way to learn the names of all the letters in the alphabet. Sing the song once and encourage those children who remember the words to join in.
- Tell the children that you will be singing the Alphabet Song again, but that this time they will be looking at the Alphabet Cards as you point out each letter and sing its name. Ask them to follow along closely and listen as you point to each letter.
- Sing the song through once as the children listen. Point to each letter on the Alphabet Cards as you sing its name. To reinforce the rhythm of the song, clap as you sing the letters that come before each pause: *G, N, Q, T, W,* and *Z.* If necessary, use **Songs Teacher Tool Card 1.**
- Now ask the children to sing with you. Continue to point to the letters and clap at the appropriate times as the children sing. Sing the song through in this manner several times.

Letter Formation Overview

If necessary, see **Classroom Support Teacher Tool Card 1** for a review of how to use the overhead projector in this activity. If you do not have an overhead projector, make the strokes and letters on the chalkboard.

Slanting Lines Begin by writing each stroke on an overhead transparency or chalkboard. Direct children's attention to the overhead or chalkboard and tell them that they are going to practice writing slanting lines. Tell them to follow the strokes you make by using their fingers to make strokes in the air. Place your pen or chalk on the starting point and have them place their fingers in the air. Say, "Start at the top and slant down this way (right)." Repeat the stroke several times. It is not necessary to use the words *left* and *right* as you make the slanting lines, nor for the children to have mastered the left-right concept. As they mimic your strokes in the air and watch you at the overhead or board, they will get the feel of the stroke.

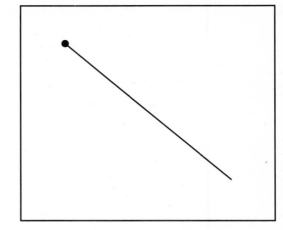

- Now ask the children to pick up their pencils and place blank sheets of paper in front of them. Place your pen or chalk on the starting point and ask the children to place their pencils at the top of the blank sheet. Make a line and ask them to follow, saying, "Start at the top, and slant down this way (right)."
- Repeat the procedure for left-slanting lines, saying, "Start at the top, and slant down this way (left)."

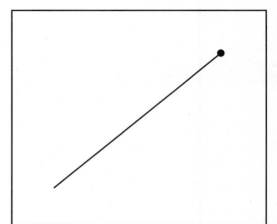

✳ WORKSHOP

Introduction to Workshop

Workshop helps students gain confidence and gives them valuable experience in working independently. Caring for their own materials also helps them develop a sense of responsibility. The early lessons are a good time to establish your classroom procedures for Workshop (and Learning Centers in general), to become acquainted with the children, and to help them work with each other. Only one activity is suggested for Workshop in the beginning lessons. As children become more independent and your classroom procedures more defined, you can offer children more activity options.

Spend some time discussing your expectations for Workshop. Have the children suggest some simple rules they should follow for this part of the day. You might want to list these suggestion on a chart. If possible, use pictures to remind children of the rules.

- Remind the children that every day at this time, there will be Workshop, a time when they can work on projects and activities on their own, or sometimes with partners. Remind children to listen to your directions first and then to take out their materials.
- Tell the children that they are going to practice making slanted line because many letters have slanted lines in them. On **Activity Sheet** 2, point to the complete *A*. Then point to the incomplete *A* and note that it is missing a line. Tell the children that by placing their pencils at the dot and following the dotted line, they will be able to draw a slanted line and so complete the letter.
- Circulate during Workshop, offering assistance. If children are able to, have them write their names at the top of their Activity Sheets. If they are not able to write their names, have them try to write the first letter. If you need to write children's names for them, encourage them to trace their names with their pencils. Or you might suggest they practice making the first letter in their name on the back of the Activity Sheet.

LESSON

3

●●● Lesson Overview

New Learning

- Phonemic awareness: listening for first, middle, and last words
- Segmentation: word substitution
- Letter formation: curves

Materials

- "This Old Man," pages 8–9 of *Pickled Peppers*
- Puppet
- Name necklaces
- Pocket Chart
- Picture Cards: *cat, fish, gate, hive, sack, sticks*
- Learning Framework Card 10
- Classroom Support Teacher Tool Card 1
- Activity Sheet 3

Prepare Ahead

- Name necklaces for each child: a 5" x 7" card with a child's name printed on it, with yarn or ribbon stapled to it

---

✷ READING THE BIG BOOK

"This Old Man"
pages 8–9 of *Pickled Peppers*

"This Old Man" is another song that children can sing over and over again. Familiar poems and songs make it easier for children to approach print in the Big Book and to make connections between the words they sing or say in poems and those words they see printed on the page. Sing songs and repeat favorite poems each day in your class to reinforce children's recognition of individual words. Songs that use numbers emphasize both the pattern of language and the sequence of numbers. You may choose to use these "number songs" to expand other mathematics activities.

- Gather the children around you and open *Pickled Peppers* to "This Old Man." Point to the title and say, "The title of this song is 'This

Old Man.'" Explain that titles are used to name poems or songs as well as books.

- Acknowledge that some children may already know the words to "This Old Man." Let them sing part of it for the class. Some children may automatically perform the motions in the song as well. Tell these children that they can be your "helpers" when the whole class learns the song and the motions tomorrow, but that for now, you want to read the words to "This Old Man."

- Read the song all the way through, then read the first verse slowly, accentuating the rhyming words and moving your finger from line to line. Explain that you are going to read the verse again, this time pointing to each word as you read it.

- Go to the second verse. Point to the first two lines of the verse and tell the children that you will read the next part of the song. Explain that sometimes all of the words of a selection are not printed on the page of a book because these words are repeated over and over. Point to the ellipsis and say, "These three dots let us know that some words are missing. When we come to these three dots, we can keep going because we'll remember the words." Read the second verse, pointing to the lines. When you come to the ellipsis, remove your hand and continue: "With a knick-knack . . ." and encourage the children to join in.

- Read the third verse in the same way.

- Point to the picture in the lower left corner of page 8. Ask a child to say what is in the picture. Reinforce the connection of the picture to the words by saying, "This is a picture of the old man in the song." Ask, "What is he playing knick-knack, paddy whack on?"

- To conclude, point to the words *this old man* and say them slowly. Remind children that spaces separate words. Ask whether anyone can count the words in the phrase *this old man.* Point to each word.

✴ PHONEMIC AWARENESS

Listening

Listening for the First, Middle, or Last Words Now that the children have had some practice listening for the position of sounds, repeat the exercise as described in Lesson 2, only this time use words and pictures instead of sounds. First have the children listen for two words as you display each word's picture on the Pocket Chart. Next, have them identify three words as the first, middle, and last words.

- Use the following Picture Cards: *cat, fish, gate, hive, sack, sticks.* Follow the same procedure as in the previous lesson. Remember to have children respond in complete sentences, using the positional words *first, middle,* and *last.*

- Repeat the exercise in which students identify the first, middle, or last word in a sequence of rhyming words. You might want to use some of the rhyming words that you will be working on in the Big Book selection to reinforce the rhymes. Try words such as *shoe, glue, two; knee, bee, tree; four, door, store.* Remember to encourage children to respond in complete sentences, using the positional words *first, middle,* and *last.*

Word Substitution Through the use of an activity such as a name poem, you can reinforce the idea that sentences are made up of separate words. When one word in the poem changes (in this case, a child's name), the sentence changes. In addition, the name poem causes the entire focus of the children's attention to change—a new name calls for a new child to respond.

In this activity you will use name necklaces. These necklaces will also be used at other times in future lessons, such as in Workshop or during letter-formation activities. Name necklaces should contain the child's first name, printed in capital and small letters. Children can wear the name necklaces when they are moving about the room, but they should place the necklaces in front of them as they are working. This will allow them to become familiar with the letters in their names.

- Distribute the children's name necklaces by holding up one necklace at a time, waiting a moment to see if the child recognizes his or her name, then saying the name, and allowing the child to claim the necklace. As you present the necklace, read the child's name again and draw attention to the letter that begins it.

- Play the game Who Ate the Cookie from the Cookie Jar? Repeat the lines with the children several times, helping them to remember the lines, until everyone knows all the words. Then try it with one child.

    If you have already distributed the name necklaces, collect them and place them in front of you. Take a name necklace from your pile and hold it up. Wait for the child whose name is on the necklace to recognize his or her name and say it. If no one recognizes the name, point to it, and say, for example, "Karey," then start the game:

Teacher: Karey ate the cookie from the cookie jar.
Karey: Who me?
Teacher: Yes you!
Karey: Couldn't be.
Teacher: Then who?

Stop here, and hold up another name necklace. Wait for the child to recognize his or her name and say it. If no one does, point to it, and say another name, for example, "Tammi," then start the game again.

Give several children a chance to recognize their names and take part in the game.

Letter Names

Alphabet Song Introduce the puppet and say that it will sometimes be a helper as the class learns more about letters.

- Remind the children that the Alphabet Song can help them remember the names and shapes of the letters in the alphabet. They can sing the song and look at the letters on the Alphabet Cards.
- Review the Alphabet Song by singing it through once with the class clapping as you say the letters *G, N, Q, T, W,* and *Z.* Using the puppet, point to each letter on the Alphabet Cards and sing its name to encourage letter recognition.
- Sing the song to *G* as the children listen. Clap on *G.* With the class, sing to *G* several times as you point to the letters. Have everyone clap on *G.*
- Now ask a child to volunteer to point to the letters and to clap as everyone else sings to *G.* If the child gets out of rhythm with the song, stop, and ask everyone to begin again and to stay with the child who is pointing. You might have the puppet point along with the child. Make sure that each volunteer succeeds in staying with the song as far as *G.* Repeat this activity several times, giving several children an opportunity to point and clap.

Letter Formation Overview

Exploring Letters Not every child will be able to make strokes with a pencil, pen, or marker at this stage. These lessons should only be viewed as an introduction to letter formation. Be supportive of children's efforts, whether or not they are successful. Start your strokes with a starting point on the overhead projector or chalkboard but do not emphasize the starting point. Allow the child to experiment with the stroke—at this point, there are no starting points or writing lines to stay within. Refer to **Classroom Support Teacher Tool Card 1** for more detailed directions on the strokes.

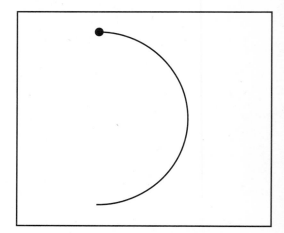

Curves Direct children to watch you and tell them that they are going to practice writing curves. Begin by writing each stroke on the overhead transparency or chalkboard, making sure the starting point is visible. First, have the children mimic the strokes you make by using their fingers to make strokes in the air.

- Place your pen or chalk on the starting point and have them place their fingers in the air. Practice the first stroke, saying, "Start here, curve around this way (right)." Repeat the stroke several times.
- Now ask the children to pick up their pencils and have their paper ready. Place your pen or chalk on the starting point and ask the

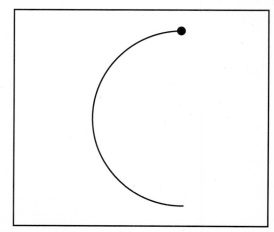

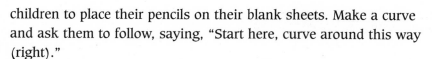

children to place their pencils on their blank sheets. Make a curve and ask them to follow, saying, "Start here, curve around this way (right)."

- Repeat the procedure for the next curve, saying, "Start here, curve around this way (left)."

✳ WORKSHOP

Continue to establish the Workshop procedures outlined in Lessons 1 and 2. If needed, refer to **Learning Framework Card 10** for more information. Review your expectations for Workshop time and your chart of rules, if you have made one.

- Have the children get Activity Sheet 3 from the designated Workshop space.
- Tell the children that they are going to practice making curved lines because many letters have curves in them. Point to the complete *G* on **Activity Sheet 3**. Then point to the incomplete *G* and note that it is not finished. Tell the children that by placing their pencils at the dot and by following the dotted line, they will be able to draw a curve, and so complete the letter. Have the children trace each dotted line, first with their finger and then with their pencil, to complete each letter.
- Remember to circulate during Workshop. For those children who are not yet writing their names, suggest they practice making the first letter in their name on the back of their Activity Sheets. Remind them that they may look at their name necklaces.
- When the children have finished their Activity Sheets, have them look for curved lines in the letters of their names on their name necklaces. Remind them that not every name has a letter with a curved line.

LESSON 4

••• Lesson Overview

New Learning

- Phonemic awareness: listening for missing sounds
- Sing Your Way to *G* game
- Letter formation: curves and circles

Materials

- "This Old Man," pages 8–9 of *Pickled Peppers*
- Puppet
- For each child, one set of Uppercase and Lowercase Letter Cards: *Aa–Dd*
- Materials for environmental sounds: same used in Lessons 1 and 2
- Four envelopes, each marked with a letter, *Aa–Dd*
- Listening Collections Audiocassette
- Activity Sheet 4

✱ READING THE BIG BOOK

"This Old Man"
pages 8–9 of *Pickled Peppers*

It is important that students become familiar with the parts of books. Take every opportunity to point out the titles of Big Books, the titles of individual selections in them, and the names of the authors and illustrators.

- Open *Pickled Peppers* to "This Old Man." Point to the title again and say it. Then point to the words below the title and say, "illustrated by Doug Cushman." Ask the children if anyone knows what "illustrated by" means. If no one does, explain that a person named Doug Cushman drew the pictures that go with "This Old Man." Say that someone who draws pictures for books is called an "illustrator." Next, ask if anyone can name the first letter of Doug Cushman's first name.

- Now play the song "This Old Man" on the Listening Collections Audiocassette or have the children sing it with you. Let your helpers perform the corresponding motions if they want to, or do them for the class yourself. Encourage the children to join in at any time.

- Tell the children that "This Old Man" has many words that rhyme.

Remind them that words that rhyme have the same last sound. Starting with the second verse, point to the couplet and read it. Tell the children that the last words in the two lines rhyme. Say, "What are the last words in these two lines?" Then go back, point to and say, *two;* point to and say, *shoe.* Say, "*Two* and *shoe* rhyme. They both end with /o͞o/." Point to the third couplet and read it. Ask if anyone knows what words rhyme. Then point to and say, *three;* point to and say, *knee.* Say, "*Three* and *knee* rhyme. They both end with /ē/." Continue through all the couplets in this manner.

- Review the rhyming words in the couplet. Point to *two* and say, "*Two* rhymes with ____," and point to *shoe.* Let the children complete your sentence. Tell them *shoe* also rhymes with *glue, blue,* and *new.* Continue reviewing each couplet.
- Conclude by singing the song.

Listening

Listening for the Missing Sound Identifying the omitted sound in a sequence is another way to give children a chance to sharpen their listening skills. Do not expect the children to identify the position of the missing sound. The goal of this activity is simply to have them hear and identify the name of the missing sound.

- Tell the children to listen closely for the sounds that you are going to make. Using the materials or recordings from earlier lessons, make (or play) two sounds. Say, "Now listen," and make just one of the same sounds. Ask, "Which sound is missing?" Model the answer for the children in a complete sentence: "The missing sound was a ____."
- Repeat this activity several times, using different sounds each time, leaving out one of the sounds, and allowing the children to identify it: "The missing sound was a ____."
- Move on to three sounds. Say, "Now listen," and make just two of these sounds. Ask, "Which sound is missing?" Remember to ask the children to use the word *sound* and to answer in complete sentences.

Word Substitution Repeat the game Who Ate the Cookie from the Cookie Jar? (See Lesson 3, Word Substitution.)

Do this as a group, using the name necklaces.

TIP FOR ENGLISH LANGUAGE LEARNERS

Return to the same activity often to provide opportunities for English Language Learners to feel comfortable with the activities. Encourage them to participate when the whole class is engaged in the activity. Watch for children who are not responding and work with them in small groups during Workshop.

LETTER NAMES AND SHAPES

Letter Names

Alphabet Song Review the Alphabet Song by singing it all the way through once with the children. Point to each letter on the Alphabet Cards as you sing its name.

Sing Your Way to G Game The Sing Your Way to *G* game provides the children with a way of finding the name of any letter they may have forgotten. You can use the puppet to help introduce this activity. Use the puppet at your discretion as the activity reappears in later lessons.

- Have the puppet point to the letter *Gg* but do not name it. Ask the children to sing the Alphabet Song with you until you reach this letter and then to stop. When you have stopped, have the puppet ask, "What is the letter?"
- Have the puppet point to other letters (*Aa–Gg*). Ask the children to sing the Alphabet Song with you to the letter indicated and then to stop. At that point, have the puppet ask for the letter name.
- Point to the letter *Gg* but do not name it. Ask a child to sing his or her way to the letter and then to stop. The child should sing the Alphabet Song, pointing to each letter and stopping as he or she names *G*.
- Ask other children to sing their way to other letters (*A–G*) and then to stop. Remind the children that they can sing their way to any letter of the alphabet by stopping when they reach the name of that letter.

Letters Aa–Dd Give each child a set of Uppercase and Lowercase Letter Cards, *Aa–Dd* only. As this activity begins, all the cards should have the capital letters facing up.

- Gather the children around you in a group. Ask them to find a *D*. Tell them that when you give the signal, they should hold up their *D* cards. If several of the children have trouble, use the Alphabet Cards and help them to sing their way to *Dd*. Say, "Does the letter on your card match the *D* on the big card?" Explain that the letter they have is called a "capital letter." Tell them to turn their cards over. Tell them the letter they see there is called a "small letter." Tell the children that the capital *D* is used at the beginning of a word and the small *d* is used everywhere else in a word. Continue with the other letters—*Aa, Bb, Cc*—and ask the children to hold up capital or small letters for each. Take note of any children who have difficulty recognizing the letters *Aa–Dd*.
- After all the children have identified their letters, hold up the envelope marked *Aa* that you prepared earlier. Ask all the children to come up and place their *Aa* Letter Cards in the envelope. Continue with all the *Bb* cards in another envelope, and so on through *Dd*.

Letter Formation Overview

More Curves and Circles Direct children's attention to the overhead projector or chalkboard and tell them that they will be practicing writing different types of curves and circles. Begin by writing each stroke on the overhead transparency or chalkboard, making sure the starting point is visible. Explain to the children that they should mimic the strokes you make on the overhead by using their fingers to make strokes in the air. Place your pen or chalk on the starting point and have them place their fingers in the air. Practice the first stroke, saying, "Start here, curve around this way (right)."

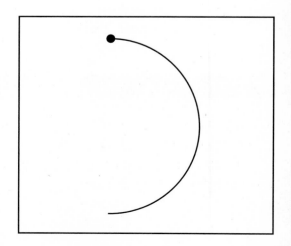

- Now ask the children to pick up their pencils and blank paper. Place your pen or chalk on the starting point and ask students to place their pencils on the paper. Now make a curve and ask them to follow, saying, "Start here, curve around this way (right)."
- Repeat the procedure for the next curve, saying, "Start here, curve around this way (left)."
- Repeat the procedure for circles, saying, "Start here and circle around this way (left)."

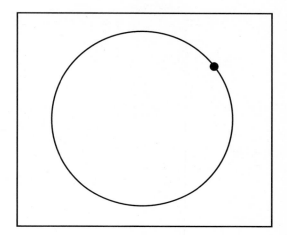

✳ WORKSHOP

Continue to establish the procedure for Workshop and to circulate among the children. Remind the children that during Workshop they are expected to work quietly on their own. Make sure that everyone has adjusted to the idea of completing activities without supervision and that they are able to work independently. Remind children that they may look at their name necklaces if they want to try to write the first letter of their name on their Activity Sheets.

- Tell the children that they are going to practice making curved strokes and circles because many letters have curves and circles in them. Point to the complete *O* and then to the incomplete *O* on **Activity Sheet 4**. Tell the children that they will be completing the letter as they have done on previous Activity Sheets, but that they will use curves and circles.
- Remember to circulate during Workshop. For those children who are not yet writing their names, take the opportunity to name all the letters in their names as you write for them. Suggest that they practice making the first letter in their name—the capital letter—on the back of the Activity Sheet.
- If children finish their Activity Sheets, have them trace their names on their name necklaces or write their names again.

LESSON 5

●●● Lesson Overview

New Learning

- Exploring Letters: *Aa*

Materials

- "This Old Man," pages 8–9 of *Pickled Peppers*
- Puppet (optional)*
- Name necklaces
- Pocket Chart
- Picture Cards: *door, gate, heaven, hive, knee, shoe, sticks, thumb, vine*

- Word Cards : *eight, five, four, he, He, knick knack, man, my, nine, old, on, one, played* (2), *seven, six, ten, This, three, two*
- For each child, one set of Uppercase and Lowercase Letter Cards: *Aa–Gg*
- Additional sets of Uppercase and Lowercase Letter Cards *Aa–Gg* in envelopes
- Envelopes or other containers, each marked with a letter, *Aa–Gg*
- Classroom Support Teacher Tool Cards 1, 2
- Home/School Connection 2

*The puppet can be used in every lesson. Keep the puppet available for use throughout the day. The puppet will not be listed in the materials section from this point on.

✳ READING THE BIG BOOK

"This Old Man"
pages 8–9 of *Pickled Peppers*

Children want to be read to, and they have an unstoppable desire to make rhymes and sing. Combining this aural/oral work with the printed word is an excellent way to help children learn the form of language. Use of the Pocket Chart will allow you to create a visual environment for the study of words and sentences. You can use this chart to display Pocket Chart Letter Cards, Word Cards, and Picture Cards. In addition, use of the Pocket Chart allows you and the children to easily manipulate letters, words, and pictures which will aid the children in print awareness and letter recognition. **Classroom Support Teacher Tool Card 2** contains additional information on the use of the Pocket Chart.

- Display the Pocket Chart so that everyone can see it. Tell the children that you will be putting some of the words from "This Old Man" in the chart. Sometimes you will use pictures instead of words. Arrange the Word and Picture Cards in order, the first word of the first line on top. Hold up one card at a time, say the word, and place the card in the chart. Continue through the second line, saying each word and placing its card in the chart. When you come to *thumb,* place the Picture Card of the thumb in the Pocket Chart. Tell the children that you will be using pictures of the rhyming words to help them remember the song.

- Pause and then read the first two lines through, pointing to each word. Ask the children to join in and finish the rest of the verse from memory: "With a knick knack . . ."
- Now hold up the *two* card. Remove the word *one* from the chart and replace it with *two.* Read the first line, pointing to each word. Continue with the second line, but when you come to *thumb,* cover it with your hand and wait. If the children say (or do not say) *shoe,* hold up the *shoe* Picture Card, and say the word. Then replace *thumb* with *shoe,* and say the lines again, encouraging the children to sing: "With a knick knack . . ."
- Continue working through the rest of the song in the same way.

✳ PHONEMIC AWARENESS

Listening

Listening for the Missing Word Tell the children to listen closely. Say three words, such as *cat, door,* and *fish.* As you say the words, put them in the Pocket Chart. Say, "Now listen," and say just two of the words and place your hand over or remove the third. Ask, "Which word is missing?" Model the answer for the children in a complete sentence, "The missing word is _____."

Repeat this activity several times, each time using three different words, leaving out one of the words, and allowing the children to identify it by saying, "The missing word is _____."

Word Substitution Continue with the game Who Ate the Cookie from the Cookie Jar? using the name necklaces. If more than one child has a name beginning with the letters *A–D,* select one of these names to use in the game. Then say, for example, "David's name begins with *D,* does anyone else have a name beginning with *D*?"

After you have repeated the game a few times, ask children to take off their name necklaces and place them on the floor in front of them. Tell them to use their fingers to trace over the letters in their names. Circulate and ask each child to name the first letter in her or his name.

LETTER NAMES AND SHAPES

Letter Names

Alphabet Song Review the Alphabet Song by singing it all the way through once with the class, clapping as you say the letters *G, N, Q, T,*

W, and *Z.* Then sing it again and point to each letter on the Alphabet Cards as you sing its name.

Sing Your Way to *G* Game Play the Sing Your Way to *G* game, asking children to sing to one of the letters between *Aa* and *Gg.* Ask the whole group to sing to the letters that you or the puppet point to before you call on individual children to do so.

Letters *Aa–Gg* Give each child Uppercase and Lowercase Letter Cards *Aa–Gg.* Allow each child, in turn, to hold up the letter and name it. Remember to help those children who find this activity difficult by having them sing their way to their letter.

- Now have all the *Aa*'s stand up and hold their cards with the capital *A's* facing out. Have the *Aa*'s sit down and the *Bb*'s stand up. Do the Sing Your Way to *G* game slowly, with the children standing up and holding up their cards when they hear their letter. Do this once or twice with the capital letters, then have the children do it with the small letters.

- Have the children help you fill envelopes with Letter Card sets *Aa–Gg.* Ask those children holding *Aa*'s to raise their hands. Have these children come up, one by one, and place their *Aa*'s in the envelope. Ask those children holding *Bb*'s to raise their hands. Have these children come up, one by one, and place their *Bb*'s in the envelope. Continue through all the letters.

    When you are done, place these envelopes, along with the additional sets, in the Workshop area.

Letter Formation Overview

During the first thirty lessons, the children will participate in many activities that teach letter recognition. These activities include songs, poems, games, matching activities, and many different types of puzzles. The lessons also include a brief overview on how to form both the capital and small letters. This is just one more way that the children can become familiar with the names of the letters. These lessons are not intended to build children's proficiency in writing letters. However, they will allow those children who have had more exposure to the letters to begin writing earlier. In the later lessons, a formal introduction to the letter strokes, including starting and ending points and directional arrows; focused practice with Exploring Sounds and Letters; and proofreading will begin for each of the letters. In the overview beginning in this lesson, use the oral descriptions to help children build the correct progression of strokes to form each letter. Because children will be watching your strokes and following along with you, it is not necessary for them to understand the concept of left and right. These terms are set off in parentheses in the descriptions. You can use them or not, depending upon the level of your students. Remember, if possible, use the overhead projector so that you and your students can form letters together. If you do not have an overhead projector, you can form the letters on the chalkboard. You may use the handwriting system outlined in detail on **Classroom Support Teacher Tool Card 1** or you may use the writing system that is standard in your school.

Exploring Letters—*Aa* Although the children will be writing letters free-form, it is a good idea to place starting points on the overhead projector or chalkboard before you begin, as a model for later lessons. First direct children's attention to the *Aa* Alphabet Card or hold one up. Note that *Aa* is red—explain that this is because *Aa* is special. It is a vowel. Tell them that they will learn more about vowels later. Name the capital letter *A* and point to it; name the small letter *a* and point to it. Tell the children that they will be writing the letter *Aa* together with you.

- Begin by placing your pen or chalk on the overhead projector or chalkboard. Have students place their fingers in the air. As you write, describe what you are doing. Say, "Start at the top, and slant down this way (left). Start at the top again, and slant this way (right). Start here and now across." Now say, "Capital *A.*"
- Repeat this activity several times, watching to see that the children are imitating your strokes in the air.
- Now ask the children to pick up their pencils and place their paper in front of them. Place a starting point. Place your pen or chalk on the overhead projector or chalkboard and ask students to place their pencils at the top of the paper. Now make a capital *A.* Say, "Start at the top, and slant down this way (left). Start at the top again, and slant this way (right). Start here and now across." Now say, "Capital *A.*"
- Repeat the steps for small *a.* Say, "Start here, around this way (left) all the way. Start here, and straight down, touching the circle." Now say, "Small *a.*"
- When the children are done, ask them to place their name necklaces in front of them. Pause and ask if anyone has an *A* as the first letter in their name. If no one answers, and there is a child in class whose name begins with *A,* point it out to the children. Also note that the name starts with a capital *A,* because capitals are used at the beginning of names. Ask if anyone else has an *a* anywhere in their name and remind them that a small *a* is used any place except at the beginning of a name.

Remind the children that Workshop is a time for quiet, independent work. You may want to review the Workshop rules briefly and discuss the responsible care of materials before going over today's activity.

- Explain to the children that in the materials section there are envelopes with a set of **Letter Cards** *Aa–Gg* for each of them. Remind the children that the Letter Cards have both capital and small letters, one on each side. During Workshop they can either turn all their cards so the capital letters are facing up or they can sing the Alphabet Song quietly to themselves, placing the Letter Cards in order. (You may want to demonstrate this.) If you believe your students can work with partners, group them for these activities and have them help each other. If they work with partners, one child can do capital letters and the other small letters. Then they can match the capital letters to the small letters. When they are done, they should put the letters back in the envelopes and then put the envelopes back in the materials section.

- Remember to circulate among the children to see if they can sing the Alphabet Song and recognize the different letters. Remind them to look at the Alphabet Cards when they need help.

Home/School Connection Home/School Connection 2 explains to the children's families that although students will be exploring writing letters they are not expected to master letter formation at this point. It also explains that you will be covering the formation of all letters again later in the year, and that you will expect the child to learn to write her or his name.

LESSON
6

••• Lesson Overview

New Learning

- Exploring letters: *Bb*

Materials

- "Hickory, Dickory, Dock," page 6 of *Pickled Peppers*
- Pocket Chart
- Word Cards for "Rain, Rain, Go Away" and "Hickory, Dickory, Dock"
- Name necklaces
- Learning Framework Card 10
- Classroom Support Teacher Tool Card 1
- Reproducible Master 1

Prepare Ahead

- For each child, a set of at least eight paper squares, each with a capital letter, a number, or a symbol, such as a star, a smile face, a heart (or use Reproducible Master 1)

✳ READING THE BIG BOOK

"Hickory, Dickory, Dock"
page 6 of *Pickled Peppers*

Developing children's print awareness is important in kindergarten. Use *Pickled Peppers* along with other Big Books to reinforce print: distinguishing words from pictures, recognizing letters, following the left-to-right progression of writing, and so forth.

Have children gather around you so that they can all see the Big Book.

- Open the book and read the poem "Hickory, Dickory, Dock" aloud.
- Read the poem through once again, this time pausing between words and pointing to the words as you read. This is a familiar poem; after a few readings, children may be ready to "read" it with you. If they are, point to each word as the children "read" it.
- To help children focus on words, read up to the last word in a line.

Ask the children what the last word in the line is. If they answer correctly, say, "Yes. The last word in the line is *dock.*" Repeat this procedure with all lines of the poem.

- Point to the pictures that accompany the poem and say that although pictures are different from words, they also help give meaning to a poem or story. Let children take turns pointing to pictures as they are mentioned in the poem. Next, ask the children to find any pictures that they do not hear mentioned in the words of the poem.

TIP FOR ENGLISH LANGUAGE LEARNERS

To encourage English Language Learners' creative and independent use of language, have them talk with a classmate about the words *mouse* and *clock.* Encourage them to talk about anything they know about a mouse or a clock. Informally monitor the children's understanding of the meanings of the words and how the words are related to the poem.

✳ PHONEMIC AWARENESS

Listening

Identifying the First, Middle, or Last Words in Sequence Now that the children have had quite a bit of practice locating sounds and words within a sequence, you might ask them to identify the entire sequence.

- Begin with three-word sequences that will sound familiar to the children. As an example, say, "Feed the mouse." Model the response you are looking for by saying, "The first word is *feed,* the middle word is *the,* and the last word is *mouse.*" Try another simple, three-word sequence in a familiar context. Ask the children for the first, middle, and last word. Remind them to use complete sentences in their responses.
- Continue with the phrase "Hickory dickory dock." Put the words in the Pocket Chart.
- Ask the children to listen again. Say longer sequences of words from the poem. Begin with "The mouse ran up the clock," enunciating each word in the sequence strongly and clearly. Ask children to say the last word. Choose another sequence such as "The clock struck one." Ask children to say the first word. If the children suggest *clock* was the first word, ask them to listen again. Say the words slowly and explain that *the* is a word, and that it is the first word in the sequence. Next, try the sequence "The mouse ran down," enunciating *the* clearly. Ask children to say the first or last words.
- When children give correct answers, point to the sequence of words in the Big Book to show the position of the words. When they make a mistake, show the word they have chosen and explain why it is the wrong answer.

Listening for Rhythm Clapping out the rhythmic beat of a poem and then segmenting it line by line will help children to hear language in parts rather than as one continuous stream of sounds.

- Teach the children this simple poem:

Rain, rain, go away.
Come again another day!

First, simply clap out the poem, word by word, until all the children have learned it.

- Put the poem in the Pocket Chart, saying each word as you do so. Now repeat the poem slowly, one line at a time, clapping word by word.

- Ask the children to do the same. Tell them that you will point to a group, and that the group should recite a line together and clap. Point to the line the group recites. Continue until everyone has had a chance to recite one line.

LETTER NAMES AND SHAPES

Letter Names

Sing Your Way to _G_ Game Play the Sing Your Way to _G_ game. Have one child wear the puppet and point to a letter (_Aa–Gg_). Let the class or a group sing to that letter and stop. If the child with the puppet forgets the letter, then you ask, "What is the letter?" and wait for the class or group to answer. Give several children a chance to play the game.

Find a Letter Remind the children that they are learning the names of all the letters of the alphabet, _a–z_, and point to the Alphabet Cards.

- Say that words are composed of letters and are found everywhere: in books; on cards, posters, and calendars; and in many other places. Tell the children that they can find letters all around the room. Say that some letters may look slightly different from those on the Alphabet Cards, but they are the same letters, _a–z_.

- Walk around the room and locate large letters, perhaps on posters, charts, or signs. If the letter begins a word, cover all of the word but the large letter. Say, "This is a letter. Can anyone tell me its name?" If no one can, name the letter, and then ask a child to point to that same letter on the Alphabet Cards.

- Identify more letters in the same manner.

- Now point to a number, perhaps on the calendar. Ask, "Is this a letter?" Reinforce the answer: "No, this is **not** a letter." Do the same thing with a picture.

- Conclude by identifying and naming two or three more letters, and then matching them with those on the Alphabet Cards.

- On the chalkboard or chart, keep a list of the letters found and the names of the children who found each letter

Letter Shapes

Exploring Letters—_Bb_ If possible, use the overhead projector in this activity so that you and your students can form letters together. You may use the handwriting system outlined in detail on **Classroom Support Teacher Tool Card 1**, or you may use the writing system that is standard in your school. Remember that at this point, children are not expected to master the writing of the letter _b_. The letter _b_ will be the focus of later lessons. This activity is intended to give the children more work with the letter so that they will learn to recognize it.

- Direct children's attention to the _Bb_ Alphabet Card. Point to the

> **TEACHING TIP**
>
> Switching between whole class, small group, and individual response makes sure all children stay engaged and gives you a chance to focus on individual children and to assess individual children's progress. Devise different ways of dividing children into groups: all girls, all children wearing sneakers, and so forth.

capital letter *B* and the small *b*. Tell the children that you will be writing the capital letter *B* first. Say, "Start at the top, and go straight down. Start at the top again and then around this way (right), in at the middle, then around this way (right), and in at the bottom. Capital *B*." Make several capital *B*'s, repeating the description of what you do each time. Have the children mimic your strokes in the air with their fingers and then use their pencils to make the strokes on blank paper.

- Go through the same steps for small *b*. Say, "Starting at the top, go straight down, back up, and around this way (right), and all the way around. Small *b*."

- When children have finished, ask them to put their name necklaces in front of them. Ask, "Does anyone have a *B* as the first letter in their name?" If there are children whose names start with *B* and no one answers, remind the children of those whose names do begin with *B*. Say, "Ben's name starts with a capital *B*, because capital letters are used at the beginning of names." Ask, "Does anyone have a *b* anywhere else in their name?" Remind them that a capital *B* is only used at the beginning of a name, but a small *b* is used anyplace else.

✱ WORKSHOP

The children are probably more comfortable with the idea of working on their own now. You may want to take a few minutes to congratulate them on their work habits or on the way they are keeping the Workshop area neat. **Learning Framework Card 10** contains more information about Workshop.

- Remind children of the work they did earlier in the day finding letters. Tell them that in the workshop area they will find sets of squares that contain either letters, numbers, or pictures. These are the squares that you prepared ahead or from **Reproducible Master 1**. The children can each get a set of cards and then look through them, sorting the letters, numbers, and pictures into separate piles. Next, they should name the letters in the letter pile. They may sing their way to the letter if they need help.

- This is a good time to see whether children are catching on to the letter names. Circulate, asking children to name their letters. If you believe your students can work with partners, make this a partner activity and have the students identify the letters for each other.

LESSON 7

Lesson Overview

New Learning

- Phonemic awareness: listening for the wrong word
- Exploring letters: *Cc*

Materials

- "Hickory, Dickory, Dock," page 6 of *Pickled Peppers*
- Name necklaces
- Classroom Support Teacher Tool Card 1
- Activity Sheet 5

✳ READING THE BIG BOOK

"Hickory, Dickory, Dock"
page 6 of *Pickled Peppers*

Gather the children around you and open *Pickled Peppers* to "Hickory, Dickory, Dock."

- Read the poem through several times, emphasizing the rhyming words, *hickory/dickory* and *dock/clock.* Read the poem again and ask the children, "What rhymes with *hickory*? What rhymes with *dock*?"
- Tell the children you might do something wrong and that you want them to raise their hands when they see or hear you do something wrong. Read the poem once, following the words with your fingers. Now start reading it backward from the last word at the bottom of the page. When children say you must start at the top, start with the last word of the first line. When children say you must start with the first word, read the first word of each line. Ask children what you should do. Emphasize that reading moves from top to bottom, left to right.
- Read the poem through again several times. If the children know the poem well enough, you can ask them to recite it slowly as you point to each word. Model this for them first. Remind them to wait until you point to a word before saying it.

✳ **PHONEMIC AWARENESS**

Listening

Listening for Word Changes By having children listen for mistakes in your reading, such as lines or words out of order, you will help them sharpen their listening skills and increase their confidence. This kind of listening activity can be done with poems that the children are already familiar with, and it can also serve as a review of past selections from *Pickled Peppers.*

- You can continue to sharpen your students' listening skills by having them listen to familiar poems that you recite incorrectly. Ask them to listen closely and to raise their hands when you make a mistake. As soon as some children have raised their hands, repeat the poem so that others can listen for the mistake. It is important to use poems that are very familiar to the children so that they can experience success.

- Try some of the following:

I'm a little teapot, short and stout
Here is my handle, here is my ketchup,
(Say, "When the words change, the poem doesn't rhyme as well, does it?")
When I get all steamed up, me hear shout,
(Say, "Two words have switched places, haven't they?")
Tip me over and pour me out.

This old man, he played one, he played knick-knack on my one,
With a knick-knack, paddy-whack, give a dog a bone . . .

This old man, he played one, he played knick-knack on my thumb,
With a pad-whack, knicky-knack, give a dog a bone . . .

This old man, he played one, he played knick-knack on my thumb,
With a knick-knack, paddy-whack, give the bone a dog . . .

This man old, he played one, he played knick-knack on my stick,
With a knick-knack, paddy-whack, give a dog a bone . . .

- To hear some of these mistakes the children will need to concentrate very hard, especially when you speak in the usual rhythm. Always take care to go back and compare your incorrect line to the correct line.

Word Substitution Any practice in which children are becoming more aware of words as separate units will help them prepare for listening to separate sounds as units within words. In the last lesson, your students broke a poem down into lines. In this lesson, they will break it down into words and work again with word substitution.

- Review the poem and clap it out, word by word.

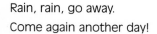

Rain, rain, go away.
Come again another day!

- Have the children sit in a circle. Move around the circle and recite the poem slowly, one word at a time. Tap a different child on the head for each word you say. Now choose a child to go around the circle, tapping others on the head. This time, the child who is tapped says the word. The child who says *day* then takes the place of the child who tapped him or her. Allow four or five children to have a turn as the "tapper."
- Ask the students to substitute a word for *rain.* Give an example first, such as, "Skunks, skunks, go away. Come again another day!" Play the tapping game with *skunks.* When a child becomes the "tapper," she or he can substitute another word for *rain.* Be prepared to help the child think of a word to use.

LETTER NAMES AND SHAPES

Letter Names

Alphabet Song Review the Alphabet Song by singing it all the way through once with the children, clapping as you say the letters *G, N, Q, T, W, Z.* Point to each letter on the Alphabet Cards as you sing its name.

Sing Your Way to *N* Game Extend the Sing Your Way to *G* game to include the letters to *N.*
- Point to, but do not name, any letter between *Gg–Nn.* Ask the children to sing the Alphabet Song with you until you reach the letter and then to stop and identify the letter.
- Point to other letters between *Gn–Nn* and ask several groups of children to sing their way to them and stop.

Find a Letter Review the list of letters found yesterday. Ask children to name the letters already on the list.

Continue having children find other letters around the room. Add these letters to the list. Then point to an Alphabet Card letter such as *Pp* and to a *p* you have written on the list. You might note that the letters look slightly different—one may be larger, smaller, a different color—but they are all *p*'s.

Letter Shapes

Exploring Letters—*Cc* Remember that the goal in Lessons 1–30 is for the children to explore the formation of the letters in order to become familiar with letter names and shapes. These lessons are not intended to build children's proficiency in letter writing. Letter formation, along with proofreading, will be covered, starting in Lesson 51. **Classroom Support Teacher Tool Card 1** contains more information about this subject.

- Direct children's attention to the *Cc* Alphabet Card. Point to the capital letter *C* and the small *c*. Tell the children that you will be writing the capital letter *C*. Say, "Start here and go around this way (left) and stop. Capital *C*."

- Make the letter several times, having the children imitate your strokes in the air with their fingers and then with their pencils on blank paper.

- Repeat the steps for small *c*. Say, "Start here and go around this way (left) and stop. Small *c*."

- Ask children to find the *Cc*'s in their name necklaces, reminding them that a capital *C* will be used as the first letter and a small *c* will be used anywhere else.

✴ WORKSHOP

Remember to be available to give help or encouragement, but allow the children to work independently as much as possible.

- Have children write their names on **Activity Sheet 5.** Help those who are having trouble. Ask these children to look at their name necklaces and to practice writing their names on the backs of their Activity Sheets.

- Show the students that Activity Sheet 5 has many pictures. Some of the pictures have letters in them. Some have numbers. Tell the children to take their time and to look carefully at all the pictures. Ask them to color in any picture that has letters in it.

LESSON 8

Lesson Overview

New Learning

- Exploring letters: *Dd*

Materials

- "Hickory, Dickory, Dock," page 6 of *Pickled Peppers*
- Name necklaces
- Pocket Chart
- Picture Cards: *cat, fish, lamp, lock, moon, rock, sack, sock, wing*
- Individual Alphabet-Sound Cards for listening: *fan, lamb, nose, pig, yaks, zipper*
- Word Cards for "Hickory, Dickory, Dock"
- For each child, one set of Uppercase and Lowercase Letter Cards: *Hh–Jj* or *Kk–Mm*
- Activity Sheet 6

✳ READING THE BIG BOOK

"Hickory, Dickory, Dock"
page 6 of *Pickled Peppers*

Gather the children around you and open *Pickled Peppers* to "Hickory, Dickory, Dock." Place the Pocket Chart so that everyone can see it.

- Ask whether anyone can recite the poem, "Hickory, Dickory, Dock," then read the poem through once and review the rhyming words: *hickory/dickory, dock/clock.*
- Put the Word Cards containing the words of the poem in the Pocket Chart, saying each word as you place it in the chart:

Hickory   dickory   dock,
The   mouse   ran   up   the   clock,
The   clock   struck   one,
The   mouse   ran   down,
Hickory   dickory   dock.

Tell the children that you are going to make the poem sound different by using Picture Cards to substitute a new rhyming word for *clock.*

- Show the children the *sock, rock,* and *lock* Picture Cards and say the name of each. Tell the children that you are going to substitute these words for *clock,* and then say the poem with the new words. Read the poem again, pointing to each card. Before you say *clock,* remove the card and allow a child to replace it with the *sock* Picture Card and say the word. Continue until you come to *clock* again and have the child replace it with the second *sock* card.

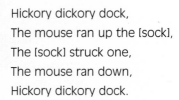

Hickory dickory dock,
The mouse ran up the [sock],
The [sock] struck one,
The mouse ran down,
Hickory dickory dock.

Reread the poem with the new words.

- Ask whether anyone wants to point to each word as the class reads it together. Make sure the children recite the poem slowly, keeping pace with the pointer and waiting to say the next word until it is indicated.
- Repeat, allowing other children to substitute the Picture Cards for *rock* and *lock.*
- Review the rhyming words, saying them together: *clock/sock/rock/lock/dock.*
- Next, ask the children whether they can think of other words that rhyme with *clock.* Say, "Can you make a word that rhymes with *clock*?" Use the words the children suggest as you recite the poem. If children cannot name any rhyming words, suggest some yourself: *knock, block, shock, stock, flock, smock,* and so on.

Listening

Substituting Rhyming Words You can extend the work with the Big Book by continuing to make rhymes. Remember that some children may not be ready to make rhymes on their own, even if they can listen for them and identify them. Giving them a visual clue will allow them to make new rhymes that match the changes you make in a familiar verse.

- Use of Picture Cards will help make this activity accessible to everyone. Put up the *cat* card and two additional Picture Cards on the Pocket Chart, such as *moon* and *lamp.*
- Tell the children that you can change the poem by saying a different word for *dock.* For example, say, "Hickory dickory dat, the mouse ran up the ____." If no one has offered the word, repeat *dat,* and start to say *ca—.* Point to the *cat* Picture Card if necessary. When the children say *cat,* repeat the two lines again, substituting *cat* to rhyme with *dat.* Ask a child to remove the *cat* card and hold it up while you lead the class in saying *dat, cat.* Replace the *cat* card with one of the

TIP FOR ENGLISH LANGUAGE LEARNERS

The Picture Cards serve as valuable visual clues for English Language Learners and will help build their English vocabularies. Review the Picture Cards you will use in the activity with English Language Learners before using them with the whole class. During the whole class activity, encourage English Language Learners to offer responses. Praise them for their efforts.

other Picture Cards. Tell the children they will help you change the
poem again and repeat the procedure.

- Continue the activity, trying the following words and pictures (either
  from the Picture Cards or the Individual Alphabet-Sound Cards):
  hickory dickory dig/ (pig); . . . *daks/* (yaks); . . . *doze/* (nose); . . .
  dan/ (fan); . . . *dipper/* (zipper); . . . *dack/* (sack); . . . *ding/* (wing); . . .
  dish/ (fish).

Word Substitution Recite the poem "Rain, Rain, Go Away" again.
Hold up an object from the room and have a child name it. Now ask the
class or the child to recite the poem, substituting the object's name in
place of rain.

Continue, using other objects. To give many children a chance, you
might want to return to this game on another day.

LETTER NAMES AND SHAPES

Letter Names

Sing Your Way to *N* Game Review the Sing Your Way to *N* game.

- Ask the whole class to sing to the letters the puppet points to before
  you call on individual children to do so.
- Choose a child to play the Sing Your Way to *N* game. Have the child
  wear the puppet and point to a letter from *Gg–Nn*. The class should
  then sing to the letter and stop. The child should ask, "What is the
  letter?" and wait for the class to answer. Continue, allowing other
  children to wear the puppet and point to a letter.

Find a Letter Go to the chalkboard and review your list of letters from
the previous lessons.

- Point to a child's name and ask, for example, "Carl, what letter did
  you find?" After the child identifies the letter, point to the next letter
  and continue down the list.
- Just as in the previous lesson, ask a few more children to find letters
  somewhere in the room. Then add the letters and the children's
  names to the list, saying, "Juana found a *b*," and so on.

Letters *Hh–Mm* Gather the children around you.

- Give each child a set of Uppercase and Lowercase Letter Cards with
  the letters *Hh–Jj* or *Kk–Mm.*
- Ask the children to look at their cards to see if they have one with
  the letter *H*. Tell them that if they do, they should hold the card up
  when you give the signal. If children are having trouble doing this,
  use the Alphabet Cards and sing your way to *H.* Point to the capital
  letter on the card and tell them that this is a capital *H.* Then tell them
  to turn their cards over and show the small *h* to the person next to
  them. Continue with the activity for the remaining letters, asking the
  children to hold up either capital or small letters for each.

Letter Shapes

Exploring Letters—*Dd* Direct children's attention to the *Dd* Alphabet Card.

- Point first to the capital *D* and then to the small *d.* Tell the children that you are going to write the capital letter *D.* Have the children announce the letter as well. Say, "Start at the top, and go straight down. Start here, around this way (right), and in at the bottom. Capital *D.*"

- Make the letter several times, having the children imitate your strokes in the air with their fingers and then on blank paper with their pencils.

- Repeat the steps for small *d.* Say, "Start here, around this way (left), and all the way around. Start here and go straight down, touching the circle. Small *d.*"

- Ask students to find *Dd*'s in their name necklaces, reminding them that a capital *D* is used as the first letter and that small *d*'s are used everywhere else. You might also have them look for *Dd*'s in the list of letters you have placed on the board for the Find a Letter activity.

✳ WORKSHOP

By now your students should be entering into Workshop quickly and heading directly to their activity. You may need to discuss procedures or rules with some individual children if they are not taking the initiative in their work. Reassure children that you will be available to help them during Workshop.

- Distribute **Activity Sheet 6.** Ask the children who can do so to put their names on Activity Sheet 6. Those who need practice can write their names on the back of the Activity Sheet.

- Hold up Activity Sheet 6 and run your finger along the path of letters from *B* to *F.* Tell the children that they can connect the letters from *A* to *G* to complete the picture of the clock. Then they can color in the picture. Remind them to start at *A* and go to the letters in order until they get to *G.* Remind the children that they can use the Alphabet Song or the Alphabet Cards to help them complete their Activity Sheets.

LESSON 9

••• Lesson Overview

New Learning

- Phonemic awareness: listening for the substituted sound
- Exploring letters: *Ee*

Materials

- "This Old Man," pages 8–9 of *Pickled Peppers*
- Name necklaces
- Pocket Chart
- Picture Cards: *bee, core, door, 5, 4, glue, knee, 1, shoe, stew, store, 3, tree, 2*
- Word Cards for "This Old Man" and "Five Little Monkeys"
- For each child, one set of Uppercase and Lowercase Letter Cards: *Hh–Jj* or *Kk–Mm*
- Rhymes and Games Teacher Tool Card 1
- Reproducible Master 2
- Activity Sheet 7

Prepare Ahead

- For each child, four squares of paper, each with a numeral 1–4 (or use Reproducible Master 2)

✳ READING THE BIG BOOK

"This Old Man"
pages 8–9 of *Pickled Peppers*

Open the Big Book and review the song "This Old Man." Ask the children to sing as you point to the words.

Use the Pocket Chart to review the activity of substituting pictures for the words that rhyme with *one, two, three,* and so on. Place the first two lines of the song in the chart, using the Picture Card for *thumb:*

This old man, he played 1,
He played knick knack on my thumb.

- Remove *1* and replace it with the Picture Card *2*. Remove the *thumb* Picture Card and replace it with the *shoe* Picture Card. With the numeral as a clue, the children should be able to recite the lines. Ask them to do so as you point to each word.

- Now tell the children you will be changing the song by adding a new rhyming word for *2*. Replace the *shoe* picture with the *glue* picture. Ask someone to name the picture, then read the lines through. Do the same with the picture of *stew*.

- Continue in the same manner with the Picture Cards for each number rhyme up to *4*: *shoe, glue, stew; knee, bee, tree; door, core, store.*

✳ PHONEMIC AWARENESS

Listening

The Ship Is Loaded with ____ Game Introduce the game, The Ship Is Loaded with ____. Tell the children they are going to pretend to load a ship with rhyming words. For this game, have the children sit in a circle and give them something to roll or toss, such as a ball. Say, "The ship is loaded with cheese." Then roll the ball to a child who must produce a rhyme for the last word, *cheese* (for example, "The ship is loaded with peas"). After the child makes the rhyme, he or she returns the ball to you. Repeat the same rhyme the child has made ("The ship is loaded with peas") and roll the ball to another child, continuing this way until the children run out of rhyming words.

- If children cannot think of a rhyme, you can help them by cuing them with a beginning sound and encouraging them to follow. **Rhymes and Games Teacher Tool Card 1** contains a complete description of the game.

- When the children have run out of rhymes for *cheese*, begin again with new cargo.

   The ship is loaded with cheese. *(peas, fleas, trees, bees, keys, . . .)*
   The ship is loaded with logs. *(dogs, hogs, frogs, . . .)*
   The ship is loaded with mats. *(cats, rats, bats, hats, . . .)*
   The ship is loaded with stars. *(cars, bars, jars, . . .)*

Word and Number Substitution This lesson lends itself to additional enumeration rhymes. These rhymes are excellent for reinforcing counting skills as well as for working with rhythm. In addition, this lesson will give children the opportunity to segment a line of a poem, reinforcing the idea of separate words.

- Teach the children the playground poem, "Five Little Monkeys":

   Five little monkeys, jumping on the bed.
   One fell off and bumped his head.
   Four little monkeys, jumping on the bed.
   One fell off and bumped his head.
   Three little monkeys, jumping on the bed.
   One fell off and bumped his head.
   Two little monkeys, jumping on the bed.

TIP FOR ENGLISH LANGUAGE LEARNERS

Give English Language Learners a chance to share their knowledge and language with other children. Encourage English Language Learners to translate the words *ship* and *cheese* into their primary languages. Invite them to talk about the meaning of each word. Recognizing minority languages is a good way to prevent inhibitions about using language. It also provides native English-speaking children with an opportunity to learn about different languages and cultures.

One fell off and bumped his head.
One little monkey, jumping on the bed.
One fell off and bumped his head.
Mama called the doctor and the doctor said:
No more monkeys jumping on the bed!

Say the poem together several times until the children know it quite well.

- Give each child four squares of paper with the numerals from 1 to 4 that you prepared ahead or from **Reproducible Master 2.** Have them place these squares of paper on the floor in front of them. Review the numbers by having the children hold up the correct square of paper when you ask for a number.

- Use the Pocket Chart to display the following Word and Picture Cards:

  5   little   monkeys   jumping   on   the   bed.

  Recite the first line of the poem, pointing to each word. Then recite the second line and when you are done, take the *5* card away. Say, "Little monkeys jumping on the bed," pointing to each word. Ask, "If one fell off and bumped his head, how many monkeys are there now?" Ask a child to hold up the paper slip with the correct number. Ask another child to bring the paper with that number on it to the chart and put it in the right place. Now read the line again, substituting the new number. Continue in this manner until you get to "1 little monkey." On "1 little monkey," place a finger over the *s* in *monkeys,* so as not to confuse any children who can read.

- Start at *5* again, and go through the poem a few more times.

LETTER NAMES AND SHAPES

Letter Names

Alphabet Song Review the Alphabet Song by singing it all the way through once with the class. Remember to point to each letter and clap as you say the letters *G, N, Q, T, W, Z.*

Sing Your Way to *T* Game Extend the Sing Your Way to *G* game to include the letters to *T.*
- Point to, but do not name, any letter between *Nn* and *Tt.* Ask the children to sing the Alphabet Song with you and the puppet until you reach the letter and then to stop and identify the letter.
- Point to other letters between *Nn* and *Tt* and ask individual children to sing their way to these letters and stop.

Find a Letter Review your list of letters from the previous lessons.
- After all the letters have been identified, select more children to find letters.
- Add these children's names and letters to the list. Remember to help those who need assistance in identifying single letters.

Letters *Hh–Mm* Gather the children around you in a group.

- Give each child a set of Uppercase and Lowercase Letter Cards with the letters *Hh–Ij* or *Kk–Mm.* Try to give individuals different sets from the ones they worked with in Lesson 8.
- Ask the children to look at their cards to see if they have one with the letter *H.* Tell them that if they do, they should hold the card up when you give the signal. If children are having trouble identifying the chosen letter, use the Alphabet Cards and sing your way to *H.* Point to the capital letter on the card and tell them that this is a capital *H.* Then tell them to turn their cards over and show the small *h* to the person next to them. Continue with the activity for the remaining letters, asking the children to hold up either capital or small letters for each.

Letter Shapes

Exploring Letters—*Ee* Direct children's attention to the *Ee* Alphabet Card.

- Note that the *Ee* card is red. Ask the children what other card was red. If someone answers *a,* say, "Yes, the *Aa* card was red. *A* and *e* are both special letters called vowels."
- Point to the capital letter *E* and the small *e.* Tell the children that you will be writing the capital letter *E.* Say, "Start at the top, and go straight down. Start here, and go straight out. Start here, and go straight out. Start here, and go straight out. Capital *E.*"
- Repeat several times, having the children imitate your strokes in the air with their fingers and then on blank paper with pencils.
- Repeat the steps for small *e.* Say, "Start here, go straight out, then around this way (left) and stop. Small *e.*"
- Ask the children to find the *Ee*'s in their name necklaces, reminding them that a capital *E* is used as the first letter and a small *e* is used anywhere else.
- Repeat the Find a Letter activity by having the children look for *Ee*'s in the room.

✳ WORKSHOP

Encourage the children to ask for your help during Workshop. Becoming aware of their own strengths and areas of need is an important part of Workshop.

- Circulate during Workshop and note children who are improving in writing their names, as well as those who still need work on their initial letters.
- Hold up **Activity Sheet 7.** Tell the children that the dog is trying to find his way to the old man who is waiting for him with a bone. Explain to the children that they should use a pencil and follow the path of letters from *A–G* until they reach the man with the bone. Remind them to follow only the letters and not the numbers or pictures.

MONITORING TIP Using Observation Log 1, record the names of children who can write their names. Give help to those who cannot.

LESSON 10

Lesson Overview

New Learning

- Exploring letters: *Ff*

Materials

- "One, Two, Buckle My Shoe," pages 12–13 of *Pickled Peppers*
- Name necklaces
- Exploring Sounds and Letters, page 3
- For each child, one set of Uppercase and Lowercase Letter Cards: *Aa–Nn*
- Activity Sheet 8
- Rhymes and Games Teacher Tool Card 2
- Home/School Connection 3

✳ READING THE BIG BOOK

"One, Two, Buckle My Shoe"
pages 12–13 of *Pickled Peppers*

You can continue to help students learn more about the parts of a book by introducing the table of contents.

- Open the Big Book to the table of contents. Remind the children that you have already read selections from *Pickled Peppers* called "I'm a Little Teapot," "Hickory, Dickory, Dock," and "This Old Man." Point to these titles in the table of contents and read them. Tell the children that today you are going to read "One, Two, Buckle My Shoe." Find the title in the table of contents and read it, then point to the numeral 12 and say it. Let the children know that this number tells you that you can find the poem on page 12. Turn to page 12 and point to the page number.
- Point to the title of the poem and read it. Then read "illustrated by Ju-Hong Chen" and ask if anyone remembers what this means. Remind the children that the illustrator drew the pictures that go with the poem.
- Read the poem, pointing to each line of text as you do so and

TIP FOR ENGLISH LANGUAGE LEARNERS

Talk more with English Language Learners about the illustrations in the selection before reading it. Show how the important aspects of the text relate to the illustrations. Associating English text with pictures helps English Language Learners to think more in English.

emphasizing the rhyming words. Say *two* and *shoe,* and remind the children that both words end with the /o͞o/ sound.

- Draw children's attention to the illustrations. Point to the word *shoe* and say it. Ask children to find the picture of the shoe. Have a child point to the picture. Continue with *door, sticks, straight* (ask them, "Are the sticks lined up straight?"), and *hen.*
- Now read the poem again, pointing word by word. Remind children that words are groups of letters. Ask children to point to a word or count the number of words in a line.
- Pocket chart activities for this selection will be covered in Lesson 11.

✳ PHONEMIC AWARENESS

Listening

Simon Says Playing the well-known Simon Says game is an excellent opportunity to work on listening skills as well as on the meaning of prepositions and positional words such as *over, behind, before, after, first, middle, last,* and so forth. If any of the children already know the game, invite them to explain it to the rest of their classmates.

In order to help the children in listening and following the directions, you should take the part of Simon until you are sure that all the children know and are comfortable with what they are to do.

- Have the children stand in a line in front of you. Explain that you will give them a direction but they are to follow the direction only if you say, "Simon says" first.
- Start with very easy directions and use "Simon says" for the first few so you can be sure the children understand that they are to perform certain actions. For example, say "Simon says take a step toward me." Wait for the children to respond and then say, "Simon says take a step back."
- When you are sure the children understand this part, try giving a direction without saying "Simon says." For example, "Step forward." Help the children understand that they are not to respond if you don't say "Simon says."
- Once you are sure all the children understand what to listen for, try easy Simon Says routines focusing on the position words listed above. Then have the children take turns being Simon. **Rhymes and Games Teacher Tool Card 2** contains instructions for this game.

Word Substitution Continue working on word substitution, this time breaking down a sentence and then changing it using the children's names. This will reinforce their ability to recognize their names as well as help them focus on words as separate units.

- Ask the children to hand you their name necklaces. Have them say the line, "One, two, buckle my shoe," with you several times. Now hold up a name necklace, and wait for the child to recognize it. Then say with the children, "One, two, buckle Sarah's shoe."
- Continue in the same manner, holding up name necklaces and substituting the child's name in the line. Soon children should be able to say the new line on their own.

Exploring Sounds and Letters, page 3

LETTER NAMES AND SHAPES

Letter Names

Sing Your Way to _T_ Game Play the Sing Your Way to _T_ game. Have one child wear the puppet and point to a letter (_Nn–Tt_), as the other children sing to the letter and stop. If the child with the puppet forgets, then you ask, "What is the letter?" and wait for the other children to answer. Give several children a chance to play.

❯ **Exploring Sounds and Letters** Distribute copies of the workbook Exploring Sounds and Letters to each child. Explain to the children that these books will be theirs to work in for the rest of the year. Show them the place where they are to keep their books when they are not using them and talk to them about how to take care of the books.

Tell the children to open Exploring Sounds and Letters to page 3. Tell them to look closely at the picture. Say, "In this picture, all of the letters from _A_ to _G_ are hidden. Take your pencil and circle as many of them as you can find."

Letter Shapes

Exploring Letters—*Ff* Direct children's attention to the *Ff* Alphabet Card.

- Point to the capital letter *F* and the small *f.* Tell the children that you will be writing the capital letter *F.* Say, "Start at the top, and go straight down. Start here, and go straight out. Start here, and go straight out. Capital *F.*"
- Make the letter several times, having the children mimic your strokes in the air with their fingers and then on blank paper with pencils.
- Repeat the steps for small *f.* Say, "Start here and go around this way (left) and straight down. Start here, and go straight across. Small *f.*"
- Ask children to find the *Ff*'s in their name necklaces and elsewhere in the room.

✱ WORKSHOP

Be sure that the children understand the directions for the activity before beginning Workshop. Children who feel confident to undertake their tasks will do so with enthusiasm.

Distribute **Activity Sheet 8.** Explain to the children that they should find the matching pairs of shoes. Point out that each shoe contains a letter—either capital or small. Tell them to draw a line connecting the capital *A* to the small *a,* the capital *B* to the small *b,* and so on. Afterwards, they can color the shoes: the *A* and *a* one color, the *B* and *b* one color, and so on.

If children have not yet worked as partners in Workshop, establish the rules for partner work and have the children play **Ordering Letters *Aa–Nn.***

- Tell children that they will each find a set of Letter Cards *Aa–Nn* in their Workshop materials area. (The cards in each set should be shuffled out of order and facing different ways.)
- Tell the children they should do two things with these cards. First, they should turn all of the cards so that they are showing either all capitals or all small letters. Then they should show the set to their partner to check.
- Next, have each child work with a partner and match each capital letter with a small letter.

Home/School Connection Home/School Connection 3 contains a note to families that describes a few games they can play with their children to reinforce learning the letters of the alphabet. The note tells families that you expect children to recognize capital and small letters *Aa–Zz,* but that so far, children have focused on letters *Aa–Nn.* Send Home/School Connection 3 home with the children.

LESSON
11

●●● Lesson Overview

New Learning

- Exploring letters: *Gg*

Materials

- "One, Two, Buckle My Shoe," pages 12–13 of *Pickled Peppers*
- Pocket Chart*
- Picture Cards: *door, 8, 5, 4, hen, 9, 1, 7, shoe, 6, sticks, straight sticks, 10, 3, 2*
- Word Cards: *A, big, Buckle, fat, Lay, my, Pick, Shut, the, them, up*
- Exploring Sounds and Letters, page 4
- For each child, one set of Uppercase and Lowercase Letter Cards: *Aa–Nn*
- Rhymes and Games Teacher Tool Card 2
- Classroom Support Teacher Tool Card 4

Prepare Ahead

- An index card with five or six letters on it, one of which is the Secret Passletter

*The Pocket Chart can be used in almost every lesson; however it will not be listed in the materials section from this point on.

✳ READING THE BIG BOOK

"One, Two, Buckle My Shoe"
pages 12–13 of *Pickled Peppers*

- Review the table of contents of *Pickled Peppers.* Find "One, Two, Buckle My Shoe" and ask a child to follow with his or her finger over to the numeral 12. Then turn to page 12 and read the poem.
- Tell the children that you will be putting "One, Two, Buckle My Shoe" on the Pocket Chart. Explain that some of the cards you will be using will have words on them, some will have numbers on them, and some will have pictures.
- Set out the following Picture Cards, face up on a desk near the Pocket Chart: *shoe, door, pile of sticks, straight sticks, hen.* Place *1/2/Buckle/my* on the chart. Ask a child to locate the Picture Card

that completes the line. When a child picks up the *shoe* Picture Card, ask him or her to place it in the correct spot on the chart. Then read the first line over again.

- Encourage the children to make some nonsense rhymes for *two*: *One, two, Buckle my goo, blue, flew, boo,* and so on. If necessary, help them create rhymes by supplying the beginning sound.
- Repeat the steps for the second line of the poem. This time, leave out *4* and ask the children for the correct number to complete the line. Remember to reread the line, and then pause and have the children think of nonsense rhymes for the number.
- Go through the third through fifth lines of the poem, leaving out a number or picture and asking the children to supply it.
- Remember that when the children are working with the cards for *sticks* or *straight* that some of them may choose the pile of straight sticks for *sticks*. Explain that they are right, but that you will save that Picture Card to use for the word *straight* in the Pocket Chart.

✳ PHONEMIC AWARENESS

Listening

Play Simon Says. For more information on playing this game, see **Rhymes and Games Teacher Tool Card 2**. This time, emphasize words that show position, such as *over, under, in front of, behind,* and *on.*

Rhythm Return to the poem "Rain, Rain, Go Away" and clap out the words. You may also want to clap out any playground chants popular at your school.

LETTER NAMES AND SHAPES

Letter Names
Sing Your Way to *G* Game Extend the Sing Your Way to *G* game to include all of the letters to *Z*.

❯ **Exploring Sounds and Letters** Have the children complete page 4 of Exploring Sounds and Letters by finding all the small letters from *a–g* on the page.

Secret Passletter Each day, choose a Secret Passletter. Have some method that will let the children know early in the day what the Secret Passletter is. For example, you might post it outside the classroom door. Then continue to use the Secret Passletter during the day. This activity will reinforce recognition of a particular letter. You can use the Secret Passletter in a variety of ways.

In this lesson, write it on an index card along with about six other letters. At various times during the day, approach children and say, "What is the Secret Passletter?" Display your index card and allow them to point to it and say the letter name. If a child approaches you with a

TEACHING TIP

As it is printed in *Pickled Peppers*, the poem uses the words for *one, two*. You also have Picture Cards with the numerals *1, 2*. Use either when putting the poem on the Pocket Chart.

TIP FOR ENGLISH LANGUAGE LEARNERS

Reinforce the meanings of the terms *over, under, in front of, behind,* and *on* for English Language Learners by using objects in the classroom to physically demonstrate the concepts. For example, place a pencil under a book as you say the word *under*. Have the children repeat the word. Repeat the procedure with the other terms. To extend the activity, say a term aloud and have a volunteer act it out using objects in the classroom. Ask the children to determine whether or not the term was accurately portrayed.

Exploring Sounds and Letters, page 4

question or asks to be excused, hold out the card and ask, "What is the Secret Passletter?" Ask visitors to use the Secret Passletter before entering the classroom.

Letter Shapes

Exploring Letters—*Gg* Remember that at this point, children are not expected to master writing the letter *g*. Later lessons will focus on the letter *g*. This exposure is to give children more work with the letter so that they will learn to recognize it.

- Direct children's attention to the *Gg* Alphabet Card. Point to the capital letter *G* and the small *g*. Form the capital *G* on the overhead projector or chalkboard. Say, "Start here, go all the way around this way (left), and then up. Start here and go straight across. Capital *G*." Have children make the letter in the air with their fingers and then on blank paper with their pencils.
- Make the letter several times.
- Repeat the steps for small *g*. Say, "Start here, go around this way (left) all the way. Start here, go straight down, touching the circle, and down around this way (left). Small *g*"

- Make sure you say the name of the letter each time you write it.
- Find capital *G*'s and small *g*'s in children's names and in objects around the room.

* WORKSHOP

You have had some time to observe the children in class and should have a good idea about how well they are handling the Workshop time. If they are comfortable and productive, you might want to offer optional activities now and then. These additional activities will not be difficult, but rather will offer the children another way to expand their Workshop time,

Make sure children know where they can get Workshop materials. Show them the place to get the Letter Cards and remind them of the activity that they can do—**Ordering Letters.** Show them places that you have established about the room—the chalkboard, an easel, an art corner—where they can make letters either with crayons or markers, or with art material such as yarn. Let children choose an activity they want to do.

- Have children try to put Uppercase and Lowercase Letter Cards *Aa–Nn* in order and use the Alphabet Song or Alphabet Cards to help them or to check their work. Have them do both capital and small letters with two different sets of cards.
- **Classroom Support Teacher Tool Card 4** contains suggestions for classroom activities for making letters.

LESSON 12

New Learning

- Exploring letters: *Hh*
- Phonemic awareness: oral blending

Materials

- "One, Two, Buckle My Shoe," pages 12–13 of *Pickled Peppers*
- Picture Cards: *door, 8, 5, 4, hen, 9, 1, 7, shoe, 6, sticks, straight sticks, 10, 3, 2*
- Word Cards: *A, big, Buckle, fat, Lay, my, Pick, Shut, the, them, up*
- Alphabet Flash Cards: *Aa–Mm*
- Learning Framework Cards, 1, 1A, 10
- Activity Sheet 9

✱ **READING THE BIG BOOK**

"One, Two, Buckle My Shoe"
pages 12–13 of *Pickled Peppers*

- Open *Pickled Peppers.* Ask if anyone can find "One, Two, Buckle My Shoe" in the table of contents. Ask another child to turn to page 12.
- Review "One, Two, Buckle My Shoe" in *Pickled Peppers,* pointing word by word.
- Now go to the Pocket Chart and set out on a low table nearby the Word and Picture Cards for the first line. Tell the children that you know the poem by heart now. Say that you are going to recite it word by word, and that you want them to help you place the cards in the Pocket Chart as you say the words.
- Say, "*one.*" Ask a child to find the Picture Card *1* and place it in the chart. Continue with *2.* Say, "*Buckle,*" and call on a child who has shown some beginning reading ability. Tell the child that the word *Buckle* is longer than the other words on the table because it has the most letters of any word on the table. Continue with the words, *my* and *shoe,* giving help and clues as needed. Finally, have a child place the *shoe* Picture Card on the chart. Reread the line slowly. Take care

to call on children whose abilities match the task so as to ensure that all children meet with success.

- Continue the activity with each line of the poem.

✴ PHONEMIC AWARENESS

Oral Blending

Word Parts Oral blending is one of the phonemic awareness activities that will be emphasized in Sounds and Letters. The goal of oral blending activities is to lead the children to understand that spoken words are made up of smaller units of sound. Because children are accustomed to producing and hearing whole words, the challenge is to find ways to get them to notice that words contain smaller units of sound—word parts and phonemes. Research shows that once children learn to think about words in terms of their component sounds, decoding makes sense to them and spelling comes more easily.

Larger pieces of words are easier to distinguish than individual phonemes, so blending syllables and word parts is the first step in leading children to become aware of the units that make up speech. The words the children will work with are sometimes broken at a syllable, sometimes at a compound part, and sometimes broken randomly. It is not necessary for children to understand what a syllable is or to know what a compound word is. In later lessons, children learn individual letter sounds and the oral blending activities will merge with regular phonics in a natural way. **Learning Framework Card 1A** contains a complete discussion of oral blending.

- Explain to the children that as they learn to read and write, they must learn to listen carefully to how words sound. Tell them that you have a listening game for them: You will say each word in two parts, and they must listen carefully to discover what the word is. Read each word, pronouncing each part distinctly and pausing cleanly at the breaks indicated (. . .). Then say that you will put the two parts together and say the whole word.

  Teacher: Dino . . . saur. I'll say the parts again. Dino . . . saur.
               Now I'll put the parts together, *dinosaur.*

  Continue with the following words:
  butter . . . fly
  alpha . . . bet

- Now ask the children to join in with you as you put the parts together. Continue to say the word parts, just once now, and then ask the children to say the whole word with you. Try the following words:

lolli . . . pop	tele . . . vision
ele . . . phant	valen . . . tine
birth . . . day	astro . . . naut

Segmentation

Word Parts This activity is the reverse of the blending activity just completed. In that activity, the children were putting word parts or syllables together into words. In this segmenting activity, they will be breaking down words into parts or syllables. It is not necessary to use the term *syllable* with the children; this is just an activity to help them hear the separate parts of words. Blending and segmenting are complementary processes in developing phonemic awareness and in learning to read and write. Whereas learning to blend syllables and phonemes into familiar words is essential to decoding, learning to segment (divide) familiar words into parts and, later, phonemes, is essential to independent spelling. **Learning Framework Card 1, Phonemic Awareness,** contains more information about this subject.

• Remind the children that yesterday they clapped out some poems, word by word. Explain that now they will be clapping out their names, part by part. Choose a child's name and say, for example, "Let's clap out Jocelyn's name. Here we go. 'Jo-ce-lyn.'" Clap and emphasize the beat of the syllables. Starting with one or two multisyllabic names will help the children quickly understand the kind of units they are listening for. Then mix one-syllable and multisyllabic names.

• Have the children clap and say the name along with you. Repeat with other children's names until everyone is clapping the right number of times with you. Point out that some names get only one clap and that other names get two or more.

Letter Names

Sing Your Way to *Z* Game Play the Sing Your Way to *G* game to the letter *Z*. Give several children a chance to work with the puppet.

Secret Passletter Determine the Secret Passletter, and give clues as to what it is. During the day, ask several children—both those who do have it and those who don't—if they have the Secret Passletter in their name necklaces. Both those who do have the day's letter and those who don't should be recognized for their ability to know.

What Is the Letter? Show Alphabet Flash Cards for the letters *Aa–Mm.* Have children respond as a group or in subgroups by calling out the letters.

TEACHING TIP

Remember to institute a wait time that is tied to something you do, such as tapping your pencil or snapping your fingers twice. The children should listen to your question, wait for your movement, and then respond together.

Letter Shapes

Exploring Letters—*Hh* Direct children's attention to the *Hh* Alphabet Card. Point to the capital letter *H* and the small *h.*

- Form the capital *H* on the overhead projector or chalkboard. Say, "Start here, straight down. Start here, straight down, then straight across the middle. Capital *H*." Have children make the letter in the air with their fingers and then on blank paper with their pencils. Make the letter several times.

- Repeat the steps for small *h.* Say, "Start here, straight down, back up, around this way (right), and straight down. Small *h.*"

- Have children look for capital *H*'s and small *h*'s in objects in the room or in their names.

✱ WORKSHOP

Even though the children are working independently, they will talk to one another as they pick out their materials and put them away or as they quietly ask each other questions. Remind children of appropriate behavior during Workshop. Refer to **Learning Framework Card 10, Workshop,** for more instructions.

- Hold up **Activity Sheet 9** and tell the children that the frame is for a picture of themselves that they will draw. First, they should draw a picture of themselves inside the frame. Then have the children write their name on the line below their picture. Help those children who need help writing their names. Have the children point to and identify the first letter of their names. Finally, in each box all around the frame, they should write the first letter of their first name. Say, "Jennifer would write a *J* in each box all the way around the frame. Pablo would write a *P* in each box all the way around the frame." Circulate during Workshop to help the children with their letters if needed.

- When the children have finished with their Activity Sheets, let them choose to do the **Ordering Letters** or **Creating Letters** game.

TIP FOR ENGLISH LANGUAGE LEARNERS

To provide English Language Learners with an opportunity to talk with English-proficient children in a natural context, have them share their pictures with a partner. Encourage them to talk about their pictures by describing picture details and what colors they used.

LESSON
13

● ● ● Lesson Overview

New Learning

- Exploring letters: *Ii*
- Oral blending
- Alphabet Cheer

Materials

- "Sleeping Outdoors," page 24 of *Pickled Peppers*
- "Sleeping Outdoors," First-Step Story 1
- Exploring Sounds and Letters, page 5
- Learning Framework Cards 1A, 8
- Rhymes and Games Teacher Tool Card 2
- Songs Teacher Tool Card 1
- Home/School Connection 4

✱ READING THE BIG BOOK

"Sleeping Outdoors"
page 24 of *Pickled Peppers*

In this lesson, your students will work with their first First-Step Story. Each child will have his or her own book to own and take care of. Illustrating, narrating, and sharing their own stories with their friends and family will give the children a sense of pride and will allow them to practice the skills and behaviors of accomplished readers and writers. First-Step Stories are sometimes reprints of selections found in *Pickled Peppers,* sometimes new stories or poems, and sometimes picture books that the children create themselves. The children's First-Step Story, "Sleeping Outdoors," is taken from *Pickled Peppers.* Your students will illustrate their First-Step Stories in Workshop, but you can also use the stories during Reading the Big Book. **Learning Framework Card 8** contains more information on how to use the First-Step Stories with your class.

- Gather the children around you. Open *Pickled Peppers* to the poem "Sleeping Outdoors." Find its title in the table of contents and locate the page number. Allow a child to help you turn to that page. Point out the names of the author and the illustrator.
- Read the poem slowly, running your finger underneath each word. Point to the parts of the pictures that match the text.

- Reread the second and fourth lines, emphasizing the words *tree* and *me.* Point to the words and ask if anyone can point to the word that rhymes with *tree.* Ask other children to volunteer words that rhyme with *tree* and *me.* Give them a beginning sound if they need help.

"Sleeping Outdoors"
First-Step Story 1

- Tell the children they will each receive their own book. Say that its title is "Sleeping Outdoors." Hand out First-Step Story 1 to each child. Explain that it does not have any pictures because each of them will become the illustrator of his or her book.
- Tell them that you will read the book together. First ask them to look at the cover and read the title, "Sleeping Outdoors." Read "by Marchette Chute" and remind them that this is the name of the person who wrote the poem in the Big Book. Then read "illustrated by" and explain that each of them will write his or her name on the blank line because they will illustrate, or draw the pictures for, this version of "Sleeping Outdoors." Have children write their names on the line.
- Ask the children to turn to the first page of "Sleeping Outdoors." When they are all in the right place, read the line, "Under the dark is a star." Hold up your version of the First-Step Story and point out the words, one by one. Read the second line, "Under the star is a tree." Encourage the children to point to each word as you read the line together. Read the next two lines in the same way, with the children pointing to the words as you read.
- Remind the children that capital letters are used at the beginning of special words such as names, and explain that capital letters are also used for words at the beginning of each line in a poem. Point to the capital letters in the Big Book and ask the children to do the same in their own books. Explain to the children that they will need to take good care of their books because they will be using them over the next few days, both during reading time and in Workshop.

✳ PHONEMIC AWARENESS

Oral Blending
Word Parts The goal of oral blending activities is to lead the children to understand that spoken words are made up of smaller units of sound. Becoming aware of syllables and word parts is the first and easiest step toward this end. Once the children are comfortable listening for word parts, they will be ready to turn their attention to sounds within word parts—phonemes. The basic procedure for oral blending in today's lessons is the same as in the previous lesson; however, the puppet gives

new dimension to the activity. **Learning Framework Card 1A** contains a complete discussion of oral blending. Remind children that you will say words in two parts and that they must listen and then put the word parts together.

- Tell the children that you want them to play the listening game again. Say that this time, the puppet wants to play, too. Say a word, pronouncing each part distinctly and pausing cleanly at the breaks indicated (. . .). Then say that the puppet will put the two parts together and say the whole word.

Teacher: Alli . . . gator. I'll say the parts again. Alli . . . gator.
         Now let's be quiet and see if the puppet can put the words together.
Puppet: Alligator

Continue with the following words:

apart . . . ment
refrig . . . erator

- Now ask the children to join in with the puppet as it puts the word parts together.

      Say the word parts, just once now, and then ask the children to say the whole word with the puppet. Try the following words:

din . . . ner	break . . . fast	en . . . ter
ex . . . it	sis . . . ter	broth . . . er
flow . . . er	laun . . . dry	sham . . . poo
spi . . . der	cy . . . clone	

Listening

Simon Says Play Simon Says again (**Rhymes and Games Teacher Tool Card 2** contains full instructions). Again emphasize words that show position—*over, under, in front of, behind*—but add *on top of, bottom of, left,* and *right;* for example, hop *on* your left foot, put your hand *on top of* your head.

LETTER NAMES AND SHAPES

Letter Names

Alphabet Cheer Teach children another version of the Alphabet Song, one based on cheers used at football and basketball games. After imitating a drum (Boom-boom Ch!), say each letter name loudly and emphatically. (**Songs Teacher Tool Card 1** contains more instructions.)

TEACHING TIP

If the children seem to understand how to blend orally, you can ask them to respond individually or in groups and say the word out loud for the class.

Boom-boom Ch! Boom-boom Ch!

A B C D

Boom-boom Ch! Boom-boom Ch!

E F G H

Boom-boom Ch! Boom-boom Ch!

I J K L

Boom-boom Ch! Boom-boom Ch!

M N O P

Boom-boom Ch! Boom-boom Ch!

Q R S T

Boom-boom Ch! Boom-boom Ch!

U V

Boom-boom Ch!

W X Y Z

Boom-boom Ch! Ch! Boom!

Secret Passletter Choose another Secret Passletter. Today you might try sitting in a circle with the children and whispering, "The Secret Passletter is _____" into the ear of the child next to you. Have the children pass the message along in whispers around the circle. Have the last child announce the Secret Passletter and see if she or he is right. If the child says the wrong letter, try the game again, this time sending the letter in the other direction. Use the Secret Passletter several times during the day.

Letter Shapes

> **Exploring Sounds and Letters** On page 5 of Exploring Sounds and Letters, have the children match small letters *a–h* with their capital forms by writing the small letters in the second part of the leaf.

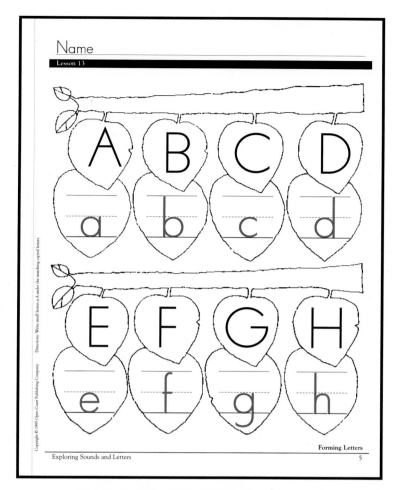

Exploring Sounds and Letters, page 5

Exploring Letters—*Ii* Remember that the goal in Lessons 1–30 is for the children to explore the formation of letters in order to become familiar with the letters' names and shapes. These lessons are not intended to build children's proficiency in writing the letters. Letter formation, along with proofreading, will begin in Lesson 51. Directions for the formation of each of the letters can be found on **Classroom Support Teacher Tool Card 1.** If you are using this style of letter formation, you might want to keep the card handy for easy reference.

- Direct the children's attention to the *Ii* Alphabet Card. Point out that *i* is red to remind us that it is a vowel, like *a.* Point to the capital letter *I* and the small *i.*
- Using the established procedure, form the capital *I* on the overhead projector or chalkboard. Make the letter several times.
- Repeat the steps for small *i.*
- Find capital *I*'s and small *i*'s in children's names and in objects around the room.

For the first time, children will begin working on a project that will last for several days. This is a big step in their independent work. Make sure that you have made arrangements for children to store their incomplete work over the next four Workshops, so that they do not lose track of their projects.

- Remind children that they will be illustrating their own book called **"Sleeping Outdoors."** Tell them that they can use crayons and draw their own pictures to help tell the story in their own way.
- Draw the children's attention to the cover of the book. Read the title and the name of the author. Then point to the line "illustrated by____" and make sure the children have all printed their own names on the line. Invite volunteers to say the line with their own names in place.
- Invite volunteers to tell what they remember about the poem. Then tell the children that their Workshop activity is to **draw a picture on the cover of the book.**
- If they have extra time, children can play the **Ordering Letters** or **Creating Letters** game.

Home/School Connection Home/School Connection 4 contains a note to families about poems and rhyming tunes. It encourages families to reinforce children's play with songs and nursery rhymes as much as possible.

TEACHING TIP

If the children have difficulty drawing, you might allow them to cut pictures out of a magazine and paste them in their books.

LESSON

14

●●● Lesson Overview

New Learning

- Exploring letters: *Jj*
- Phonemic awareness: oral blending

Materials

- "Sleeping Outdoors," page 24 of *Pickled Peppers*
- "Sleeping Outdoors," First-Step Story 1
- Learning Framework Card 1A

✳ READING THE BIG BOOK

"Sleeping Outdoors"
page 24 of *Pickled Peppers*
First-Step Story 1

Encourage children to follow in their First-Step Stories as you read in *Pickled Peppers.*

- Have the children get their copies of First-Step Story 1, "Sleeping Outdoors," and gather around you.
- Open *Pickled Peppers* to page 24. Point to the title and read "Sleeping Outdoors." Ask the children if they can find the same title on their own books. Ask them to point to it.
- Point to the author's name and read it. Ask the children to point to the author's name in their books. Now ask them to point to their names as illustrators of their own books.
- Read the poem "Sleeping Outdoors" from *Pickled Peppers* as the children follow along in their books. Read each line slowly and pause to remind the children to turn the page. Read the poem several times.
- Ask a child to come up and point to the capital letter in the first word of each line in the poem. Say, "Yes, capital *U* is the first letter in *Under,* and it is a capital because it starts a new line in the poem," and so on.
- Talk about the meaning of *Under.* Ask, "What does the book say is *under* the dark? What is *under* the star? What is *under* the tree? And what is *under* the blanket?" Point to the picture of the child in the Big Book and ask the children, "What are some of the things under *me*?"

- Ask for volunteers to read their books to the class. Let each volunteer "read" one page.
- Tell the children that they will work on their books again during Workshop.

✴ Oral Blending

Word Parts The basic procedure for oral blending in today's lesson is the same as in the previous lesson, with the puppet giving new dimension to the activity. Throughout the lessons, children will become more and more engaged in oral blending, ultimately offering the parts of the word for their classmates to blend. The puppet encourages children's responses. First, they respond as a chorus to the teacher's prompts; then they respond individually; then a child and the puppet will give parts of the word; and, finally, in later lessons, pairs of children will give both parts of the word for others to blend. **Learning Framework Card 1A** contains more information on oral blending.

- Reintroduce the puppet as your helper. Explain that today you are going to say part of a word and the puppet will say another part. Tell the children that then they can put the parts together and say the word back to you. (If the children don't seem ready for this, go back to saying the word together as a class and try this activity another day.)
- Practice a few times together.
  Teacher: pow
  Puppet: der
  Teacher: What's the word?
  Everyone: powder

Practice with a few more words:
porcu . . . pine
gir . . . raffe

Continue with the following words:

pop . . . corn	pop . . . sicle
tri . . . cycle	tri . . . angle
bum . . . blebee	bump . . . er
cir . . . cus	cir . . . cle
sug . . . ar	can . . . dy

Listening

Simon Says Play Simon Says again. This time emphasize short prepositions or words that show position, for example, *in, on, with.*

Letter Names

Alphabet Cheer Do the Alphabet Cheer the children learned in the previous lesson. This time, point to the letters on the Alphabet Cards as you say them. Repeat the cheer again and have one child point to the letters in each line.

Boom-boom Ch! Boom-boom Ch!
A B C D
Boom-boom Ch! Boom-boom Ch!
E F G H
Boom-boom Ch! Boom-boom Ch!
I J K L
Boom-boom Ch! Boom-boom Ch!
M N O P
Boom-boom Ch! Boom-boom Ch!
Q R S T
Boom-boom Ch! Boom-boom Ch!
U V
Boom-boom Ch!
W X Y Z
Boom-boom Ch! Ch! Boom!

Secret Passletter Choose a Secret Passletter and include it in activities throughout the day.

Letter Shapes

Exploring Letters—*Jj* Direct children's attention to the *Jj* Alphabet Card. Point to the capital letter *J* and the small *j*.

- Using the established procedure, form the capital *J* on the overhead projector or chalkboard. Have the children make the letter in the air with their fingers and then on blank paper with their pencils. Make the letter several times.
- Repeat the steps for small *j*.
- Look for capital *J*'s and small *j*'s in objects around the room and in children's names.

Make sure that children are storing their First-Step Stories in the Workshop area or in some other place you have designated so that they do not lose track of their projects.

- Read the first line of the poem "Sleeping Outdoors." Ask the children questions about the dark: When is it dark? What places are dark: closets? movie theaters? attics? basements? How does it feel to be in the dark? Does a light in the dark make you feel good? What other things light up the dark besides stars? flashlights? lamps? head-lights?

- Recite the first line of the poem again. Let children illustrate the first page and then put their books away until tomorrow.

- If they have extra time, children can play the **Ordering Letters** or **Creating Letters** game. Include any additional Workshop activities from your own Learning Centers that you think are appropriate.

TIP FOR ENGLISH LANGUAGE LEARNERS

Have English Language Learners practice using and producing language to communicate ideas. Encourage the children to tell what they have heard classmates say during the discussion. Then ask them to add anything they want to add about their own feelings and ideas. Praise the children's listening and speaking efforts.

LESSON
15

●●● Lesson Overview

New Learning

- Exploring letters: *Kk*
- Phonemic awareness: oral blending

Materials

- "Sleeping Outdoors," First-Step Story 1
- Exploring Sounds and Letters, page 6
- Listening Collections Audiocassette
- Songs Teacher Tool Card 4
- Observation Log 1, Reproducible Master 28

Prepare Ahead

- An index card with vowels on it, one of which is the Secret Passletter

---

✱ READING THE BIG BOOK

"Sleeping Outdoors"
First-Step Story 1

Have children get their copies of First-Step Story 1, "Sleeping Outdoors," and gather around you. Using the version of "Sleeping Outdoors" found in *Pickled Peppers,* read each line slowly and have children follow along in their individual copies, pointing to each word as you read if they are able to do so. Remember to cue them about when to turn the page.

- Draw the children's attention to *Pickled Peppers.* Ask for a volunteer to point to any word on the "Sleeping Outdoors" page. Read the word the child pointed to and then read the entire line. Repeat this activity several times.
- Point to the word *under.* Point to an object in the room and ask a child to name what is under it. Or place things one on top of the other and ask, "What is under the book?" (eraser), "What is under the paper?" (pencil), etc. Then reverse the question: "What is on top of the eraser?" (book), "What is on top of the pencil?" (paper).
- Tell the children that they will work on their stories again during Workshop.

---

* Oral Blending

Word Parts This activity is similar to previous oral blending activities. Explain that you are going to say part of a word and the puppet will say another part.

- Tell the children that when the puppet asks what the word is, they should put the word parts together and say the whole word back to you.

    Teacher: De

    Puppet: licious. What's the word?

    Everyone: Delicious

    Practice with the following words:

    ba . . . nana

    pump . . . ernickel

- Now that the children have warmed up, ask them individually to put the parts together and say the word. Continue with the following words:

    bi . . . cycle   go . . . rilla

    res . . . taurant   ham . . . burger

    grand . . . ma   centi . . . pede

    gro . . . ceries

Listening

Simon Says Play Simon Says again. This time, emphasize descriptive words, for example, take a *big* step.

Letter Names

For children to understand how the alphabet works, they must appreciate that the vowels behave differently than other letters, in both spelling and sound. You can initiate this understanding by introducing the vowels as a special subset among letters. In the upcoming lessons, the children will pay special attention to the vowels, learning to name them and to listen for their long sounds in words. This is important preparation for the How the Alphabet Works activities that begin in Lesson 21. Note, too, that extra attention to the names and sounds of the vowels is especially valuable for children for whom English is not the first language.

Vowel Song Explain to the children that there are some special letters in the alphabet called vowels. Say, "Sometimes you can hear the names of these vowels in words. To make it easier for you to remember them as a group, vowels are colored red on the Alphabet Cards." Point to each vowel on the Alphabet Cards and say its name.

- Listen to the Vowel Song on the Listening Collections Audiocassette or consult **Songs Teacher Tool Card 4** for the words. Sing the song to

MONITORING TIP For the next five days, observe four or five children a day during the lesson. Call on individual children to determine if they can orally blend word parts. Do this each day until you have checked every child. Record observations on Observation Log 1, Reproducible Master 28.

the class, pointing to the Alphabet Cards for *a, e, i, o,* and *u* as you sing them.

- Now tell the children to sing the song with you, very slowly, so that you have time to point to each letter as it is sung.

I can name the vowels for you
And you can name them too! Hoo!
A-E-I-O-U!
A-E-I-O-U!
A-E-I-O-U!
And you can name them too! Hoo!

Sing the song together several times until all of the children have caught on to the rhythm and remember the names of the vowels.

Secret Passletter Choose a vowel as a Secret Passletter for the day. Place the Secret Passletter and the other vowels on your index cards, so that the children are focusing on the vowels when you ask them for the Secret Passletter.

Letter Names
❯ **Exploring Sounds and Letters** All of the animals pictured on page 6 of Exploring Sounds and Letters sleep outdoors: the bird, crab, dog, frog, hen, insect. Point out this connection between the picture and the poem. Then have the children draw a line from the animal to its home and match small letters with capitals. Tell them that they can trace over the capital and small letters for practice.

Letter Shapes
Exploring Letters—*Kk* Using the *Kk* Alphabet Card, point out the capital letter *K* and the small *k*.

- Following the established procedure, form the capital *K* on the overhead projector or chalkboard. Have the children form the letter in the air with their fingers and then on blank paper with their pencils.
- Repeat the steps for small *k*.
- Look for capital *K*'s and small *k*'s around the room and in children's names.

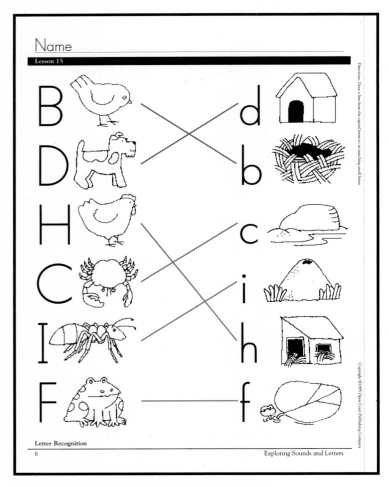

Exploring Sounds and Letters, page 6

✳ WORKSHOP

- Remind the children that they are working on their **"Sleeping Outdoors" First-Step Stories.**
- Review the second line of the poem "Sleeping Outdoors": "Under the star is a tree." Talk about trees, asking the children such questions as: What do different types of trees look like? Do you have a favorite tree? Do you have a tree in your yard or on your street? What kind is it?
- Make sure that the children have crayons. Read the second line of the poem again. Have the children illustrate page 3 in their books and put them away.
- If they have extra time, children can play the **Ordering Letters** or **Creating Letters** game. Include any additional Workshop activities from your Learning Centers that you think are appropriate.

TIP FOR ENGLISH LANGUAGE LEARNERS

Draw English Language Learners into group discussions to reinforce that their ideas are valid and worth attention. Encourage the children to express their knowledge of trees and praise their speaking efforts.

LESSON 16

Lesson Overview

New Learning

- Listening for vowel sounds
- Exploring letters: *Ll*

Materials

- "Walk Along," pages 18–19 of *Pickled Peppers*
- "Sleeping Outdoors," First-Step Story 1
- Exploring Sounds and Letters, page 7
- For each child, one set of Uppercase and Lowercase Letter Cards: *Ee–Ll*
- Listening Collections Audiocassette
- Songs Teacher Tool Cards 4 and 5

Prepare Ahead

- An index card with vowels written in small letters

✳ READING THE BIG BOOK

"Walk Along"
pages 18–19 of *Pickled Peppers*

Open *Pickled Peppers* to "Walk Along" and read the title. Explain to the children that "Walk Along" is a song that they can sing together. Say that first, you will read some of the words to them, and then you will sing it for them. If you prefer, you can use the Listening Collections Audiocassette and play the song for the class. Read the first three verses of the song.

- Read the first three verses again. As you read, show the children that they can perform some of the actions in the song as follows (use Songs Teacher Tool Card 5):

Come on, Judy, and hush your talking, (wave arm, put finger to lips)
Let's clap hands and we'll go walking. (clap to the beat)
Walk along, Judy, with your red dress on. (walk in place)
Walk along, Judy, with your red dress on. (walk in place)

. . . Let's snap our fingers and we'll go walking. (snap to the beat)
Note: If the children are not yet able to snap their fingers, simply have them
mimic the movement instead of trying to teach them to snap.
. . . Let's shake out our legs and we'll go walking. (shake legs)
. . . Let's shake our hips and we'll go walking. (twist to the beat)
. . . Let's shake our arms and we'll go walking. (shake arms around)

- Have the children stand up and perform the actions in the song as
  you sing it or play it on the Listening Collections Audiocassette.
  Follow along in *Pickled Peppers,* pointing to each word with your
  finger.
- Repeat the song several times, having the children sing along and act
  out the parts.

**TIP FOR ENGLISH
LANGUAGE LEARNERS**

Acting out the words to a song or poem is an
effective way to build the vocabularies of English
Language Learners. During Workshop, review the
song and actions with children so that they will be
more familiar with them in subsequent lessons.

✳ PHONEMIC AWARENESS

✳ Oral Blending

Word Parts This activity is similar to previous oral blending activities,
except the first part of the word gives little clue to the remainder.
Because of this, the children will have to listen carefully.
- With this first set of words that begin with only the initial consonant
  and vowel, the children receive the strongest clue to the whole word
  from the second part of the word.
- Explain that you are going to say part of a word and the puppet will
  say another part. Tell the children that you want them to put the
  parts of the word together and say it back to you.

Teacher: Dy
Puppet: namite. What's the word?
Everyone: Dynamite

Practice with the following words:

li . . . brary	high . . . way	mo . . . torcycle
mi . . . croscope	go . . . pher	pea . . . nut
wai . . . ter	bea . . . ver	lo . . . comotive
mi . . . crophone	sci . . . entist	si . . . deways

MONITORING TIP Remember to keep
monitoring children's oral blending skills.

Listening for Long Vowel Sounds

In learning to read, children must understand that letters and groups of letters represent individual sounds. The first step in learning to match single sounds to their letter forms is to be able to hear individual sounds, separately, within words. Long vowel sounds are one of the easiest sounds to hear, and so they are perfectly suited for this beginning sound-recognition activity. You have already introduced vowels as a special subset of the alphabet. And you have explained to the children that you can sometimes hear the name of the vowel in the word. The best way to demonstrate this is by having the children listen for the vowel sounds within open-syllable words. That is, words in which the first or the last sound the children hear is a long vowel.

Give children plenty of practice in listening for and identifying the long vowels sounds. If they are not catching on, slow down and return to simple listening, without asking them to identify specific vowels. Being able to hear individual phonemes as distinct units of sound is an important starting point to reading. With this foundation, children will be able to complete some basic exercises, starting in Lesson 21, that highlight the way in which phonemes are joined together in different ways to represent the speech sounds they hear every day.

Listen for Vowels—Long *a* Tell children that words are made up of sounds. Say, "If you listen closely, you can hear sounds in words. The set of letters called vowels are special because many times you can hear their names in words."

- Go to each vowel on the Alphabet Cards, have the children name it, and then give an example of a word in which you can hear the vowel's name. Say, "What letter is this? We can hear *a*'s name in the word, *tray.* Can you hear the *a* in *tray*?"

  Continue with *e* and *tree, i* and *sky, o* and *go, u* and *use.*

- Now tell children that you will say some words and you want them to listen for the vowel *a* to say its name. Tell them that they should put their thumbs up when they hear the /ā/ sound. Say, "*Bay.* Can you hear the vowel sound /ā/?"

  Tell the children to wait until you give a signal before they respond. Then try a few more words with /ā/, for example, *lay, say.*

- Now tell the children that you will say a list of words. Some of the words will have the /ā/ sound and some will not. Ask them to repeat the word and then give a thumbs-up sign if they hear the /ā/ sound in the word. Say that they should say /ā/ when you give the signal. Try the following words:

a	day	way	lay
low	so	say	grow
gay	age	ate	toe
know	hoe	high	pie
pay	may	my	me

Letter Names

Vowel Song Remind the children that sometimes you can hear the names of vowels in words. Point to the vowels on the Alphabet Cards and name them.

- Sing the "Vowel Song" again (refer to **Songs Teacher Tool Card 4** for instructions). Point to the Alphabet Cards on *A, E, I, O,* and *U.*
- Sing the song very slowly and let the children take turns pointing to the Alphabet Cards as the class sings.

❯ **Exploring Sounds and Letters** In the Exploring Sounds and Letters activity on page 7, children circle the small letters that match each of the capital letters.

Secret Passletter Have a child choose another vowel as the Secret Passletter for the day. Remember to use your index card with the vowels on it, so that children are focusing on the vowels when you ask them for the Secret Passletter. Today you might want small letter vowels on the index card.

Exploring Sounds and Letters, page 7

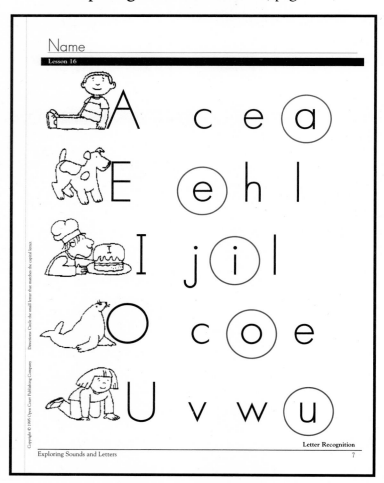

Show Me Game Give each child Uppercase and Lowercase Letter Cards *Ee–Ll.* Say a letter such as "capital *I*" or "small *h.*" Children should find the letter and then, on your signal, hold the Letter Card so that the correct letter is facing you.

Letter Shapes

Exploring Letters—*Ll* Using the *Ll* Alphabet Card, point out the capital letter *L* and the small *l.*

- Form the capital *L* on the overhead projector or chalkboard. Make the letter several times, first having children form the letter in the air with their fingers and then on blank paper with their pencils.
- Repeat the steps for small *l.*
- Look for capital *L*'s and small *l*'s around the room and in children's names.

✳ WORKSHOP

- Tell the children that they will be illustrating the last two lines of their "Sleeping Outdoors" First-Step Stories. Have them take out their books. Some children may be able to read along with you now, so encourage them to do so.
- Ask children to think about snuggling under a blanket. Ask them such questions as the following: What color blanket do you have on your bed; what is your favorite color?
- Make sure the children have crayons. Recite the third and fourth lines of the poem, and have the children illustrate the pages of their books.
- If they have extra time, children can play the **Ordering Letters** or **Creating Letters** game. Include any additional activities from your Learning Centers that you think are appropriate.

LESSON

17

●●● Lesson Overview

New Learning

- Exploring letters: *Mm*

Materials

- "Sleeping Outdoors," page 24 of *Pickled Peppers*
- "Sleeping Outdoors," First-Step Story 1
- For each child, one set of Uppercase and Lowercase Letter Cards: *Ee–Ll*
- Listening Collections Audiocassette
- Songs Teacher Tool Card 6
- Rhymes and Games Teacher Tool Card 3
- Reproducible Masters 3, 4
- Home/School Connection 5

Prepare Ahead

- Construction paper or Reproducible Masters 3 and 4, markers, glue, and glitter for use in Workshop

---

✳ READING THE BIG BOOK

"Sleeping Outdoors"
page 24 of *Pickled Peppers*
First-Step Story 1

Tell children to get their First-Step Story, "Sleeping Outdoors," and gather around you. Read the poem from *Pickled Peppers.* Have each child open her or his First-Step Story and, as you read each line slowly, have them follow along, pointing to each word. Make sure the children are turning the pages at the proper time.

- Invite volunteers to come to the front of the class and share their drawings as the class reads the poem.
- Tell children that they are going to practice reading their books so that when they have finished illustrating them, they can take them home to share. Have children read their books and show their drawings to a partner. If this is the first time the children are sharing, set some ground rules for sharing, both for the sharer and the audience. Children should not be embarrassed by their work. The environment

should be one of acceptance and support. This should prevail whenever the children share their work with classmates. Let each partner
take some time explaining his or her illustrations.

✳ PHONEMIC AWARENESS

✳ Oral Blending

This is similar to previous oral blending activities. In this set of
words beginning with a consonant and vowel, the second part of the
word does not give a strong clue to the word. Therefore, the children
must listen very carefully.

Tell the children you are going to say part of a word and the puppet
will say another part. Explain that you want them to put the parts of the
word together and say it back to you.

Teacher: wea
Puppet: sel. What's the word?
Everyone: weasel

Continue with the following words:

wea . . . ver	co . . . la
figh . . . ter	si . . . lent
ri . . . der	ta . . . ble
ra . . . dar	ma . . . ple
migh . . . ty	cei . . . ling

Listening for Long Vowel Sounds

Listening for Long *e* Remind children that you are listening for the
vowel sounds in words. Go to the Alphabet Cards and review the vowel
names and the words from yesterday. "You can hear the *a* in *tray.* You
can hear the *e* in *tree.* You can hear the *i* in *pie.* You can hear the *o* in
go. You can hear the *u* in *use.*"

Now tell children that you will say some words and you want them to
listen for the vowel *e* to say its name. Give each child an *Ee* Uppercase
and Lowercase Letter Card. Tell them that they should repeat the word
after you, then, on your signal, hold up the cards if they hear the /ē/
sound. Have them finish by saying the /ē/ sound. Try the following
words:

see	so	bow	**bee**
eat	ate	toe	now
day	**ease**	**knee**	know
she	**he**	hoe	**flee**

"Apples and Bananas" The song "Apples and Bananas" will help children listen for and say vowels. In each verse of the song, some of the
vowel sounds are replaced with a new vowel sound. (The song can be
found on **Songs Teacher Tool Card 6** and on the Listening Collections
Audiocassette.)

• Tell the children they are going to hear a song named "Apples and
Bananas" that will help them hear and say the special letters called
vowels.

- Sing or play the song for the children:

> I like to eat, eat, eat
> apples and bananas.
> I like to eat, eat, eat
> apples and bananas.
> In the next verse, some of the vowels are replaced with /ā/.
> I like to ate, ate, ate
> ayples and baynaynays.
> In the next verse, some of the vowels are replaced with /ē/.
> I like to eat, eat, eat
> eeples and beeneenees.

And so on.

- Sing the song together, announcing the vowel sound for each new verse and pointing to the Alphabet Card. For example, say, "And now let's sing for /ī/." Go through all the vowel sounds slowly.

LETTER NAMES AND SHAPES

Vowel Names
Vowel Song   Sing the "Vowel Song" again.

Letter Names
Secret Passletter   Have a child choose another vowel as the Secret Passletter for the day.

Show Me Game   Give each child Uppercase and Lowercase Letter Cards *Ee–Ll.* Say a letter such as "capital *I*" or "small *h.*" Tell the children to find the letter and then, on your signal, hold up the Letter Card so that the correct letter is facing you.

Letter Shapes
Exploring Letters—*Mm*   Remember that at this point, letter-writing activities are meant only to develop in children a certain level of comfort and experience with letter formation. The letters will appear in later lessons, lending more careful attention to their formation.
- Using the *Mm* Alphabet Card, point to the capital letter *M* and the small *m.*
- Using the established procedure, form the capital *M* on the overhead projector or chalkboard.
- Make the letter several times, first having children form the letter in the air with their fingers and then on blank paper with their pencils.
- Repeat the steps for small *m.*
- Find capital *M*'s and small *m*'s in children's names and around the room.

Remember, the letter-recognition activities are not meant to create letter-writing proficiency in children. But the combination of activities, including singing, writing, letter puzzles and other worksheets, plus the Fine Art activities will promote letter recognition. The following includes another letter activity you might want to add to your collection of letter-recognition activities.

- Because children are now halfway through the alphabet in **Exploring Letters,** this is a good time to review some letter shapes. Explain to the children that they will be making their own **Letter Lines.** Hold up a strip of colored construction paper that has been marked with the capital letters *A–G* or use **Reproducible Masters 3** and **4.** Tell the children that in Workshop, they can write over the letters in glue and then sprinkle them with glitter. Remind them to say each letter's name as they work on it. Store the Letter Lines. In subsequent lessons, the children will make additional glitter letters. You will want to staple them together, matching up the lines, to make a complete Letter Line for each child to take home.

- Introduce the **Hop Along** game (use the Hop Along Game Mat). The object of the game is to move one's marker from the bunny to the carrot at the end of the trail. When a child's marker lands on a letter, the child must name (1)

  the letter or (2) the sound of the letter, as designated by you. Demonstrate both levels. Explain that if a player does not correctly name the letter or sound, he or she must either (1) go back a space at a time until he or she is able to answer correctly for a letter, or (2) lose the next turn. (It is up to you to decide which rule would be best for your group. Or you may decide on a new rule.) There are additional spaces designated for losing a turn (sad face) and for getting a free turn (happy face). Explain the game to the children. Circulate around the room and help the children learn the game.

- You might want to establish a Game Corner and include the Hop Along game as part of Workshop. A description of Hop Along can also be found on **Rhymes and Games Teacher Tool Card 3.** Put Hop Along in the Game Corner and have it available as an activity during Workshop.

Home/School Connection Home/School Connection 5 contains a note to the families explaining the First-Step Stories, in this case, "Sleeping Outdoors." Send this note home with the book.

LESSON
18

● ● ● Lesson Overview

New Learning

- Exploring letters: *Nn*

Materials

- "Walk Along," pages 18–19 of *Pickled Peppers*
- Picture Cards: *black, blue, bow, brown, dress, green, orange, pants, pink, purple, red, shirt, shoe, shorts, skirt, sock, white, yellow*
- Word Cards: *along, on, Walk, with, your*
- Exploring Sounds and Letters, page 8
- For each child, one set of Uppercase and Lowercase Letter Cards: *Ee–Ll*
- For each child, Uppercase and Lowercase Letter Card: *Ii*
- Classroom Support Teacher Tool Card 1
- Reproducible Masters 5, 6

Prepare Ahead

- Name cards for each child for the Pocket Chart; you may use your set of name necklaces
- Construction paper or Reproducible Masters 5 and 6, markers, glue, and glitter for Workshop

---

✳ READING THE BIG BOOK

"Walk Along"
pages 18–19 of *Pickled Peppers*

Open *Pickled Peppers* to the song "Walk Along." Read through the first verse, pointing to each word. When you come to the words *red dress,* ask a child to point to the red dress in the picture in *Pickled Peppers.* Then ask the children if anyone in the class is wearing red. If someone is wearing anything red—shoes, socks, or shirt—substitute that child's name and the name of the article of clothing in the verse and then sing it again as a group.

- Continue this procedure with the next three verses.
- Now tell the children that you have a game for them. When you sing a verse, they will need to guess who "so-and-so" is. Sing a verse,

using the words *so-and-so* for a child's name, and then name something being worn by that child. If you say, for example, "Walk along, so-and-so, with your blue bow on," the children have to look for the child with the blue bow and name her.

- Place all the color Picture Cards in one area on a low table and all the other Picture Cards in another area. Have the children hold their name cards. Now invite the children to gather around the Pocket Chart. Place the words in the chart, saying each one slowly: *Walk/along/*(child's name)*/with/your/*(Picture Card) *red/*(Picture Card) *dress/on.* Read this line over a few times. Ask the children if anyone wants to read the line on his or her own.

- Now ask a child to come up and change some of the words and pictures. First, have the child replace the name card with her or his own name. Next, remove the color card, and ask the child to replace it with a new one. Then have the child replace the clothing card. Now, ask the child to recite the new line as you point to each word or picture. Help if necessary. Give several children a chance to change the line.

> **TIP FOR ENGLISH LANGUAGE LEARNERS**
>
> English Language Learners may need additional practice using the names of colors. As part of the discussion about the song, point to articles of clothing in the illustrations and have children name the color of each. Then have English Language Learners classify classroom items by color.

✳ PHONEMIC AWARENESS

✳ Oral Blending

Word Parts The children may notice the consonant and long vowel sound at the end of each word in this set. The first part of the word should give a strong clue to what the whole word is.

Tell the children that the puppet is going to say part of a word and you will say another part. Explain that you want them to put the word together and say it back to you.

Puppet: pota
Teacher: to. What's the word?
Everyone: potato

Continue with the following words:

occu . . . py	toma . . . to	avoca . . . do
Colora . . . do	zucchi . . . ni	chimpan . . . zee
magni . . . fy	satis . . . fy	mug . . . gy
multi . . . ply	dictionar . . . y	

Listening for Long Vowel Sounds

Listening for Long *i* Remind children that you are listening for the vowel sounds in words. Go to the Alphabet Cards, and review the vowel names and the words from yesterday. Make sure that each child has an *Ii* Uppercase and Lowercase Letter Card.

- Now tell the children to listen for the vowel *i* to say its name /ī/.
- Say that when you say the word, you want them to repeat it, hold up their *Ii* Letter Cards if the word has a long *i* sound, and then say /ī/. Try the following words:

try	cry	fry	fly	buy
bye	shy	my	sigh	pie
flow	throw	glow	bow	crow
die	guy	sly	lie	why

"Apples and Bananas" The song "Apples and Bananas" provides the children with strong support in using the same vowel sound in different consonant contexts. If you sing the song slowly, it is easy for children to make the vowel sound replacements. Sing the song together, and point to the appropriate Alphabet Card before each new verse.

LETTER NAMES AND SHAPES

Letter Names

Alphabet Cheer Return to the Alphabet Cheer. If you have musical instruments in your class, encourage children to make music while they cheer. Individual children can take turns being the "band leader" and point to the letters on the Alphabet Cards.

Secret Passletter Have a child choose another vowel as the Secret Passletter for the day.

Show Me Game Give each child Uppercase and Lowercase Letter Cards *Ee–Ll.* Say a letter such as "capital *I*" or "small *i.*" Tell the children that they should find the letter and then, on your signal, hold the Letter Card so the correct letter is facing you.

Letter Shapes

Exploring Letters—Nn Using the *Nn* Alphabet Card, point out the capital letter *N* and the small *n.*

- Using the established procedure, form the capital *N* on the overhead projector or chalkboard. Refer to **Classroom Support Teacher Tool Card 1** for complete instructions on forming the letters.
- Make the letter several times, first having children form the letter in the air and then on paper.
- Repeat the steps for small *n.*
- Look for capital *N*'s and small *n*'s in children's names and in things in the room.

❯ **Exploring Sounds and Letters** Open Exploring Sounds and Letters to page 8. Have children copy the *Ll, Mm,* and *Nn* letters.

✳ WORKSHOP

Remember to offer additional activities only if the children are comfortable and productive during Workshop.

- Continue with the glitter **Letter Line** activity for letters *H–N,* using **Reproducible Masters 5** and **6**. Review the procedure for the children (see Workshop in Lesson 17) and then keep their Letter Lines to be assembled later.
- Encourage children use the areas of the room—chalkboard, easel— designed to allow them to create letters.
- For each child, have Uppercase and Lowercase Letter Card sets from *Ee–Ll,* shuffled and out of order. Have the children put the letters in order. Then encourage pairs of children to match capital and small letters.
- Have the **Hop Along** Game Mat available so that children can play the game described in Lesson 17.

Exploring Sounds and Letters, page 8

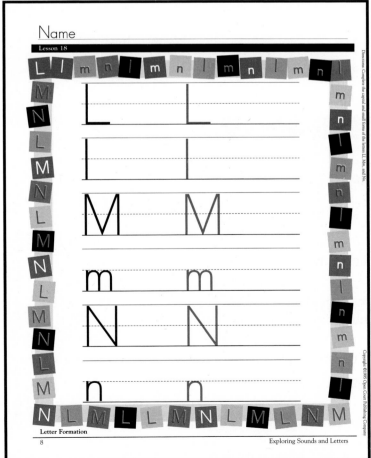

LESSON
19

● ● ● Lesson Overview

New Learning

- Exploring letters: *Oo*

Materials

- "Walk Along," pages 18–19 of *Pickled Peppers*
- Picture Cards: *black, blue, bow, brown, dress, green, orange, pants, pink, purple, red, shirt, shoe, shorts, skirt, sock, white, yellow*
- Word Cards: *along, on, Walk, with, your*
- For each child, one set of Uppercase and Lowercase Letter Cards: *Ii–Oo*
- Reproducible Masters 7, 8
- Home/School Connection 7

Prepare Ahead

- Construction paper for Letter Lines, or use Reproducible Masters 7, 8

✳ READING THE BIG BOOK

"Walk Along"
pages 18–19 of *Pickled Peppers*

Open *Pickled Peppers* to the song "Walk Along." Read through the verses, then have the children stand and act out the song.

- Play the game from Lesson 18 in which the children must find "so-and-so."
- Repeat the activity from Lesson 18 in which the children come to the Pocket Chart and change words in the line, "Walk along, Judy, with your red dress on."
- Remind children to look for individual letters in the words of the song.

✱ Oral Blending

Word Parts This activity is similar to previous oral blending activities. As in earlier activities, the children may notice the consonant and long vowel sound at the end of each word in this set. However, this time, the first part of the word does not give a strong clue to what the whole word is.

Puppet: rain
Teacher: bow. What's the word?
Everyone: rainbow

Continue with the following words:

rai . . . ny	can . . . dy
clou . . . dy	hap . . . py
san . . . dy	win . . . dy
quick . . . ly	bubb . . . ly
win . . . dow	pil . . . low

Listening for Long Vowel Sounds

Listening for Long *o* Remind children that you are listening for the long vowel sounds in words.

- Go to the Alphabet Cards, and review the vowel names and the words *tray, tree, pie, go,* and *use.*
- Tell children that you will say some words and that you want them to listen for the vowel *o* to say its name, /ō/. Tell them that they should put their thumbs up when they hear the /ō/ sound. Try the following words:

may	play	snow	show	so
flow	throw	glow	grow	gray
go	no	new	flew	blew
blow	slow	dough	foe	pay

"Apples and Bananas" Sing the song "Apples and Bananas" with the children. Remember to point to a new vowel Alphabet Card before you begin each verse.

Vowel Names

Secret Passletter Choose a vowel not yet used as the Secret Passletter for the day.

MONITORING TIP You should complete the monitoring of the children's oral blending of word parts. Record your observations on Observation Log 1, Reproducible Master 28.

TIP FOR ENGLISH LANGUAGE LEARNERS

Return to the same activity often to provide opportunities for English Language Learners to feel comfortable with the activities. Encourage them to participate when the whole class is engaged in the activity. Watch for children who are not responding and work with them in small groups during Workshop.

Letter Names

Alphabet Cheer Do the Alphabet Cheer. Hand out two Uppercase and Lowercase Letter Cards to each child. After the cheer, play the game of Give me an *N*. Everyone with an *N* should stand and shout "*N!*" Repeat with other letters the children have learned.

Show Me Game Give each child Uppercase and Lowercase Letter Cards *Ii–Oo*. Say a letter such as "capital *I*" or "small *m*." Tell the children to find the letter and then, on your signal, hold the Letter Card so that the correct letter is facing you.

Letter Shapes

Exploring Letters—*Oo* Using the *Oo* Alphabet Card, point out the capital letter *O* and the small *o*. Remind students that *o* is a vowel.

- Form the capital *O* on the overhead projector or chalkboard. Remember, as you make the letter, use the terms *left* and *right* only if the children are familiar with them. They will be watching your strokes on the overhead projector or chalkboard for the direction.
- Make the letter several times, first having children form the letter in the air and then on blank paper.
- Repeat the steps for small *o*.
- Find capital *O*'s and small *o*'s in children's names and around the room.

✱ WORKSHOP

- Continue with the glitter **Letter Line** activity for the letters *O–T*, using **Reproducible Masters 7** and **8**.
- Encourage children use the areas of the room—chalkboard, easel— designed to allow them to create letters.
- For each child, have Uppercase and Lowercase Letter Card sets from *Ii–Oo* shuffled and out of order. Have the children work in pairs to place the letters in order and play the **Show Me** game described in Lesson 18.
- Have the **Hop Along Game Mat** available for children to play the game. Make sure children who go to the Game Corner know how to play the game. (See Rhymes and Games Teacher Tool Card 3.)

Home/School Connection Skip Home/School Connection 6 for now and distribute Home/School Connection 7. It contains a note to families that describes a few more games they might play with their children to reinforce learning the alphabet. Explain to families that you are expecting children to recognize capital and small letters *Aa–Zz*. Suggest that they find ways to help their children learn the letters. You will use Home/School Connection 6 in Lesson 22.

LESSON
20

●●● Lesson Overview

New Learning

- Exploring letters: *Pp*

Materials

- "Bluebird, Bluebird," page 26 of *Pickled Peppers*
- Exploring Sounds and Letters, page 9
- For each child, one set of Uppercase and Lowercase Letter Cards: *Ii–Oo*
- For each child, Uppercase and Lowercase Letter Card: *Uu*

Prepare Ahead

- Construction paper for Letter Lines or use Reproducible Masters 9, 10

✳ READING THE BIG BOOK

"Bluebird, Bluebird"
page 26 of *Pickled Peppers*

Open *Pickled Peppers* to the table of contents and find "Bluebird, Bluebird." Ask if anyone can help you find the page number, then turn to that page.

- Read through the song several times, pointing to each word.
- Remind children that words are made up of separate groups of letters and that words are separated by spaces. Read the first two lines of the song. Ask children to count the words in these lines. See if they are able to point to some words in the song.

✱ PHONEMIC AWARENESS

✱ Oral Blending

Word Parts With this set of words, children may notice that when the second half of the word changes, they are blending an entirely new word.

- Say the first part of the word, and have the puppet say the second part. Then have the class put the word together and say it back to you.

  Teacher: rock
  Puppet: y. What's the word?
  Everyone: rocky

  Continue with the following words:

rock . . . et	rock . . . er	rock . . . ing
be . . . tween	be . . . hind	be . . . fore
be . . . cause	be . . . gin	neigh . . . bor
neighbor . . . hood	neighbor . . . ly	plan . . . ter
plan . . . et	plann . . . ing	

Listening for Long Vowel Sounds

Listening for Long *u* Move on to listening for the /ū/ vowel sound in words. Go to the Alphabet Cards and review the vowel names and the identifying words. Give children a *Uu* Uppercase and Lowercase Letter Card to hold up when they hear the /ū/ sound. Try the following words:

try	cry	cue	pew	view
shy	my	menu	few	nephew
unit	unite	buy	guy	hue
fuel	mule	tie	why	

"Apples and Bananas" Sing the song together, and point to the *Uu* Alphabet Card to announce a new verse.

LETTER NAMES AND SHAPES

Letter Names

Sing Your Way to *G* Game Play the Sing Your Way to *G* game, choosing any letter from *a–z*. Try to focus in on those letters that the children have the most difficulty recognizing.

❯ **Exploring Sounds and Letters** Tell children to open Exploring Sounds and Letters to page 9. Show them that if they connect the dots, from letter to letter, in order from *A–N,* they will complete the picture of the bluebird. Tell children to color the bird blue after they have completed the drawing.

Show Me Game Give each child Uppercase and Lowercase Letter Cards *Ii–Oo.* Say a letter such as "capital *I*" or "small *m.*" Tell the children that they should find the letter and then, on your signal, hold the Letter Card so that the correct letter is facing you.

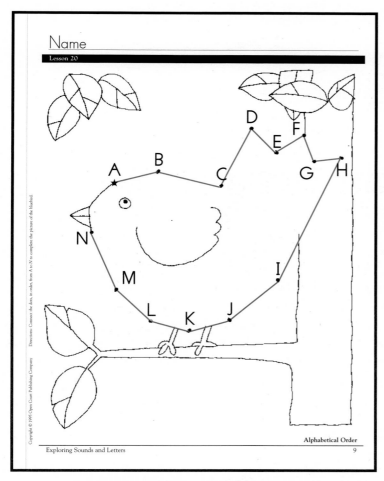

Exploring Sounds and Letters, page 9

Letter Shapes

Exploring Letters—*Pp* Using the *Pp* Alphabet Card, point out the capital letter *P* and the small *p*.

- Using the established procedure, form the capital *P* on the overhead projector or chalkboard.
- Make the letter several times, first having children form the letter in the air and then on blank paper.
- Repeat the steps for small *p*.
- Find capital *P*'s and small *p*'s in the room or in children's names.

✱ WORKSHOP

- Continue with the glitter **Letter Line** activity for letters *U–Z,* using **Reproducible Masters 9** and **10.**
- For each child, have Uppercase and Lowercase Letter Card sets from *Ii–Oo* shuffled and out of order. Have the children work as partners to place the letters in proper order and match capital and small letters. Children may also want to play the **Show Me** game with a partner.
- Make the **Hop Along** game available.

MONITORING TIP Recheck to see if children can write their names. During Workshop and when children are working, help those who cannot write their names. Use Observation Log 1 to record the names of all children who can write their names.

LESSON
21

● ● ● Lesson Overview

New Learning

- How the Alphabet Works
- Initial consonants
- Exploring letters: *Qq*

Materials

- "Bluebird, Bluebird," page 26 of *Pickled Peppers*
- Word Cards for "Bluebird, Bluebird"
- For each child, one set of Letter Cards: *Ii–Oo*
- Learning Framework Card 5
- Songs Teacher Tool Card 7
- Classroom Support Teacher Tool Card 1

✳ READING THE BIG BOOK

"Bluebird, Bluebird"
page 26 of *Pickled Peppers*

The goal of this activity is to demonstrate the concept that the same printed word stands for the same spoken word in every instance.

- Open *Pickled Peppers* to "Bluebird, Bluebird" and read the song to the children. Ask a child to come forward and point to each line as the two of you sing the song together. Pause before the second verse and ask another child to come forward and point to the words as you sing the song. (The music can be found on Songs Teacher Tool Card 7.)

- Place in your lap the Word Cards for the first and second lines of the song and have the Word Cards for the third and fourth lines on a nearby table that the children can see. Place the words *Bluebird/ bluebird/Go/through/my/window/* in the Pocket Chart. Say each word as you place it in the chart.

- Read the third line of the song. Ask the children what the difference is between the first line and the third. Reread if necessary. Explain that the lines must be exactly alike.

- With this clue and using line one as a model, have the children place the Word Cards for the third line in the chart, one at a time.

- Do the same with the fourth line. Remind the children that when the lines are the same, they will have the same words in the same order.

- Reorder two words in one of the lines and ask the children if it is the same.

- Place the words for the remaining lines and then read the whole song.
- Reread the first verse, reciting the first two lines and pointing to each word. Invite a child to point to each word in the third and fourth line as the class says it. Continue with other children for the remaining lines. Leave the words in the Pocket Chart for the next lesson.

TIP FOR ENGLISH LANGUAGE LEARNERS

English Language Learners will benefit from multiple exposures to the song. The repetition of the words and actions in the song will help reinforce the connection between the words and their meanings.

✳ PHONEMIC AWARENESS

✳ Oral Blending

Initial Consonants As the focus of this lesson shifts to phonemes, the blending activity marks an important transition. The goal of this activity is to show the children that the initial consonant of a word can be broken off and put back on. Rhyming words are useful in helping the children recognize this initial sound. Make sure when you say the initial consonants that you emphasize the phoneme.

Teacher:	/l-l-l/
Everyone:	/l/
Puppet:	ocket
Teacher:	What's the word?
Everyone:	locket
Teacher:	Again, with me: /l/ . . . ocket

Continue with the following words:

/r/ . . . ocket	/p/ . . . ocket	
/m/ . . . ountain	/f/ . . . ountain	
/s/ . . . andal	/h/ . . . andle	/k/ . . . andle
/n/ . . . oodle	/p/ . . . oodle	/d/ . . . oodle

✳ HOW THE ALPHABET WORKS: PART 1

The beginning lessons in this Sounds and Letters module focused on giving children a solid foundation in learning to recognize letter forms and to listen and attend to sounds. This next segment of lessons, entitled How the Alphabet Works: Part 1, complements this important foundation. These lessons will help children understand that letters work together in a systematic way to connect spoken language to written words. The purpose of the lessons is to engage children in experiences that will help them develop some fundamental understandings, including:

- a limited number of letters combine in different ways to make many different words;
- words are composed of sounds, and letters represent those sounds;
- anything that can be pronounced can be spelled;
- letters and sounds can be used to identify words; and
- meaning can be obtained by using letters and sounds to figure out words.

In Lessons 22–25, you will give each child a Letter Card to use in the activities. In Lessons 26–30, you will give them each an Alphabet-Sound Card to use in the activities, because in these lessons they will be associating the sound with the name of the letter. **Learning Framework Card 5** has more information about these activities.

I Can Spell Anything The goal of this lesson is to reinforce for the children the idea that anything that can be pronounced can be spelled with the letters they already know.

- Have the children give you a word. Tell them you know how to spell that word. Write the word on the chalkboard. Show them that the word contains the letters shown on the Alphabet Cards.
- Create opportunities for the children to help you. For instance, "I think this word starts with a *p*. Which letter is a *p*?" Point to the appropriate Alphabet Card.
- When you are done, have the children spell the word again, letter by letter, and say the word.
- Continue, encouraging children to come up with some difficult or "big" words.

LETTER NAMES AND SHAPES

Letter Names

Show Me Game Give each child Uppercase and Lowercase Letter Cards *Ii–Oo*. Name a letter such as "capital *I*" or "small *m*." Children should find the letter and then, on your signal, hold their Letter Cards so that the correct letter is facing you.

Letter Shapes

Exploring Letters—*Qq* Using the *Qq* Alphabet Card, point out the capital letter *Q* and the small *q*.

- Refer to **Classroom Support Teacher Tool Card 1** to form the capital *Q* on the overhead projector or chalkboard. Have the children say the letter name with you.
- Make the letter several times, first having children form the letter in the air and then on blank paper.
- Repeat the steps for small *q*.

✳ WORKSHOP

Make sure that the children are aware of the activities that are available to them in the Learning Centers.

- Have the children finish their **Letter Lines.**
- Encourage the children to use the areas of the room such as the chalkboard or easel that are designed to allow them to create letters.
- Have a set of Uppercase and Lowercase Letter Cards *Ii–Oo* for each child, shuffled and out of order so they can play the **Ordering Letters** game.
- Make the **Hop Along** game available.

LESSON
22

• • • ## Lesson Overview

New Learning

- How the Alphabet Works
- Exploring letters: *Rr*

Materials

- "Bluebird, Bluebird," page 26 of *Pickled Peppers*
- Word Cards for "Bluebird, Bluebird"
- Exploring Sounds and Letters, page 10
- Uppercase and Lowercase Letter Cards: *Bb, Dd, Ff, Hh, Ll, Mm, Nn, Pp, Rr, Ss*, and *Tt* (one card for each child and two of each letter for you; vowels for you)
- For each child, one set of Uppercase and Lowercase Letter Cards: *Ii–Oo*
- Songs Teacher Tool Card 7
- Learning Framework Card 5
- Home/School Connection 6

Prepare Ahead

- Capital letters and small letters of *Ii–Oo* for **Match My Letter**
- Various Special Letter materials for Workshop activities: headline letters from newspapers, large letters from magazines and other sources, letter cutouts and stencils, handwritten letters on index cards, plastic letters
- Special Letter containers and glue

✳ READING THE BIG BOOK

"Bluebird, Bluebird"
page 26 of *Pickled Peppers*

This lesson focuses on the children's oral/aural knowledge of the song to diagnose problems they may have with the order of printed words. The lesson will help children learn the importance of word order and the correspondence of printed words to spoken words.

- Review "Bluebird, Bluebird" by reading it once in *Pickled Peppers* and then singing it with the children. (See Songs Teacher Tool Card 7.)
- Review the first verse of the song as you put the words in the Pocket Chart.
- Hide all the lines of the song except lines one and two by turning the cards over.

- Change a word in lines one and two. For example say, *dickory* for *window.* Read it aloud a few times. Ask children which word is wrong. Then reveal lines two and three of the poem by turning the cards over. Read the lines, again changing a word. Ask the children which word is different.
- Repeat the substitution activity several times.

✱ PHONEMIC AWARENESS

✱ Oral Blending

Initial Consonant Continue the activity in which the children blend the initial consonant sound with the rest of the word. This time, say the initial consonant sound, then have the puppet say the remainder of the word. Have the children put the word together and say it.

Teacher:	/m-m-m/
Everyone:	/m-m-m/
Puppet:	eatball
Teacher:	What's the word?
Everyone:	meatball

Continue with the following words:

/f/ . . . ootball	/d/ . . . ickory	/h/ . . . ickory
/f/ . . . ellow	/y/ . . . ellow	/m/ . . . ellow
/b/ . . . umpy	/l/ . . . umpy	/g/ . . . rumpy
/t/ . . . omato	/p/ . . . otato	

✱ HOW THE ALPHABET WORKS: PART 1

In How the Alphabet Works, you are introducing the children to the idea that letters and their associated sounds work together in a systematic way to create words. The activities in this section will help children gain insight into that system. Refer to **Learning Framework Card 5** for more information. In this lesson, each child will become a "Letter Expert" on a certain letter. Assign at least two children to each letter so that they can work together.

I'm a Letter Expert

- The following subset of letters will be used in the How the Alphabet Works lessons: *Bb, Dd, Ff, Hh, Ll, Mm, Nn, Pp, Rr, Ss,* and *Tt.*
- Give each child an Uppercase and Lowercase Letter Card with one of the letters from the above subset. Tell the children that they are going to become experts on their letter's name, shape, and, later, sound. Assign the letters quickly. Avoid drilling the children. Simply make sure they understand that they are responsible for a particular letter and that they know who else in the class has the same letter and will be part of their group. If you do not have twenty-two children in your class, arrange any leftover Letter Cards on the chalkboard, and tell the children that you will be the Letter Expert for these letters, and for all the vowels.

- After each child in a group has been given a letter, do a quick rehearsal of all the group letters. Call on someone from each group to say, "Our letter is _____." Explain to the children that each day you will hand out their Special Letters and that they should place them in front of them.
- Make a set of Letter Cards for yourself that contains two cards for each letter. Shuffle these cards and put them in your lap. Hold the cards up one by one, and ask the children in that Letter Expert group to hold up their Special Letters and say the letter name when you give the signal.

TEACHING TIP

First call on the whole group, for example, the *Bb* Letter Experts. Ask the question, "What is your Special Letter?" and then call on someone from within the group to answer so that all the children will listen.

LETTER NAMES AND SHAPES

Letter Names

❯ **Exploring Sounds and Letters** Have the children complete the letter maze on page 10 of Exploring Sounds and Letters. Explain that the chef needs to find his big pot in order to cook the stew. Tell the children to follow the letters *I–O* with their pencils to help the chef reach the pot.

TIP FOR ENGLISH LANGUAGE LEARNERS

Before completing this page, discuss the illustration with English Language Learners. Point to the chef, cat, and various objects in the picture as you name each. Provide time for children to practice naming the objects to help them build their English vocabularies.

Exploring Sounds and Letters, page 10

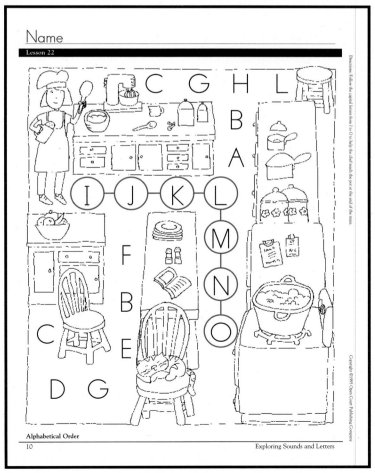

Match My Letter Using the capital and small letters of *Ii–Oo* that you prepared ahead, give half the children capital letters and the other half the matching small letters. Tell the children with capital letters that they will need to walk around the group and try to find the small-letter partners to their letters. Say that when they find the person with the matching letter, they should join hands and raise their cards. Check to make sure correct matches have been made. Redistribute the cards and repeat, letting the children with small letters do the searching.

Letter Shapes

Exploring Letters—*Rr* Remember that at this point, children are not expected to master writing the letter *r*. The letter *r* will be the focus of later lessons. This activity is intended to give children more work with the letter so that they will learn to recognize it.

- Using the *Rr* Alphabet Card, point out the capital letter *R* and the small *r*.
- Form the capital *R* on the overhead projector or chalkboard. Have the children say the letter name with you.
- Make the letter several times, first having children form the letter in the air and then on blank paper.
- Repeat the steps for small *r*.
- Find *Rr*'s in children's names and around the room.

✳ WORKSHOP

For the next few lessons, children will be focusing on their Special Letter as a part of their Letter Expert activities. Gather a set of materials such as letters from newspapers or plastic letters that the children can search through to find their Special Letter. Then give each Letter Expert group a large plastic bucket, paper bag, or special place to store the Special Letters they find.

- Place the Special Letter materials in the Workshop area. Tell the children to get in their Letter Expert groups and sort through the materials, looking for their Special Letter. They can work together to decorate the container, gluing their Special Letters to the outside.
- Have the children use the areas of the room such as the chalkboard or easel that you have designated as a place for them to create their Special Letters.
- Have Uppercase and Lowercase Letter Cards *Ii–Oo* for each child, shuffled and out of order so that children can play the **Ordering Letters** game.
- Have the **Hop Along** game ready to play.

Home/School Connection At this point you can distribute Home/School Connection 6. It contains a note to families that explains the objectives of How the Alphabet Works.

LESSON 23

• • • Lesson Overview

New Learning

- How the Alphabet Works
- Exploring Letters: *Ss*

Materials

- "Bluebird, Bluebird," page 26 of *Pickled Peppers*
- Name necklaces
- Word Cards for "Bluebird, Bluebird"
- Uppercase and Lowercase Letter Cards: Corresponding to Special Letters and the vowels
- Uppercase and Lowercase Letter Cards: *Dd, Hh, Ll, Pp, Tt, Vv, Zz*
- Activity Sheet 10

Prepare Ahead

- Special Letters (on brightly colored paper), three for each Letter Expert group

---

✳ READING THE BIG BOOK

"Bluebird, Bluebird"
page 26 of *Pickled Peppers*

Review "Bluebird, Bluebird" by singing it together, and pointing to the lines in *Pickled Peppers.* Children have been working with the repeating lines of the first verse for three days. They should be ready to place the words on the Pocket Chart without much help from you. Place the words /*Bluebird*/*bluebird*/*Go*/*through*/*my*/*window*/ on a low table and out of order. Tell the children that you will be saying each line and that they will place the words on the chart. Say, "*Bluebird.*" Ask a child to find the word. If the child chooses *bluebird,* tell him or her that this is the first word, so the child should find the *bluebird* with the capital *B.* Have the word placed in the chart. Continue on with the rest of the words for the first two lines, calling on other children to place them on the first two lines of the Pocket Chart.

- When you finish each set of lines, place the cards for the next two lines on the table and call on more children to choose the words as you say them. The completed Pocket Chart looks like this:

Bluebird, Bluebird,
Go through my window.
Bluebird, Bluebird,
Go through my window.
Bluebird, Bluebird,
Go through my window.
Oh, Johnny what a day.

- Now read the second verse of "Bluebird, Bluebird" in *Pickled Peppers,* pointing to each word as you read it. Read the second verse one more time, pointing to a different child to say each word as you point to it. Allow children to place the words of the second verse on the Pocket Chart using the same procedure used for the first verse. If necessary, place the first line yourself so that children can use it as a model.

✳ PHONEMIC AWARENESS

✳ Oral Blending

Initial Consonants Say the initial consonant sound and have the puppet say the rest of the word. Then have the class put the word together and say it back to you.

Teacher:　　/m/
Puppet:　　oney. What's the word?
Everyone:　money

Try the following words:

/m/ . . . arket	/b/ . . . etter	/m/ . . . orning
/l/ . . . etter	/l/ . . . umpy	/s/ . . . ample
/l/ . . . unch	/l/ . . . oose	/b/ . . . unch
/g/ . . . oose	/b/ . . . asket	/s/ . . . addle
/b/ . . . umpy		

✳ HOW THE ALPHABET WORKS: PART 1

In How the Alphabet Works, you will begin to introduce the children to the idea that letters and their associated sounds work together in a systematic way to create words. The activities in this section will help children gain insight into that system. Though they have not yet attached sounds to the letters, the following activity will help children focus on the importance of the order of letters in words.

Letter Order

Make a Word Remind children to sit in their Letter Expert groups. Give each group Uppercase and Lowercase Letter Cards that match their Special Letters. As you hand out each card, say the name of the letter on the card and ask the children to hold up their hands if it is their letter. Have the letter cards for the vowels easily accessible.

- Write the word *most* on the chalkboard in extra large lowercase letters and say it. Ask if any group has the first letter in the word. When they volunteer, ask a child from that group to come up and stand in front of the *m* on the chalkboard, holding the Special Letter. Continue with the other letters. Produce the letter card for *o* and choose someone to hold the card and get in the proper position. When the children are in the proper order, stand behind them and tap each child on the head, saying "*m-o-s-t* spells *most*."

- If children have ordered themselves incorrectly, spell out the word on the chalkboard and say it. Then spell out the word they have formed and try to say it. When they understand their mistake, point to the letters on the chalkboard one by one, and walk them through it so that they can order themselves correctly.

- Erase the *m* on the chalkboard and replace it with *p.* Ask the group, "Which Letter Card does not match the letter on the chalkboard?" When the *m* child sits down, ask if there is a Letter Expert group with the letter *p.* Ask a child from that group to come up and stand in front of the *p* on the chalkboard, holding the *Pp* Letter Card. Now stand behind them and tap each child on the head, saying "*p-o-s-t* spells *post*." Explain that when the first letter of the word changed, the group had spelled a different word.

- You can reinforce the importance of the order of letters if you reorder the children at the front of the class to spell a whole new word. Say, "Let's mix up these letters and see what happens." Erase *post* from the chalkboard. Write an extra large *s* and ask the child with the *Ss* Letter Card to take the first position. Then write an extra large *t,* an *o,* and a *p,* instructing the children to line up accordingly. Say, "Let's see what we've spelled now." Stand behind the children and tap each child on the head, saying "*s-t-o-p* spells *stop*."

- Continue the procedure with the words *pots, spot,* and *tops.*

- To involve children from each letter group, continue with *tip, pit, pet, net, pat*, and *bat.*

LETTER NAMES AND SHAPES

Letter Names

Alphabet Cheer Review the Alphabet Cheer just one time.

Boom-boom Ch! Boom-boom Ch!
A B C D
Boom-boom Ch! Boom-boom Ch!
E F G H
Boom-boom Ch! Boom-boom Ch!
I J K L
Boom-boom Ch! Boom-boom Ch!
M N O P
Boom-boom Ch! Boom-boom Ch!
Q R S T

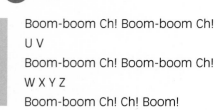

Boom-boom Ch! Boom-boom Ch!

U V

Boom-boom Ch! Boom-boom Ch!

W X Y Z

Boom-boom Ch! Ch! Boom!

Hand each child one of the *Dd, Hh, Ll, Pp, Tt, Vv,* or *Zz* Uppercase and Lowercase Letter Cards. Now ask the children to listen to and chant the Alphabet Cheer. At the end of the corresponding *Boom-boom Ch!* line, say, "Did you say *d*?" and have the children with *d*'s hold them up and say, "*d*!" Continue with the cheer, saying, "Did you say *h*? . . . Did you say *l*? . . ." and so on.

Exploring Letters—*Ss* Remember that the goal in Lessons 1–30 is for the children to explore the formation of the letters in order to become familiar with their names and shapes. These lessons are not intended to build children's proficiency in letter writing. Letter formation, along with proofreading, will begin in Lesson 51.

- Using the *Ss* Alphabet Card, point out the capital *S* and the small *s*.
- Using the established procedure, form the capital *S* on the overhead projector or chalkboard. Remember to have the children say the letter.
- Make the letter several times, first having children form the letter in the air and then on blank paper.
- Repeat the steps for small *s*.
- Remember to have children who have an *S* or *s* in their name point to it on their name necklaces and raise their hands.

✳ WORKSHOP

Remind the children that as Letter Experts, they will be working with their Special Letters in Workshop.

- Stage a **Letter Hunt.** Tell the children that hidden around the room are the Special Letters they have been working with. Explain that these letters are on brightly colored paper and show the children an example. (These are the letters you prepared ahead.) Review each group's Special Letter if necessary. Each group must find three copies of its letter. When you give the signal, the Letter Experts must move quietly about the room, looking for their Special Letters. If they find a different group's Special Letter, they must remain silent and pass by it. When they have found all three of their Special Letters, they should return to their places. Then distribute Activity Sheet 10. Have the children find their Special Letter in the words on the page and circle each one.
- Be sure to post letters in open sight and in easy to reach places. Afterwards, children should **decorate the letters** for Show and Tell in Lesson 29.

LESSON 24

••• Lesson Overview

New Learning

- How the Alphabet Works
- Exploring letters: *Tt*

Materials

- "Rhyme Stew," page 10 of *Pickled Peppers*
- Exploring Sounds and Letters, page 11
- Alphabet Flash Cards
- Three of each Uppercase and Lowercase Letter Card: *Bb, Dd, Ff, Hh, Ll, Mm, Nn, Pp, Rr, Ss,* and *Tt* (three of each vowel card for you)

Prepare Ahead

- Hide around the room three copies of the Letter Cards for each Special Letter.

✳ READING THE BIG BOOK

"Rhyme Stew"
page 10 of *Pickled Peppers*

Open *Pickled Peppers* to the table of contents and find "Rhyme Stew." Ask whether anyone can tell what page number the poem is on, and then turn to that page. First, read the poem through slowly, pointing to each word.

- Starting with the first line, read the poem again, reviewing the rhyming words in each line.
- Point to the pictures and ask whether anyone can find the pictures that go with the rhyming words.
- Conclude by reading the poem one more time all the way through, encouraging the children to join in when they can.

✳ PHONEMIC AWARENESS

✳ Oral Blending

Initial Consonants Say the initial consonant sound and have the puppet say the rest of the word. Then have the class put the word together and say it back to you.

Teacher: /m/
Puppet: agazine. What's the word?
Everyone: magazine

Try the following words:

/m/ . . . istake	/m/ . . . iddle	/m/ . . . aybe	
/l/ . . . azy	/l/ . . . esson	/l/ . . . isten	/l/ . . . onely
/b/ . . . owling	/b/ . . . akery	/b/ . . . ottle	/b/ . . . attle

TEACHING TIP
After oral blending, you may want to review the words and clarify meaning as needed. Then choose a few words for children to use in sentences.

MONITORING TIP During the next four or five days, observe the children to see how they do in oral blending of initial consonant sounds. Observe four or five children a day either during the oral blending or during Workshop. Record your observations on Observation Log 1. If some children are having trouble, create a group during Workshop and have the group do additional blending work.

✳ HOW THE ALPHABET WORKS: PART 1

Though they have not yet attached the sound to their Special Letter, children can learn from this activity that the order of letters is very important to the spelling of words. This lesson will focus on these concepts:

- letters can be used to identify words
- letters combine in certain order to make words

The children will identify their letters in words, and then place the letters of words in the correct order.

Letter Order

Make a Word Give the children in each Letter Expert group three Uppercase and Lowercase Letter Cards for their Special Letter and ask one child in each group to name the Special Letter. Ask another child from each group to stand, hold their group's letter up before the class, but remain silent.

- Ask the class if anyone can name the letter.
- Write the word *farm* on the chalkboard in large lowercase letters and say it. Ask whether any group has the first letter in the word as its Special Letter. If a group has the letter, ask a child from that group to come up and stand in front of the *f* you have written on the chalkboard, holding his or her letter so that the class can see it. Continue with the other letters with you holding the *a.* When the children are in the proper order in front of the letters, say, *"f-a-r-m* spells *farm."* Have the children spell the word.
- If the children have ordered themselves incorrectly, spell out the word on the chalkboard and say it. Spell out the word they have ordered and try to say it. When they understand their mistake, point to the letters on the chalkboard one by one, and help them order themselves correctly.
- Continue the procedure with the following words:

hall	middle	lesson	bottle
peppermint	telephone	timer	

Letter Names

Review the Alphabet Song or Alphabet Cheer.

❯ **Exploring Sounds and Letters** Ask the children to open Exploring Sounds and Letters to page 11 and take out their crayons. Point to the pot of stew on the page and have the children notice that several capital letters are cooking in the pot. Review which letters they are. On the bottom of the page are several small letters. The children should first circle a letter in the pot with one color and then circle its matching small letter with the same color. Using a different color, they should circle another capital letter in the pot and then circle its matching small letter with the same color, and so on. If the children do not have crayons, tell them to circle the capital letter in the pot and draw a line to its matching small letter.

Alphabet Flash Cards Use the Alphabet Flash Cards to review the letters.

Letter Shapes

Exploring Letters—*Tt* Using the *Tt* Alphabet Card, point out the capital *T* and the small *t*. Using the established procedure, form the capital *T* on the overhead projector or chalkboard.

- Make the letter several times, first having children form the letter with their fingers in the air and then with their pencils on blank paper.
- Repeat the steps for small *t*.
- Look for *Tt*'s in children's names and in objects around the room.

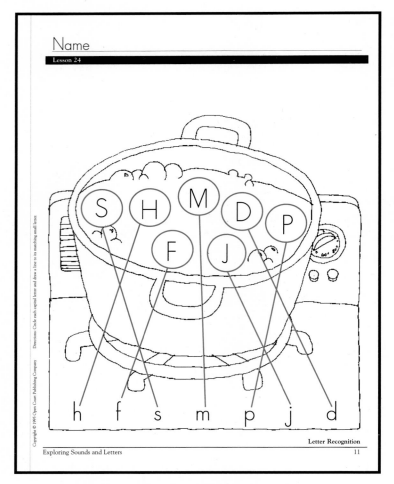

Name _____

Lesson 24

Exploring Sounds and Letters, page 11

Letter Recognition

Exploring Sounds and Letters

11

✳ WORKSHOP

- Tell the children that you have hidden around the room three copies of each Letter Expert group's Special Letter for a **Letter Hunt**. Review each group's Special Letter if necessary. Say, "When I give the signal, I want each of you to work with the others in your Letter Expert group to find all three copies of your Special Letter. If you find another letter, pass by it."

- When the groups have found all three of their Special Letters, the children can get together in their Letter Expert groups and place the letters in their Special Letter container.

LESSON
25

Lesson Overview

New Learning

- How the Alphabet Works
- Exploring letters: *Uu*

Materials

- "Rhyme Stew," page 10 of *Pickled Peppers*
- Picture Cards: *beans, cook, dice, feet, hook, hot, jeans, meat, moon, pot, rice, spoon, stew*
- Word Cards: *a, for, Let's, make, rhyme, you*
- Uppercase and Lowercase Letter Cards for the Special Letters (the vowel cards for you)
- Alphabet Flash Cards

Prepare Ahead

- Large sheets of colored poster paper for group collage
- Old magazines or other sources of letters that can be cut up

---

✶ READING THE BIG BOOK

"Rhyme Stew"
page 10 of *Pickled Peppers*

- Open *Pickled Peppers* to the table of contents and find "Rhyme Stew" again. Turn to the poem and read it slowly, pointing to each word.
- Sprinkled throughout the large illustration that accompanies the poem are pictures of the two rhyming words from each line of the poem (except for the word *you* in line one). Call the children's attention to the illustration on page 11. Point to the cook and say, "I see a picture of a *cook.* What word from the poem rhymes with *cook?* Can you find a picture of it on this page?" Wait for the children to point out the picture of the hook on the string. Congratulate them. Then have the children find pictures of the other pairs of rhyming words from the poem.
- Tell the children that they may find pictures of additional words that rhyme with the words from the poem. They may enjoy looking for these additional rhyming words. (For example, they may find cook/hook/book; meat/feet/beet; rice/dice/mice; peas/sneeze/fleas; noodle/doodle/poodle; and so on.)
- Assemble the Word and Picture Cards for the first seven lines of "Rhyme Stew." The words *Let's/make/a/rhyme/for/you* are all on

separate Word Cards. Place these words in the Pocket Chart, one by one, saying each word as you place it. The last two rhyming words in each line (except for *you*) are on labeled Picture Cards: /stew/hot/pot/cook/hook/ and so forth. Keep the Picture Cards for the first word of each pair in your lap and place the other Picture Cards on a nearby low table.

- Read the line *Let's make a rhyme for you* on the Pocket Chart. Find the Picture Card that rhymes with *you* (*stew*) and place it in the Pocket Chart. Point to the words and read the line with the children.

- Now remove *you,* and replace it with *hot.* Read the line as it is, "Let's make a rhyme for *hot. Stew.*" Ask, "Is that right?" When the children respond with a resounding "No!" ask a child to find the picture whose name rhymes with *hot* (*pot*). Place that Picture Card in the Pocket Chart in place of *stew.* Now read the line again and allow the children to join in. Continue in the same manner until you have covered the first seven lines of the poem.

---

* PHONEMIC AWARENESS

* Oral Blending

Initial Consonants This activity is similar to previous oral blending activities, only this time the children will work with somewhat harder-to-blend stop consonants. Give the initial consonant sound and have the puppet say the rest of the word. Remember to emphasize the phoneme.

Teacher:	/t/
Everyone:	/t/
Puppet:	eapot. What's the word?
Everyone:	Teapot

Continue with the following words:

/t/ . . . elephone	/t/ . . . oothache	/t/ . . . ornado
/t/ . . . attletale	/p/ . . . eppermint	/p/ . . . opsicle
/p/ . . . opcorn	/p/ . . . otato	/k/ . . . upboard
/k/ . . . upcake	/k/ . . . aterpillar	/k/ . . . alendar

MONITORING TIP Observe four or five children today to see how they are progressing with oral blending. Record your observations on your Observation Log 1, Reproducible Master 28.

---

* HOW THE ALPHABET WORKS: PART 1

Letter Order

Make a Word This exercise will help the children see that a change in the order of any letter of a word changes the word. Give the children in each Letter Expert group the Uppercase and Lowercase Letter Card for their Special Letter.

- Write the word *most* on the chalkboard in large lowercase letters and say it. Ask whether any Letter Expert group has the first letter in the word for its Special Letter. If a group does have the *m,* ask a child from that group to come up and stand in front of the *m* on the chalkboard, holding an *Mm* Letter Card. Continue with the other letters with you holding the *o.* When the children are in the proper order, go behind them, saying "*m-o-s-t* spells *most.*"

- Erase the *m* on the chalkboard and replace it with *p.* Ask the class which child now needs to sit down because that letter does not match the letter on the chalkboard. When the *m* child sits down, ask if there is a Letter Expert group with the letter *p.* If there is, ask a child from that group to come up and stand in front of the *p* on the chalkboard, holding the *Pp* Letter Card. Now say, "*p-o-s-t* spells *post.*" Explain that when the first letter of the word changed, the group made a different word.

- You can reinforce the importance of the order of letters if you reorder the children standing at the front of the class to make a whole new word. Say, "Let's mix up these letters and see what happens." Erase *post.* Write a large lowercase *s* and ask the child with the *s* to take the first position. Then write a large *t,* an *o,* and a *p* until the children are all lined up again. Say, "Let's see what we've spelled now." Spell the word, "*s-t-o-p* spells *stop.*"

- Continue the procedure with the words *pots, spot,* and *tops.*

- To engage all the Letter Expert groups, continue with *hip, tip, pit, pet, net (ten), hat, fat, bat,* and *pat (tap).*

✱ LETTER NAMES AND SHAPES

Letter Names
Alphabet Song Repeat the Alphabet Song or Alphabet Cheer.

Alphabet Flash Cards Use the Alphabet Flash Cards to review the letters.

Letter Shapes
Exploring Letters—*Uu* Using the established procedure, form the capital *U* on the overhead projector or chalkboard.

- Repeat the procedure for small *u.*

✱ WORKSHOP

Pass out a large sheet of colored poster paper to each Letter Expert group. Explain that each group should look through the materials that you have assembled and try to find examples of their Special Letter. They should cut out the letters and paste them on the poster paper to **make a large collage of their letter.** They can also draw their Special Letters if they want to. The collage should be saved for Show and Tell in Lessons 29 and 30.

LESSON
26

●●● Lesson Overview

New Learning

- Exploring letters: *Vv*

Materials

- "Rhyme Stew," page 10 of *Pickled Peppers*
- Picture Cards: *beans, bowl, doodle, fur, hole, jeans, noodle, peas, potatoes, sneeze, stir, tomatoes*
- Word Cards: *a, for, Let's, make, rhyme, you*
- Exploring Sounds and Letters, pages 12–13
- Alphabet Flash Cards
- Individual Alphabet-Sound Cards: *Bb, Dd, Ff, Hh, Ll, Mm, Nn, Pp, Rr, Ss*, and *Tt* (one card for each child; vowels for you)

Prepare Ahead

- Construction paper, glitter, sequins, yarn, and glue

✳ READING THE BIG BOOK

"Rhyme Stew"
page 10 of *Pickled Peppers*

Open *Pickled Peppers* to the table of contents and find "Rhyme Stew" again. Have a child point to the page number, say it, and help you turn to that page. Review the poem, reading it slowly and pointing to each word.

- Assemble the remaining Word and Picture Cards for "Rhyme Stew." The words and pictures *Let's/make/a/rhyme/for/beans/jeans/* should be up on the chart from the last lesson. Continue with the activity from that lesson for other rhyming words in the poem.
- Remove the Picture Card *beans* and replace it with *peas.* Then find the picture whose name rhymes with *peas.* Continue with other picture cards.

✷ Oral Blending

Initial Consonants Say the initial consonant sound and have the puppet say another part. Then have the children put the word together and say it back to you.

Teacher:	/p/
Everyone:	/p/
Puppet:	ocket. What's the word?
Everyone:	pocket

Continue with the following words:

/p/ . . . acket	/p/ . . . oster
/k/ . . . oaster	/t/ . . . oaster
/t/ . . . angle	/d/ . . . angle
/d/ . . . oodle	/p/ . . . oodle
/p/ . . . aper	/t/ . . . aper
/t/ . . . able	/p/ . . . oison
/p/ . . . oultry	

TEACHING TIP
Remember, you may want to review the words and their meanings.

MONITORING TIP Observe another four or five children today. Record your observations on Observation Log 1.

The children have been introduced to the idea that letter order is very important. Now they will be introduced to the idea that each letter has a corresponding sound.

You will find it helpful to use the Individual Alphabet-Sound Cards during these exercises. On the back of each card is a picture that represents the sound the letter makes. You will take the children through brief spelling exercises in which they blend some sounds to create a word. You should not dwell on the blending nor ask the children to do so; simply use it to introduce the idea that words are composed of sounds and that letters represent those sounds.

To keep confusion to a minimum and to emphasize that sounds combine to make words, use long vowels whenever possible.

Sounds in Words

- Explain that every letter has at least one sound. Then demonstrate by holding up the *Mm* Individual Alphabet-Sound Card and saying, "The sound of this letter is /m/." Hold up the long *e* Individual Alphabet-Sound Card and say, "A sound for this letter is /ē/." The word we can make from putting these sounds together is /m/ /ē/, *me.*"
- Now explain that the children will learn the sound that goes with their Special Letter. Give each child an Individual Alphabet-Sound

Card for his or her Special Letter. Have the children turn over their Individual Alphabet-Sound Cards and look at the pictures on the back. Each letter has a picture of something that makes the letter's sound. For instance, the picture for *Pp* is popping popcorn, because popcorn goes /p/ /p/ /p/ when it pops. The children will need to become the experts on this letter's sound. Move around the Letter Expert groups and assign the sounds to letters. This should be done quickly. Give yourself the Individual Alphabet-Sound Cards for the vowels.

- Ask each child, "What is your Special Letter's sound?" and wait for him or her to say it. Do a quick rehearsal after each group has its letter. Call on a child from each group to say, "Our letter's name is ___ and our letter's sound is ___."

- Say, "Let's look at the word *me* again." Say, "The sounds /m/ /ē/ make *me*." Repeat, and ask the children to raise their hands if they have the letter for the sound of /m/ when you say it. Remind the children that the picture on the back of the card will help them remember their sounds.

- For the remaining words on the list, write the word on the chalkboard and then say it sound by sound. Ask the children to hold up the picture of their sound if they hear you say it. You will take care of the vowels. Always end by saying, "*N-o* spells *no*; the sounds /n/ /ō/ say *no*." Make sure the children join in to say their group's sound when it occurs. Try these words:

| mold | so | sold | tree | fee | mild |
| beet | deep | steep | post | host | |

LETTER NAMES AND SHAPES

Letter Names

❯ **Exploring Sounds and Letters** Have the children open Exploring Sounds and Letters to pages 12–13. Tell them to match the capital and small forms of the letters *Ss, Tt, Uu* and *Vv,* by coloring the correct petals on each flower. They should then copy each letter on the writing lines at the top of the page.

Alphabet Flash Cards Use the Alphabet Flash Cards to review the letters.

Letter Shapes

Exploring Letters—*Vv* Using the established procedure, form a capital *V.* Repeat the procedure for small *v.*

✳ WORKSHOP

- Have each Letter Expert group go on a **Letter Walk** around the room during Workshop time to find examples of its Special Letter.
- Each child should write her or his **Special Letter** with markers or crayons on the construction paper that you prepared ahead. Let the children decorate their letter if they want with the glitter, yarn, etc., that you prepared ahead. The Letter Expert groups should sort through the materials, looking for their Special Letters.

TEACHING TIP

Circulate during Workshop time. Stop to ask the groups what their Special Letter sound is.

Exploring Sounds and Letters, page 12

Exploring Sounds and Letters, page 13

LESSON
27

●●● Lesson Overview

New Learning

- Exploring letters: **Ww**

Materials

- "Rhyme Stew," page 10 of *Pickled Peppers*
- Picture Cards for the rhyming words of "Rhyme Stew"
- Word Cards: *a, for, Let's, make, rhyme, you*
- Alphabet Flash Cards
- Individual Alphabet-Sound Cards: **Bb, Dd, Ff, Hh, Ll, Mm, Nn, Pp, Rr, Ss,** and **Tt** (one card for each child; vowels for you)

✱ READING THE BIG BOOK

"Rhyme Stew"
page 10 of *Pickled Peppers*

Review the poem in *Pickled Peppers*.

- Place the Word Cards for the first line of the poem in the Pocket Chart, saying each word as you do so.
- When you put the Picture Card or Word Card in the chart, ask the children for a rhyme that begins with a particular sound. For example, place the words *Let's/make/a/rhyme/for/you/* on the chart. Ask the children for a rhyme for *you* that begins with /t/. Then a rhyming word that begins with /s/; it does not matter if the words are nonsense words.
- Continue the activity with the rest of the poem.

TIP FOR ENGLISH LANGUAGE LEARNERS

Provide an opportunity for English Language Learners to add meaning to the vocabulary associated with the poem. Encourage the children to illustrate two rhyming words in the poem. The children may choose any pair that they like. Have them write the words as labels under each illustration. Illustrating favorite words helps to make the words personally meaningful for the children.

✱ PHONEMIC AWARENESS

✱ Oral Blending

Initial Consonants This oral blending activity is similar to those in previous lessons, but this time let the puppet say the initial consonant. You say the rest of the word, and then ask the rest of the children, "What's the word?" Call on another child to put the word together and say it back to you.

Puppet: /t/

Everyone: /t/

Teacher: icket. What's the word?

Everyone: ticket

Try the following words:

/p/ . . . icket	/t/ . . . ickle
/p/ . . . ickle	/p/ . . . oppy
/k/ . . . opy	/t/ . . . aste
/p/ . . . aste	/k/ . . . astle
/k/ . . . arton	/k/ . . . ettle
/k/ . . . etchup	/k/ . . . itten

✱ HOW THE ALPHABET WORKS: PART 1

TEACHING TIP

If you think the children are ready, call on individuals to put the word together. Alternate between whole-class response and individual response.

MONITORING TIP At this time, you should complete the monitoring of the children's oral blending of initial consonant sounds. Record your observations on Observation Log 1. Work with any children who are having problems.

The goal of this lesson is to show that words are composed of sounds and that letters represent those sounds.

Words, Letters, and Sounds

Distribute the Individual Alphabet-Sound Cards to the proper Letter Expert groups. Say the word and write it on the chalkboard. Have the children with the Alphabet-Sound Cards that contain the letters in the word come to the front of the room and hold out their cards, with you holding the vowels. Say the word again as you point to the cards.

pint

mild

mind   (After the children have spelled and pronounced *mind,* have the child holding *m* sit down and ask a child with *f* to come forward. Ask the children how this changes the word.)

find

bold

hold

bolt

need

eel

peel

street

TEACHING TIP

Even though only one child from a Letter Expert group will come forward, all the children in the group should say their letter's sound when it occurs in the word. Always end the activity by saying the sounds in the word one by one and then saying the entire word.

LETTER NAMES AND SHAPES

Letter Names

Alphabet Song   Review the Alphabet Song or Alphabet Cheer.

Alphabet Flash Cards   Use the Alphabet Flash Cards to review the letters.

Letter Shapes

Exploring Letters—*Ww* Using the established procedure, show the children how to form a capital *W.*

* Repeat the procedure for small *w.*

✱ WORKSHOP

Remind the children that they should continue to collect and create materials on their **Special Letters.** Tell them that in a few days, they will have a chance to show the rest of the class what they know about their letter. They can show the pictures of letters they have collected from newspapers and magazines, the words that contain their Special Letters, their decorated construction paper letters, their Special Letter collage, and, of course, their Special Letter containers. The children can look through the materials and find more examples of their letter to add to their group collage.

TEACHING TIP

Circulate and review with each group their letter name and its sound. Ask each group to think about why their letter's shape is special. Does it have a curved line in it? Does it have a straight or slanted line? Does it have a circle?

LESSON 28

Lesson Overview

New Learning

- Exploring letters: *Xx*

Materials

- "Trees," First-Step Story 2
- Exploring Sounds and Letters, pages 14–15
- Alphabet Flash Cards
- Individual Alphabet-Sound Cards: *Bb, Dd, Ee, Ff, Hh, Ll, Mm, Nn, Oo, Pp, Rr, Ss, Tt*

✳ USING FIRST-STEP STORIES

"Trees"
First-Step Story 2

Tell the children that today they are going to read a poem called "Trees." Explain that there are many different types of trees, such as maple, elm, walnut, and palm. Say that some trees are strong and good for climbing. There are trees that make fruit such as apples or lemons. There are trees that have big seeds or nuts such as chestnuts or walnuts. There are giant trees that are very tall and old such as redwood trees. Ask the children if they can describe kinds of trees that they have seen.

- Tell the children you want them to pretend to be like trees. Have them stand in a circle. Act out the poem and have children follow along.
- Read the poem aloud.

> **TIP FOR ENGLISH LANGUAGE LEARNERS**
>
> You may wish to read this poem to English Language Learners a day or so in advance of when it is read to the larger group. During the initial reading, the children have the opportunity to learn the movements associated with the poem and clarify any confusion. When you read the poem again with the larger group, they may feel freer to participate.

Elm trees stretch and stretch so wide, their limbs reach out on every side.
(Stretch out your arms and legs.)

Pine trees stretch and stretch so high, they nearly reach up to the sky.
(On your tiptoes stretch up with hands extended to the ceiling.)

Willows droop and droop so low, their branches sweep the ground below.
(Bend down to the floor and sweep your arms back and forth.)

- Gather the children around and distribute copies of First-Step Story 2, "Trees." Tell the children that they are going to create their own books about trees. They will illustrate the book by drawing pictures of the trees in the poem. Explain that this is why there is no name printed after "illustrated by" on the cover. In Workshop, the children will write their names in this space. Recite "Trees" one more time, encouraging the children to follow along in their own books. Give them a signal when it is time to turn the pages.

✳ PHONEMIC AWARENESS

✳ Oral Blending

Initial Consonant Continue work in oral blending, this time using one-syllable words. Have the puppet say the initial consonant sound and you say the rest of the word. Then have the children put the word together and say it back to you.

Puppet: /s/
Teacher: ing. What's the word?
Everyone: sing

Continue with the following words:

/k/ . . . ing	/r/ . . . ing
/s/ . . . eal	/r/ . . . eal
/f/ . . . eel	/r/ . . . at
/f/ . . . at	/h/ . . . at
/f/ . . . ool	/p/ . . . ool
/k/ . . . ool	

✳ HOW THE ALPHABET WORKS: PART 1

The goals of this lesson are to show that letters and sounds can be used to identify words, and that meaning can be obtained by using letters and sounds to figure out words.

Sounds in Words Distribute the Individual Alphabet-Sound Cards to the Letter Expert groups. Call out the letters of the word *bee* and have a child come to the front and hold the Individual Alphabet-Sound Card *Bb.* Invite volunteers to hold *Ee* cards. Sound out the word, then write it on the chalkboard. Have the children show that the letters are the same as the word you wrote on the chalkboard. Move from *bee* to *see* by asking the child with the *Bb* card to sit down and having a child with *Ss* come up. Say the word as *see* and then again as *bee.* Proceed with the activity, using the following words:

tee	me	he	
most	post		
old	fold	told	sold
peel	feel	reel	
teen	seen		

Remember that even though only one child from a Letter Expert group will come forward, all the children in the group should say their letter's sound when it occurs in a word. Always end by saying the sounds of the word one by one and then saying the entire word.

Letter Names

Alphabet Song Review the Alphabet Song or Alphabet Cheer.

❯ **Exploring Sounds and Letters** For a review of the capital and small forms of letters *Ss–Zz,* have children open their Exploring Sound and Letters to pages 14–15. Point out that every monkey in the trees has a capital letter on it. Point out, too, that on the ground are monkeys with small letters on them. Tell the children to draw a line from the monkey with the capital letter to its matching small letter.

Exploring Sounds and Letters, page 14

Exploring Sounds and Letters, page 15

Alphabet Flash Cards Use the Alphabet Flash Cards to review the letters.

Letter Shapes

Exploring Letters—*Xx* Using the established procedure, form the capital *X* on the overhead projector or chalkboard. Repeat the procedure for small *x*.

✳ WORKSHOP

- Ask children to take out the **First-Step Story, "Trees."** Have them print their names in the space next to "illustrated by," then illustrate the cover of their books.
- After children are done with their First-Step Stories, they should go through their Special Letter containers with their **Letter Expert groups** and organize their materials for Show and Tell in Lesson 29. You might want to hand out envelopes. Children can place loose letter samples or the words that contain their Special Letters in the envelopes.

MONITORING TIP Over the next three days, check individual children on their recognition of both capital and small letters. Record your results on Observation Log 1.

LESSON
29

●●● Lesson Overview

New Learning

- Exploring letters: *Yy*

Materials

- "Trees," First-Step Story 2
- Individual Alphabet-Sound Cards: *Bb, Dd, Ff, Hh, Ll, Mm, Nn, Pp, Rr, Ss,* and *Tt* (one card for each child)
- For each child, Uppercase and Lowercase Letter Card sets *Pp–Zz*

✳ USING FIRST-STEP STORIES

"Trees"
First-Step Story 2

Act out the poem "Trees" with the class again, as described in Lesson 28.

- Have the children gather around as you hold up a copy of First-Step Story 2, "Trees." Say, "In the poem there were rhyming words. Can anyone hear the rhyming words?" Go over the poem again, using your finger to point out each word. Emphasize *wide/side/high/ sky/low/below/*. Remind the children that *wide* and *side* rhyme because they both end with the same sounds, /ī/ /d/. Tell them that they can create more rhyming words by putting a new sound in front of *ide*. Say /t/ and *ide*. Then *tide*. Give another initial consonant sound and see if a child can create the new rhyming word.

- Have children discover other words that rhyme with *wide (tide, side, hide, ride, guide)*; with *high (sigh, buy, die, guy, lie, pie)*; and with *low (toe, show, go, no)*.

> **TIP FOR ENGLISH LANGUAGE LEARNERS**
>
> Reinforce the meanings of the terms *wide, side, high, low,* and *below* for English Language Learners by using objects in the classroom to physically demonstrate the concepts. Have the children repeat each word as you state it aloud and provide a visual example. To extend the activity, say a term aloud and have a volunteer act it out using objects in the classroom.

✳ Oral Blending

Initial Consonants This oral blending activity is similar to previous activities. This time, have the children concentrate on words beginning with *b, c,* and *d.*

Teacher:	/b/
Puppet:	at. What's the word?
Everyone:	bat

Continue with the following words:

/k/ . . . at	/b/ . . . ank
/d/ . . . ay	/k/ . . . ute
/k/ . . . lown	/d/ . . . og
/b/ . . . and	/d/ . . . ive
/d/ . . . ark	/b/ . . . oat
/k/ . . . ook	/k/ . . . omb

This is an excellent opportunity to allow the Letter Expert groups to show what they have learned about their Special Letters. Encourage all the children in a group to say something about their letter. You might do half of the groups today, and the other half in the next lesson.

Show and Tell Have a Letter Expert group come to the front of the room. Ask a child to say the name of the group's Special Letter. Then you might ask another child to show his or her decorated letter, or you might ask another child to hold up the group's collage while a second child points out all the letters. Hand one of the children an Uppercase and Lowercase Letter Card and ask her or him to show the class the capital and small letter.

End the Show and Tell by having one member of each group hold the Individual Alphabet-Sound Card for the group's Special Letter, point to the letter, name it, and then say its sound. Ask the whole class to name the letter and then say its sound.

Letter Names

Catch Me If You Can Tell the children that you will be singing the Alphabet Song, but that somewhere you will make a mistake. (If necessary, use Songs Teacher Tool Card 1.) Say that as soon as they catch the mistake, they should raise their hands. Sing the Alphabet Song, but leave a letter out. Try to do this as slyly as possible. When a child catches you, ask if he or she can name the letter you left out.

Letter Shapes

Exploring Letters—*Yy* Using the established procedure, form the capital *Y*. Repeat the procedure for small *y*.

✱ WORKSHOP

Children can now illustrate page 2 of "Trees," but first, read the lines on page 2 to them and act it out. Ask the children to think about what elm trees look like with their limbs stretched so wide. Say, "Can you draw them?" After the children are finished with their drawing, collect their books and save them for the next lesson.

When the children are finished, have them work on one of the following activities:

- For each child, have Uppercase and Lowercase Letter Card sets *Pp–Zz* shuffled and out of order so the children can play the **Ordering Letters** game.
- Make the game **Hop Along** available.

MONITORING TIP Over the next three days, check individual children on their recognition of both capital and small letters. Record your results on Observation Log 1.

LESSON
30

●●● Lesson Overview

New Learning

- Exploring letters: *Zz*

Materials

- "Trees," First-Step Story 2
- Exploring Sounds and Letters, pages 16–17
- Alphabet Flash Cards
- Individual Alphabet-Sound Cards: *Bb, Dd, Ff, Hh, Ll, Mm, Nn, Pp, Rr, Ss,* and *Tt* (one card for each child)
- For each child, sets of Uppercase and Lowercase Letter Cards *Pp–Zz*
- Classroom Support Teacher Tool Card 1

✳ USING FIRST-STEP STORIES

"Trees"
First-Step Story 2

Act out the "Trees" poem with the children again. Then read the poem through slowly, encouraging the children to follow along in their own books, pointing to each word. Note any child who seems unable to follow and any child who is able to turn the pages without prompting.

✳ PHONEMIC AWARENESS

✳ Oral Blending

Final Consonant In this series of oral blending activities, children will be blending the first part of a word with the final consonant sound. Say the first part of the word yourself and have the puppet say the final consonant sound.

Teacher: Superma

Puppet: /n/. What's the word?

Everyone: Superman

Continue with the following words:

watermelo . . . /n/	telepho . . . /n/
cartoo . . . /n/	napki . . . /n/
bubblegu . . . /m/	astronau . . . /t/
doughnu . . . /t/	raincoa . . . /t/
grapefrui . . . /t/	footprin . . . /t/

✱ HOW THE ALPHABET WORKS: PART 1

Remember, this is an excellent opportunity to allow the Letter Expert groups to show off what they have learned about their letter. Do the second half of the groups today. If necessary, lead each group in sharing its materials with the class.

Show and Tell Ask different members of the group to share some of the Special Letter materials with the class.

End the Show and Tell session by having one member of each group hold the Individual Alphabet-Sound Card for the group's letter, point to the letter, name it, and then say its sound. Ask the whole class to name the letter and then say its sound.

LETTER NAMES AND SHAPES

Letter Names
Alphabet Song Review the Alphabet Song or Alphabet Cheer.

❯ **Exploring Sounds and Letters** Have children open Exploring Sounds and Letters to pages 16–17. Explain to the children that they should connect the dots on page 16 from *A* to *M* to complete the picture. Then tell them to connect the dots on page 17 from *N* to *Z* to complete the picture.

Alphabet Flash Cards Use the Alphabet Flash Cards to review the letters.

Letter Shapes
Exploring Letters—Zz Using the established procedure, form the capital *Z* on the overhead projector or chalkboard. If necessary, see **Classroom Support Teacher Tool Card 1** to refresh your memory of the procedure. Repeat the procedure for small *z*.

TIP FOR ENGLISH LANGUAGE LEARNERS

Have English Language Learners practice using and producing language to communicate ideas. Pair English Language Learners with a native English speaker in their Show and Tell group. Have them practice what they will say during Show and Tell to develop the confidence they need to speak in front of the class. Informally monitor their conversations to assess their understanding of the materials to be shared. Then encourage English Language Learners to volunteer to be a group spokesperson.

Exploring Sounds and Letters, page 16

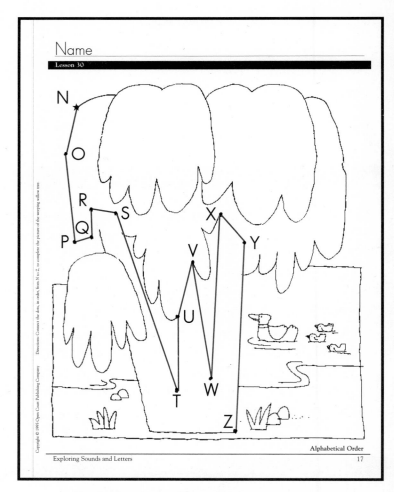

Exploring Sounds and Letters, page 17

✳ WORKSHOP

- Tell the children that they can now illustrate page 3 of their First-Step Story **"Trees."** First, however, read the lines on page 3 to them and act them out. Ask them what they think pine trees look like. Can they draw them? After the children are finished drawing, collect their books and save them for the next lesson.

    When the children are finished, have them work on one of the following activities:
- For each child, have Uppercase and Lowercase Letter Card sets *Pp–Zz,* shuffled and out of order so the children can play the **Ordering Letters** game.
- Make the game **Hop Along** available.

MONITORING TIP Check individual children on their recognition of both capital and small letters. Record your results on Observation Log 1.

LESSON 31

●●● Lesson Overview

New Learning

- /s/
- Initial /s/

Materials

- "Trees," First-Step Story 2
- Exploring Sounds and Letters, pages 18–19
- For each child, Uppercase and Lowercase Letter Card: *Ss*
- Classroom Support Teacher Tool Card 1
- Home/School Connection 8

✱ USING FIRST-STEP STORIES

"Trees"
First-Step Story 2

- Using a copy of First-Step Story 2, read the poem "Trees" while the children follow along in their own books. Give them the signal you have established when you want them to turn the pages.
- Ask for volunteers to come to the front of the room and talk about their illustrations.
- Read the first two lines and ask if anyone can identify the rhyming words.

✱ PHONEMIC AWARENESS

✱ Oral Blending

Initial Consonant Now that the children are familiar with the way the oral blending activities work, you can easily switch back and forth in your techniques. Sometimes you may say both parts of the word and sometimes you may work with the puppet. You will also want to alternate between individual and whole-class responses. This will require all children to remain attentive and to participate.

Teacher: /s/
Everyone: /s/
Puppet: imple
Teacher: What's the word?
Everyone: simple

Continue with the following words:

/s/ . . . ilent	/s/ . . . illy
/s/ . . . entence	/s/ . . . eagull
/s/ . . . andwich	/s/ . . . ailboat
/s/ . . . ubmarine	/s/ . . . omebody
/s/ . . . unflower	/s/ . . . paceship
/s/ . . . tomach	/s/ . . . chool

✱ HOW THE ALPHABET WORKS: PART 2

Lessons 31–50 include a special set of activities called How the Alphabet Works: Part 2. These activities serve as an introduction to the alphabetic principle. They are complementary to and extend the How the Alphabet Works: Part 1 activities in Lessons 21–30. These introductory lessons ensure that your students will have the basic understanding required before working through the alphabet, letter by letter, and attaching sounds to each letter. Starting with *s,* children will attach sounds to a few chosen letters and listen for and identify those sounds in the initial and final positions of words. They will compare one sound to another. They will learn to identify words by looking for the letters that represent their initial and final sounds.

In Lesson 45, the children will be introduced to the convention that each vowel has a short sound in addition to its long sound. The use of short vowels allows more straightforward exploration of the alphabetic principle, as it makes available many words that do not involve silent letters or other special spelling conventions.

The Sound of *s*

Introducing *Ss* Introduce the letter *s.* Point to the *Ss* Alphabet Card and name the letter. Turn the *Ss* card over so the children can see the picture of the sausages. Point to the picture and say, "The sound of the letter *s* is /s/. The word *sausages* starts with the /s/ sound."

- Hold up the *Ss* Alphabet Card and say /s/ /s/ /s/ /s/ /s/. Tell the children that there is a short poem that will help them remember the /s/ sound for the letter *s:*

Sue buys sausages on Saturday.
Sam cooks sausages on Sunday.
The sausages sizzle /s/ /s/ /s/ /s/ /s/ /s/ when hot.
Sam eats sausages, but Sue does not.

TEACHING TIP

As you introduce the sounds in How the Alphabet Works: Part 2, turn over the appropriate Alphabet Cards that are displayed in the classroom.

- Ask the children if they can hear the many /s/ sounds in the poem. Recite the poem several times, emphasizing the initial /s/ sound, and asking children to join in where they can.

Name Some _s_ Words Brainstorm to create a list of words that begin with /s/. Write the words on the chalkboard or a chart. Let children participate as much as they can. Make sure you include in your list children's names that begin with _s_.

Listening for Initial /s/ Remember to establish a signal that the children understand as the signal to respond. When you indicate the response signal, children will show their card if they think the word begins with /s/.

- Give each child an _Ss_ Uppercase and Lowercase Letter Card. Look at the picture on the Alphabet Card for _s_. Ask each of the children to say the /s/ sound as they take their cards.
- Now tell the children that you will say a word, and that you want them to listen for the first sound. If it is /s/, they should hold up the _Ss_ card when you give the signal.

Try the following words:

see	sake	so	make
say	soak	may	poke
sigh	pole	my	sink
sight	soap	might	sip
meat	sap	seat	map
seal	seek	sail	seen

Linking the Sound to the Letter

Word Pairs In this activity, you will write pairs of words on the chalkboard, one word of each pair should begin with /s/, the other should not. Say the word beginning with /s/, and ask children to identify it. Remind them to listen for the /s/ sound and then to think about which letter makes that sound.

- Write _see, bee_ on the chalkboard. Ask the children, "Which word says _see_? If you think it is this one (point to _see_), raise your hand. If you think it is this one (point to _bee_), raise your hand." Ask someone to come up and point to the word and to circle the letter that makes the /s/ sound at the beginning of the word. Try these words:

fit	sit	so	no
mix	six	September	November
sand	hand		

- If children are having trouble, remind them that the words you are looking for begin with the /s/ sound, so the correct word will begin with the letter that makes that sound, _s_.

Writing *Ss* Remember, if possible, to use the overhead projector so that you and the children can form letters together. If you do not have an overhead projector, you can form the letters on the chalkboard. You may use the letter formation system outlined in detail on **Classroom Support Teacher Tool Card 1** or use the writing system that is standard in your school. This section should just be a review of *Ss* so that children can use it in their Exploring Sounds and Letters activity.

- Using the established procedure, review how to form a capital *S*.
- Review the steps for forming small *s*.
- Remind children that the letter *s* makes the /s/ sound.

❯ **Exploring Sounds and Letters** Have children open Exploring Sounds and Letters to pages 18–19. Explain that some of the things in the pictures on the pages begin with the /s/ sound. Ask the children to write the letter *s* under each picture that begins with /s/.

- Show the children the *s* on the top of the page so they have a model to look at as they make their letters. Have the children write a capital and small letter *s* on the lines at the top of page 18.
- Review each picture, one by one, and ask children if it begins with /s/. If yes, have them write an *s* on the line below the picture.
- After children have finished, be sure to go over the pictures as a class and name them. Each time you say an *s* word, ask the children to repeat the word and listen for the /s/ sound.

Exploring Sounds and Letters, page 18

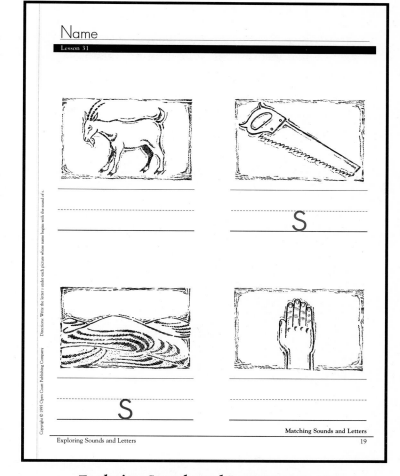

Exploring Sounds and Letters, page 19

Copyright © 1995 Open Court Publishing Company

✳ WORKSHOP

- Have the children complete their illustrations for **"Trees,"** in their First-Step Stories. Remind them that they will be illustrating the last page, which is about willow trees. If possible, show them a picture of willow trees.
- Children may wish to share their First-Step Stories with a partner when they are finished. Assign partners, and explain that as they look through each other's books, they should tell one thing they like about their partner's drawings. Suggest that they might talk about the colors they like or a certain part of the drawing, but it should be a positive remark.

Home/School Connection Have the children take Home/School Connection 8 home to their families, along with their completed First-Step Story, "Trees."

LESSON 32

••• Lesson Overview

New Learning

- /s/
- Initial /s/ sound

Materials

- "Los Pollitos," pages 22–23 of *Pickled Peppers*
- For each child, Uppercase and Lowercase Letter Card: *Ss*
- Listening Collections Audiocassette
- Songs Teacher Tool Card 8
- Activity Sheet 11

✱ READING THE BIG BOOK

"Los Pollitos" ("The Baby Chicks")
pages 22–23 of *Pickled Peppers*

Open *Pickled Peppers* to the table of contents and find "Los Pollitos," which is Spanish for "The Baby Chicks." Have a child find the number of the page on which the song can be found. Say the number and turn to the page. Point to and read the title of the song in Spanish and then in English. Explain to the children that people around the world speak different languages, and that this song was originally written in Spanish. Show them that it is written in the Big Book in both English and Spanish.

- If you are comfortable doing so, first read the song in Spanish and then in English. (If you are not, play the song on the Listening Collections Audiocassette.) If appropriate to your class, ask the children if anyone can speak a language other than English. If any of the children can speak another language, ask them to say hello in that language.
- Read the English version of the song two or three more times, pointing word by word.
- If your class is counting now, you may want to have them count the chicks along the border. If you have students who speak Spanish, ask them to count in Spanish, if they can.

- The music for "Los Pollitos" is on **Songs Teacher Tool Card 8** and can be found on the Listening Collections Audiocassette.
- Sing the song in English several times, until most children know the words.

✻ PHONEMIC AWARENESS

✻ Oral Blending

Initial Consonant Vary your techniques as you blend more words that have the initial /s/ sound. Write *s* on the chalkboard. Emphasize the /s/ sound.

Puppet: /s/ (and point to the *s* on the chalkboard)
Everyone: /s/
Teacher: pider. What's the word?
Everyone: spider

Continue with the following words:

/s/ . . . ticky	/s/ . . . aw
/s/ . . . unday	/s/ . . . addle
/s/ . . . omeplace	/s/ . . . weatshirt
/s/ . . . eat	/s/ . . . aturday
/s/ . . . tudent	/s/ . . . uitcase
/s/ . . . tamp	/s/ . . . oap
/s/ . . . ukey	/s/ . . . ally

✻ HOW THE ALPHABET WORKS: PART 2

The Sound of *s*

✻ **Reviewing *Ss*** Review the letter *s*. Hold up or point to the *Ss* Alphabet Card and say /s/ /s/ /s/ /s/ /s/ /s/:

> Sue buys sausages on Saturday.
> Sam cooks sausages on Sunday.
> The sausages sizzle /s/ /s/ /s/ /s/ /s/ /s/ when hot.
> Sam eats sausages, but Sue does not.

Listening for Initial /s/ Give each child an Uppercase and Lowercase Letter Card for *Ss.* Look at the picture on the *Ss* Alphabet Card. Ask the children to say the /s/ sound as they take their cards.

Tell the children that you will say a word, and that you want them to listen for the first sound. Say, "If it is /s/, hold up the *Ss* card when I give you the signal. Try the following words:

sat	tail	mat	salt	may	sap
say	map	sigh	may	sight	say
sand	saw	hand	save	safe	sing
sad	ring	sack	see	sail	sent

I'm Thinking of Something That Starts with _____ Game Look around the room until you see something that starts with /s/ that will be easily recognized by the children. Say, "I'm thinking of something that starts with /s/." Then begin to give a series of clues. You might direct the children's attention to one part of the room, or talk about the object's size or color. For example, for *sock* you might say, "It is something you wear."

Linking the Sound to the Letter

Word Pairs Write pairs of words on the chalkboard, one beginning with /s/, one not. For each pair, say the word beginning with /s/. Remind children to listen for the /s/ sound and to think about which letter makes that sound.

- Write *pit, sit* on the chalkboard.
- Ask the children, "Which word says *sit*? If you think it is this one (point to *pit*) raise your hand. If you think it is this one (point to *sit*) raise your hand." Ask children why they chose one or the other word.

  Try other word pairs:

sat	rat	**same**	tame
moon	**soon**	**see**	tree
mile	**smile**	**sit**	pit

- Remind the children that the words you are looking for begin with the /s/ sound, so the correct word will begin with the letter that makes the /s/ sound.

✱ WORKSHOP

- Put copies of **Activity Sheet 11** in the Workshop area. Explain to the children that the little chick in the picture is trying to find its way back to its mother. Tell them that they should use their pencils to trace the chick's path, and that they should circle the objects they see in the picture that start with /s/.
- Have materials on hand so that children can practice making their *s* shapes in a variety of ways. Suggest that they might finger-paint their *s*'s or decorate large paper cutouts of *s*'s.

LESSON
33

●●● Lesson Overview

New Learning

- /s/
- Final /s/

Materials

- "Los Pollitos," pages 22–23 of *Pickled Peppers*
- Word Cards for the first verse of "Los Pollitos"
- Exploring Sounds and Letters , pages 20–21
- For each child, Uppercase and Lowercase Letter Card: *Ss*
- For each child, one set of Uppercase and Lowercase Letter Cards: *Aa–Zz*
- Rhymes and Games Teacher Tool Card 3

Prepare Ahead

- Blank Pocket Chart Word Cards and marker

✳ READING THE BIG BOOK

"Los Pollitos" ("The Baby Chicks")
pages 22–23 of *Pickled Peppers*

Depending upon the makeup of your class, you may want to spend more time on the Spanish version of the song in this lesson.

- Review "Los Pollitos" in *Pickled Peppers,* first finding it in the table of contents and then turning to the page where it begins. Read the English version, pointing to each word.
- Put the Word Cards for the first four lines of the song on the Pocket Chart.

Baby   chicks   are   singing,
pío,   pío,   pío
mamma   we   are   hungry
mamma   we   are   cold

- Have the blank Word Cards and a marker ready. Say, "The chicks are hungry," and point to *hungry.* Say, "The chicks are cold," and point to *cold.* Explain that the words *hungry* and *cold* describe how the

chicks feel. Call on individual children and ask them to think of other words that might describe how the chicks feel at different times. If they need help, you may give them clues: "How do you feel when you need a drink of water?" or "How do you feel when you need to go to sleep?" When the children volunteer a word, write it on a card, and ask the children to read the changed line: "mamma we are thirsty," or tired, or hot, and so on.

✽ PHONEMIC AWARENESS

✽ Oral Blending

Final Consonant Listening for a final consonant sound is much more difficult than listening for initial sounds, so you may want to provide children with more classroom support. During Workshop, you can work with children who need more help.

Have the puppet say the first part of words and you say the final consonant /s/.

Puppet: octopu
Teacher: /s/. What's the word?
Everyone: octopus

Continue with the following words:

somepla . . . /s/	choi . . . /s/
practi . . . /s/	ambulan . . . /s/
firepla . . . /s/	triceratop . . . /s/
brontosauru . . . /s/	tyrannosauru . . . /s/
circu . . . /s/	happine . . . /s/
senten . . . /s/	platypu . . . /s/
jui . . . /s/	

✽ HOW THE ALPHABET WORKS: PART 2

The Sound of *s*

Reviewing *Ss* Review the /s/ sound:

> Sue buys sausages on Saturday.
> Sam cooks sausages on Sunday.
> The sausages sizzle /s/ /s/ /s/ /s/ /s/ /s/ when hot.
> Sam eats sausages, but Sue does not.

Tell children they can hear the /s/ sound in parts of words other than the beginning. Repeat *eats.* Emphasize the middle /s/ sound in *sausages.*

Listening for Final /s/ Give each child an Uppercase and Lowercase Letter Card for *Ss*. Look at the picture on the *Ss* Alphabet Card. Ask the children to say the /s/ sound as they take their cards.

Tell the children that you will say a word, and that you want them to listen for the /s/ sound at the end of the word. Say that if they hear the /s/ sound, they should hold up the *Ss* card when you give the signal. Try the following words:

fuss	groan	**bus**	**grace**	**gas**	**lace**
mass	rain	man	cane	**kiss**	**case**
can	**face**	**class**	**trace**	**brass**	train
grass	drain	**grease**	**dress**	green	**mess**

Linking the Sound to the Letter

Word Pairs This activity follows the same procedure used in earlier lessons, except that it requires children to identify a word based on its final sound.

- Write *toss, tot* on the chalkboard. Say, "Which word says *toss*? *Toss* has an /s/ sound at the end." Ask the children whether they can hear the /s/ sound at the end of *toss.* Ask them what letter they should look for.

  Then write the following words:

pat	**pass**	**bus**	but
miss	mitt	elephant	**elephants**
gas	gap		

- For each pair, have children come up and point to the correct word. Have them trace over the *s* with their fingers.

Writing Ss Using the established procedure, review with the children how to form a capital *S* and small *s.*

❯ **Exploring Sounds and Letters** Tell the children to look at the first pair of pictures on pages 20–21 of Exploring Sounds and Letters and identify the one ending with the /s/ sound. Point to each picture and name it, but do not identify the /s/ sounds. Ask the children to write an *s* under the pictures that end with the /s/ sound. Then have the children practice writing capital *S* and small *s* on the lines at the top of page 20.

✳ WORKSHOP

- Introduce your students to the **Bus Stop** game. Use the Bus Stop Game Mat and the pack of Uppercase and Lowercase Letter Cards. Unlike the Hop Along game, Bus Stop has no letters printed in the spaces. When a player lands on a space, he or she must draw a card from the pack and identify the letter on the card.
- To play the game, a player spins the spinner, moves a marker the correct number of spaces, and, if not on a "lose turn" space, draws a card. If a player cannot correctly identify the letter on the card, the player forfeits the next turn.
- If a player lands on a "free turn" space, the player may spin again and choose a card after landing on another space farther along the trail. If a player lands on a "lose turn" space, no card may be drawn

Exploring Sounds and Letters, page 20

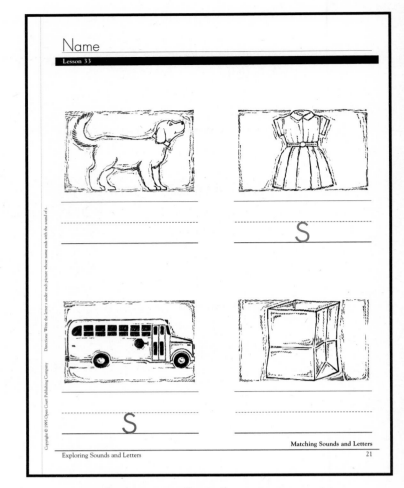

Exploring Sounds and Letters, page 21

and the player must lose one turn before spinning again. As you demonstrate the game, make sure children understand which spaces are "free turns" and which are "lose turns."

- A player wins by being the first to reach the bus stop.
- Have **Bus Stop** available in the Workshop Game Corner. **Rhymes and Games Teacher Tool Card 3** contains instructions for more challenging levels of the game.
- For each child, have Uppercase and Lowercase Letter Card sets *Aa–Zz,* shuffled and out of order so they can play the **Ordering Letters** game. Have the children sort the cards, as in earlier Workshops.
- Make the **Hop Along** game available.
- Let children use designated areas of the room such as the chalkboard or easel to create *s*'s.

LESSON
34

Lesson Overview

New Learning

- /m/
- Initial /m/

Materials

- "Los Pollitos," pages 22–23 of *Pickled Peppers*
- Word Cards for the second verse of "Los Pollitos"
- Exploring Sounds and Letters, pages 22–23
- For each child, Uppercase and Lowercase Letter Card: *Mm*
- For each child, one set of Letter Cards: *Aa–Zz*
- Classroom Support Teacher Tool Card 1

Prepare Ahead

- Blank cards and a marker

✳ READING THE BIG BOOK

"Los Pollitos"
pages 22–23 of *Pickled Peppers*

Read "Los Pollitos" one or two times. Each time, stop at "pío, pío, pío" and allow the children to recite these words as a group.

- Give special attention to the second verse of the song, reading it through several times while pointing to each word.
- Place the Word Cards for the second verse on the Pocket Chart.
- Have blank cards and a marker ready. Say, "Mamma looks for wheat," and ask a child to point to *wheat.* Say, "Mamma looks for corn," and ask another child to point to *corn.* Explain that the words *wheat* and *corn* name things the chicks can eat. Call on individual children and ask them to think of other words for food. Say that they can name any kind of food, not just food for chicks. When the children volunteer a word, write it on a card, and ask them to read the changed line: "Mamma looks for pizza," or apples, or hot dogs, and so on.

✱ Oral Blending

Initial Consonant Using the techniques from earlier lessons, have the children blend words with the initial /m/ sound.

Puppet:	/m/
Everyone:	/m/
Teacher:	eatball. What's the word?
Everyone:	meatball

Continue with the following words:

/m/ . . . ustache	/m/ . . . ustard
/m/ . . . onkey	/m/ . . . other
/m/ . . . onster	/M/ . . . acDonald
/m/ . . . edicine	/m/ . . . easure
/m/ . . . ayonnaise	/m/ . . . ultiple
/m/ . . . ushroom	/m/ . . . usic

The goal in this section is to provide the children with a solid foundation for hearing sounds in words. Starting with a small set of letters, children listen for and identify those sounds in the initial and final positions of words. They compare one sound to another. They learn to identify words by looking for the letters that represent their initial and final sounds.

The Sound of *m*

Introducing *Mm* Point to the *Mm* Alphabet Card and name the letter. If you do not have the picture side showing, turn the card over.

- Hold up the *Mm* Alphabet Card and say /m/ /m/ /m/ /m/ /m/ /m/. Read the poem for /m/:

For Muzzy, the Monkey,
bananas are yummy.
She munches so many,
they fill up her tummy.
She says /m/ /m/ /m/ /m/ /m/!

- Ask the children if they can hear the /m/ sounds at the beginning of many of the words in the poem. Recite the poem again, asking children to join in where they can. Let them know that the picture on the card can help them remember /m/.

Listening for Initial /m/ Give each child the Uppercase and Lowercase Letter Card for *Mm.* Look at the picture on the *Mm* Alphabet Card. Ask the children to say the /m/ sound as they take their cards.

Explain to the children that you will say a word, and that you want them to listen for an /m/ sound at the beginning of the word. Tell them that if they hear the /m/ sound, they should hold up the *Mm* card. Try the following words:

me	mite	may	mix	my	mild
hi	milk	hold	make	mold	man
mat	march	sat	money	hat	moon
hiss	soon	miss	mud	mop	mug
mood	hug				

I'm Thinking of Something That Starts with _____ Game Think of something that starts with /m/ that the children can see in the classroom. Say, "I'm thinking of something that starts with /m/." And then begin to give a series of clues. For example, for a picture of the moon, you might say, "I'm thinking of something that is on the bulletin board, can be seen at night, and begins with /m/."

Linking the Sound to the Letter

Writing *Mm* For this activity, you may use the letter formation system outlined in detail on **Classroom Support Teacher Tool Card 1** or use the writing system that is standard in your school.

- Using the established procedure, review with the children how to form a capital *M*.
- Review the steps for making small *m*.
- Remind children that the letter *m* makes the /m/ sound.

Word Pairs Write a pair of words on the chalkboard, one beginning with /m/, one not. For each pair, say the word beginning with /m/, point to each of the words, and have children identify the correct word by signaling thumbs-up when you point to it.

he	me	man	pan
dad	mad	Monday	Tuesday
large	medium	money	honey

Remind the children that the words you are looking for begin with the /m/ sound, so the correct word will begin with the letter *m*.

❯ **Exploring Sounds and Letters** Have children open Exploring Sounds and Letters to pages 22–23. Explain that the names of some of the pictures on the pages start with the /m/ sound. Ask the children to write the letter *m* under the pictures whose names start with /m/. Name each pair of words and have children write an *m* under the word whose names begins with the /m/ sound. Then have them practice writing capital *M* and small *m* on the lines at the top of page 22.

Exploring Sounds and Letters, page 22

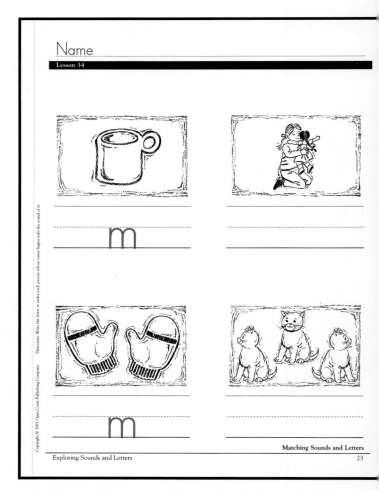

Exploring Sounds and Letters, page 23

Copyright ©1995 Open Court Publishing Company

✳ WORKSHOP

- For each child, have Uppercase and Lowercase Letter Card sets *Aa–Zz,* shuffled and out of order, so the children can reorder them.
- Make the **Hop Along** and **Bus Stop** games available.
- Encourage children to use designated areas of the room such as the chalkboard or easel to create *m's.*

LESSON
35

Lesson Overview

New Learning

- /m/
- Final /m/

Materials

- "Los Pollitos," pages 22–23 of *Pickled Peppers*
- Exploring Sounds and Letters, pages 24–25
- Individual Alphabet-Sound Cards: *Mm* and *Ss*
- For each child, Uppercase and Lowercase Letter Card: *Mm*
- For each child, one set of Uppercase and Lowercase Letter Cards: *Aa–Zz*
- Rhymes and Games Teacher Tool Card 3

✳ READING THE BIG BOOK

"Los Pollitos"
pages 22–23 of *Pickled Peppers*

Open *Pickled Peppers* to "Los Pollitos" and read it through. Sing it with the children. (If necessary, use Songs Teacher Tool Card 8.)

Tell the children that they are going to make a game out of "Los Pollitos." Have them stand in a circle, with one child in the middle. Explain that the child in the middle represents the hen and the rest of them are the chicks. In the first verse, the children should walk around the hen, moving their elbows up and down to imitate baby chicks. For the second verse, the circle should stop moving, and the hen should walk around looking for food and feeding the chicks. For the third verse, the chicks should sit down and close their eyes to rest, while the hen walks around giving them comfort.

✳ PHONEMIC AWARENESS

✳ Oral Blending

Final Consonant Continue the oral blending activities, this time with the final /m/ sound. Write the letter *m* on the chalkboard.

Puppet:	classroo
Everyone:	/m/
Teacher:	What's the word?
Everyone:	classroom

Continue with the following words:

eardru . . . /m/	nightti . . . /m/
thunderstor . . . /m/	broo . . . /m/
ga . . . /m/	sli . . . /m/
handso . . . /m/	bedti . . . /m/
costu . . . /m/	bubblegu . . . /m/
daydrea . . . /m/	

✱ HOW THE ALPHABET WORKS: PART 2

The Sound of *m*

Reviewing *Mm* Review the letter *m.* Point to the *Mm* Alphabet Card and name the letter.

- Hold up or point to the *Mm* Alphabet Card and say /m/ /m/ /m/ /m/ /m/ /m/. Recite the poem, adding some actions. Encourage the children to join in.

For Muzzy, the Monkey, (wiggle fingers under arms)
bananas are yummy. (rub tummy)
She munches so many, (pretend to eat)
they fill up her tummy. (circle arms out in front of tummy)
She says /m/ /m/ /m/ /m/ /m/!

- Repeat the poem again, and ask everyone to say /m/ /m/ /m/ /m/ /m/! as loud as they can.

Listening for Final /m/ Hearing the final consonant sound is somewhat more difficult than hearing the initial consonant sound in words.

- Give each child an Uppercase and Lowercase Letter Card for *Mm.* Look at the picture on the *Mm* Alphabet Card. Ask the children to say the /m/ sound as they take their cards.
- Tell the children that you will say a word, and that you want them to listen for an /m/ sound at the end of the word. Say that if they hear /m/, they should hold up the *Mm* card when you give the signal.

aim	slick	name	trim	fame	trick
face	lime	came	lick	case	lack
lame	ram	lace	cram	tame	clam
time	claim	dime	game	slime	tam
slim	take				

Linking the Sound to the Letter

Writing *Mm* Review the established procedures for forming capital *M* and small *m*.

Word Pairs Write pairs of similar looking words on the chalkboard, one pair at a time. Say the word ending with /m/ for each word pair. Then, ask the children to identify the word you said by signaling thumbs-up when you point to it.

at	**am**		**mom**	mop
bat	**ham**		**storm**	stool
dream	drool		**bathroom**	backyard

Ask children to come up and point to the correct word and then to trace with their fingers the letter that makes the final /m/ sound.

❯ **Exploring Sounds and Letters** Have the children open Exploring Sounds and Letters to pages 24–25. Explain that some of the words on the pages end in the /m/ sound. Point to each pair of pictures and name each one. Ask the children to write an *m* under the picture whose name ends with the /m/ sound. Have them practice writing the letters on page 24.

Exploring Sounds and Letters, page 24

Exploring Sounds and Letters, page 25

- Introduce the **Roller Ride** game. Use the Roller Ride Game Mat with the *Mm* and *Ss* Individual Alphabet-Sound Cards. If a child draws an *Ss* card, he or she must say a word beginning with /s/. If a child draws an *Mm* card, he or she must say a word beginning with /m/. This game should provide a fun challenge for children who are doing well with identifying letter sounds. The rules for Roller Ride are essentially the same as the rules for Bus Stop introduced in Lesson 34. The "stop" and "wait" spaces serve the same function as "lose turn" spaces. Instructions for this game, including more challenging variations, can be found on **Rhymes and Games Teacher Tool Card 3.**

- For each child, have Uppercase and Lowercase Letter Card sets *Aa–Zz,* shuffled and out of order so the children can play the **Ordering Letters** game.

- Make the **Hop Along, Bus Stop,** and **Roller Ride** games available.

- Encourage children use designated areas of the room such as the chalkboard or easel to create *m's.*

LESSON
36

●●●● Lesson Overview

New Learning

- Comparing /m/ and /s/

Materials

- "There Was Once a Fish," page 25 of *Pickled Peppers*
- Exploring Sounds and Letters, pages 26–27
- For each child, Uppercase and Lowercase Letter Card: *Mm* and *Ss*
- For each child, one set of Uppercase and Lowercase Letter Card: *Aa–Zz*
- Reproducible Master 11

Prepare Ahead

- Two baskets or other containers, one labeled with the letter *m*, one with the letter *s*
- Make a copy of Reproducible Master 11 for each child; cut out the squares if the children do not yet have scissors skills

---

✱ **READING THE BIG BOOK**

"There Was Once a Fish"
page 25 of *Pickled Peppers*

Open *Pickled Peppers* to the table of contents and find "There Was Once a Fish." Ask a child to point to the page number. Say the number and turn to that page. Read the title of the poem and the name of the illustrator.

- Read the poem a few times, pointing to each word and emphasizing the rhyming words. Repeat each couplet and ask the children to listen for the rhyming words.
- Say, "*fish* and *wish* rhyme." Explain that you are going to say other pairs of words, and that you want them to signal thumbs-up if the words rhyme, thumbs-down if not.

First couplet:

fish	vest
fish	dish
fish	swish
fish	fit

Second couplet:

sea	knee
sea	weep
sea	me
sea	tree

Save the last two couplets for the next lesson.

- Ask individual children to come up and identify pictures that tell about certain parts of the poem. Say, for instance: "Where is the picture of the fish being brought to another person?" "Where is the picture of the fish when he is caught on the line? Does he look happy?" "In what picture does the fish look most happy?" Ask the children to name other things that might be in the sea with the fish.
- Read the poem through two or three more times, encouraging children to join in where they can.

✳ PHONEMIC AWARENESS

✳ Oral Blending

Initial Consonant Isolation Explain to the children that the puppet has a new game. When he hears a word, he likes to repeat only the first sound. Tell them to listen closely and, when you give the signal, to help the puppet.

Teacher:	sailor
Puppet:	/s/
Teacher:	meatball
Puppet:	/m/
Teacher:	On the next word, help the puppet out.
Teacher:	mister
Everyone and Puppet:	/m/

Continue with the following words:

mail	sight	might	milk	silk	seat
meat	mole	sail	satin	seal	meal

✳ HOW THE ALPHABET WORKS: PART 2

The Sounds of *m* and *s*

Reviewing *Mm* and *Ss* Point out the Alphabet Card for *Mm*. Ask the children to describe the picture. Recite the poem stressing the /m/ sound. Ask the children to follow along with their actions and their very loud /m/ /m/ /m/!

> For Muzzy, the Monkey, (wiggle fingers under arms)
> bananas are yummy. (rub tummy)
> She munches so many, (pretend to eat)
> they fill up her tummy. (circle arms out in front of tummy)
> She says /m/ /m/ /m/ /m/ /m/!

Ask the children if they can hear the /m/ sounds. Remind them that some of the words have the /m/ sound in the middle, such as *yummy* and *tummy*.

Now point out the Alphabet Card for *Ss* and have the children describe the picture. Then recite the poem stressing the /s/ sound.

> Sue buys sausages on Saturday.
> Sam cooks sausages on Sunday.
> The sausages sizzle /s/ /s/ /s/ /s/ /s/ /s/ when hot.
> Sam eats sausages, but Sue does not.

Listening for Initial /m/ and /s/ Give each child one *Mm* and one *Ss* Uppercase and Lowercase Letter Card. Tell them that you will say a word and that they should repeat it. Say that if a word starts with the /s/ sound, on your signal, they should hold up their *Ss* Letter Card. If it starts with the /m/ sound, they should hold up their *Mm* Letter Card. Try the following words:

men	sight	met	seat	map	meat
mat	mean	sat	me	set	see
sit	so	sock	soap	may	mope
say	Sue	my	might	sigh	man

Listening for Final /m/ and /s/ Sounds Tell children that you will say a word and that they should repeat it. Say that, this time, if a word ends with the /s/ sound, on your signal, they should hold up their *Ss* Letter Card. If it ends with the /m/ sound, they should hold up their *Mm* Letter Card. Try these words:

aim	rice	fame	nice	face	twice
came	ice	case	I'm	race	time
lace	chime	lame	dime	loom	dice
loose	lime	blame	slime	bloom	slim
room	him	rhyme	house		

Linking the Sound to the Letter

Word Pairs Write on the chalkboard a pair of words, one beginning with *m,* the other beginning with *s.* Say the word beginning with *m* for each word pair. Have children identify the word that you said by signaling thumbs-up when you point to it. For example, point to the first word pair and ask, "Which word says *mat*?" Point to each word and have the children signal the correct one. Then repeat the activity using words beginning with *s.*

sat	mat		sad	mad
Monday	Sunday		may	say
seat	meat			

- Continue the activity asking children to signal thumbs-up for words that end in /s/ and then for those that end in /m/.

him	hiss	clam	class
bus	bum	plum	plus
mom	moss		

➤ **Exploring Sounds and Letters** Ask the children to open Exploring Sounds and Letters to pages 26–27. Explain that the pictures on the pages all begin with either *s* or *m.* Go through the pictures one by one with the children. Name each picture. Have the children write *s* under the pictures whose names begin with the /s/ sound and write *m* under the pictures whose names begin with the /m/ sound. After the activity, review their work.

✳ WORKSHOP

- Describe the following activity to the children as an alternative activity for Workshop. If the children have scissors skills, you may wish to keep **Reproducible Master 11** intact, otherwise cut out the individual pictures on the master. Tell the children that they will each get a set of twelve pictures. Say that if a picture starts with /s/ they should put it in the *s* pile; if it starts with /m/, they should put it in the *m* pile.
- For each child, have Uppercase and Lowercase Letter Card sets *Aa–Zz,* shuffled and out of order so they can play the **Ordering Letters** game.
- Make the games **Hop Along, Bus Stop,** and **Roller Ride** available.
- Encourage children to use designated areas of the room such as the chalkboard or easel to create *M*'s and *S*'s.

Exploring Sounds and Letters, page 26

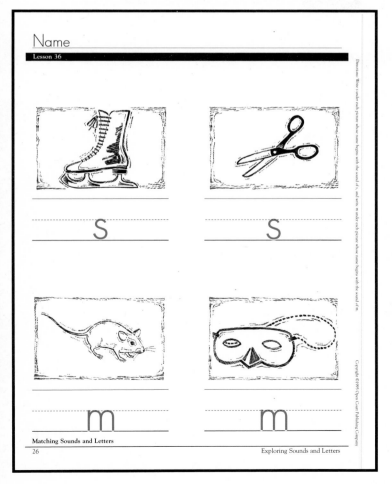

Exploring Sounds and Letters, page 27

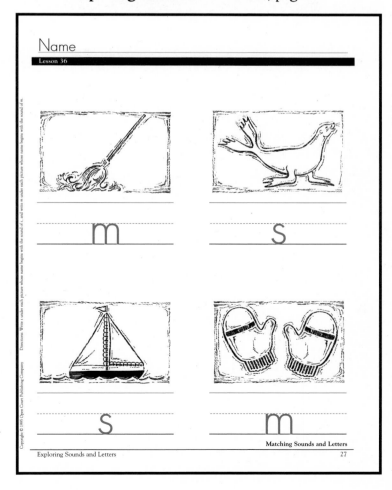

LESSON
37

●●● Lesson Overview

New Learning

- *Dd*
- /d/
- Initial /d/

Materials

- "There Was Once A Fish," page 25 of *Pickled Peppers*
- Exploring Sounds and Letters, pages 28–29
- Individual Alphabet-Sound Card: *Dd*
- For each child, Uppercase and Lowercase Letter Cards: *Dd* and *Ss*
- For each child, one set of Uppercase and Lowercase Letter Cards: *Aa–Zz*

✳ READING THE BIG BOOK

"There Was Once a Fish"
page 25 of *Pickled Peppers*

Read the poem, one couplet at a time. Review the rhyming words in each couplet. Explain that you are going to say pairs of words and that children should use the thumbs-up signal when they hear a rhyme, and thumbs-down when they do not:

Third couplet:

line	fine
line	look
line	pine
line	fight

Fourth couplet:

you	who
you	stew
you	tulip
you	brew

✱ Oral Blending

Initial Consonant Use the puppet to concentrate on blending words that begin with /d/. Explain that you will say the first sound of a word and that the puppet will say the rest of the word. Then everyone should say the whole word.

Teacher: /d/
Puppet: inosaur. What's the word?
Everyone: dinosaur

If you think they are ready, ask individual children to put some of the words together. Alternate between individual and whole-class response. Continue with the following words:

/d/ . . . ishwasher	/d/ . . . andelion
/d/ . . . oughnut	/d/ . . . ynamite
/d/ . . . angerous	/d/ . . . ictionary
/d/ . . . inner	/d/ . . . ragon
/d/ . . . onkey	/d/ . . . affodil
/d/ . . . ragonfly	/d/ . . . ungeon
/d/ . . . iamond	/d/ . . . evelop

The Sound of *d*

Introduce *Dd* Point to the *Dd* Alphabet Card and name the letter.

Tell the children that there is a short poem that will help them remember the sound for letter *d*. Read the poem and say /d/ /d/ /d/ /d/ /d/:

Dinah, the dancing dinosaur,
Had huge and clumsy feet
They went /d/ /d/ /d/ /d/ /d/
As Dinah kept the beat.

Ask the children if they can hear the /d/ sound in *Dinah* and *dinosaur*. Recite the poem again, asking children to stamp their feet and say /d/ /d/ /d/ /d/ /d/ with you.

Listening for Initial /d/ Sound Give each child one *Dd* and one *Ss* Uppercase and Lowercase Letter Card. Explain to the children that you will say a word, and that you want them to repeat it. Say that, on your signal, they should hold up the *Dd* Letter Card if the word starts with /d/, and the *Ss* Letter Card, if the word begins with /s/.

deep	sip	deal	dip	deer	dope
dare	soap	say	so	sigh	doe
day	don't	die	do	dime	dude
sign	dunk	sing	sunk	ding	son
song	done				

Silly Sentences Make silly sentences with the children that involve *d* words. Keep extending the sentences:

Dinah dances.

Dinah the dinosaur dances.

Dinah the dinosaur dances with difficulty.

David and Dinah the dinosaurs dance with difficulty.

David the dragon and Dinah the dinosaur dance with difficulty . . . and so on.

Linking the Sound to the Letter

Word Pairs Write on the chalkboard a pair of similar-looking words, one beginning with the /d/ sound, one not. Say the word beginning with *d* for each word pair. Have children identify the word you said by using the thumbs-up signal when you point to it.

dig	pig	**deep**	peep
dad	mad	**did**	hid
donkey	monkey	**dinosaur**	monster

Writing *Dd* Using the established procedure, review with the children how to form a capital *D.*

- Review the steps for small *d.*
- Remind children that the letter *D* makes the /d/ sound.

❱ **Exploring Sound and Letters** Have the children open Exploring Sounds and Letters to pages 28–29, and instruct them to find the initial /d/ pictures as before. Name each picture, and tell the children to write the letter *d* under each picture whose name begins with the /d/ sound. After the activity, be sure to review their work. Then have them write capital *D* and small *d* on the lines at the top of page 28.

✱ WORKSHOP

- For each child, have Uppercase and Lowercase Letter Card sets *Aa–Zz,* shuffled and out of order so the children can play the **Ordering Letters** game.
- Make the games **Hop Along, Bus Stop,** and **Roller Ride** available. Add the *Dd* Individual Alphabet-Sound Card to Roller Ride.
- Encourage children to use designated areas of the room such as the chalkboard or easel to create *D's.*

TIP FOR ENGLISH LANGUAGE LEARNERS

Pair English Language Learners with native English speakers to play one of the review games. Informally assess their understanding of the letters reviewed by monitoring their conversations during the game.

Exploring Sounds and Letters, page 28

Exploring Sounds and Letters, page 29

LESSON
38

●●● Lesson Overview

New Learning

- Final /d/

Materials

- "Higglety, Pigglety, Pop!" page 39 of *Pickled Peppers*
- Exploring Sounds and Letters, pages 30–31
- For each child, Uppercase and Lowercase Letter Cards: *Dd* and *Mm*
- Home/School Connection 9

✳ READING THE BIG BOOK

"Higglety, Pigglety, Pop!"
page 39 of *Pickled Peppers*

Open *Pickled Peppers* to "Higglety, Pigglety, Pop!" Read the title of the song and the name of the illustrator. Read the song several times, pointing to each word. Ask children to listen for the rhyming words. Explain that you are going to say pairs of words and that you want them to signal thumbs-up when they hear a pair that rhymes, and thumbs-down when they hear a pair that does not rhyme. Try the following words:

pop	mop		pop	top
pop	tap		pop	flop
pop	put		pop	hop
hurry	flurry		hurry	scurry
hurry	happy		hurry	worry
hurry	hilly		hurry	blurry

> **TIP FOR ENGLISH LANGUAGE LEARNERS**
>
> Talk more with English Language Learners about the poem's illustration before reading the poem. Show how the important aspects of the text relate to the pictures. Associating text with pictures helps English Language Learners to think more in English.

✳ PHONEMIC AWARENESS

✳ Oral Blending

Final Consonant Now concentrate on the final /d/ sound for oral blending. Say the first part of a word and have the puppet supply the final consonant sound.

Teacher:	lemona
Puppet:	/d/
Teacher:	What is the word?
Everyone:	lemonade

Continue with the following words:

birdsee . . . /d/	noseblee . . . /d/
gingerbrea . . . /d/	afrai . . . /d/
grandchil . . . /d/	diamon . . . /d/
chalkboar . . . /d/	cornfiel . . . /d/
reboun . . . /d/	confuse . . . /d/
playgroun . . . /d/	respon . . . /d/

✱ HOW THE ALPHABET WORKS: PART 2

The Sound of *d*

Reviewing Dd Review the letter *Dd.* Read the poem for the *Dd* Alphabet Card again:

> Dinah, the dancing dinosaur,
> Had huge and clumsy feet
> They went /d/ /d/ /d/ /d/ /d/
> As Dinah kept the beat.

Recite the poem again, asking children to stamp their feet and shout /d/ /d/ /d/ /d/ /d/.

Listening for Final /d/ Give each child one *Dd* and one *Mm* Uppercase and Lowercase Letter Card. Say a word and have the children repeat it. Then have them hold up the *Dd* Letter Card if the word ends with /d/ and the *Mm* Letter Card if it ends with /m/.

aid	groom	ad	greed	odd	grade
nod	raid	need	ride	seed	rhyme
seem	time	beam	tide	bead	hide
dead	home	reed	roam	rude	foam
room	food				

Linking the Sound to the Letter

Word Pairs Write on the chalkboard a pair of words, one ending with /d/, one not. Say the word ending with /d/ for each word pair. Then have children identify the word you said by using the thumbs-up signal when you point to it.

him	**hid**		man	**mad**
mud	mug		seem	**seed**
golf	**gold**		hunter	**hundred**
postman	**postcard**			

Writing Dd If you feel your class needs the review, review the formation of the letters capital *D* and small *d.*

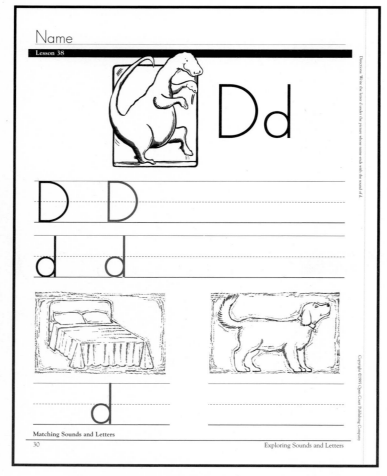

Exploring Sounds and Letters, page 30

Exploring Sounds and Letters, page 31

❯ **Exploring Sounds and Letters** Have children open Exploring Sounds and Letters to pages 30–31, and explain that some of the pictures on the pages end in the /d/ sound. Point to each picture and say the name. Ask the children to write the letter *d* under each picture whose name ends with the /d/ sound. After the activity, be sure to review the children's work.

✱ WORKSHOP

- For each child, have Uppercase and Lowercase Letter Card sets *Aa–Zz,* shuffled and out of order so the children can play the **Ordering Letters** game.
- Make the games **Hop Along, Bus Stop,** and **Roller Ride** available.
- Children love to work at the chalkboard like the teacher. Invite them in small groups to practice writing *Ss's, Mm's,* and *Dd's* on the chalkboard. They might work in pairs, one child writing a capital, and the other its matching small letter.

Home/School Connection Home/School Connection 9 informs families that their children are starting to learn the sounds of the letters, especially /s/, /m/, and /d/. Send it home with the children.

LESSON 39

●●● Lesson Overview

New Learning

- Comparing /d/, /m/, and /s/

Materials

- "Higglety, Pigglety, Pop!" page 39 of *Pickled Peppers*
- Picture Cards: *knot, pail, pie, pig, post, pot, tail, tie, toast, wig*
- Word Cards: *dog, eaten, has, Higglety, mop, pigglety, pop, The, the,*
- Exploring Sounds and Letters, pages 32–33
- For each child, Uppercase and Lowercase Letter Cards: *Dd, Mm,* and *Ss*
- For each child, one set of Uppercase and Lowercase Letter Cards: *Aa–Zz*

✳ READING THE BIG BOOK

"Higglety, Pigglety, Pop!"
page 39 of *Pickled Peppers*

- Open *Pickled Peppers* to "Higglety, Pigglety, Pop!" Reread the song.
- Using Word Cards put the first two lines of the song in the Pocket Chart. Read them, pointing to each word. Tell the children that you will need their help changing some of the rhyming words. Hold the first column of the Picture Cards listed below in your lap. Place the other Picture Cards on a nearby low table.

pie	*tie*
post	*toast*
pot	*knot*
pail	*tail*
pig	*wig*

- Take out the *pop* Word Card, put in the *pie* Picture Card, and say the new line. Then read the next line, pausing before *mop.* Remove *mop,* and ask a child to go to the table and find a Picture Card that will make a new rhyme.
- Continue in this way, working through the other rhyming Picture Cards.

> **TIP FOR ENGLISH LANGUAGE LEARNERS**
>
> Give English Language Learners a chance to share their knowledge and language with other children. Encourage English Language Learners to translate the words dog, pig, and cat into their primary languages. Recognizing minority languages is a good way to prevent inhibitions about using language. It also provides native English-speaking children with an opportunity to learn about different languages and cultures.

* Oral Blending

Initial Consonant Isolation Continue working with words that contain initial /d/, /m/, or /s/ sounds. Vary the techniques you use. Have the puppet say the word and the children say the initial consonant sound. Then have the children repeat the word.

Puppet: Daisy
Everyone: /d/
Everyone: daisy

Continue with the following words:

dancer . . . /d/	distance . . . /d/	mole . . . /m/
muscular . . . /m/	separate . . . /s/	salamander . . . /s/
marble . . . /m/	salad . . . /s/	make . . . /m/
date . . . /d/	daring . . . /d/	double . . . /d/

The Sounds of *d, m,* and *s*

Reviewing *Dd, Mm,* and *Ss* Review the names of the three letters *Dd, Mm,* and *Ss,* by pointing to the Alphabet Cards and their pictures. Reread the poems for the sounds of /d/, /m/, and /s/. (See pages 124, 136, and 149 of this book.)

Listening for Final /d/, /m/, and /s/ Sounds Give each child one *Dd,* one *Mm,* and one *Ss* Uppercase and Lowercase Letter Card. Tell them to set the *Ss* card aside for now. You will only be using the *Dd* and *Mm* cards at first. Tell the children that you will say a word and you want them to listen for the last sound. Say that if they hear /d/ at the end, they should hold up the *Dd* card. If they hear the /m/ at the end, they should hold up the *Mm* card. Try the following words:

aid	bead	add	reed	odd	grade
nod	raid	need	ride	seed	rhyme
seem	time	beam	tide		

Continue the activity with /d/ and /s/. Have children set aside their *Mm* cards, and use the cards for *Dd* and *Ss.*

bud	lad	bus	lace	mad	raid
mass	race	kiss	case	kid	fad
clad	face	class	made	grade	mess
grass	dress				

Linking the Sound to the Letter

Word Pairs In this activity you will write sets of letters on the chalkboard, say them, and then ask the children how to make them complete words.

Write sets of letters on the chalkboard, for instance, *at.* Say *at.* Ask,

"How can we make this *sat*?" Try the following words:

op	mop	ay	day
ick	sick	otor	motor
agger	dagger		

❯ **Exploring Sounds and Letters** Ask the children to open Exploring Sounds and Letters to pages 32–33. Explain that the pictures on the pages all end with either /d/, /s/, or /m/. Say each picture name. Then have the children complete the word by writing either a *d, s,* or *m* at the end of the word. Make sure to review their work when the children have finished.

✳ WORKSHOP

- For each child, have Uppercase and Lowercase Letter Cards *Aa–Zz,* shuffled and out of order so the children can play the **Ordering Letters** game.
- Make the games **Hop Along, Bus Stop,** and **Roller Ride** available.
- Children love to work at the chalkboard like the teacher. Invite them in small groups to practice writing *Ss*'s, *Mm*'s, and *Dd*'s on the chalkboard. They might work in pairs, one child writing a capital, and the other its matching small letter.

MONITORING TIP Observe again any children who did not successfully recognize their capital and small letters *Aa–Zz* in previous monitorings. Note their progress on Observation Log 1, Reproducible Master 28.

Exploring Sounds and Letters, page 32

Exploring Sounds and Letters, page 33

LESSON
40

●●● Lesson Overview

New Learning

- *Pp*
- /p/
- Initial /p/
- Comparing /p/, /s/, and /d/

Materials

- "Peter Piper," page 40 of *Pickled Peppers*
- Exploring Sounds and Letters, pages 34–35
- For each child, Uppercase and Lowercase Letter Cards: *Dd*, *Pp* and *Ss*
- For each child, one set of Uppercase and Lowercase Letter Cards: *Aa–Zz*

✱ READING THE BIG BOOK

"Peter Piper"
page 40 of *Pickled Peppers*

- Open *Pickled Peppers* and turn to "Peter Piper." Read the poem through slowly, pointing to each word. Explain that this is often a difficult poem to recite because there are so many /p/ sounds. It is called a tongue-twister.

    Look at the first line and count the number of *p*'s. Ask a child to help you count the *p*'s in the second line, and so on.

- Ask the children to say *Peter Piper*. Ask them to look at the picture and point out the pickled peppers. Tell the children that you want them to review the sounds they have already learned for the letters *s, m,* and *d.* Hold up (or point to the Alphabet Card for) each letter, and ask the class to say its sound. Now tell the class that you want them to change Peter Piper's name by changing the first /p/ sounds to /s/, /d/, or /m/, depending upon which letter you point to.

    Help them the first few times: *Seter Siper/Meter Miper/ Deter Diper.* Try this a few times until children catch on.

- Now try the same sounds with *pickled peppers*: *sickled seppers/mickled meppers/dickled deppers.*

✳ Oral Blending

Initial Consonant Work with words that begin with /p/. Remember to vary your technique.

Everyone and Puppet: /p/
Teacher: uppet. What's the word?
Everyone: puppet

Continue with the following words:

/p/ . . . addle	/p/ . . . uddle
/p/ . . . irate	/p/ . . . umpkin
/p/ . . . ussywillow	/p/ . . . izza
/p/ . . . ocket	/p/ . . . orcupine
/p/ . . . ineapple	/p/ . . . imento
/p/ . . . istachio	/p/ . . . orpoise

The Sound of p

Introducing Pp Introduce the letter *Pp.* Point to the *Pp* Alphabet Card and name the letter. Read the poem for the /p/ sound:

> Popcorn! Popcorn! Ping and Pong shouted,
> Let's pop some in a pot, because we like it hot!
> /p/ /p/ /p/ /p/ was the sound it made.

Ask the children if they can hear the /p/ sound. Repeat the poem again, asking children to join in where they can.

Listening for /p/, /s/, and /d/ Give each child a *Pp, Dd* and *Ss* Uppercase and Lowercase Letter Card. Tell children to set the *Dd* card aside for now. You will only be using the *Pp* and *Ss* at first. Tell the children that you will say a word and you want them to listen for the first sound. If it is /p/, they should hold up the *Pp* card. If it is /s/, they should hold up the *Ss* card. Try the following words:

paw	peel	saw	seal	some	sole
son	pole	pun	pore	some	poke
sack	soak	pack	sigh	pat	pie
pal	pea	pail	see	sail	seek

- Continue the activity with *Pp* and *Dd.* Have children set aside their *Ss* cards, and listen for /p/ or /d/.

pot	pose	dot	dose	pace	post
place	pore	pay	door	day	part
date	dart	pin	dad	pill	pad
pig	pan				

Pp **Words** Make sentences with the children that involve *Pp* words. Keep extending the sentences. "Peter picked pansies," "Peter and Pam picked purple pansies," and so on.

Linking the Sound to the Letter

Word Pairs Write pairs of words on the chalkboard, one of which starts with *p*. For example, write *pot* and *cat*. Ask the children, "Which word says *pot*?" Then as you point at each word ask again, "Does **this** word say *pot* or does **this** word sat *pot*?" Continue with the word pairs below, asking the children to identify, with the thumbs up signal, the words that begin with /p/. Try:

pat	hat	**pail**	sail
pay	day	**poke**	coke
Pam	Sam	**parrot**	carrot

Writing *Pp* Have the children practice writing the letter *p*.
- Review the steps for forming a capital *P*.
- Remind children that the letter *P* makes the /p/ sound.
- Review small *p*.

❯ **Exploring Sounds and Letters** Ask the children to turn to pages 34–35 in Exploring Sounds and Letters. Explain that many of the pictures begin with the /p/ sound. Ask the children to write *p* under the pictures whose names start with /p/. After the activity, go over all the picture names and ask the children to listen for the beginning sounds. Then have them write capital *P* and small *p* on the lines at the top of page 34.

✳ WORKSHOP

- Have Uppercase and Lowercase Letter Cards *Aa–Zz* for each child, shuffled and out of order so they can play the **Ordering Letters** game. Tell the children to put them in order. If the children are working with partners, one child can do capital letters and the other child can work with the small letters.
- Make the games **Hop Along**, **Bus Stop**, and **Roller Ride** available.
- Encourage the children to use designated areas of the room such as the chalkboard or easel to create their *Pp*'s.

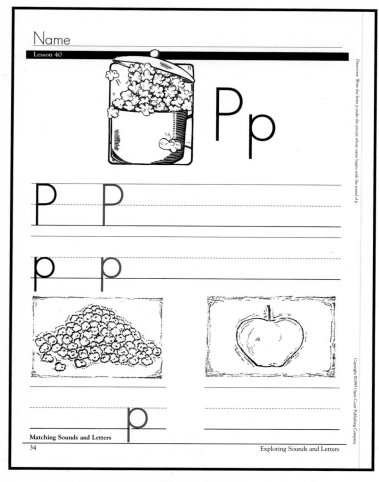

Directions: Write the letter p under the picture whose name begins with the sound of p.

Name

Lesson 40

P p

P   P

p   p

p

Matching Sounds and Letters

34

Exploring Sounds and Letters, page 34

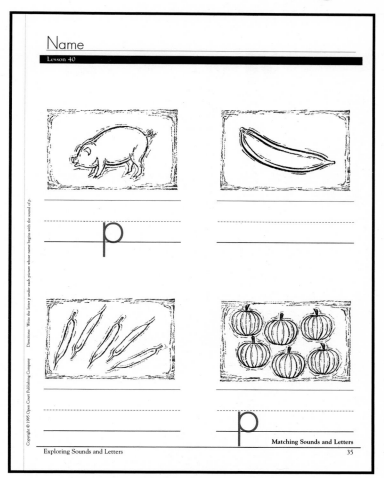

Directions: Write the letter p under each picture whose name begins with the sound of p.

Name

Lesson 40

p

p

Matching Sounds and Letters

35

Exploring Sounds and Letters, page 35

LESSON

41

●●● Lesson Overview

New Learning

- Final /p/
- /p/, /m/, and /d/

Materials

- "Peter Piper," page 40 of *Pickled Peppers*
- Word Cards for first line of "Peter Piper"
- Exploring Sounds and Letters, page 36–37
- For each child, one set of Uppercase and Lowercase Letter Cards: *Dd, Mm, Pp*
- For each child, one set of Uppercase and Lowercase Letter Cards: *Aa–Zz*

Prepare Ahead

- A paper bag and Pocket Chart Letter Cards: one each of *Hh, Ii, Oo, Rr*; two of *Pp*; three each of *Dd, Mm*

✳ READING THE BIG BOOK

"Peter Piper"
page 40 of *Pickled Peppers*

This activity will help children attend to the importance of the order of words.

- Read "Peter Piper" slowly, pointing to each word. Explain that the word *peck* means a large amount, so Peter must have picked a lot of peppers.
- Put the first line of "Peter Piper" on the Pocket Chart.
- Change the order of the words and read the poem all the way through with the new first line. Encourage the children to discuss how this makes the line different. What does it do to the sentence?
- Try this several times.

✳ PHONEMIC AWARENESS

✳ Oral Blending

Final Consonant Blend word parts for words ending in the /p/ sound, using the techniques from earlier lessons.

Puppet: antelo
Child: /p/
Teacher: What's the word?
Everyone: antelope

Continue with the following words:

ro . . . /p/	ho . . . /p/	mo . . . /p/	ty . . . /p/
ri . . . /p/	lam . . . /p/	dam . . . /p/	ram . . . /p/
tar . . . /p/	har . . . /p/	shar . . . /p/	microsco . . . /p/

✳ HOW THE ALPHABET WORKS: PART 2

Remember that Lessons 31–50 are meant to give the children a taste of how the letter-sound correspondences work. They will be working with both short and long vowels as they create new words by changing initial and final consonants.

The Sound of *p*

Introducing *Pp* Review the short poem for the letter *Pp*. Hold up the *Pp* Alphabet Card and say /p/ /p/ /p/ /p/ /p/ /p/:

Popcorn! Popcorn! Ping and Pong shouted,
Let's pop some in a pot, because we like it hot!
/p/ /p/ /p/ /p/ was the sound it made.

Repeat the poem, emphasizing the initial /p/ sounds and asking the children to pop up and down in their chairs on /p/ /p/ /p/ /p/ /p/ /p/.

Listening for Final /p/ Give each child one *Pp*, one *Mm*, and one *Dd* Uppercase and Lowercase Letter Card. Have the children put their *Dd* card aside. Explain to the children that you will say a word and that you want them to repeat it. Say that, on your signal, they should hold up the *Pp* Letter Card if the word ends with /p/ and the *Mm* card if the word ends with /m/.

deep	sip	dome	dip	dime	dope
groom	tip	reap	time	rhyme	tap
sheep	sap				

Repeat the activity for words ending with /d/ and /p/. The children can put aside their *Mm* cards.

seed	lip	feed	slip	flip	wipe
ripe	leap	cap	keep	hip	trip
hid	grid	ship	drip	did	dad

Linking the Sound to the Letter

Grab Bag of Letters   Using the paper bag and Pocket Chart Letter Cards you prepared ahead, place two copies each of the *Pp, Dd,* and *Mm* Pocket Chart Letter Cards in the bag. Place the bag beside the Pocket Chart.

- Tell the children that you are going to place two Letter Cards in the Pocket Chart, and that you want them to make words by adding letters from the bag to the end of the two letters on the chart.
- Put the letters *d* and *i* in the chart. Say *"di"* (short *i* sound). Call on a child to reach into the bag for a letter and place it after *di.* Say, "Can you say the new word?" Help if necessary.
- Now remove the letter, and ask another child to reach into the bag. When the *Pp, Dd,* and *Mm* cards have been used, return them to the bag and continue the activity using the following sets of letters to make short vowel words:

  hi...d   hi...m   hi...p   ri...d
  ri...m   ri...p   mo...d   mo...m   mo...p

Writing Pp   Using the established procedure, review with the children formation of *P* and *p.*

❯ **Exploring Sounds and Letters**   Have children open Exploring Sounds and Letters to pages 36–37. Explain that some of the pictures on the pages end with the /p/ sound, others end with the /m/ sound. Ask the children to write the letter *p* under the pictures whose names end with /p/ and *m* under those whose names end with /m/. Say all the names of the pictures one by one to the children.

After children have finished, be sure to go over the pictures as a class and name them. This will help any children who may have identified the pictures incorrectly.

✳ WORKSHOP

- For each child, have Uppercase and Lowercase Letter Cards *Aa–Zz,* shuffled and out of order so they can play **Ordering Letters.** Tell the children to put them in order. If they are working with partners, one can do capital and one small letters.
- Make the **Hop Along, Bus Stop,** and **Roller Ride** games available.
- Let children use designated areas of the room to practice making *p*'s.

TIP FOR ENGLISH LANGUAGE LEARNERS

Encourage conversational practice to find out about language in a friendly, unintimidating way. Pair English Language Learners with native English speakers. Have partners talk with each other as they order the letters. Informally monitor the children's conversations to assess their progress.

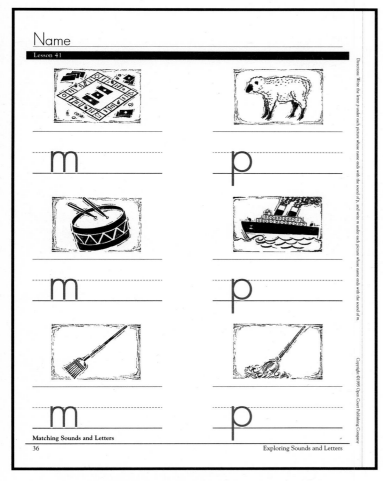

Name

Lesson 41

m

p

m

p

m

p

Matching Sounds and Letters

36

Exploring Sounds and Letters

Exploring Sounds and Letters, pages 36

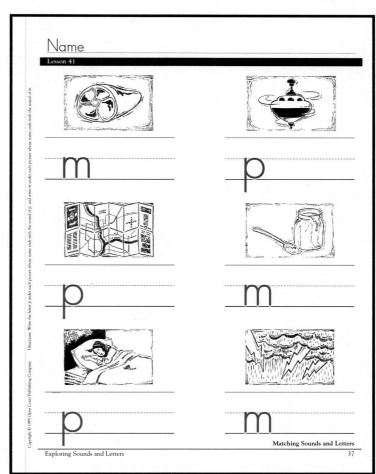

Name

Lesson 41

m

p

p

m

p

m

Exploring Sounds and Letters

Matching Sounds and Letters

37

Exploring Sounds and Letters, pages 37

LESSON

42

● ● ● Lesson Overview

New Learning

- Initial /t/
- /t/

Materials

- "Peter Piper," page 40 of *Pickled Peppers*
- Word cards for the first line of "Peter Piper"
- Exploring Sounds and Letters, pages 38–39
- For each child, Uppercase and Lowercase Letter Card: *Tt*
- Reproducible Master 12

Prepare Ahead

- T Tree materials: a large, many-twigged tree branch; bucket of sand; circles and squares of colored construction paper in varying sizes; hole punch; short lengths of yarn; magazines; crayons; markers; glitter; glue

---

✳ READING THE BIG BOOK

"Peter Piper"
page 40 of *Pickled Peppers*

- Reread "Peter Piper" in *Pickled Peppers.* Use Word Cards to put the first line of the poem on the Pocket Chart.
- Ask children to count the number of *p*'s in each line. (If the children are not able to count, have them point to the *p*'s.) Say, "How many words start with *p*?"
- Read the poem again, then have individual children say it as fast as they can.

✳ PHONEMIC AWARENESS

✳ Oral Blending

Initial Consonant Vary your techniques as you have the children blend words that have the initial /t/ sound.

/t/ . . . angle   /t/ . . . ortoise   /t/ . . . able

/t/ . . . otal   /t/ . . . iger   /t/ . . . erritory

/t/ . . . emper   /t/ . . . elegram   /t/ . . . elephone

/t/ . . . elevision

✳ HOW THE ALPHABET WORKS: PART 2

The Sound of *t*

Introducing *Tt* Introduce the letter *t*. Hold up or point to the letter *Tt* Alphabet Card and say, "/t/ /t/ /t/ /t/ /t/ /t/":

> Tom Tuttle's timer ticks like this: /t/ /t/ /t/ /t/ /t/ /t/.
> Tonight Tom Tuttle wants tomatoes on toast.
> He sets his timer. Listen carefully /t/ /t/ /t/ /t/ /t/ /t/.
> What sound would the timer make if you set it? /t/ /t/ /t/ /t/ /t/.

Repeat the poem several times. Then have the children join in.

Listening for Initial /t/ Give each child a *Tt* Uppercase and Lowercase Letter Card. Explain to the children that you will say a word, and that you want them to repeat it. Say that, on your signal, they should hold up the *Tt* Letter Card if the word starts with /t/:

tip	**tin**	**trip**	pin	rip	pest
sit	**test**	**town**	**tar**	**trade**	**tab**
raid	**tack**	**tad**	sack	**time**	**tap**

I'm Thinking of Something That Starts with _____ Game Review the past sounds you have used in this game. Ask children to close their eyes. Tell them that you are going to think of things having to do with food and eating that start with certain sounds. Say that you will give them clues, and as soon as they think they know what you are thinking of, they should raise their hands. You will need to announce the sound each time:

> "I am thinking of something that starts with /t/":
>
> You do this to bread in the morning. (toast)
> You sit here to eat. (table)
> You chew food with these. (teeth)
> You lick your lips with this. (tongue)
>
> "I am thinking of something that starts with [/p/, /m/, /s/, /d/]." (Give clues for):
>
> pretzel
> potato chips

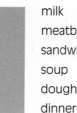

milk
meatball
sandwich
soup
doughnut
dinner

Linking the Sound to the Letter

Word Pairs Write two words on the board, one beginning with /t/, one not. Say the word beginning with /t/. Ask individual children to come to the chalkboard and circle the word you said and underline the letter that makes the /t/ sound. Try these words:

tail	sail	**top**	mop
pear	**tear**	**ticket**	picket
Sunday	**Tuesday**	**table**	able

Writing *Tt* Use the overhead projector or the chalkboard so that the children can form letters with you.
- Review how to form a capital letter *T*.
- Review how to form a small *t*.

❯ **Exploring Sounds and Letters** Ask children to turn to pages 38–39 in Exploring Sounds and Letters. Have children practice writing the capital and small forms of *Tt* in the space provided. Explain that some of the pictures on the pages begin with the /t/ sound. Name the pictures. Ask the children to write a *t* under the pictures whose names start with /t/. After the activity, go over all the picture names and ask the children to listen for the beginning sounds.

✳ WORKSHOP

- Make a **T Tree** and have the children decorate it with pictures or drawings of things that start with /t/. Place the branch you have prepared in the bucket of sand. Set out the materials.
- Tell the children they are going to decorate a T Tree. Explain that they can look through the magazines for pictures of things that start with /t/, cut them out, and glue them onto the colored construction paper pieces that you prepared ahead. Say that, if they prefer, they can draw their own *t* pictures. You can also use **Reproducible Master 12.** Tell the children that some of the pictures on the master start with /t/, but others do not. Say that they can cut out these *t* pictures and paste them onto the construction paper pieces. Tell them to save the other pictures and place them in a can or basket that you have provided. They will be used in Lesson 45.
- Circulate during Workshop to see that children are using the correct pictures. Use a punch to make holes in the paper pieces and show the children how to string the yarn through the holes. Let them decorate the tree.
- Continue to have the standard Workshop activities available.

TIP FOR ENGLISH LANGUAGE LEARNERS

Pair English Language Learners with native English speakers to complete the T tree. Have native English speakers share words that begin with /t/ with English Language Learners and help them to locate appropriate pictures. Informally assess children's vocabularies by monitoring their conversations during the activity.

Name

Lesson 42

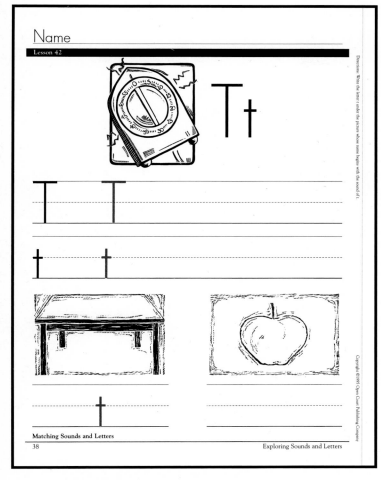

Directions: Write the letter t under the picture whose name begins with the sound of t.

Matching Sounds and Letters

38

Exploring Sounds and Letters

Exploring Sounds and Letters, page 38

Name

Lesson 42

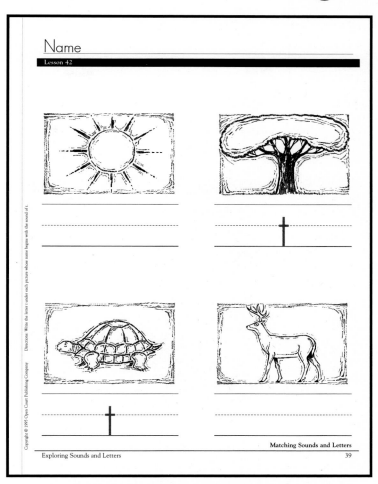

Directions: Write the letter t under each picture whose name begins with the sound of t.

Exploring Sounds and Letters

Matching Sounds and Letters

39

Exploring Sounds and Letters, page 39

LESSON
43

●●● Lesson Overview

New Learning

- Final /t/

Materials

- "Peter Piper," page 40 of *Pickled Peppers*
- Pocket Chart Letter Cards: one each of *c, e, h, i, n, o, s, u;* two each of *D, M, S, T, P*
- Word Cards: *Peter, Piper*
- For each child, Uppercase and Lowercase Letter Card: *Tt*
- Exploring Sounds and Letters, pages 40–41

✳ READING THE BIG BOOK

"Peter Piper"
page 40 of *Pickled Peppers*

- Reread "Peter Piper" in *Pickled Peppers.*
- Review the /t/ sound, along with /p/, /d/, /m/, and /s/.
- Put the Word Cards *Peter Piper* in the Pocket Chart
- Place two of each of the following Pocket Chart Letter Cards on a low table nearby: *T, S, M, D.*
- Ask the children whether anyone can change "Peter Piper" into "Teter Tiper." Ask a volunteer to place the correct letters over the capital *P*'s to make the change.
- Ask children to make other changes, using any combination of the letters *T, S, M,* and *D.*

✳ PHONEMIC AWARENESS

✳ Oral Blending

Final Consonant Use the puppet to help the children concentrate on blending the first part of words with the final consonant sound /t/. Try the following words:

ba . . . /t/	acroba . . . /t/	figh . . . /t/
tonigh . . . /t/	nightligh . . . /t/	deli . . . /t/
boa . . . /t/	mas . . . /t/	naviga . . . /t/
straigh . . . /t/	concentra . . . /t/	celebra . . . /t/
overcoa . . . /t/		

---

* HOW THE ALPHABET WORKS: PART 2

The Sound of *t*

Reviewing *Tt* Review the letter *Tt*. Hold up the *Tt* Alphabet Card and say /t/ /t/ /t/ /t/ /t/ /t/. Read the poem:

> Tom Tuttle's timer ticks like this: /t/ /t/ /t/ /t/ /t/ /t/.
> Tonight Tom Tuttle wants tomatoes on toast.
> He sets his timer. Listen carefully /t/ /t/ /t/ /t/ /t/ /t/.
> What sound would the timer make if you set it? /t/ /t/ /t/ /t/ /t/.

Repeat several times until children can join in.

Listening for Final /t/ Give each child a *Tt* Uppercase and Lowercase Letter Card. Explain to the children that you will say a word, and that you want them to repeat it. Say that, on your signal, they should hold up the *Tt* Letter Card if the word ends with /t/.

pit	dust	hit	pot	hip	hot
hat	tot	sat	top	mat	hop
man	hut	mute	hum	but	pet

Linking the Sound to the Letter

Grab Bag of Letters Place Pocket Chart Letter Cards *p* and *t* in a paper bag. Put the Pocket Chart Letter Cards *i* and *p* in the Pocket Chart. Say *"ip"* (short *i* sound). Invite a child to reach into the bag for a letter and then place it on the chart in front of the letters already there. Say, "Can you say the new word?" Help if necessary. Now remove the initial letter, and ask another child to reach into the bag. When the *p* and *t* cards have both been used, return the letters to the bag and continue the activity with the following sets of letters to make short vowel words:

p . . . ot	t . . . ot	p . . . in	t . . . in
p . . . en	t . . . en		

Continue by reviewing words that end with *p* and *t*:

hi . . . t	pi . . . t	si . . . t	si . . . p
cu . . . t	pu . . . t	po . . . t	po . . . p

Writing *Tt* Review with the children how to form capital *T* and small *t*.

❯ **Exploring Sounds and Letters** Have children open Exploring Sounds and Letters to pages 40–41. Have children practice writing the capital and small forms of *Tt* in the space provided. Explain that some of the pictures on the pages have names that end with the /t/ sound. Ask the children to write a *t* under the pictures whose names end with /t/. Review the picture pairs one by one with the children before they write their letters.

After children have finished, be sure to go over the pictures as a class and name them. This will help any children who may have identified the pictures incorrectly.

✱ **WORKSHOP**

- Have children continue making decorations for the class **T Tree.**
- Encourage the children to use other Workshop and Learning Center activities if they finish working on the T Tree.

TIP FOR ENGLISH LANGUAGE LEARNERS

To help English Language Learners feel more at ease, continue to let them work with a partner during the activity.

Exploring Sounds and Letters, page 40

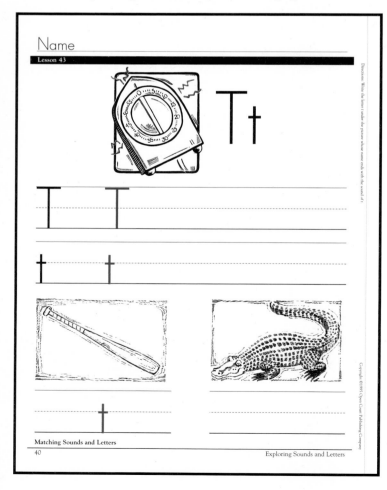

Exploring Sounds and Letters, page 41

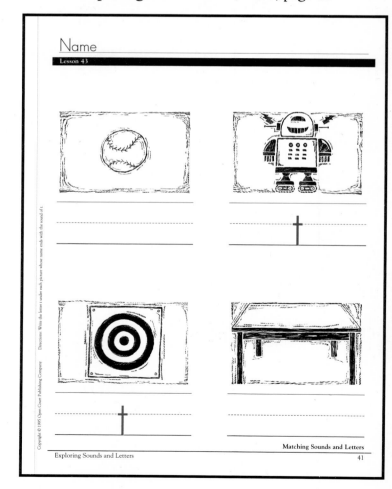

LESSON
44

Lesson Overview

New Learning

- Initial /h/
- /h/

Materials

- The Top and the Tip," page 16 of *Pickled Peppers*
- "The Top and the Tip," First-Step Story 3
- Exploring Sounds and Letters, pages 42–43
- For each child, Uppercase and Lowercase Letter Card: *Hh*
- Learning Framework Card 8

✳ READING THE BIG BOOK

"The Top and the Tip"
page 16 of *Pickled Peppers*

In this lesson, the children will work with another First-Step Story. First-Step Stories are sometimes reprints of the selections found in *Pickled Peppers,* sometimes new stories or poems, and sometimes picture stories that the children write and draw themselves. These personal books allow the children to practice the skills and behaviors of accomplished readers and writers. The First-Step Story used in this lesson is based on the poem "The Top and the Tip" in *Pickled Peppers.* For more information about how to use the First-Step Stories with your class, see **Learning Framework Card 8.**

- Open *Pickled Peppers* to the table of contents and point to "The Top and the Tip." Ask the children if someone can point to the page number. Say the number and then turn to it. Read the title, pointing to each word. Read the author's name and then read *Illustrated by Roz Schanzer.* Remind the children that illustrators are the people who draw pictures to go along with stories and poems.
- Read through the poem slowly, running your finger under each word as you do so. Ask the children if they see anything in the picture that the words describe and have them point out these pictures. Explain that all illustrators choose to draw pictures about a story or poem in their own way.

"The Top and the Tip"
First-Step Story 3

- Give each child his or her own copy of the First-Step Story "The Top and the Tip." Have the children follow along, pointing to each word as you read the poem in *Pickled Peppers.* Go slowly, and note if children are able to follow. Use the established signal to let them know when to turn the pages.
- Talk about the meaning of *top* and *tip.* Ask children to point to the tops of their shoes or to the tips of their fingers. You might hold up some everyday objects such as a bottle and ask, "What is the top of the bottle?" (bottle cap), "What is the tip of a pencil?" (the point), etc.
- Tell the children to place their First-Step Story aside. Explain that they will work with them again in Workshop.

❋ Oral Blending

Initial Consonant Blend words with the initial /h/ sound. Use a variety of techniques.

Puppet	/h/
Everyone:	/h/
Teacher:	ouse. What's the word?
Everyone:	house

Ask individual children or the entire class to respond. Continue with the following words:

/h/ . . . andkerchief	/h/ . . . ail
/h/ . . . urricane	/h/ . . . appiness
/h/ . . . oneysuckle	/h/ . . . orse
/h/ . . . elicopter	/h/ . . . aystack

The Sound of *h*

Introducing *Hh* Point to the *Hh* Alphabet Card and say the letter. Turn the card over so that the picture side is showing. Read the poem for /h/:

Harry the Hound Dog
hurries around.
/h/ /h/ /h/ /h/ /h/ /h/
is his hurrying sound.

Tell the children to listen for the /h/ sound in the following words: *Harry, hound, hurry.*

Ask children a series of questions so that they can practice the /h/ sound. Wait for them to reply: /h/ /h/ /h/ /h/ /h/ /h/. Try these questions:

What sound do you make when you pedal your bike as hard as you can?

What sound do you make when you run very fast?

Listening for Initial /h/ Give each child an *Hh* Uppercase and Lowercase Letter Card. Tell the children that you will say words and that some of them start with the /h/ sound. Ask them to hold up their *Hh* cards when they hear the /h/ sound. Try the following words:

hat	**hot**	**hit**	pot	**hip**	pen
sat	**hen**	mat	**hope**	man	**hand**
hut	**hop**	**hum**	bum		

Silly Sentences Make silly sentences with the children that involve *h* words. Keep extending the sentences: Harry hiked on the highway. Harry and Hannah hiked on the highway. Harry and Hannah hurriedly hiked on the highway.

Linking the Sound to the Letter

Word Pairs Use the techniques as in earlier lessons. Ask the children to listen for the initial /h/ sound in the following pairs of words. Say the word that begins with /h/ and then ask individual children come to the board, circle the word you say, and underline the letter that makes the /h/ sound.

blustery	**history**	**hand**	send
dad	**had**	March	**harsh**
hatch	match		

Writing *Hh* Review with the children how to form capital *H* and small *h.*

❯ **Exploring Sounds and Letters** Have children open Exploring Sounds and Letters to pages 42–43. Have children practice writing the capital and small forms of *Hh* in the space provided. Explain that some of the pictures on the pages begin with the /h/ sound. Ask the children to write the letter *h* under the pictures whose names start with /h/. Go over the pictures as a class and name them. When the children have completed the page, review the picture names as a class. Each time you say an *h* word, ask the children whether they can hear the /h/ sound at the beginning of the word.

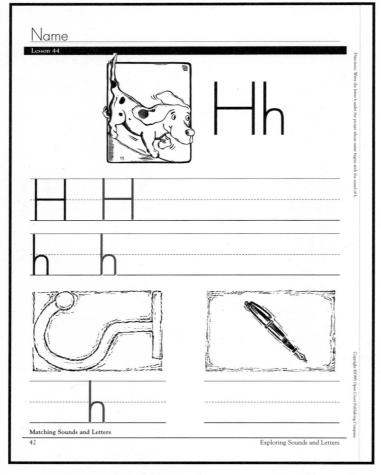
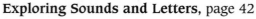

Exploring Sounds and Letters, page 42

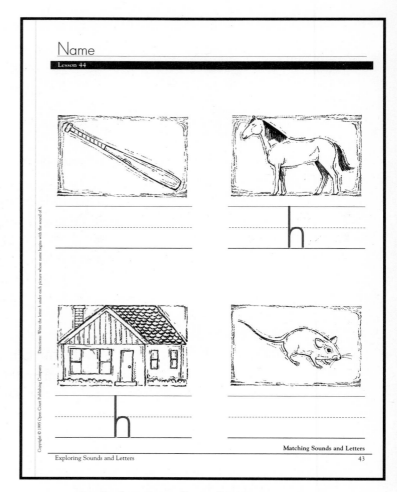

Exploring Sounds and Letters, page 43

- Tell the children that they will be illustrating their **First-Step Story, "The Top and the Tip."** Explain that you want them to write their names in the space after the words *Illustrated by,* because they will be the illustrators. Remind the children that the poem is all about what is on the tops and tips of things. Point out that the cover contains several incomplete drawings. Say that they can complete the drawings by coloring in the missing tops and tips.

- Continue to have the other Workshop or Learning Centers activities available for the children.

LESSON

45

●●● Lesson Overview

New Learning

- Short *a*

Materials

- "The Top and the Tip," page 16 of *Pickled Peppers*
- "The Top and the Tip," First-Step Story 3
- Pocket Chart Letter Cards: *a, h, m, p, s, t*; two of *d*
- Word Cards: *a, is, of, the, tip, top,*
- *Exploring Sounds and Letters,* pages 44–45
- Learning Framework Card 8
- Activity Sheet 12

✻ USING THE FIRST-STEP STORIES

"The Top and the Tip"
First-Step Story 3

Make sure children have their own First-Step Stories with them as you go over the poem in *Pickled Peppers.* Encouraging children to point to words along with you will help them understand that text flows from left to right. For more information on how to use the First-Step Stories with your class, see **Learning Framework Card 8.**

- Ask children to open their First-Step Story to page 2. Using *Pickled Peppers,* read the first line of "The Top and the Tip," pointing to each word. Signal the children when to turn the pages in their books, and continue reading.

- Put the words *is, the, top, of, a* in the Pocket Chart. Leave a space at the beginning.

- Have children think of objects that are on the top of something and name them. If they have problems, help them out. For example, say, "What is on top of my head?"

- Change *top* in the Pocket Chart to *tip.* Repeat the activity.

TIP FOR ENGLISH LANGUAGE LEARNERS

To help English Language Learners build confidence, allow them to express their ideas without interruption.

✳ Oral Blending

Using techniques from earlier lessons, continue the oral blending activities, this time with words containing the initial short *a* sound.

/a/ . . . m	/a/ . . . dd	/a/ . . . sk
/a/ . . . pple	/a/ . . . ccident	/a/ . . . fter
/a/ . . . crobat	/a/ . . . stronaut	/a/ . . . thlete

The Sound of Short *a*

Introducing Short *a* Point to the long *Aa* Alphabet Card and remind children that the letters called vowels are special because they sometimes say their names in words such as *tray, play, day.* Say, "When the *a* says its name, /ā/, it is called long *a*. That is why the red *a* is long." Point to it. Explain that vowels are also special because sometimes they also say different sounds. Say, "Sometimes *a* has a different sound." Point to the picture of the lamb on the short *a* card and say that the *a* in lamb makes the /a/ sound. Explain that this different sound is called short *a*. Tell the children to listen to the poem that will help them remember short *a*:

I'm Pam the lamb, I am.
This is how I tell the farmer where I am:
/a/ /a/ /a/ /a/ /a/ /a/
I'm Pam the lamb, I am.
This is how I tell my friends where I am:
/a/ /a/ /a/ /a/ /a/ /a/

Repeat the poem, and ask everyone to say /a/ /a/ /a/.

Listening for Short *a* Explain that you will say several words. Some will have the long *a* sound; some will have the short *a* sound. Ask the children to raise their hands when they hear the short *a* sound:

raid	rake	**rack**	**sack**	**back**	**add**
bake	aid	**tack**	**mad**	take	made
tape	**pad**	**tap**	paid	lake	

Linking the Sound to the Letter

Grab Bag of Letters Tell the children that you are going to place some letters in the Pocket Chart, and that you want them to make words out of these letters by putting one of the letters from the paper bag in front of the letters on the chart. Put the letters *a* and *d* in the chart. Put the letters *s, m, d,* and *p* in the bag. Say /a/ /d/. Call on a child to reach into the bag for a letter and to place it in the chart in front of *a* and *d.* Say, "Can you say the new word?" Help the child sound the word out if necessary. Remove the letter and ask another child to reach into the bag. Try the following words. Then repeat the exercise with the letters *a* and *t* on the chart and the letters *s, m, p,* and *h* in the bag.

s . . . ad   m . . . ad   d . . . ad   p . . . ad
s . . . at   m . . . at   p . . . at   h . . . at

Always sound out the word, letter by letter.

Writing *Aa* Review the formation of capital *A* and small *a.*

❯ **Exploring Sounds and Letters** Have children open Exploring Sounds and Letters to pages 44–45. Have children practice writing the capital and small forms of *Aa* in the space provided. Explain that some of the pictures on the page have names with the short *a* sound and some have names with the long *a* sound. Tell them to write the letter *a* under each picture whose name has the short *a* sound in it. Name each picture for the children. Review the words when everyone has finished.

Exploring Sounds and Letters, page 44

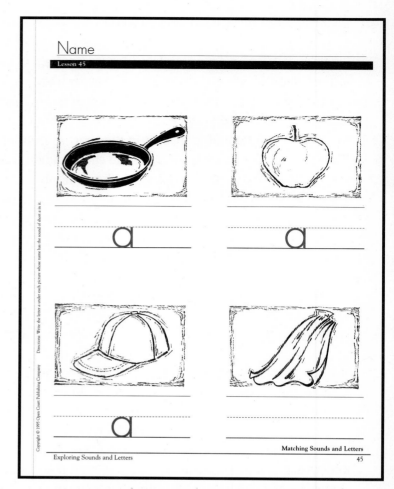

Exploring Sounds and Letters, page 45

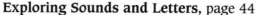

✳ WORKSHOP

- Tell the children that they will have two pages to illustrate in their **First-Step Story, "The Top and the Tip."** Hold up a First-Step Story, turn to page 2, and read the first line: "Hair is the top of a person." Point to page 3 and read the next line: "a chimney's the top of a house." Tell the children that they can use their crayons or markers to illustrate these lines in any way that they wish.

- Gather the *h* pictures (hand, hook, hat, hen) that were left over from Reproducible Master 12 in the **T Tree** activities in Lesson 42. Have duplicates of **Activity Sheet 12** and the four pictures available in Workshop. There is one word in each of the six boxes on the Activity Sheet. Have the children match each of the four pictures to a word and glue the picture in the correct box. Remind the children to pay attention to the first sound in the word and the last sound in the word to figure out which word names the picture. Circulate during Workshop, giving children clues about the words: What is this? A hat? What sound does *hat* end in? Is there a word with *t* at the end? Remind them that two boxes on the Activity Sheet will remain empty.

LESSON
46

Lesson Overview

New Learning

- Short *a*

Materials

- "The Top and the Tip," page 16 of *Pickled Peppers*
- "The Top and the Tip," First-Step Story 3
- Exploring Sounds and Letters, page 46
- Race Track Game Mat
- Rhymes and Games Teacher Tool Card 3

✻ USING THE FIRST-STEP STORIES

"The Top and the Tip"
First-Step Story 3

- Go over the poem again, first using the version in *Pickled Peppers* and having the children follow along in their own First-Step Story.
- Talk about the following lines of the poem:

a cover's the top of a book,
the tail is the tip of a mouse.

- Ask children about these lines: How is a cover the "top" of a book? Why is the tail the "tip" of a mouse?

✻ PHONEMIC AWARENESS

✻ Oral Blending

Continue working with short *a,* using a variety of techniques. This time have the children blend the final consonants.

pa . . . /d/	sa . . . /d/	ha . . . /d/
ma . . . /d/	la . . . /d/	ha . . . /t/
ma . . . /t/	sa . . . /t/	pa . . . /t/
ma . . . /p/	sa . . . /p/	ta . . . /p/

The Sound of Short *a*

Introducing Short *a* Remind children that they learned that vowels sometimes make a long sound (point to the long *a* Alphabet Card) and sometimes make a short sound (point to the short *a* Alphabet Card). Recite the poem that will help them remember short *a,* and ask them to join in where they can:

I'm Pam the Lamb, I am.
This is how I tell the farmer where I am:
/a/ /a/ /a/ /a/ /a/ /a/
I'm Pam the Lamb, I am.
This is how I tell my friends where I am:
/a/ /a/ /a/ /a/ /a/ /a/

- Repeat the poem, and ask everyone to say /a/ /a/ /a/ /a/ /a/ /a/.
- Go around the group, and ask individual children to make the lamb sound (/a/).

Listening for Short *a* Tell children that you are once again going to say several words, some with the long *a* sound, and some with the short *a* sound. Tell them that when they hear the long *a* sound they should reach their arms up so that they are long, and when they hear the short *a* sound, they should scrunch up so that they are short. Try these words:

cat	pat	came	tame	tail
tan	pan	ran	man	fan

Linking the Sound to the Letter

Writing *Aa* Review the formation of capital *A* and small *a.*

❱ **Exploring Sounds and Letters** Have children open Exploring Sounds and Letters to page 46. Explain that for each picture on the page, there are two words. Say that all the words use letters that they have been practicing. Tell them to circle the word that names the picture. Have them practice writing the word in the space provided. As a clue, remind them to pay attention to the first and last sounds of the picture name.

- Today the children return to their **First-Step Story, "The Top and the Tip,"** to illustrate lines three and four. Read the third line of the poem on page 4: "a cover's the top of a book." Point to page 5, and read the fourth line: "the tail is the tip of a mouse."
- Introduce the **Race Track** game as another option for Workshop. Use the Race Track Game Mat and the pack of Uppercase and Lowercase

---

TIP FOR ENGLISH LANGUAGE LEARNERS

Return to the same activity often to provide opportunities for English Language Learners to feel comfortable with the activities. Encourage them to participate when the whole class is engaged in the activity. Watch for children who are not responding and work with them in small groups during Workshop.

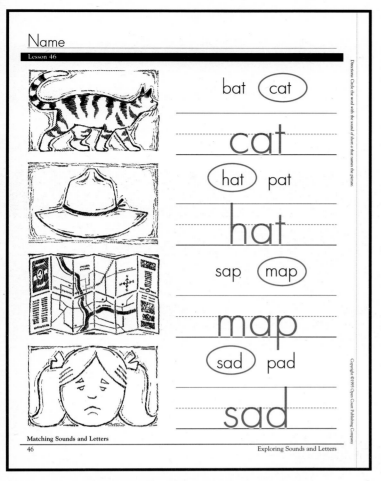

Exploring Sounds and Letters, page 46

Letter Cards. The rules for this game are essentially the same as the rules for the **Bus Stop** game (see pages 133–134). Each player spins the spinner, moves a marker the correct number of spaces, and, if the player does not land on a "lose turn" space, draws a card. If the player cannot answer correctly for the drawn card, the player must forfeit the next turn. If a player lands on a "free turn" space, the player may spin again and choose a card after landing on another space further along. If a player lands on a "lose turn" space, no card may be drawn, and the player must lose one turn before spinning again. The first player to cross the finish line is the winner. Make sure the children understand the "lose turn" and "free turn" spaces before they begin the game. You may want to start simply by having children choose a Letter Card and name the letter. Later, the children can name the letter and give the sound of the letter. Instructions for this game and the different levels of the game can be found on **Rhymes and Games Teacher Tool Card 3.** Choose the level you feel is appropriate.

LESSON
47

●●● Lesson Overview

Materials

- "The Top and the Tip," page 16 of *Pickled Peppers*
- "The Top and the Tip," First-Step Story 3
- Picture Cards: *cat, hat, sad, van*
- Exploring sounds and Letters, page 47

✳ **USING FIRST-STEP STORIES**

"The Top and the Tip"
First-Step Story 3

- Go over the poem again, first using the version in *Pickled Peppers* and having the children follow along in their First-Step Stories.
- Review the fifth and sixth lines in the poem:

> The sky is the top of the world,
> the top of the sky is space,

- Discuss the meaning of these lines with the children.

✳ **PHONEMIC AWARENESS**

✳ Oral Blending

Continue working with short *a,* using a variety of techniques.

c . . . ash	c . . . an	c . . . alf
c . . . ast	l . . . ast	l . . . augh
l . . . amb	b . . . ack	b . . . ath
t . . . ab	r . . . aft	r . . . ag

MONITORING TIP Check children again on their recognition of letters. Make sure children who are having trouble are playing games and participating in activities during Workshop that will reinforce letter recognition.

✳ HOW THE ALPHABET WORKS: PART 2

The Sound of Short *a*

Reviewing Short *a* Remind children that they learned about the different sounds that vowels make; sometimes long, sometimes short. Recite the poem that will help them remember short *a*, and ask them to join in where they can:

> I'm Pam the Lamb, I am.
> This is how I tell the farmer where I am:
> /a/ /a/ /a/ /a/ /a/ /a/
> I'm Pam the Lamb, I am.
> This is how I tell my friends where I am:
> /a/ /a/ /a/ /a/ /a/ /a/

- Repeat the poem and ask everyone to say /a/ /a/ /a/ /a/ /a/ /a/.
- Go around the group and ask the children to make the lamb sound (/a/).

Listening for Short *a* Tell the children that you are again going to say several words. Some will have the long *a* sound, some will have the short *a* sound. When they hear the long *a* sound, they should reach their arms up so that they are long. When they hear the short *a* sound, they should scrunch up so that they are short.

cat	pat	came	pan	tail
pane	tan	ran	tame	rain

Linking the Sound to the Letter

Final Consonants Display the Picture Cards *cat, hat, van,* and *sad.* Write the word pairs listed below on the board. Ask the children which word stands for each picture. For example, point to *cat* and say, "Does **this** say *cat*? or (as you point to *can*) does **this** say *cat*?"

Pictures:	Words:	
cat	cat	can
hat	hat	ham
van	van	vat
sad	sad	sat

❯ **Exploring Sounds and Letters** Have children open Exploring Sounds and Letters to page 47. Explain that for each picture on the page there are two words. Name each picture for the children. Tell them to circle the word that names the picture. Have them practice writing the word in the space provided.

Exploring Sound and Letters, page 47

✱ **WORKSHOP**

- Today, children illustrate the fifth and sixth lines of their **First-Step Story.** Remind them that they can be as creative as they like when illustrating. Ask them to imagine what they might see in outer space.
- Continue to have the other activities available during Workshop.

TIP FOR ENGLISH LANGUAGE LEARNERS

Before English Language Learners complete these lines in their First-Step Story, pair them with native English speakers to discuss what they might see in outer space. Provide pictures and photographs of space scenes to stimulate conversation. Help children to identify objects in the pictures and photographs.

LESSON
48

●●● Lesson Overview

New Learning	Materials
• Short *o*	• "The Top and the Tip," page 16 of **Pickled Peppers**
	• "The Top and the Tip," First-Step Story 3
	• Pocket Chart Letter Cards: *d, h, m, o, p* (2), *s , t* (2)
	• Word cards for the last two lines of "The Top and the Tip"
	• Exploring Sounds and Letters, page 48
	• Home/School Connection 10

✷ USING FIRST-STEP STORIES

"The Top and the Tip"
First-Step Story 3

Return to "The Top and the Tip" one last time. This time, give children some practice recognizing the common words *the, of,* and *is.* Using the Pocket Chart, you can remove these words from the last two lines of the poem, then ask the children to complete the poem by putting the words back in the right places.

- Go over the poem again, first using *Pickled Peppers* and having the children follow along in their First-Step Story.
- Point out and emphasize the words *the, of, a,* and *is.*
- Review the last two lines:

a flower's the top of the stem,
the nose is the tip of the face.

- Talk about what the lines mean and how the children might illustrate them.
- Tell children to place their First-Step Stories aside. Explain that they will be completing their books in Workshop.

✳ Oral Blending

Initial Consonant Take the children through a brief session of oral blending as a warm-up for the short *o* sound. Use any of the techniques from earlier lessons. Try the following words with short *o*:

b . . . ond	l . . . ock	r . . . ock	d . . . ock	t . . . ock
f . . . ond	m . . . ock	s . . . ock	t . . . op	p . . . op

The Sound of Short o

Reviewing Long *o* Remind children that the vowels are special because they have both short and long sounds. Point to the long *o* Alphabet Card and remind children that *o* sometimes says its name in words like *toe, blow, row.* Explain that when *o* says its name, it is called "long *o*." That is why the red *o* on the card is long. Point to it.

Introducing Short *o* Point to the picture of the frog on the short *o* Alphabet Card and say that the *o* in *frog* makes a different sound. Explain that this different sound is called short *o.* Tell the children to listen to the poem that will help them remember short *o*:

> Bob the Frog did not feel well at all.
> He hopped to the doctor's office.
> "Say /o/, Mr. Frog. /o/ /o/ /o/."
> "My head is hot, and my throat hurts a lot."
> "Say /o/, Mr. Frog. /o/ /o/ /o/."

Remind children that when they go to the doctor, they probably open their mouths and say (make the short *o* sound) too. Ask the children to do so now. Then ask if they can hear the short *o* sound in *Bob, frog, not,* and *hop.* Repeat the poem again, asking children to open their mouths like Bob the Frog and say /o/ /o/ /o/.

Listening for Short *o* Explain that you will say several words. Some will have the long *o* sound; some will have the short *o* sound. Ask the children to raise their hands when they hear the short *o* sound:

top	hop	rope	hope	mope	soap
mop	stop	dot	shop	don't	sock

Linking the Sound to the Letter

Grab Bag of Letters Tell the children that you are going to place some letters in the Pocket Chart, and that you want them to make words by taking letters out of a bag and placing them before the letters on the chart. Put *o, p* in the chart and the letters *s, m, p, t,* and *h* in the bag. Say *op,* using the short sound of *o.* Call on a child to reach into the bag for a letter and to place it in the chart as the first letter. Ask, "Can you say the new word?" Help the child sound out the word if necessary. Now remove the letter and ask another child to reach into the bag. When the children have used all of the letters from the bag, repeat the activity using the letters *o, t* on the chart and the letters *d, p, t,* and *h* in the bag.

   _op   sop . . . mop . . . pop . . . top . . . hop

   _ot   dot . . . pot . . . tot . . . hot

Always sound out the word, letter by letter.

Writing *Oo* Review the formation of capital *O* and small *o*.

❯ **Exploring Sounds and Letters** Have children open Exploring Sound and Letters to page 48. Explain that for each picture on the page there are two words. Name each picture for the children. Tell them to circle the word that names the picture. Have them practice writing the word in the space provided. Remind them to pay attention to the first and last sounds for a clue.

Exploring Sounds and Letters, page 48

- Today, the children will complete their **First-Step Story,** "The Top and the Tip," by illustrating the last two pages. Explain to them that, if they like, they can draw a picture of themselves to illustrate the last page. Say that, if they do, they should sign their name underneath it.
- Encourage the children to share their books with each other after they are finished.
- Continue to have the other activities available for the children during Workshop.

Home/School Connection   Home/School Connection 10 can be sent home with the completed First-Step Story, "The Top and the Tip."

LESSON
49

●●●● Lesson Overview

New Learning	Materials
	• "Higglety, Pigglety, Pop!" page 39 of *Pickled Peppers*
	• Exploring Sounds and Letters, page 49
	• For each child, one set of Uppercase and Lowercase Letter Cards: *Aa–Zz*
	• Game mats

✳ **READING THE BIG BOOK**

"Higglety, Pigglety, Pop!"
page 39 of *Pickled Peppers*

Now that the children have some practice with short *o* and short *a,* return to "Higglety, Pigglety, Pop!"

• Open *Pickled Peppers* to "Higglety Pigglety Pop!" Reread the song.

• Point to the words *pop, dog,* and *mop* and say them. Ask the children if they can change all of these into short *a* words. Point to *pop* and say *pap,* and so on. Then read the whole song through, having the children substitute the short *a* words when you give the signal.

✳ **PHONEMIC AWARENESS**

✳ Oral Blending

Take the children through a brief session of oral blending as a warmup for the short *o* sound. Use any of the techniques from earlier lessons. Try the following words with short *o*:

```
s . . . ob      s . . . od      s . . . ock
d . . . ot      d . . . ock     d . . . on      d . . . ot
p . . . od      p . . . ot      p . . . ocket
```

The Sound of Short *o*

Reviewing Short *o* Remind children what they have learned about the different sounds that vowels make: sometimes they are long, sometimes they are short. Once again, recite the poem that will help them remember short *o,* and ask them to join in where they can:

> Bob the Frog did not feel well at all.
> He hopped to the doctor's office.
> "Say /o/, Mr. Frog. /o/ /o/ /o/."
> "My head is hot, and my throat hurts a lot."
> "Say /o/, Mr. Frog. /o/ /o/ /o/."

- Repeat the poem, and ask everyone to say /o/ /o/ /o/.
- Review the poem one last time. Tell the children that you are going to recite each word of the poem and then pause. If they hear the short *o* sound in a word, they should say /o/ when you come to that part.

Listening for the Short *o* Sound Practice listening for short *o* and long *o* again. Remind the children that some words will have the long *o* sound; some will have the short *o* sound. When they hear the long *o* sound, they should reach their arms up so that they are long. When they hear the short *o* sound, they should scrunch down so that they are short.

cot	comb	pot	roam	pole	Tom
hot	mom	home	dome	not	dot

❯ **Exploring Sounds and Letters** Have children open Exploring Sounds and Letters to page 49. Explain that some of the pictures on the page have the short *o* sound in the middle and some have the long *o* sound in the middle. Name each picture. Tell them to circle the pictures whose names have the short *o* sound and write an *o* beneath those pictures.

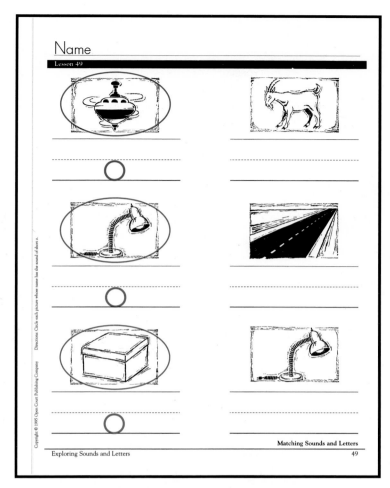

Exploring Sounds and Letters, page 49

- For each child, have Uppercase and Lowercase Letter Cards *Aa–Zz,* shuffled and out of order for the **Ordering Letters** game. Tell the children to put them in order. If the children are working with partners, one can do capital letters and one small letters.
- Make the games **Hop Along, Bus Stop, Roller Ride,** and **Race Track** available.
- Encourage children to use designated areas of the room to make letters.

LESSON
50

●●● Lesson Overview

New Learning

- Comparing short **o** and short **a**

Materials

- "Higglety, Pigglety, Pop!" page 39 of **Pickled Peppers**
- For each child, Individual Alphabet-Sound Cards: short **o** and short **a**

✱ READING THE BIG BOOK

"Higglety, Pigglety, Pop!"
page 39 of *Pickled Peppers*

- Open *Pickled Peppers* to "Higglety, Pigglety, Pop!" Reread the song.
- Point to the words *pig, cat,* and *pop* and say them. Ask the children if they can turn all of these into short *o* words. Point to *cat* and say *cot* to demonstrate.
- Read the whole song through, having the children substitute the short *o* sound in all the words you indicate.
- Read the song through once more, adding *Higglety* and *Pigglety* to the words to be changed.

✱ PHONEMIC AWARENESS

✱ Oral Blending

Take the children through a brief session of oral blending as a review of the short *a* and short *o* sounds. Use techniques from earlier lessons. Try the following words with short *o* and short *a*:

ba . . . g	bo . . . g	ba . . . t	ma . . . t	mo . . . p
ma . . . p	mo . . . m	ma . . . d	stam . . . p	stom . . . p

The Sound of Short *o* and Short *a*

Reviewing Short *a* Review short *a*, pointing to the Alphabet Card and using the short *a* poem:

I'm Pam the Lamb, I am.
This is how I tell the farmer where I am:
/a/ /a/ /a/ /a/ /a/ /a/
I'm Pam the Lamb, I am.
This is how I tell my friends where I am:
/a/ /a/ /a/ /a/ /a/ /a/

Reviewing Short *o* Review short *o*, pointing to the Alphabet Card and using the short *o* poem:

Bob the Frog did not feel well at all.
He hopped to the doctor's office.
"Say /o/, Mr. Frog. /o/ /o/ /o/."
"My head is hot, and my throat hurts a lot."
"Say /o/, Mr. Frog. /o/ /o/ /o/."

Ask individual children to complete the following: "The lamb says _____ ;" "The frog says _____ ;" "The short *a* says _____ ;" "The short *o* says _____ ."

TIP FOR ENGLISH LANGUAGE LEARNERS

Reread the song on page 39 of *Pickled Peppers*. Encourage children to raise their hand every time they hear an /o/ word as you read aloud.

Listening for Short *o* and Short *a* In this activity, children will listen carefully and discriminate between short *o* and short *a* sounds in the middle of words. Say a word and have children repeat it. They can also hold up their short *o* or short *a* Individual Alphabet-Sound Cards for the sound they hear.

- Hold up the Individual Alphabet-Sound Card for short *a* and ask the children to say the sound. If they hesitate ask them, "What sound does the lamb make?" Repeat this with the Individual Alphabet-Sound Card for short *o*. If necessary, repeat this several times until the children are sure of each sound.
- Now hand each child an Individual Alphabet-Sound Card for short *a* and short *o*. Tell children that you are going to say words that have either short *a* or short *o* in the middle. Say that when they hear each word, they are to hold up the card that tells the sound they hear in the word:

cap	sock	cot	spot	rat	pot
rot	pat	rock	mat	rack	mop
sack	mad	sat			

Linking the Sound to the Letter

Word Changes In this activity, write one word on the board, ask a child to say it, and then change it into another by changing the vowel.

Write *map* on the board. Ask the children "What does this word say?" Change the letter *a* to an *o* and ask, "Now what does this word say?" Continue with these words:

tap	top	cot	cut
hot	hat	pat	pot
rock	rack	black	block

✳ WORKSHOP

Have several activities available for the children to use during Workshop.

LESSON
51

••• Lesson Overview

New Learning

- Writing *Aa*

Materials

- "The Big Horned Toad," page 17 of *Pickled Peppers*
- Picture Cards: *apple, alligator, astronaut*
- Exploring Sounds and Letters, pages 50–51
- Alphabet Card: Long *a* and Short *a*
- Individual Alphabet-Sound Cards: Long *a* and Short *a*
- Learning Framework Card 7
- Classroom Support Teacher Tool Card 1
- Reproducible Master 13

✱ READING THE BIG BOOK

"The Big Horned Toad"
page 17 of *Pickled Peppers*

Open *Pickled Peppers* to the table of contents. Ask the children if anyone remembers what this section of a book is called. Point to the name of the poem, "The Big Horned Toad," and ask for a volunteer to point to the page number. Say the page number and turn to that page.

- Read the name of the poem and the names of the author and the illustrator. The artwork that accompanies this selection will probably elicit quite a reaction from children, so you may want to look at it before showing it to the children. Ask children if they have ever seen anything like this horned toad before. Say, "How do you think its skin feels? What is it doing with its tongue?" Ask them if the picture is scary or funny to them.

- Read the poem through slowly, pointing to each word as you say it. Repeat the words, "He's not quite green and he's not quite yellow." Ask the children how they would describe the color of the horned toad. Point to the words *lumpy* and *bumpy* and ask the children what these words mean.

- Read the poem through one more time.

TIP FOR ENGLISH LANGUAGE LEARNERS°

Spend some time with English Language Learners discussing the illustration that accompanies the poem before reading it. Show how the important aspects of the text relate to the illustration. Associating English text with pictures helps English Language Learners to think more in English. Help children identify the animals and plants in the illustration, such as the toad, toad's tongue, bugs, and grass.

✳ Oral Blending

Vowel Replacement Continue to have the children work on oral blending. This time, have them replace initial short vowel sounds, using words in which the second part of the word gives a strong clue as to the pronunciation of the entire word. After the first word, use new short vowel sounds to replace the original and make nonsense words. Ask the children to repeat the sound.

- Have the puppet say the initial vowel sound.
- Have the children repeat the initial sound.
- Say the second part of the word.
- Then, on your signal, have everyone blend the parts into a whole word.

Puppet: /a/
Children: /a/
Teacher: lligator. What's the word?
Everyone: alligator

Continue using these words:

/a/ . . . lligator	/o/ . . . lligator
/e/. . . ggplant	/a/ . . . ggplant
/a/ . . . lphabet	/o/ . . . lphabet
/e/ . . . lephant	/o/ . . . lephant
/o/ . . . ctopus	/a/ . . . ctopus

Letter Names, Shapes, and Sounds

This lesson begins a new series of lessons in which each letter of the alphabet receives separate attention. The activities in these lessons differ from the alphabet activities in earlier lessons in the following ways:

- **Aiming for mastery.** Previous activities have aimed at helping children develop an understanding of letter-sound principles. By participating in these activities, some children may have mastered letter recognition and printing. The aim of these new lessons is for every child to achieve mastery.
- **Accuracy in printing.** Children will learn to print within guidelines.
- **Daily work in Exploring Sounds and Letters.** For each letter, there is at least one Exploring Sounds and Letters page.

The Sound of Short *a*

Warmup If the children need to review the alphabet, lead them through the Alphabet Cheer.

Reviewing Long *a* Display the long *a* Alphabet Card. Ask a child to name the letter and explain why it is special. Ask another child what sound the long *a* makes.

Reviewing Short *a* Now display the short *a* Alphabet Card. Ask children if they remember what sound the short *a* makes. Have the children recite the poem for short *a* with you:

I'm Pam the Lamb, I am.
This is how I tell the farmer where I am:
/a/ /a/ /a/ /a/ /a/ /a/.
I'm Pam the Lamb, I am.
This is how I tell my friends where I am:
/a/ /a/ /a/ /a/ /a/ /a/.

Show children the *apple, astronaut,* and *alligator* Picture Cards. Say the word on each card and ask children to listen for the short *a* at the beginning of the word. Have them repeat the words.

Listening for Long *a* and Short *a* Say, "The letter *a* sometimes is a____(pause and hold up the long *a* Alphabet-Sound Card) long *a,* and sometimes it is a____(pause and hold up the short *a* Alphabet-Sound Card) short *a*."

- Ask the children to stand in a circle. Explain that you are going to say some words and that you want them to listen to each one carefully. Say, "When I give you the signal, I want you to raise your hands as high over your heads as you can if you hear a long *a* sound and to scrunch down all the way to the floor if you hear a short *a* sound."

- Remind the children that some words have either the long *a* or short *a* sound in the beginning, then say these words:

at   April   astronaut   ache

Remind the children that some words have the long *a* or short *a* sounds in the middle or at the end, then say these words:

say   sat   bat   bay   ray   rat
fat   play   pay   pat   hat   lay
day

Linking the Sound to the Letter

Writing *Aa* Use the overhead projector or the chalkboard so that you and the children can form letters together. You may use the handwriting system outlined in detail on **Classroom Support Teacher Tool Card 1** or use the system that is standard in your school. The Exploring Sounds and Letters page for each letter gives the children a place to practice some of their letters. During Lessons 50–90, children will review lines and starting points to help them with their letter formation.

- Review with the children how to form a capital *A.* Use the oral description from earlier lessons or from **Classroom Support Teacher Tool Card 1,** as the children imitate your strokes in the air.

- Have children take out Exploring Sounds and Letters and turn to pages 50–51. Point out the letters and the picture of the lamb at the top of the page. Then ask the children to write their own capital *A's* in the space provided. Help them form the letters by showing them your strokes on the overhead projector or chalkboard.

- Review how to form small *a.* Follow the same procedure, having children form the letters in the air and then write them in Exploring Sounds and Letters.

❯ **Exploring Sounds and Letters** Have the children focus on the pictures on pages 50–51. Tell them that some picture names have the short *a* sound, and some have the long *a* sound. Name each picture. Ask the children to write the letter *a* if the picture name has the short a sound.

Exploring Sounds and Letters, page 50

Exploring Sounds and Letters, page 51

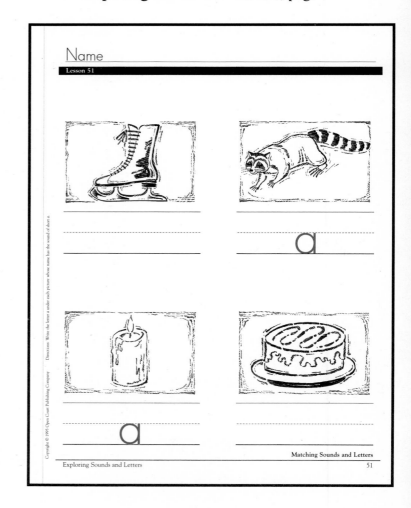

- Have the children start a **Letter Book.** Explain that as they learn each new letter, they can add it to their Letter Books. You can use **Reproducible Master 13** for the pages of the Letter Book or make them from construction or writing paper. Tell the children that they can write the letters on the top of the pages and then write words or draw pictures of things that start or end with the letters.

- Have other activities available for children during Workshop. Incorporate into Workshop activities from your own Learning Centers and use ideas from the Workshops in the Discovery Modules. Make sure to **create a writing center and a reading center** for children to use during Workshop.

LESSON
52

••• Lesson Overview

New Learning

- Initial **b**
- /b/
- Writing **Bb**

Materials

- "The Big Horned Toad," page 17 of *Pickled Peppers*
- Picture Cards: *bat, beans, bed, bee, bow, bowl*
- Exploring Sounds and Letters, pages 52–53
- Alphabet Card **Bb**
- Alphabet Flash Cards
- For each child, Uppercase and Lowercase Letter Card: **Bb**
- Learning Framework Card 10
- Classroom Support Teacher Tool Card 1

✷ **READING THE BIG BOOK**

"The Big Horned Toad"
page 17 of *Pickled Peppers*

Open *Pickled Peppers* to the table of contents. Ask for a volunteer to help you find the poem "The Big Horned Toad" and its page number. Say the page number and turn to that page.

- Remind the children that they know the sound of short *a*. Read the poem through, emphasizing the rhyming words *grass* and *pass*. Ask the children if they hear the short *a* sound in the words.
- Ask children to talk about their favorite part of the poem. Ask if anyone can recite it.
- Read the poem through one more time to end the session.

✷ **PHONEMIC AWARENESS**

✷ Oral Blending

Vowel Replacement Continue oral blending, having the children replace intitial short vowel sounds and create nonsense words, as in the previous lesson.

/a/ . . . pple	/o/ . . . pple	
/e/ . . . levator	/a/ . . . levator	/o/ . . . levator
/i/ . . . gloo	/a/ . . . gloo	/o/ . . . gloo
/o/ . . . pposite	/a/ . . . pposite	/e/ . . . pposite

LETTER NAMES, SHAPES, AND SOUNDS

The Sound of *b*

Warmup Review the alphabet by using the Alphabet Flash Cards. When you come to a letter that the children have learned the sound of, ask them to say the sound. Point to the picture on the appropriate Alphabet Card to remind them of the sound.

Reviewing *b* Point to the *Bb* Alphabet Card and say the letter name. Turn the card over and display the picture for the letter. Say the sound of *b,* /b/, and tell the children there is a poem that will help them remember the sound:

> Bobby loves his basketball.
> He bounces it all day.
> The ball goes: /b/ /b/ /b/ /b/ /b/ /b/
> As it bounces on its way.

Repeat the poem, emphasizing the initial /b/ sounds. Ask the children to pretend they are bouncing a ball and say /b/ /b/ /b/ /b/ /b/ /b/.

Listening for Initial *b* Remind children that the letter *b* makes the /b/ sound. Say, "Listen for the /b/ sound at the beginning of the following words." Hold up the Picture Cards and name them: *bat, bed, bee, bowl, beans, bow.* Emphasize the /b/ sound. Give each child a *Bb* Uppercase and Lowercase Letter Card. Explain that you are going to say some words, and that after you say each one, you will point to someone who will repeat the word. Tell the children to listen carefully and hold up their cards if the word starts with the /b/ sound.

Try the following words:

basket
battle
bat
fat
Bob (Ask the children if they heard the /b/ at the beginning and the end.)
bird
herd
hoot
boot
box
fox
fall

I'm Thinking of Something That Starts with_____Game Locate something in the room that begins with /b/ and is easily seen by everyone. Say, "I'm thinking of something in the room that begins with the /b/ sound. Look around and raise your hand when you think you know what it is." At first, give no hints and allow the children to name anything that starts with /b/. If they name something that does not start with /b/, say that word and then isolate the initial consonant. For instance, "*Door.* No, *door* starts with the /d/ sound. What starts with the /b/ sound?" The hints you give should become more and more specific until the children find the right word. Hints that are too specific will produce the answer too quickly. This defeats the purpose of having the children think about /b/ words.

Linking the Sound to the Letter

Writing *Bb* Demonstrate how to form a capital *B.* Use the oral descriptions from earlier lessons or **Classroom Support Teacher Tool Card 1,** as children imitate your strokes in the air.

- Follow the same steps for small *b.*
- Have children take out Exploring Sounds and Letters and turn to page 52. Point out the letter and the picture of the ball at the top of the page. Remind children that the letter *b* makes the /b/ sound, like a ball bouncing. Point to the completed capital *B.* Help them form the letter, by showing them your strokes on the overhead projector or chalkboard as they write two capital *B*'s.
- Follow the same steps for small *b,* having children write in the air and then complete the rows in Exploring Sounds and Letters by writing two small *b*'s.

❯ **Exploring Sounds and Letters** Have the children focus on the pictures on page 52–53 in Exploring Sounds and Letters. Tell them that some of the pictures start with the /b/ sound. Ask them to write the letter *b* under a picture only if the picture name starts with the /b/ sound. Name each picture. Review the children's work when they have finished.

✳ WORKSHOP

Allow children to choose which activities they want to do, including their **Letter Books.** Let them know that they can move from one activity to another. Refer to **Learning Framework Card 10** for more information about Workshop.

Exploring Sounds and Letters, page 52

Exploring Sounds and Letters, page 53

LESSON
53

●●●● Lesson Overview

New Learning

- *Bb*
- /b/

Materials

- "The Big Horned Toad," page 17 of *Pickled Peppers*
- Exploring Sounds and Letters, pages 54–55
- Alphabet Cards: *Bb, Dd, Mm, Ss, Tt,*
- Uppercase and Lowercase Letter Cards: *Bb, Cc, Ff, Jj, Nn, Rr, Vv, Ww, Zz*
- For each child, one set of Uppercase and Lowercase Letter Cards: *Aa–Zz*
- Rhymes and Games Teacher Tool Card 3
- Game Mats

✳ READING THE BIG BOOK

"The Big Horned Toad"
page 17 of *Pickled Peppers*

Open *Pickled Peppers* to "The Big Horned Toad."

- Remind the children that they have already found two rhyming words, *grass* and *pass,* in the poem. Ask them if they can hear other words that rhyme. Read the first two lines of the poem again, emphasizing *fellow* and *yellow.* Say, "Can you name the rhyming words?"
- Encourage children to say new rhymes for *fellow* and *yellow.* Tell them that you will give them a beginning sound, and that you want them to use it to create a new rhyme. Hold up the *Bb* Alphabet Card and say /b/ /b/ /b/. Ask the children to repeat the sound, and then say *bellow.* Try /m/ for *mellow.* Tell the children that you want them to try other sounds to make rhymes that are not really words: /t/, /d/, /s/.
- Read the poem through one more time to end the session.

✳ PHONEMIC AWARENESS

✳ Oral Blending

Vowel Replacement In this activity, have children blend the initial short vowel sound with the remainder of the word, using words in which the remainder gives only a weak clue as to the pronunciation of the word.

Give the initial short vowel sound, and then have the puppet give the remainder. Ask everyone to say the whole word. Remind the children that the words they make when they change the initial short vowel sound are nonsense words.

Teacher: /o/
Puppet: tter
Everyone: otter

/o/ . . . tter	/a/ . . . tter	/e/ . . . tter
/a/ . . . ddition	/e/ . . . ddition	/o/ . . . ddition
/e/ . . . nter	/a/ . . . nter	/o/ . . . nter

LETTER NAMES, SHAPES, AND SOUNDS

The Sound of *b*

Warmup Another way to review the alphabet is by using the Alphabet Rap.

Hand each child a *Cc, Ff, Jj, Nn, Rr, Vv, Ww,* or *Zz* Uppercase and Lowercase Letter Card. Now ask the children to listen as you say the **Alphabet Rap**. Stress the last letter in each line. Tell the children that when they hear their letters, they should hold their cards up. Repeat the rap and have the children join in as a group.

This *A B C*
is just for me,
And *D E F*
is next you see,
G H I J
comes after that
K L M N
I've got down pat.
O P Q R
S T U V
are all that's left
except *W*
X Y and *Z.*

Reviewing *Bb* Point to the *Bb* Alphabet Card and name the letter again. Review the short poem for *b.* Hold up the *Bb* Alphabet Card so the children can see the picture and say /b/ /b/ /b/ /b/ /b/ /b/:

Bobby loves his basketball.
He bounces it all day.
The ball goes: /b/ /b/ /b/ /b/ /b/ /b/
As it bounces on its way.

Repeat the poem, emphasizing the initial /b/ sounds. Ask the children to pretend they are bouncing a ball and say /b/ /b/ /b/ /b/ /b/ /b/.

Listening for Final /b/ Give each child a *Bb* Uppercase and Lowercase Letter Card. Explain that you are going to say some words and that after you say each one, you will point to someone, who will repeat the word. Say that you want everyone to listen carefully and to hold up their *Bb* cards if the word ends with /b/.

Try the following words:

cob	**lob**	let	**tub**	**club**	**tab**
tan	**rob**	**sob**	**bib**	rid	**rib**
crib					

Linking the Sound to the Letter

Word Pairs Write two words, one ending in /b/, one not, on the chalkboard. Say the word that ends with /b/ and ask a volunteer to come to the board and circle that word and to underline or trace over the letter that makes the /b/ sound.

rib	rip	son	sob
tab	tan	hub	hut
rob	rod		

❯ **Exploring Sounds and Letters** Have children open Exploring Sounds and Letters to pages 54–55. Tell them to look at the pictures on the pages and circle every picture whose name begins with /b/. First let children work on their own. Then name everything in each picture: *bug, toad, bee, fox, bird, duck, bat, bear, ball, buggy, bone, bunny, barn, cow, toad, snake.* If the children have not circled something that begins with /b/, have them do so. Give them time to write anything they choose on the bottom of the page; however, encourage them to write *b*'s or *b* words.

TIP FOR ENGLISH LANGUAGE LEARNERS

Before English Language Learners complete the pages, work with them in small groups to identify the animals pictured. Encourage them to share how to say the names of these animals in their primary languages. Recognizing minority languages is a good way to prevent inhibitions about using language. It also provides native English-speaking children with an opportunity to learn about different languages and cultures.

Exploring Sounds and Letters, page 54

Exploring Sounds and Letters, page 55

✱ WORKSHOP

- Introduce the game **Make Tracks** to the children. Use the Make Tracks Game Mat. The rules for this game are the same as those for the **Bus Stop** game. Use the level of the game that you think is appropriate for the children. Review **Rhymes and Games Teacher Tool Card 3** for information on how to switch some of the levels of the games.

- Have children add *Bb* to their **Letter Books.** Tell them that under each picture on the *b* page, they can write the letter *b* or a word that starts with *b.*

- For each child, have Uppercase and Lowercase Letter Card sets from *Aa–Zz,* shuffled and out of order, so they can play the **Ordering Letters** game. If the children are working with partners, have one do capitals and one do small letters.

- Encourage children to use designated areas of the room to make letters.

- Make the games **Hop Along, Bus Stop, Roller Ride,** and **Race Track** available.

LESSON
54

••• Lesson Overview

New Learning

- Writing *Cc*
- /k/

Materials

- "Bluebird, Bluebird," page 26 of *Pickled Peppers*
- Exploring Sounds and Letters, pages 56–57
- Alphabet Flash Cards
- For each child, one Upercase and Lowercase Letter Card: *Cc*
- Listening Collections Audiocassette
- Songs Teacher Tool Card 7
- Classroom Support Teacher Tool Card 1

✳ READING THE BIG BOOK

"Bluebird, Bluebird"
page 26 of *Pickled Peppers*

Return to the song "Bluebird, Bluebird" and read it through several times.

- Ask the children if anyone can say the beginning sound in the word *bluebird*. Ask if anyone can name the first letter in the word *bluebird*.
- Listen to the song on the Listening Collections Audiocassette. **Songs Teacher Tool Card 7** contains directions for a ring game the children can play with the song. Have them play the game a few times.

✳ PHONEMIC AWARENESS

✳ Oral Blending

Vowel Replacement Continue oral blending with initial short vowel words. Explain to the children that they must listen carefully because the second part of the word will not give them a strong clue as to the pronunciation of the whole word.

- Give the initial short vowel sound of each word, and then have the puppet give the remainder.

- Ask everyone to say the whole word. Remind the children that the words they make when they change the initial short vowel sound are nonsense words.

/a/ . . . pple	/o/ . . . pple	/e/ . . . pple
/a/ . . . fter	/o/ . . . fter	/e/ . . . fter
/o/ . . . strich	/a/ . . . strich	/e/ . . . strich

LETTER NAMES, SHAPES, AND SOUNDS

The Sound of c

Warmup Review the alphabet by using the Alphabet Flash Cards. When you come to a letter that the children have learned the sound of, ask them to say the sound. Point to the picture on the appropriate Alphabet Card to remind them of the sound.

Reviewing c Point to the Alphabet Card *Cc* and turn it over to show the picture for the letter. Say the sound of *c*, /k/. Review the short poem for /k/.

> Carlos clicks his camera
> /k/ /k/ /k/ /k/ /k/ /k/ it goes.
> The pictures come out crisp and clear.
> So give a smile, /k/ /k/ /k/ Carlos is here!

Repeat the poem, emphasizing the initial /k/ sounds. Ask the children to join in on /k/ /k/ /k/ /k/ /k/ /k/.

Listening for Initial /k/ Give each child a *Cc* Uppercase and Lowercase Letter Card. Explain to the children that you are going to say some words and that you want them to listen for the beginning sounds. Tell them that if they hear a /k/ sound at the beginning of a word, they should hold up their *Cc* cards.

comet	cold	coin	coal	bat	cash
carry	care	damp	candy	tube	cow

I'm Thinking of Something That Starts with____ Game Play the I'm Thinking of Something That Starts with____ game, as described on page 204, this time choosing something in the room that begins with the /k/ sound.

Linking to the Letter

Making New Words Write the word *at* on the board and say it. Explain to the children that you want them to help you change *at* into *bat.* Say, "If we want to change this word into /b/-/short a/-/t/, we have to put the /b/ sound at the beginning. What letter do we need for that sound?" Wait for the children to supply the letter *b.* Then change *bat* to *cat,* and then to *hat.* Continue, working with word sets such as: *op, bop, cop, hop.*

Writing Cc Review with the children how to form a capital *C*. Use the oral descriptions from earlier lessons or **Classroom Support Teacher Tool Card 1,** as the children imitate your strokes in the air.

- Have the children open Exploring Sounds and Letters to page 56. Point out the letter and the picture of the camera at the top of the page. Remind children that the letter *c* sounds like the click of the camera, /k/. Have them complete two capital *C*'s.
- Review the steps for forming small *c*. Follow the same procedure, having children write in the air and then complete two small *c*'s.

❯ **Exploring Sounds and Letters** Have the children focus on the pictures on pages 56–57 in Exploring Sounds and Letters. Explain that some of the pictures start with the /k/ sound. Tell the children to write the letter *c* under the picture only if it starts with the /k/ sound. Name each picture. Review their work when they have finished.

✳ WORKSHOP

Allow the children to choose activities they want to do. Remind them that they can move from one activity to another.

Exploring Sounds and Letters, page 56

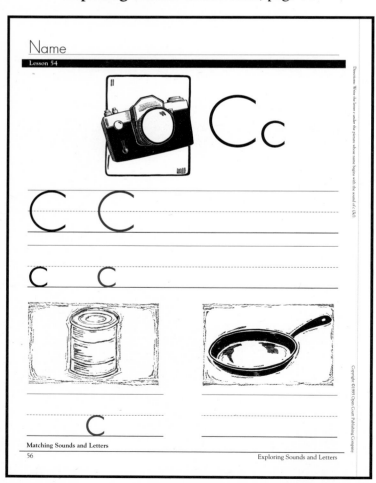

Exploring Sounds and Letters, page 57

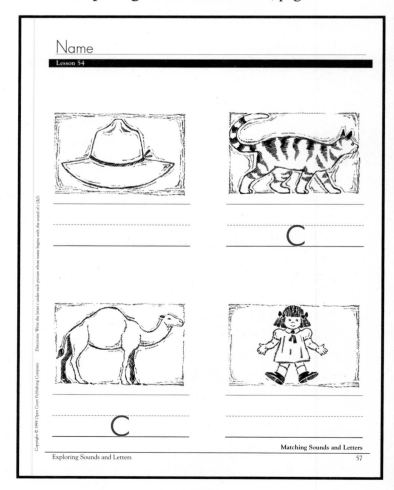

LESSON 55

Lesson Overview

New Learning

- Writing *Cc*
- /k/

Materials

- "Los Pollitos," pages 22–23 of *Pickled Peppers*
- Picture Cards: *bat, beans, bed, bee, bow, bowl, can, cap, cat, coat, cook, core, corn, cup*
- Exploring Sounds and Letters, pages 58–59
- Uppercase and Lowercase Letter Cards: *Aa–Zz*
- For each child, Uppercase and Lowercase Letter Cards: *BB, Cc*
- Listening Collections Audiocassette
- Songs Teacher Tool Card 8

✳ READING THE BIG BOOK

"Los Pollitos"
pages 22–23 of *Pickled Peppers*

Return to "Los Pollitos." Read the song through several times. Listen to the song on Listening Collections Audiocassette and see **Songs Teacher Tool Card 8** for instructions for the game that children can play with the song. Have them play the game a few times.

✳ PHONEMIC AWARENESS

✳ Oral Blending

Vowel Replacement In this oral blending activity, the children will work with multisyllable words that end in a long vowel sound. Have the children continue blending, this time with long vowel sounds. Tell children that you are practicing replacing vowels, but that the words you are saying may be nonsense words, like in the song, "Apples and Bananas."

coff . . . /ē/	coff . . . /ō/	coff . . . /ā/
berr . . . /ē/	berr . . . /ō/	berr . . . /ā/
marr . . . /ē/	marr . . . /ō/	marr . . . /ā/
scar . . . /ē/	scar . . . /ō/	scar . . . /ā/

LETTER NAMES, SHAPES, AND SOUNDS

The Sound of c

Warmup If the children need to review the alphabet, have them repeat the Alphabet Rap with you. Distribute some of the Uppercase and Lowercase Letter Cards and tell the children to hold up their cards on cue.

Reviewing c Display the Alphabet Card *Cc* and turn it over to show children the picture. Say the sound of *c*, /k/. Review the short poem for /k/:

Carlos clicks his camera
/k/ /k/ /k/ /k/ /k/ /k/ it goes.
The pictures come out crisp and clear.
So give a smile, /k/ /k/ /k/ Carlos is here!

Repeat the poem, emphasizing the initial /k/ sounds, and asking the children to join in on /k/ /k/ /k/ /k/ /k/ /k/.

Listening for Initial /k/ Hold up the following Picture Cards and name them: *core, cook, coat.* Ask children if they can hear the /k/ sound at the beginning of each word.

Give each child one *Bb* and *Cc* Uppercase and Lowercase Letter Card. Tell the children that you are going to hold up Picture Cards and say the words on them, and that you want them to listen for the beginning sound of each word. Say, "If you hear a /b/, hold up the *Bb* card; if you hear a /k/, hold up the *Cc* card." Shuffle the following Picture Cards so they are out of order: *bee, bat, bed, bowl, beans, bow, core, cook, coat, corn, cup, cat, cap, can.* Hold up the cards one by one and say the word on each. Cue the children to hold up their cards.

Silly Sentences Play the Silly Sentences game by making a sentence that is full of /k/ sounds.

Linking to the Letter

❯ Exploring Sounds and Letters Have the children open Exploring Sounds and Letters to pages 58–59. Explain that on page 58 the Prince has to find his way to the castle, which starts with the /k/ sound. Say that he must follow the path, stepping only on the stones with pictures whose names begin with /k/. If he chooses the wrong path, he might meet a ferocious lion or dragon. Tell the children to start at the beginning and find each stone that has a /k/ picture on it, circle it, and help

Exploring Sounds and Letters, page 58

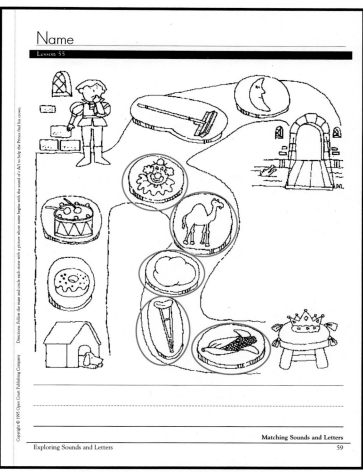

Exploring Sounds and Letters, page 59

the Prince find the castle. Let children try to do this on their own. When they have finished, go over the page and identify all the /k/ stones. Then explain that on page 59 the Prince has to find his crown, stepping only on the stones that have a /k/ picture on them. Tell children to circle the pictures whose names begin with the /k/ sound to help the Prince find his crown. If some children have not circled a /k/ stone, have them do so. Then have them write /k/ words or make a row of capital *C's* on the bottom of the page.

✳ **WORKSHOP**

Encourage children to choose the activities they want to do. Remind them that they can move from one activity to another.

LESSON
56

●●● Lesson Overview

New Learning

- *Dd*
- /d/

Materials

- "Hickory, Dickory, Dock," page 6 of *Pickled Peppers*
- Pocket Chart Letter Cards: *a, d* (2), *h, m, o, p* (2), *s*
- Picture Cards: *cat, coat, cook, core, corn, cup, deer, dish, dog, dollar, door, duck*
- Word Cards: *Dad, had, a, hat, cat, bat, mat*
- Exploring Sounds and Letters, pages 60–61
- Alphabet Flash Cards
- For each child, Uppercase and Lowercase Letter Cards: *Cc* and *Dd*

✳ READING THE BIG BOOK

"Hickory, Dickory, Dock"
page 6 of *Pickled Peppers*

- Return to "Hickory, Dickory, Dock." Read the poem through several times and ask the children to listen for the /k/ sounds.
- Say each word of the poem slowly. Ask children to give the thumbs-up signal if they hear the /k/ sound anywhere in the word and the thumbs-down signal if they do not hear the sound.

✳ PHONEMIC AWARENESS

✳ Oral Blending

Vowel Replacement Continue to have the children work on oral blending, using single-syllable words that end in a vowel.

Blend the following words in the usual manner, using the puppet if you wish, and alternating between whole class and individual responses.

h . . . /ē/	h . . . /ō/	h . . . /ā/	h . . . /ī/
m . . . /ē/	m . . . /ī/	m . . . /ō/	m . . . /ā/
kn . . . /ē/	kn . . . /ō/		

LETTER NAMES, SHAPES, AND SOUNDS

The Sound of *d*

Warmup Take the children through a quick review of the alphabet, using the Alphabet Flash Cards. Hold up cards in random order, with the capital/small letter combination showing. If the sound of a letter was introduced in earlier lessons, have the children review the sound.

Reviewing Dd Because the children have learned the letter *d* and its sound before, ask them if anyone can name the letter or say its sound. Ask for volunteers to say words that start with *d*.

• Review the short poem for /d/.

> Dinah, the dancing dinosaur,
> had huge and clumsy feet.
> They went /d/ /d/ /d/ /d/ /d/ /d/
> As Dinah kept the beat.

• Repeat the poem, emphasizing the initial /d/ sounds. Ask the children to stomp their feet on /d/ /d/ /d/ /d/ /d/ /d/.

Listening for the Initial Sound Have the children review initial consonant sounds.

• Hold up and say the words on the following Picture Cards: *deer, door, duck, dish, dog, dollar.* Tell the children to listen for the /d/ sound at the beginning of each word.

• Give each child one *Cc* and one *Dd* Letter Card. Hold up and say the words on the *Dd* Picture Cards again, but this time intersperse them with the *Cc* Picture Cards—*core, cook, coat, corn, cup, cat*—from the previous lesson. Have children repeat each word after you say it and hold up the *Dd* card when they hear /d/ at the beginning of the word and the *Cc* card when they hear /k/ at the beginning of the word.

Linking the Sound to the Letter

Grab Bag of Letters and Words Have the children play Grab Bag.

• Put the letters *ad* on the Pocket Chart and the letters *d, s, h, m,* and *p* in the bag.

• Invite a volunteer to choose a letter from the bag and put it in front of *ad* on the chart.

• Have the children sound out the word on the chart.

• Repeat the exercise until all of the possible words have been made.

• Continue the exercise by placing the letters *op* on the chart and the letters *h, m,* and *p* in the bag.

dad	sad	had	mad
pad	hop	mop	pop

• Next use Word Cards to make sentences such as *Dad had a hat*.

• Replace *hat* with *cat, bat,* and *mat*. Read each sentence.

Writing *Dd* Review with the children how to form a capital *D,* using the oral descriptions from earlier lessons or **Classroom Support Teacher Toolcard 1,** as children imitate your strokes in the air.

- Review the steps for forming small *d.*
- Have children open Exploring Sounds and Letters to page 60. Ask them to write capital and lowercase *Dd* on the page.

➤ **Exploring Sounds and Letters** Have the children focus on the pictures on page 60 and on page 61 in Exploring Sounds and Letters. Explain that some of the pictures start with the /d/ sound. Ask the children to write the letter *d* under a picture only if the picture name begins with the /d/ sound. Name each picture. Let children write *d*'s under the pictures whose names start with the /d/ sound. Review the children's work when they have finished.

Exploring Sounds and Letters, page 60

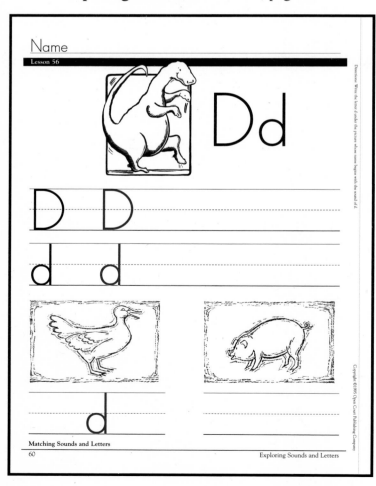

Exploring Sounds and Letters, page 61

✳ WORKSHOP

- Have the children work on the *Dd* page of their **Letter Books.**
- Have other activities available for children during Workshop. Incorporate Workshop activities into your other Learning Centers and use ideas from the Workshops in the Discovery Modules. Make sure to create a writing center and a reading center for children to use during Workshop.

TIP FOR ENGLISH LANGUAGE LEARNERS

Provide an opportunity for English Language Learners to practice using creative language in conversation. Pair English Language Learners with native English-speaking children. Have the children share their Letter Books. Exchanging information during Workshop reinforces what children are learning and helps to build friendships.

LESSON
57

● ● ● Lesson Overview

New Learning

- *Ee*
- Short *e* and long *e*

Materials

- "Old MacDonald," pages 14–15 of *Pickled Peppers*
- Pocket Chart Letter Cards: *a, b, e, m, p, s, t*
- Picture Cards: *eagle, easel, eel, elephant, elk, envelope,*
- Exploring Sounds and Letters, pages 62–63
- Individual Alphabet-Sound Cards: Long *e* and Short *e*
- Listening Collections Audiocassette
- Songs Teacher Tool Card 9
- Home/School Connection 11

✳ READING THE BIG BOOK

"Old MacDonald"
pages 14–15 of *Pickled Peppers*

- Tell the children that today they are going to learn the song "Old MacDonald." Ask whether anyone knows the song. If they do, have them sing it.
- Open *Pickled Peppers* and turn to "Old MacDonald." Read through the song, pointing to the pictures of the animals mentioned in each verse. Ask the children if they see any other animals in the picture that you did not mention when you read the verse.
- Sing the song with the children. The Listening Collections Audiocassette and **Songs Teacher Tool Card 9** contain more information.
- Sing the song several times, encouraging the children to say the names of the animals and make the sounds.

✳ Oral Blending

Vowel Replacement Have the children blend the following words in the usual manner, using the puppet if you wish, and alternating between whole class and individual responses.

b . . . /ē/	b . . . /ī/	b . . . /ā/
d . . . /ā/	d . . . /ō/	d . . . /ī/
sh . . . /ē/	sh . . . /ō/	sh . . . /ī/

LETTER NAMES, SHAPES, AND SOUNDS

The Sound of Long *e* and Short *e*

Warmup Take the children through a quick review of the alphabet, using the Alphabet Flash Cards. Hold up the cards in random order, showing the small letters. Review the sounds of letters already introduced.

Introducing Long *e* Point to the long *e* Alphabet Card. Name the letter and its sound. Turn over the Alphabet Card to show the picture. Ask the children if they remember why the letter *e* is special.

Show the children the Picture Cards for *eagle, easel,* and *eel.* Say the word on each card and ask children to listen for the /ē/ at the beginning of the word. Have them repeat the words.

Introducing Short *e* Point to the short *e* Alphabet Card. Remind children that sometimes the special letters called vowels make another sound. Say, "The letter *e* can say its name, but it can also make the sound /e/." Recite the poem for short *e*:

Jen's pet hen likes to peck, peck, peck /e/ /e/ /e/
She pecks at a speck on the new red deck /e/ /e/ /e/
This is how her pecking sounds: /e/ /e/ /e/ /e/ /e/ /e/
When she pecks at a speck on the hen house deck.

- Show the children the Picture Cards for *elephant, envelope, elk.* Say the word on each card and ask children to listen for the /e/ at the beginning of the word. Have them repeat the words.
- Continue the short *e* activity by saying some single-syllable words. Ask the children to listen carefully for the short *e* in the middle of the word. Ask children to repeat the word, and then say the short *e* sound. Try these words: *jet, bet, set, bed, red, deck, peck*

Listening for Short *e* and Long *e* Say "The letter *e* sometimes is a _____ (pause and hold up the long *e* Alphabet-Sound Card) long *e* and sometimes it is a _____ (pause and hold up the short *e* Alphabet-Sound Card) short *e*."

Remind the children that some words have the short *e* sound at the beginning of the word and some words have the long *e* sound at the beginning. Then say these words:

eagle	eat	elevator	elbow
ever	each	enter	east

Tell the children you will say some words and they should reach up as high as they can if they hear a long *e* at the beginning of a word. If they hear a short *e* at the beginning of a word, they should scrunch down very short. Remind children that some words have the short *e* or long *e* sound in the middle or at the end. Tell the children to get ready to stretch up long or scrunch down short depending on whether they hear long *e* or short *e.* Then say these words:

see	set	we	wet	bet
bee	beat	knee	net	neck

Linking the Sound to the Letter

Grab Bag of Letters and Words Play Grab Bag in the usual way. Put the letters *e* and *t* in the Pocket Chart or on the chalkboard. Pronounce *et* for the children. Have in a bag, the letters *p, m, s,* and *b.* Make the words *pet, set, bet,* and *met.* Change the vowel to *a* and make the words *bat, mat, sat, pat.*

Writing *Ee* When using Exploring Sounds and Letters, always remember to name each picture at the top of the page before children begin writing.
- Using the established procedure, review how to form a capital *E.* Have children complete two capital *E*'s.
- Review the steps for forming small *e.* Have the children complete two small *e*'s.

❯ **Exploring Sounds and Letters** Have the children focus on the pictures on pages 62–63 in Exploring Sounds and Letters. Explain that some of the pictures have the short *e* sound in them. Ask the children to write the letter *e* under each picture whose name contains the short *e* sound.

Exploring Sounds and Letters, page 62

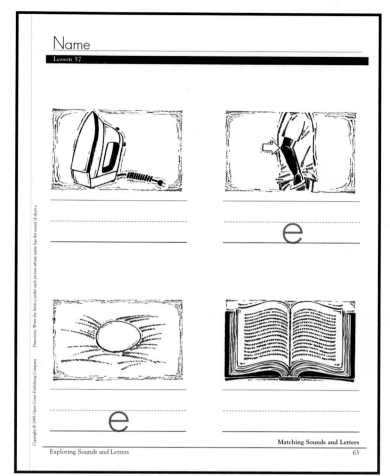

Exploring Sounds and Letters, page 63

✱ WORKSHOP

- Have children complete the *Ee* page of their **Letter Books.**
- Have the materials available for the children to play the various letter recognition games such as **Ordering Letters.**
- Make the games **Hop Along, Bus Stop, Roller Ride, Race Track,** and **Make Tracks** available in the Game Corner.
- Let children use the designated areas of the room to make letters.

Home/School Connection Send Home/School Connection 11 home to the parents. It suggests games families can play together to reinforce letter sounds.

LESSON
58

●●● Lesson Overview

New Learning

- *Ee*
- Short *e*, long *e*

Materials

- "Old MacDonald," pages 14–15 of *Pickled Peppers*
- One set of Uppercase and Lowercase Letter Cards: *Aa–Zz*

✳ READING THE BIG BOOK

"Old MacDonald"
pages 14–15 of *Pickled Peppers*

Open *Pickled Peppers* to "Old MacDonald" and sing the song again.

- Tell the children that you are going to sing the song again, but that this time you will use the long vowel sounds from the Alphabet Cards instead of *E-I-E-I-O.* Say, "What are all the vowels?" Sing the song again and invite children to join in when you sing the vowels.
- First review the consonant sounds the children have learned in the past few lessons: /b/, /k/, and /d/. Ask the children to name animals whose names begin with each of these sounds. Suggest, for example, *bird, cow,* and *dog.*
- Next sing the song substituting an animal the children have just named for the animals mentioned in "Old MacDonald":

Old MacDonald had a farm, A-E-I-O-U.
And on his farm he had a bird, A-E-I-O-U.
With a /b/ /b/ here and a /b/ /b/ there,
Here a /b/, there a /b/ everywhere a /b/ /b/.
Old MacDonald had a farm, A-E-I-O-U.

- Continue with other animals.

* Oral Blending

Vowel Replacement Have the children work on oral blending using your usual procedure. Use single-syllable words that begin with short vowels.

/i/ . . . n	/o/ . . . n	/a/ . . . n
/i/. . . f	/o/ . . . ff	
/i/ . . . s	/a/ . . . s	/u/ . . . s

The Sound of Short *e* and Long *e*

Warmup Have the children warm up by playing the Sing Your Way to _____ game. Place all the Uppercase and Lowercase Letter Cards in a bag. Ask a child to draw a card out and hold it up but not name it. Then have the children sing their way to that letter. If the children know the sound of the letter, ask a volunteer to say it.

Reviewing Long *e* Review long *e*. Hold up the long *e* Alphabet Card.

Reviewing Short *e* Review the short poem for short *e* . Hold up the *Ee* Alphabet Card:

Jen's pet hen likes to peck, peck, peck /e/ /e/ /e/
She pecks at a speck on the new red deck /e/ /e/ /e/
This is how her pecking sounds: /e/ /e/ /e/ /e/ /e/ /e/
When she pecks at a speck on the hen house deck.

Repeat the poem, emphasizing the initial /e/ sounds, and asking the children to peck at the ground with their fingers on /e/ /e/ /e/ /e/ /e/ /e/.

Listening for Short *e* and Long *e* Provide the children with more practice listening for short and long *e*'s. Explain that you are going to say some words, and that some of them will have the long *e* sound and some will have the short *e* sound. Tell them that when they hear the long *e* sound, they should stretch their arms up so that they are long, and that when they hear the short *e* sound, they should scrunch down so that they are short. Use the following words:

bet	beat	met	meat	net
neat	seat	set	peck	peek

TIP FOR ENGLISH LANGUAGE LEARNERS

Return to the same activity often to provide opportunities for English Language Learners to feel comfortable with the activities. Encourage them to participate when the whole class is engaged in the activity. Watch for children who are not responding and work with them in small groups during Workshop.

Linking the Sound to the Letter

Word Pairs Write one word on the board, ask a child to say it, and
then change it into another word by changing the vowel sound.

Always say the word with the short *e* sound. Continue with other
words:

set	sat	not	net
bet	bat	pet	pot
peck	pack		

＊ WORKSHOP

Have several activities available to the children. At times during
Workshop, meet with individuals or with small groups to discuss their
work. Work with those children who may need extra help or extra
challenges.

LESSON
59

Lesson Overview

New Learning

- *Ff*
- /f/

Materials

- "Old MacDonald," pages 14–15 of *Pickled Peppers*
- Picture Cards: *feet, fern, fish, fork, four, fur*
- Exploring Sounds and Letters, pages 64–65
- Alphabet-Sound Card: *Ff*
- For each child, Uppercase and Lowercase Letter Card: *Ff*

Prepare Ahead

- Gather all the Picture Cards whose picture names begin with letters *a–e, h, m, p, s,* and *t* for use in Workshop

---

✱ READING THE BIG BOOK

"Old MacDonald"
pages 14–15 of *Pickled Peppers*

- Sing the first three verses of "Old MacDonald" with the children.
- Have the children think of new animals and new sounds the animals might make. Sing the song again, using the new animals and sounds.

✱ PHONEMIC AWARENESS

✱ Oral Blending

Vowel Replacement Continue the oral blending activity. This time, start with a word with an initial short vowel sound and have the children create nonsense words.

/u/ . . . p   /a/ . . . p   /e/ . . . p   /o/ . . . p
/a/ . . . t   /e/ . . . t   /o/ . . . t

The Sound of *f*

Warmup For warmup, repeat the activity from the previous lesson, Sing Your Way to _____ game.

Introducing Ff Display the *Ff* Alphabet Card and say its sound. Show the picture side of the card and recite the poem for /f/:

Franny the fan spins oh, so fast
Spreading fresh air with a regular blast.
When Franny the fan goes round and round
/f/ /f/ /f/ /f/ /f/ /f/ is her fast fan sound.

Repeat the poem, emphasizing the initial /f/ sound and asking the children to join in on /f/ /f/ /f/ /f/ /f/ /f/.

Listening for Initial /f/ Ask children to listen for the initial /f/ sound then hold up and name the Picture Cards: *feet, fern, fur, fork, fish, four.* Have children repeat each word, emphasizing the /f/ sound.

Give each child an *Ff* Uppercase and Lowercase Letter Card. Tell the children that you are going to say words and that you want them to hold up the card when they hear a word that begins with the /f/ sound:

fame	blame	**fish**	beat	**feet**	**feel**
fit	bit	**fin**	**fist**	**fall**	ball
fat	box	**fox**			

Words, Words Ask children to say words that begin with the /f/ sound. Write the words on the board. Add words to the list during the day.

Linking the Sound to the Letter

Writing Ff Demonstrate how to form a capital *F*, using the oral descriptions from earlier lessons or **Classroom Support Teacher Toolcard 1,** as children imitate your strokes in the air. Repeat the steps for small *f*.

❯ **Exploring Sounds and Letters** Have the children focus on the pictures on pages 64–65 in Exploring Sounds and Letters. Explain that some of the pictures begin with the /f/ sound. Ask the children to write the letter *f* under each picture whose name begins with the /f/ sound. Have children write capital *F*'s and small *f*'s at the top of page 64, as in past lessons.

Exploring Sounds and Letters, page 64

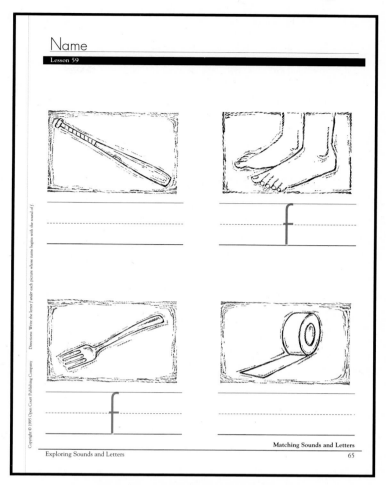

Exploring Sounds and Letters, page 65

Add the **What Sound Is It?** game to Workshop. Place all of the Picture Cards you have used so far for the letters *a–e, h, m, p, s,* and *t* in the Workshop area. Have the children sort the pictures into piles according to their initial sounds. You will need to eliminate some of the Picture Cards that aren't appropriate (such as *eight*) or are unrecognizable (such as *pickled pears* and *plum bun*).

LESSON 60

●●● Lesson Overview

New Learning

- *Ff*
- /f/

Materials

- "Old MacDonald," pages 14–15 of *Pickled Peppers*
- Picture Cards: *feet, fern, fish, fork, four, fur*
- Exploring Sounds and Letters, pages 66–67
- For each child, Uppercase and Lowercase Letter Card: *Ff*

✱ READING THE BIG BOOK

"Old MacDonald"
pages 14–15 of *Pickled Peppers*

Open *Pickled Peppers* to "Old MacDonald" and sing the song again with the class.

- Make the children aware of the animals that live on the farm by pointing to their pictures: a cow, a pig, a duck, a horse, and chickens.
- Ask them to imagine that old MacDonald only had animals on his farm whose names started with the letter *f*. Explain that there would be no cow, no pig, no duck, no horse, and no chickens. Ask, "What kind of animals or insects would he have?"
- Ask the children to name some animals whose names start with the letter *f*, (for example: frog, fish, falcon, fawn, firefly, flamingo, flea, fly, fox). Enunciate the name of the animal and write the names on the chalkboard as children say them. If the children cannot think of many *f* animals, give them clues. Point out that *farm* also starts with the letter *f*.
- Now sing "Old MacDonald" together using the *f* animals and using the /f/ sound as the sound of each animal.

✳ Oral Blending

Using Phonics You can now begin oral blending activities that involve some written work. Merging oral blending with written work at the board creates a natural progression from a purely oral activity to phonics. At this point, you will still be giving the children parts of words to blend. But after children have successfully blended one word, you will change the initial consonant, ask for its sound, and ask the children to blend the new word. This activity mirrors what you have been doing in other activities, such as Grab Bag of Letters. With this practice under their belts, children will be able to graduate to true phonics in later lessons during which they will be given single letters, identify their sounds, and then blend them to form words.

- This oral blending activity is similar to the others, except that in this activity you will work at the chalkboard with sounds represented by their spellings. You will blend initial consonants with the rest of the word. Say the initial sound of a word, /w/. Write it on the chalkboard. Say the remainder of the word, *ishing* and write it on the chalkboard. Ask the children to put the parts of the word together and say it back to you.

Teacher: /w/
Teacher: ishing. What's the word?
Everyone: wishing

- Now erase the *w* and write an *f*. Say, "Now the word starts with the letter *f*. It doesn't start with a /w/ sound, it starts with _____? Yes, /f/ . . . ishing. What is the new word?"

- Because you will be using as replacements letter sounds that the children are already familiar with, they should be able to identify the new sounds and then blend the new word. Try the following word changes:

/r/ . . . ailing	/s/ . . .ailing	/m/ . . . ailing
/l/ . . . etter	/b/ . . . etter	
/s/ . . .ingle	/m/ . . . ingle	/t/ . . . ingle
/w/ . . . illing	/f/ . . . illing	
/m/ . . . angle	/d/ . . . angle	/t/ . . . angle

Letter Names, Shapes, and Sounds

Warmup For warmup, repeat the activity from the previous lessons, Sing Your Way to _____ game.

The Sound of *f*

Introducing Ff Display the *Ff* Alphabet Card and say its sound. Show the picture side of the card. Recite the poem for /f/:

Franny the fan spins oh, so fast
Spreading fresh air with a regular blast.
When Franny the fan goes round and round
/f/ /f/ /f/ /f/ /f/ /f/ is her fast fan sound.

Repeat the poem, emphasizing the initial /f/ sound and asking the children to join in on /f/ /f/ /f/ /f/ /f/ /f/.

Review the Picture Cards for *f: feet, fern, fish, fork, four, fur.*

Silly Sentences Game Play the Silly Sentences game by making a sentence that is full of /f/ sounds.

Listening for Final /f/ Give each child an *Ef* Uppercase and Lowercase Letter Card. Tell them you are going to say words and that you want them to hold up the card when they hear a word that ends with the /f/ sound. Try these words:

half	hat	cat	**calf**	**laugh**	latch
muff	**puff**	pet	**leaf**	**reef**	red
tough	**rough**	**huff**			

Linking the Sound to the Letter

❯ **Exploring Sounds and Letters** Have the children look at the pictures on pages 66–67 of Exploring Sounds and Letters and circle the items that begin with the /f/ sound. First let children work on their own. Then review the objects on the pages: *frog, fish, fly, fox, pig, cat, fox, fence, flag, flamingo, chicken, and sheep.* If some children think an item begins with /f/ and they have not circled it, have them do so. Give them time to write anything they would like at the bottom of the page; but encourage them to write *f*'s or *f* words.

TIP FOR ENGLISH LANGUAGE LEARNERS

Before English Language Learners complete the pages, work with them in small groups to identify the animals pictured. Encourage them to share how to say the names of these animals in their primary languages. Recognizing minority languages is a good way to prevent inhibitions about using language. It also provides native English-speaking children with an opportunity to learn about different languages and cultures.

✳ WORKSHOP

Have children complete the *Ef* page of their **Letter Books.**
- Make various letter recognition games available such as the **Ordering Letters** game.
- Make the games **Hop Along, Bus Stop, Roller Ride, Race Track,** and **Make Tracks** available.
- Let children use the designated areas of the room to make letters.
- Add to the **What Sound Is It?** game, the Picture Cards for words that begin with *f.*

Exploring Sounds and Letters, page 66

Exploring Sounds and Letters, page 67

LESSON
61

••• Lesson Overview

New Learning

- *Gg*
- /g/

Materials

- "To Market, to Market," page 7 of *Pickled Peppers*
- Picture Cards: *gate, goat, goose, green, guitar*
- Exploring Sounds and Letters, pages 68–69
- For each child, one Uppercase and Lowercase Letter Card: *Gg*
- Game Mats

Prepare Ahead

- Using consonants already introduced, prepare two sets of cards: one with capital letters and one with the corresponding lowercase letters. Make enough cards so each child has one card, either a capital letter or one of the corresponding lowercase letters.

✳ READING THE BIG BOOK

"To Market, to Market"
page 7 of *Pickled Peppers*

- Open *Pickled Peppers* to the table of contents and find the page number for "To Market, to Market." Turn to the page and read the title of the poem and the name of the illustrator.
- Point to the illustration and ask the children whether they can use it to predict what the poem is going to be about.
- Read the poem to the children two or three times.
- Draw the children's attention to the illustration again. Remind them of their predictions, stressing those that were correct. Ask the children which is the pig and which is the hog. Ask if anyone knows what a *plum bun* is. If no one does, tell them the answer.
- Read the poem again, emphasizing the rhyming words: *pig/jig; hog/jog; bun/done.*

Oral Blending

Initial Consonant Replacement Have the children make new words by replacing the initial consonant with a new one. Use multisyllabic words. Say *matter.* Write *m* on the chalkboard. Say, "*Matter* begins with *m* and makes the sound /m/. Write the rest of the word on the chalkboard. Point to *m* again and pronounce it. Then point to the rest of the word and pronounce it. Then ask the children to say the whole word.

> *Teacher:* /m/
> *Teacher:* atter. What's the word?
> *Everyone:* matter

- Erase the *m* and write *b* in its place. Say, "Now the word begins with the letter *b,* so it doesn't start with /m/ any more. What sound does it start with? What's the new word?" Allow for wait time.
- Because you will be using as replacements only those letter sounds with which the children are already familiar, they should be able to identify the new sounds and then blend the new word. Try the following word changes:

/m/ . . . atter	/b/ . . . atter	/f/ . . . atter
/s/ . . . ound	/m/ . . . ound	/h/ . . . ound
/h/ . . . arry	/b/ . . . arry	/m/ . . . arry

Note: When you write names on the board, remind children that they need capital letters.

Segmentation

Restoring Final Word Parts In this activity, the children focus on the last part of a syllable. Tell children that the puppet sometimes forgets parts of words. Explain that you want them to listen as you say a word, listen to the puppet, and then say the part of the word he has forgotten. Then say the whole word. Model this for them.

> *Teacher:* cat
> *Puppet:* /k/
> *Everyone:* at
> *Everyone:* cat

Use the following words:

| /h/at | /m/at | /s/ink | /p/ink | |
| /m/ink | /p/itch | /h/itch | /m/itch | /d/itch |

Warmup Divide the class evenly into two groups. Use the sets of capital and lowercase letters you have prepared ahead of time. Give each child in one group a lowercase letter, and the other group the matching capital letters. Explain that, when you give the signal, you want them to go about the room, looking at each other's letters until they find the partner for their letter. Tell them to hold their hands in the air when they have found their partners. When everyone has found a partner, go around the room, pointing to the partners, and having each pair say its letter and the letter's sound.

The Sound of g

Introducing g Display the *Gg* Alphabet Card and say /g/. Turn the card over and show the picture for the /g/ sound, then recite the poem for /g/:

> Gary is a gopher
> Who gulps green grapes all day.
> When he gulps and giggles,
> /g/ /g/ /g/ /g/ /g/ /g/ is what he'll say.

Repeat the poem emphasizing the initial /g/ sounds, and asking the children to join in on /g/ /g/ /g/ /g/ /g/ /g/. Remind children that the Alphabet Card and its picture will help them remember the sound of the letter.

Listening for Initial and Final /g/ Hold up the following Picture Cards and say the word on each card. Ask the children to listen for the /g/ sound at the beginning of each: *green, goat, guitar, goose, gate.*
- Give each child a *Gg* Uppercase and Lowercase Letter Card. Ask them to listen to each word you say and, if the beginning sound is /g/, to hold up their cards and say /g/. Try these words:

sought	**got**	set	**get**	**gill**
sill	**game**	same	**grit**	sit

- Now ask children to listen for the /g/ sound at the end of words. Tell them to hold up their card and say /g/ when they hear the /g/ sound at the end. Try the following words:

hog	**dog**	dot	**log**	lot	
big	**pig**	pot	**peg**	**leg**	let

Silly Sentences Game Have the children play the Silly Sentences game by making a sentence that is full of /g/ sounds. For example, *Gary the Gopher got grapes.* Help the children expand the sentence.

Linking the Sound to the Letter

Writing Gg Review with the children how to form a capital *G*.
- Tell the children to take out their Exploring Sounds and Letters workbook and turn to page 68. Work with them as they complete a line of capital *G*'s.
- Repeat for small *g*.

❯ **Exploring Sounds and Letters** Have children open Exploring Sounds and Letters to pages 68–69. Point to and name each picture. Ask children to write the letter *g* under each picture whose name begins with the /g/ sound.

✳ WORKSHOP

- Have children add *Gg* to their **Letter Books**.
- Encourage children to work on the **Ordering Letters game** and other letter recognition games.
- Play the **What Sound Is It?** game, adding the Picture Cards for words whose names start with /g/ to the set for the children to sort.
- Make the games **Hop Along, Bus Stop, Roller Ride, Race Track,** and **Make Tracks** available. Each of these games or game mats can be used for any variation of the games you choose. In each case, the children spin a spinner or roll the dice and move along a path. You and your students may find it fun to make up new games with rules different from the ones presented in earlier lessons.
- Let children use designated areas of the room to practice their letters.

Exploring Sounds and Letters, page 68

Exploring Sounds and Letters, page 69

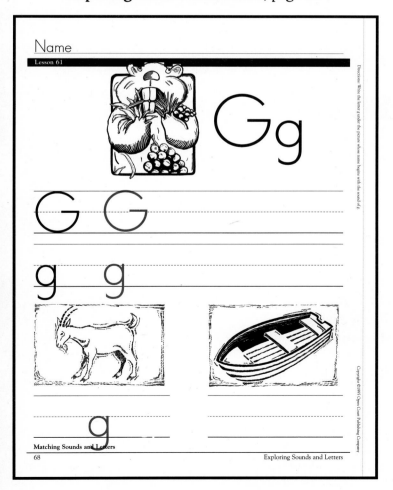

LESSON
62

●●●● Lesson Overview

New Learning

- *Hh*
- /h/

Materials

- "To Market, to Market," page 7 of *Pickled Peppers*
- Picture Cards: *hat, hen, hive, hook, horse, house*
- Exploring Sounds and Letters, pages 70–71
- For each child, one Uppercase and Lowercase Letter Card: *Hh*
- *Pickled Peppers* Poster
- Reproducible Master 29

Prepare Ahead

- Writing folders, one for each child

✱ READING THE BIG BOOK

"To Market, to Market"
page 7 of *Pickled Peppers*

- Open *Pickled Peppers* to "To Market, to Market." Point to the title and to the name of the illustrator. Remind the children what illustrators do. Read the poem aloud. Because many children may be familiar with the poem, invite them to participate.
- Read the poem again, this time emphasizing the rhyming words: *pig/jig; hog/jog; bun/done*. Now say *pig* and ask the children for a word that rhymes with *pig*. You may want to help them out by giving them initial sounds. For example, say /w/. Then ask, "What word rhymes with *pig* and starts with /w/?"
- Do the same with *hog* (*log, dog, fog*, etc.) and *bun* (*sun, done, run*, etc.).

Oral Blending

Initial Consonant Replacement Have the children make new words by replacing the initial consonant with a new one. Say *game*. Write *g* on the chalkboard. Say, "*Game* begins with the letter *g* that makes the sound /g/." Write the rest of the word on the chalkboard. Point to *g* again and pronounce it. Then point to the rest of the word and pronounce it. Finally, ask the children to pronounce the whole word.

Teacher: /g/
Teacher: ame
Everyone: game

- Erase the *g*, and write *t* in its place. Say, "Now the word begins with the letter *t*, so it doesn't start with the /g/ sound any more. What sound does it start with? What's the new word?" Allow for wait time.
- Try the following word changes:

g . . . ame	t . . . ame	s . . . ame
t . . . aking	b . . . aking	m . . . aking
m . . . ender	s . . . ender	f . . . ender

Segmentation

Restoring Final Word Parts Explain to the children that in this activity, they once again must help the puppet. Remind them that the puppet is forgetful, and sometimes leaves off the ends of words.

Teacher: poke
Puppet: /p/
Everyone: oke
Everyone: poke

Use the following words:

/m/ . . . ill	/f/ . . . at	/b/ . . . eat
/s/ . . . eal	/s/ . . . ink	/h/ . . . oops
/h/ . . . air	/b/ . . . in	/h/ . . . ow

Warmup Take the children through a quick Warmup by having them recite the alphabet. Have the children sit with you in a circle. Say *A* and tap the child next to you on the shoulder. That child should say *B* and tap the next child. Continue around the circle until you have reached *Z*.

The Sound of *h*

Reviewing *h* Display the *Hh* Alphabet Card and say /h/. Ask the children if anyone remembers the poem for /h/. Have those who remember it recite the poem. If no one remembers it, say it yourself.

Harry the Hound dog
Hurries around
/h/ /h/ /h/ /h/ /h/ /h/
Is his hurrying sound.

Repeat the poem, emphasizing the initial /h/ sounds, and asking the children to pant like Harry on /h/ /h/ /h/ /h/ /h/ /h/.

Listening for Initial /h/ Hold up each of the following Picture Cards and say the word on the back of each: *hat, horse, house, hive, hen, hook.*
- Ask children to listen for /h/ at the beginning of each word.
    Tell children that /h/ is a special sound that is only at the beginning of a word.
- Give each child an *Hh* Uppercase and Lowercase Letter Card. Tell them that you will say some words and that they should hold up their *Hh* cards every time they hear the sound of *h* at the beginning of a word.

at	**hat**	am	**ham**	
is	**his**	him	**hike**	like
sill	**hill**			

Words, Words Ask the children to list as many words that begin with /h/ that they can think of. Write the words on the board, and add words to the list as children think of more during the day.

Pickled Peppers **Poster** Hang the poster on the wall. Future lessons will assume the poster is displayed in a place where children can see it. Invite the children to gather around the poster and look at it. Encourage them to describe what they see. Ask a child to point out Harry the Hound dog. Ask another child what letter comes before *h* in the alphabet? Have the children find the gopher and the letter *g*. Let the children know they are welcome to study the poster whenever they have time. They may enjoy challenging each other to letter hunts.

Linking the Sound to the Letter
Word Changes Write the word *at* on the chalkboard and say it. Ask the children if anyone knows how to change *at* into *hat*. Say, "If we want to change this into *hat*, we have to put the /h/ sound at the beginning. What letter do we need?" Continue by changing *am* to *ham*, *oil* to *foil*, *mouse* to *house*.

Writing *Hh*
- Review with the children how to form a capital *H*.
- Have children take out Exploring Sounds and Letters and turn to page 70. Lead them in completing a line of capital *H*'s as in past lessons.
- Repeat for small *h*.

❯ Exploring Sounds and Letters Have the children focus on the pictures on pages 70-71 in Exploring Sounds and Letters. Explain that some of the picture names start with the sound of *h*. Name each picture. Ask the children to write the letter *h* under each picture whose name begins with /h/.

✱ WORKSHOP

- Create a **writing folder** for each child. Tell children that they can always use their writing folder during Workshop time to write or draw by themselves on topics of their choice. You might want to model a writing process for them by selecting a topic and drawing a picture about the topic on the board. Keep the children's writing folders stored in a place where they can find and use them easily.
- Have several activities or centers available for the children to use. During Workshop, find time to meet with individuals or small groups to have them share their work. Always make time to work with children who need extra help or extra challenges.

MONITORING TIP Monitor children's oral blending during Workshop. Record your comments on Observation Log 2, Reproducible Master 29.

Exploring Sounds and Letters, page 70

Exploring Sounds and Letters, page 71

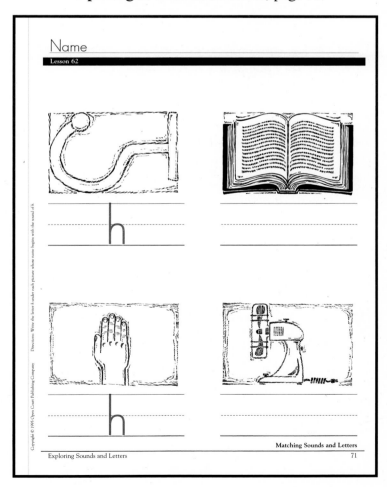

LESSON
63

● ● ● Lesson Overview

New Learning

- *Ii*
- Long *i* and short *i*

Materials

- "To Market, to Market," page 7 of *Pickled Peppers*
- Pocket Chart Letter Cards: *b, f, i, n, p, t*
- Picture Cards: *ice, ice cream, inch, infant, insect, iron,*
- Exploring Sounds and Letters, pages 72–73
- For each child, one Uppercase and Lowercase Letter Card: *Ii*
- Game Mats

✳ READING THE BIG BOOK

"To Market, to Market"
page 7 of *Pickled Peppers*

- Open *Pickled Peppers* to "To Market, to Market." Read the poem, and invite the children to join in.
- Read the poem again. This time point to, but do not say, the rhyming words. *To market, to market, to buy a fat* (point to the word *pig*).
- Explain to the children that you are going to read the poem again, but that you are first going to name something that can be purchased in a market. say, "When we come to *jiggety jig,* I want you to change it to rhyme with the new word." Model for them:

To market, to market, to buy a fat cake.
Home again, home again, jiggety (jake).

- Help children with the initial sound if they need it. Continue with others:

To market, to market, to buy a fat bean.
Home again, home again, jiggety (jean).
To market, to market, to buy a fat hen.
Home again, home again, jiggety (jen).
To market, to market, to buy a fat cow.
Home again, home again, jiggety   (jow).

✻ PHONEMIC AWARENESS

Oral Blending

Initial Consonant Replacement In this activity, use multisyllablic words, including some that begin with stop consonants (that is, consonants that can't be elongated such as *b, d, p, t, k*). Because stop consonants are more difficult to blend than are other consonants, the children may need more practice with this activity.

- Begin by saying the initial sound of the word *paper,* /p/. Write the letter *p* on the chalkboard. Say the remainder of the word *aper* and write it on the board. Ask the children to put the parts together and say the word back to you.
  Teacher: /p/
  Teacher: aper. What's the word?
  Everyone: paper

- Now erase the *p,* and write a *t.* Say, "Now the word starts with the letter *t,* so it doesn't start with /p/ anymore. What sound does it start with? Yes, /t/ . . . aper. What's the new word?"
  Try the following word changes:

/p/...aper	/t/...aper	/k/...aper
/h/...andle	/k/...andle	
/s/...ailor	/t/...ailor	

Segmentation

Restoring Final Word Parts Continue to have the children help the puppet. Again, remind them that the puppet sometimes forgets and leaves off the ends of words.

  Teacher: hitch
  Puppet: /h/
  Everyone: itch
  Everyone: hitch

Use the following words:

hall	tall	hair	hate
bear	fair	farm	

Warmup Take the children through a review of the alphabet using the Alphabet Cards. Stop on some of the letters whose sounds the children have already learned and invite volunteers to say the sound. Point to the picture on the Alphabet Card as a reminder of the sound.

The Sounds of Long and Short *i*

Introducing Long *i* Point to the Long *i* Alphabet Card. Ask if anyone can tell you the name of the letter and say its sound. Remind children that *i* is a vowel, and that vowels are special letters because they can say their names.

Show the children the Picture Cards for long *i*: *ice cream, ice, iron.* Say the words on the cards and ask children to listen for the /ī/ at the beginning of each word. Have them repeat the words.

Introducing Short *i* Point to the Short *i* Alphabet Card. Remind children that a vowel can make a sound other than its name, and that the short sound of *i* is /i/. Recite the poem for short *i*:

> Here sits Pickles the Pig.
> Tickle Pickles, and she'll get the giggles.
> This is the sound of Pickles' giggles:
> /i/ /i/ /i/ /i/ /i/

- Show the children the Picture Cards for short *i*: *inch, infant, insect.* Say the word on each Picture Card and ask children to listen for /i/ at the beginning of word. Have them repeat the words.
- Give each child one *Ii* Uppercase and Lowercase Letter Card. Explain that you are going to say some words and that you want them to listen carefully for /i/ in each word and hold up their letter cards each time they hear the sound of short *i*. Remind them that the /i/ sound might be at the beginning of the word or it might be in the middle. Try these words:

it	**sit**	us	**fit**	bus	**in**
an	**bin**	ban	tan	**tin**	**fin**	grin

Listening for Long and Short *i* Point to the Long *i* Alphabet Card and say, "Remember, sometimes the letter *i* says its name, /ī/." Point to the Short *i* Alphabet Card and say, "And sometimes it says another sound, /i/."

- Make sure each child has an *Ii* Uppercase and Lowercase Letter Card. Tell the children that you are going to say some words, and that they should listen carefully for the beginning sounds of each. Say, "When you hear /ī/ hold your *Ii* card up high and say /ī/, and when you hear /i/, scrunch down and say /i/."
Try the following words:

inch	ice	iron	infant	
iceberg	island	ill	ice cream	insect

- Remind children that the long *i* sound can come at the end of words. Tell them to listen for the long *i* or short *i* sounds in the middle or at the end of the following words and to stretch up for long *i* or scrunch down for short *i* as they did before:

sigh	sit	why	wit
white	buy	bite	night
nick	tick	tie	

Pickled Peppers **Poster** Have the children look for the capital *I*, which stands for the sound of long *i* and for the animal that stands for the sound of short *i*. Then invite volunteers to point them out and tell which they are pointing to.

Linking the Sound to the Letter

Grab Bag of Letters Review the consonants already introduced, while still concentrating on the short *i* sound. Before the activity begins, put the Pocket Chart Letter Cards *t, p, b,* and *f* in a bag.

Put *i* and *n* in the Pocket Chart. Say them. Then add a letter from the bag to the chart. For example, add *t* in front of *i n,* making *tin.* Call for a volunteer to pull a letter from the bag and replace the *t* on the chart. Ask the child to say the sound of the letter and then to say the word. Continue until all the letters have been used.

Writing *Ii* Review with the children how to form a capital *I*.
- Have children take out Exploring Sounds and Letters and turn to page 72. Work with them as they complete a line of capital *I*'s as in past lessons.
- Repeat for small *i*.

➤ **Exploring Sounds and Letters** Have the children focus on the pictures on pages 72-73 in Exploring Sounds and Letters. Explain that some of the pictures show things whose names have the short *i* sound. Ask the children to write the letter *i* under each picture whose name has the /i/ sound.

✳ **WORKSHOP**

- Work with individuals or small groups of children who are having difficulties with the sounds of letters *a–h.*
- Have children add *Ii* to their **Letter Books.**
- Encourage children to play the **Ordering Letters** game.
- Add the Picture Cards for words whose names start with long and short *i* to the **What Sound Is It?** game for children to sort.
- Make the games **Hop Along, Bus Stop, Roller Ride, Race Track,** and **Make Tracks** available.
- Have the children add to their **writing folders.**

TIP FOR ENGLISH LANGUAGE LEARNERS

Encourage conversational practice to find out about language in a friendly, unintimidating way. Pair English Language Learners with native English speakers. Have partners talk with each other as they order the letters. Informally monitor the children's conversations to assess their progress.

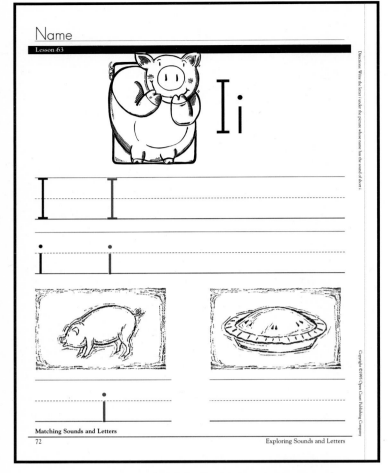

Exploring Sounds and Letters, page 72

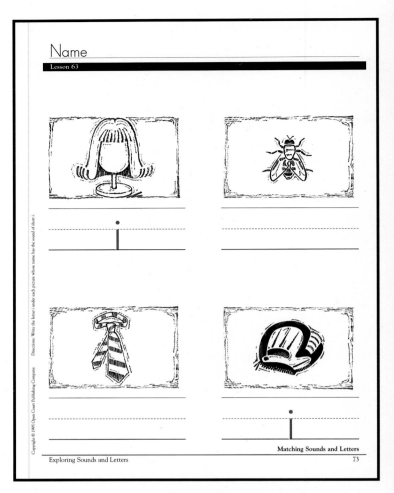

Exploring Sounds and Letters, page 73

LESSON
64

Lesson Overview

Materials

- "To Market, to Market," page 7 of **Pickled Peppers**
- For each child, one Uppercase and Lowercase Letter Card: **Ii**
- Activity Sheet 13

✱ READING THE BIG BOOK

"To Market, to Market"
page 7 of *Pickled Peppers*

- Repeat the rhyming activity from Lesson 63 in which you substitute items you might buy at a market for the word *pig* in the poem. Tell the children that you will name another thing purchased at the market, and that you want them to change *jiggety jig* to make it rhyme with the new word. Try:

To market, to market, to buy a fat horse.
Home again, home again, jiggety (**jorse**).
To market, to market, to buy a fat corn.
Home again, home again, jiggety (**jorn**).
To market, to market, to buy a fat goat.
Home again, home again, jiggety (**joat**).
To market, to market, to buy a fat goose.
Home again, home again, jiggety (**juice**)

- Children often like to revisit selections they have worked with in the past. Invite a volunteer to tell you which selection he or she would like to revisit. Read the poem or sing the song with the children.

Oral Blending

Initial Consonant Replacement, Phonics Method Continue to use multisyllabic words that begin with stop consonants which are more difficult to blend. Following the procedure used in earlier lessons, write *picket* on the board.

Teacher : /p/
Teacher: icket. What's the word?
Everyone: picket

Now erase the *p*, and write *t*. Say, "Now the word starts with the letter *t*, so it doesn't start with /p/ anymore. What sound does it start with? What's the new word?"
Try the following word changes:

/p/...icket	/t/...icket	/p/...ickle	/t/...ickle
/p/...arrot	/k/...arrot	/p/...ower	/t/...ower

Segmentation

Initial Consonant Sounds Tell children that they must help the puppet again, but that this time it is forgetting the first part of words. Model this for children:

Teacher: fox
Puppet: ox
Teacher: /f/ /f/ /f/ /f/ ox. You forgot the /f/.

Have children supply both the whole word and the initial sound the puppet forgets. Try these words.

Teacher: feel
Puppet: eel
Everyone: /f/ /f/ /f/ eel. You forgot the /f/.

fold	fat	fair	farm
sand	seal	sink	

Warmup Quickly review the alphabet with the children by leading the children in the Alphabet Cheer.

The Sounds of *i*

Reviewing Long *i* Review the long *i* sound by displaying the Long *i* Alphabet Card and remind the children that long vowels say their names.

Reviewing Short *i* Review the short *i* sound by displaying the Short *i* Alphabet Card and leading the children through the poem:

Here sits Pickles the Pig.
Tickle Pickles, and she'll get the giggles.
This is the sound of Pickles' giggles:
/i/ /i/ /i/ /i/ /i/

Repeat the poem, emphasizing the short *i* sounds, and asking the children to giggle on /i/ /i/ /i/ /i/ /i/ the way Pickles does. Remind the children to look at the Alphabet Card if they have difficulty remembering /i/.

Listening for Long and Short *i* Using the procedure established in earlier lessons, have the children practice listening for short and long *i* sounds again. Remind them that when they hear you say the long *i* sound, they should hold their *Ii* Uppercase and Lowercase Letter Cards up high and say /ī/, and that when they hear /i/, they should scrunch down and say /i/. Remind them to wait for your signal before responding. Try these words:

mitt	light	might	pin	kit	sit
kite	sight	right	sip	hit	

Linking the Sound to the Letter

Word Pairs Write two words on the board, one containing a short *i* sound, one not. Say the word with the short *i* sound in the middle, and ask the children to find that word.

Write *miss* and *moss* on the board. Ask the children, "Which word says *miss*?" Repeat with other pairs, such as the following:

sat	sit	bit	bat
pot	pit	pack	pick

✳ WORKSHOP

- Give the children copies of **Activity Sheet 13** to complete. Name all the pictures on the sheet before children begin. Have them write *i* under any picture whose name has the short *i* sound.
- As always, have other activities available for children during Workshop and remember to incorporate into Workshop ideas from your other Learning Centers and activities from the Discovery Modules. Especially be sure to have a writing center and a reading center for children to use doing Workshop.

MONITORING TIP Monitor children on oral blending during Workshop. Record your comments on Observation Log 2, Reproducible Master 29.

LESSON

65

● ● ● Lesson Overview

New Learning

- *Jj*
- /j/

Materials

- "To Market, to Market" page 7 of *Pickled Peppers*
- Picture Cards: *jam, jar, jeans, jellyfish, judge, juice*
- Exploring Sounds and Letters, pages 74–75
- For each child, one Uppercase and Lowercase Letter Card: *Jj*

Prepare Ahead

- Sets of Uppercase and Lowercase Letter Cards for each letter whose sound has been introduced
- Bags to place the Letter Cards in
- Make up half as many bags of cards as you have students in class so that the children can work with partners.

✳ READING THE BIG BOOK

"To Market, to Market"
page 7 of *Pickled Peppers*

- Open *Pickled Peppers* to "To Market, to Market." Read the poem once for review.
- Tell the children that as they read the first verse of the poem today, you want them to change the beginning sounds of *jiggety* and *jig*. Explain that you will point to an Alphabet Card, and that they should use the sound of the letter on the card. Model their response by pointing to the *Hh* Alphabet Card and saying *higgety-hig*.
- Go through the activity several times, pointing to Alphabet Cards for all the consonants that you have covered to date.
- Choose another volunteer to tell which selection he or she would like to revisit.

✳ PHONEMIC AWARENESS

Oral Blending

Initial Consonant Replacement In this activity, you will have the children begin blending single-syllable words. Use the same procedure as in earlier lessons. Remember to give the children the initial consonant sound and then the remainder of the word. Always help them with the replacement consonant and ask them to blend the new word.

Try the following word changes:

/s/ . . . un	/b/ . . . un	/f/ . . . un
/d/ . . . ine	/f/ . . . ine	/m/ . . . ine
/t/ . . . ake	/f/ . . . ake	/m/ . . . ake

Segmentation

Initial Consonant Sounds Tell the children that the puppet seems to be forgetful again, and that they will have to help it the way they did before, by giving it the beginning sounds of words. Model the children's response.

Teacher: heart

Puppet: eart

Everyone: /h/ /h/ /h/ /h/ /h/ eart. You forgot the /h/.

Ask a volunteer to point to the Alphabet Card for the letter that makes the /h/ sound. Ask the children to tell you what they remember about *h* and the /h/ sound. Then continue having them help the puppet. Use these words:

sand	hoops	fair	fate
hill	fat	tow	hitch

Letter Names, Shapes, and Sounds

Warmup For a quick review, have the children sit in a circle with you and have each child say a letter, then tap the shoulder of the next child. The next child should then say the letter that comes next in the alphabet.

Review any of the consonant substitution activities the children have done.

The Sound of *j*

Introducing *j* Display the *Jj* Alphabet Card and say the sound of the letter, /j/. Show the picture for the /j/ sound and teach the short poem for /j/:

Jenny and Jackson like to have fun.
They play jacks, jump rope, and juggle in the sun.
Each time they jump, their feet hit the ground.
/j/ /j/ /j/ /j/ /j/ is the jumping-rope sound.

Repeat the poem, emphasizing the initial /j/.

Listening for Initial /j/ Hold up and name each of these Picture Cards: *jam, jar, judge, jeans, juice, jellyfish.* Ask the children to listen for the /j/ sound at the beginning of the words.

- Give each child a *Jj* Uppercase and Lowercase Letter Card.
- Have the children hold up their *Jj* cards each time they hear the /j/. Try these words:

green	jail	jeans	Gail	Jill
Jake	jam	Jim	gas	

I'm Thinking of Something That Starts with _____ Play the I'm Thinking of Something That Starts with _____ game, using words that begin with /j/. This time, choose objects that are outside of the room, but give the children some clues to what you are thinking of. You might try the following objects and clues:

something you drink in the morning: *juice*
something you put on your toast: *jam* or *jelly*
the sound bells make: *jingle*
this part of your face (point to it): *jaw*

If you have children in your class whose names begin with /j/, you might want to use their names in the game.

Pickled Peppers Poster Ask the children to look on the poster and point to the letter that makes the sound /j/. Repeat asking for the letter that makes the /b/ sound.

Linking the Sound to the Letter

Word Pairs Write the words *jacket* and *packet* on the board. Say, "Which word says *jacket?*"

- Ask a child to come to the board and point to the right word.
- When the child points to *jacket,* say, "Right! The /j/ sound begins *jacket."*
- Then point to *packet* and ask the children what they think it says.
- Throughout the activity, always say the word with initial /j/. Then ask children what they think the other words say. Try with these words:

join	coin	**Jill**	pill	**Jake**	cake
jam	ham	**jingle**	mingle		

Writing Jj Demonstrate how to form a capital *J,* using the established method.

- Have children take out Exploring Sounds and Letters and turn to page 74. Work with them as they complete a line of capital *J*'s, as in past lessons.
- Repeat for small *j.*

❯ **Exploring Sounds and Letters** Focus the children's attention on the pictures on pages 74-75 of Exploring Sounds and Letters. Point out that some of the pictures show things whose names begin with /j/. Ask the children to write the letter *j* under each picture whose name begins with /j/.

- Introduce the **Letters in a Row** game. Have the children choose partners. Give each pair of children a paper bag with the Letter Card sets you prepared ahead of time. Have one child from each pair take a card out of the bag, say the name of the letter, and say its sound. If the partners agree that this is the correct letter name and sound, the first child gets another turn and chooses another card. If the letter name and sound are said incorrectly, the second child takes a turn at choosing a card. Tell the children to raise their hands and ask for help if they can't agree on the letter name or sound. Challenge the children to see how many letters in a row they can name.
- Have other activities available for children during Workshop such as **Game Corner, Creating Letters, Letter Books, writing folders.**
- Work in small groups with children who are having difficulty with Oral Blending.

Exploring Sounds and Letters, page 74

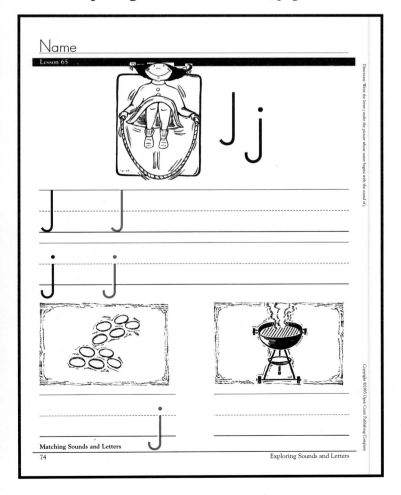

Exploring Sounds and Letters, page 75

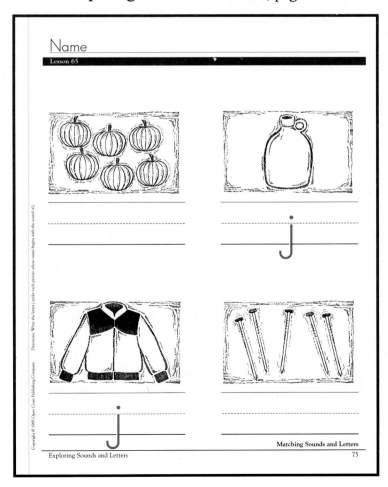

LESSON
66

••• Lesson Overview

New Learning

- *Kk*
- Initial /k/

Materials

- "To Market, to Market," page 7 of *Pickled Peppers*
- Picture Cards: *kangaroo, keys, kitchen, kite, kittens, koala*
- Exploring Sounds and Letters, pages 76–77
- For each child, Uppercase and Lowercase Letter Cards: *Jj* and *Kk*

✱ READING THE BIG BOOK

"To Market, to Market"
page 7 of *Pickled Peppers*

- Have the children sit in a circle and tell them that today you want them to change the beginning sounds of *jiggety jog* again. Model the responses you want by saying /d/ then *diggety dog*. Go around the circle, giving each child one of the consonants covered to date.
- Revisit selections the children have done before.

✱ PHONEMIC AWARENESS

✱ Oral Blending

Initial Consonant Replacement In this activity, the children will blend single-syllable words, starting with words with the more easily blended initial consonants. Remember to give the children the initial consonant sound and then the remainder of the word. Then help them with the replacement consonant and ask them to blend the new word. Use the procedures established in earlier lessons.

Try the following word changes:

/f/ . . . eat	/n/ . . . eat	/s/ . . . eat
/k/ . . . atch	/b/ . . . atch	/h/ . . . atch
/h/ . . . uff	/m/ . . . uff	/b/ . . . uff

Segmentation

Initial Consonant Sounds Tell the children that the puppet is forgetful again, and that they must help by saying the parts of words that it leaves off.

Teacher: ball
Puppet: all
Everyone: /b/ /b/ /b/ /b/ all. You forgot the /b/.

Try these words:

hall	tall	call
mall	bat	bend
beat	bin	bear

LETTER NAMES, SHAPES, AND SOUNDS

Warmup Choose an activity to help the children prepare for the lessons that follow.

- For a quick review, have the children play the tapping game again. Tell the children that this time, they should each say three letters in a row before tapping another child on the shoulder. Try to give everyone a chance to recite.
- Randomly point to Alphabet Cards for letter sounds that the children have learned. Have the children say each sound as you point to the cards.

The Sound of *k*

Introducing *k* Display the *Kk* Alphabet Card and say /k/. Show the picture for the sound of *k* and explain that this sound is the same as the one they learned for the letter *c.* Ask children if they remember the sound of *c* and its poem. Review the poem for /k/:

Carlos clicks his camera
/k/ /k/ /k/ /k/ /k/ /k/ it goes.
The pictures come out crisp and clear.
So give a smile, /k/ /k/ /k/ Carlos is here!

Repeat the poem emphasizing the initial /k/.

Listening for Initial /k/ and /j/ Hold up and name each of these Picture Cards: *kangaroo, keys, kitchen, kite, kittens, koala.* Ask the children to listen for /k/ at the beginning of each word.

- Give each child one *Kk* and one *Jj* Uppercase and Lowercase Letter Card. Tell them you are going to say words, and that when they hear you say a word beginning with /k/, they should hold up the *Kk* card and say /k/ when you give the signal.
- When they hear /j/, they should hold up the *Jj* card and say /j/.
- Remember to allow for wait time. Use the following words:

keyhole	kelp	jeans
kettle	kazoo	jangle
June	kind	kaleidoscope
kite	kayak	jog
jet	keep	

***Pickled Peppers* Poster** Have the children look for the letter *k* (capital or small) on the *Pickled Peppers* poster and point it out. Ask whether anyone knows what other letter makes the same sound as *k*. Ask for a volunteer to find the *c* (capital or small).

Linking the Sound to the Letter

Word Pairs Write *kite* and *bite* on the board.

- Ask the children, "Which one says *kite*?" Call on a volunteer to go to the board and point to the word.
- Say, "Right! *Kite* has the sound /k/." Have everyone say *kite*.
- Point to *bite* and say, "What do you think this word says." Call on a child to answer.
- Remember to say the words beginning with /k/ or /j/ after the children identify them. Then have everyone say the word with you. Continue with these words:

jail	sail	kiss	miss
keep	deep	kitten	mitten

Writing *Kk* Demonstrate how to form a capital *K*, using the established procedure.

- Have children open Exploring Sounds and Letters workbook and turn to page 76. Work with them as they complete a line of capital *K*'s as in past lessons.
- Repeat for small *k*.

❯ **Exploring Sounds and Letters** Focus children's attention on the pictures on pages 76–77 in Exploring Sounds and Letters. Have the children write the letter *k* under pictures whose names begin with /k/.

✱ WORKSHOP

Have a variety of activities available for children during Workshop such as **Game Corner, Creating Letters, Letter Books, Letters in a Row,** and other activities to reinforce letter recognition and sounds.

Home/School Connection Home/School Connection 12, which will be sent home in Lesson 68, asks you to select some of the children's work from Workshop for them to take home and share with their families. Talk with each child about what she or he wants to choose from Workshop to take home.

Exploring Sounds and Letters, page 76

Exploring Sounds and Letters, page 77

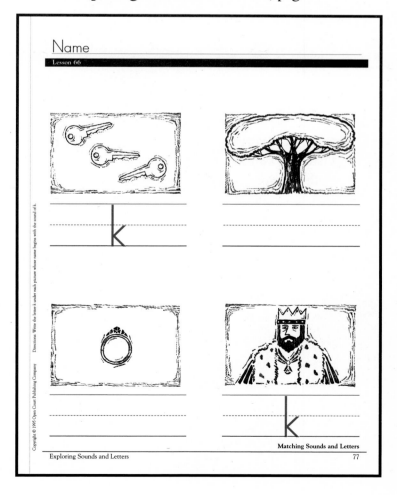

LESSON
67

● ● ● Lesson Overview

New Learning

- Final /k/

Materials

- "Walk Along," pages 18–19 of *Pickled Peppers*
- Pocket Chart Letter Cards: *b, d, f, i, k, m, n*
- For each child, Uppercase and Lowercase Letter Card: *Kk*
- For each child, Uppercase and Lowercase Letter Cards: *Cc, Ff, Jj, Nn, Rr, Vv, Ww, Zz*
- Listening Collections Audiocassette
- Songs Teacher Tool Card 5

✳ READING THE BIG BOOK

"Walk Along"
pages 18–19 of *Pickled Peppers*

- Open *Pickled Peppers* to "Walk Along." Play the song on the Listening Collections Audiocassette and have the children join in.
- With everyone standing up, have the children walk in place for the first verse and then show the children that they can act out some of the words as follows:

Come on, Judy, and hush your talking, (wave arm, put finger to lips)
Let's clap hands and we'll go walking. (clap to the beat)
Walk along, Judy, with your red dress on. (walk in place)
Walk along, Judy, with your red dress on. (walk in place)

Let's snap our fingers and we'll go walking. (snap to the beat)
Let's shake out our legs and we'll go walking. (shake legs)
(**Note:** See Songs Teacher Tool Card 5 for music and movements.)

- Play the game of finding "so-and-so," as you did in earlier lessons with "Walk Along." Sing a verse, use "so-and-so" for the name, and then mention an article of clothing (and its color) being worn by

TEACHING TIP

Some children may not yet have the ability to perform actions such as finger snapping. Encourage them to try, and praise their efforts.

someone in the class. If you say, "Walk along, *so-and-so,* with your green shirt on," the children have to look around for the child with the green shirt and name her or him.

✳ Oral Blending

Initial Consonant Replacement Continue to have the children blend single-syllable words.

- Try the following word changes:

/j/ . . . im	/h/ . . . im	/t/ . . . im
/f/ . . . it	/h/ . . . it	/s/ . . . it
/f/ . . . an	/p/ . . . an	/m/ . . . an
/d/ . . . an		

Remind children that names use capital letters.

Segmentation

Initial Consonant Sounds Today have the children focus on initial consonant sounds. Tell them that the puppet will join in saying the beginning sounds of words.

Teacher: sand
Puppet and Everyone: /s/

Use the following words:

sand	tall	seal	teal	meal
tall	mat	sink	mall	sat

Warmup Hand each child one of the following Uppercase and Lowercase Letter Cards: *Cc, Ff, Jj, Nn, Rr, Vv, Ww, Zz.* Ask the children to listen as you repeat the Alphabet Rap. Stress the last letter in each line. Tell the children that when they hear their letters, they should hold up their Letter Cards. Repeat the rap and invite the children to join in.

The Sound of *k*

Reviewing *k* Point to the *Kk* Alphabet Card, say /k/, and review the short poem. Encourage children to recite along with you.

Carlos clicks his camera
/k/ /k/ /k/ /k/ /k/ /k/ it goes.
The pictures come out crisp and clear.
So give a smile, /k/ /k/ /k/ Carlos is here!

Listening for Final /k/ Give each child a *Kk* Uppercase and Lowercase Letter Card. Tell the children that you are going to say words that end with /k/. Begin by saying the word *pack*. Say, "Where is the sound /k/? At the beginning or end?" Explain that when they hear a word ending with the sound /k/, they should hold up their cards and on your signal, say /k/. Use the following words:

tack	poke	tap	coat
rack	bike	rat	bite
sack	seat	sat	seek

Linking the Sound to the Letter

Grab Bag of Letters and Words   Put the Pocket Chart Letter Cards *ind* in the Pocket Chart or write them on the board. Have the Pocket Chart Letter Cards *k, b, f, m* in a bag. Have a child pick a letter from the bag and place it in front of *ind*. Have the child blend the word. Continue forming the words *kind, bind, find, mind*.

✳ WORKSHOP

- Have the children play with letters to **make words** in the Pocket Chart.
- Have other activities available for children during Workshop such as **Game Corner, Creating Letters, Letter Books.**
- If some children have not yet decided what to take home, talk to them about what they want to choose from Workshop to take home to their families.

LESSON

68

●●● Lesson Overview

New Learning

- *Ll*
- Initial /l/

Materials

- "Walk Along," pages 18–19 of *Pickled Peppers*
- Picture Cards: *black, blue, bow, brown, dress, green, ladybug, lamp, lion, lock, lockers, orange, pants, pink, purple, red, shirt, shoe, shorts, skirt, sock, white, yellow*
- Word Cards: *Walk, along, Judy, with, your, on*
- Exploring Sounds and Letters, pages 78–79
- Alphabet Flash Cards
- For each child, Uppercase and Lowercase Letter Card: *Ll* or *Mm*
- Home/School Connection 12

Prepare Ahead

- Name necklaces
- Examples of the children's work from Workshop

✱ READING THE BIG BOOK

"Walk Along"
pages 18–19 of *Pickled Peppers*

- Open *Pickled Peppers* to "Walk Along." Point to and say the title and the names of the author and illustrator. Read through all the verses.
- Place all the color Picture Cards in one area of a low table, all the clothing Picture Cards in another area, and have the children hold their name necklaces (from Lesson 3). (If the children no longer have their original name cards, be sure to make new name cards in advance.)
- Gather the children around the Pocket Chart. Place the following words in the chart, saying each one slowly:
  Walk/along/Judy/with/your/red (color card)/*dress* (clothes card)/*on.*
  Read this line over a few times. Ask for volunteers to read the line on their own.

- Ask individual children to change the line by changing the words and pictures. First, take out *Judy* and allow a child to replace it with her own name. Next, remove the red color card, and allow another child to replace it with a different color card. Then call on a third child and allow him to replace the dress clothing card. Now, ask for a volunteer to recite the new line as you point to each word or picture. Help the child, if necessary. Give several children a chance to do this.

✳ PHONEMIC AWARENESS

✳ Oral Blending

Initial Consonant Replacement Use single-syllable words, some of which begin with stop consonants, which are more difficult to blend. Remember to give the children the word in two parts: the initial consonant sound and the remainder. Then help them with the replacement consonant and ask them to blend the new word.

Try the following word changes:

/r/ . . . ake	/k/ . . . ake	/t/ . . . ake
/m/ . . . uff	/k/ . . . uff	/p/ . . . uff
/r/ . . . an	/t/ . . . an	/k/ . . . an	/p/ . . . an

Segmentation

Initial Consonant Sounds Again, have children respond with the puppet, focusing on the initial consonant.

Teacher: mash
Puppet and *Everyone:* /m/ /m/ /m/ ash. /m/

Use the following words:

/m/ . . . ash	/l/ . . . ash	/m/ . . . ore	/p/ . . . ore
/t/ . . . ore	/s/ . . . ore	/m/ . . . itt	/s/ . . . it
/p/ . . . it	/l/ . . . it		

LETTER NAMES, SHAPES, AND SOUNDS

Warmup Review the alphabet by using the Alphabet Flash Cards. When you come to a letter the children have learned the sound of, ask them to say the sound. Point to the picture on the Alphabet Card to remind them of the sound.

The Sound of *l*

Introducing *l* Display the *Ll* Alphabet Card and say /l/. Show the picture for /l/ and introduce the short poem:

Look! It's Leon the Lion.
Leon loves to lap water from lakes.
This is the lapping sound Leon makes:
/l/ /l/ /l/ /l/ /l/ /l/.

Repeat the poem again, emphasizing the initial /l/.

Listening for Initial /l/ and /m/ Hold up and name each of the following Picture Cards: *ladybug, lamp, lion, lockers, lock.* Ask the children to listen for /l/ at the beginning of the words. Have them repeat the word and the /l/ sound as they see each Picture Card.

Give half the children *Ll* and half *Mm* Uppercase and Lowercase Letter Cards. Tell them that you are going to say words that begin with /m/ or /l/. Follow the procedure from earlier lessons. Try these words:

list	mend	mist	lick	link
like	mink	Mike	lend	mast	last

Catching the Letter Train Game Have the children sit in a circle and play the Catching the Letter Train Game. Tell them that you are the engine of the L train. Explain that instead of saying /ch/ /ch/ /ch/, this train says /l/ /l/ /l/. Lead the children in saying this sound until everyone is involved—then give them the signal to stop. Next, say that to get on the L train, everyone needs a ticket, and that a ticket is a word beginning with /l/. Explain that when you stop behind someone and ask for a ticket, she or he should say a word that starts with /l/. Stop at one child and ask for a ticket. When the child gives a word, she or he "gets on the train" and walks behind you. To keep the action going and to involve more children, you can stop and ask two or three children at a time to give their *l*-word tickets.

Linking the Sound to the Letter

Writing Ll Demonstrate how to form a capital *L*, using the established procedure.

- Have children open Exploring Sounds and Letters to page 78. Work with them as they complete a line of capital *L*'s, as in past lessons.
- Repeat for small *l*.

❯ **Exploring Sounds and Letters** Focus the children's attention on the pictures on pages 78–79 of Exploring Sounds and Letters. Proceed as in earlier lessons.

✱ **WORKSHOP**

Have a variety of activities available for children during Workshop such as **Game Corner, Creating Letters, Letter Books.**

Home/School Connection Have the children finish preparing the examples of their work to take home to their families. Send the work home along with Home/School Connection 12.

TEACHING TIP
If some children have a difficult time generating words, brainstorm words with the class before playing the game.

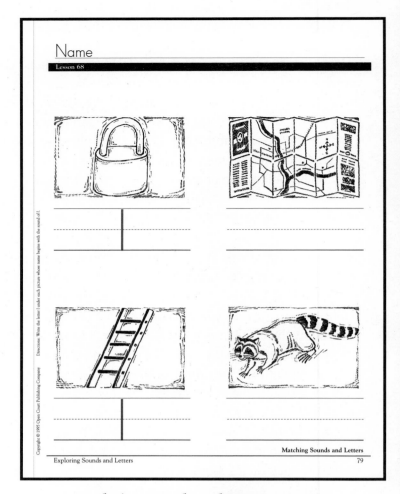

Exploring Sounds and Letters, page 78

Exploring Sounds and Letters, page 79

LESSON

69

● ● ● ● **Lesson Overview**

New Learning

- Final /l/

Materials

- "If You Should Meet a Crocodile," page 38 of *Pickled Peppers*
- Pocket Chart Letter Cards: *a, b, c, f, h, l* (2), *m*
- Picture Cards: *ladybug, lamp, lion, lock, lockers*
- Exploring Sounds and Letters, pages 80–81
- For each child, Uppercase and Lowercase Letter Card: *Ll*
- Game Mats

✱ **READING THE BIG BOOK**

"If You Should Meet a Crocodile"
page 38 of *Pickled Peppers*

- Open *Pickled Peppers* to the table of contents and find "If You Should Meet a Crocodile." Ask a volunteer to help you find the page number. Turn to the page. Point to and say the title and the name of the illustrator. Point to "Anonymous" and explain that this means that no one knows who wrote the poem. Read the poem through two or three times, emphasizing the rhyming words.

- After a few readings, ask whether anyone can say the rhyming words: *crocodile/smile/Nile*; or *dinner/thinner*; or *stroke/poke*.

- Explore the children's understanding of the meaning of the poem. Ask them leading questions such as, "What does 'Ignore the welcome in his smile' mean?" "Does anyone know what the Nile is?" Have a map of Africa or Egypt ready to show them where the Nile is.

- Consider creating a small display on crocodiles. Include books, pictures, and plastic models. This will provide an excellent opportunity to integrate science activities into the language arts lessons.

TIP FOR ENGLISH LANGUAGE LEARNERS

Point to a word in the poem, read it aloud, and have volunteers act it out. Repeat the activity so that the words have been acted out several times. Invite English Language Learners to participate by acting out words that have already been acted out by other classmates.

✱ Oral Blending

Initial Consonant Replacement Continue to blend single-syllable words using words with initial stop consonants.

Try the following word changes:

/b/ . . . ack	/t/ . . . ack	/p/ . . . ack	/k/ . . . atch
/p/. . . atch	/k/ . . . ill	/p/. . . ill	/t /. . . ill /g/. . . ill

Segmentation

Initial Consonant Sounds Have children respond with the puppet, focusing on the initial consonant.

Teacher: sand

Puppet and Everyone: /s/ /s/ /s/ /s/ /s/ /s/ and. /s/

Use the following words:

/s/ . . . ame	/s/ . . . eat	/m/ . . . ake	/s/ . . . ake
/l/ . . . ake	/m/ . . . ice	/l/ . . . ice	/m/ . . . eal
/p/ . . . eal	/s/ . . . eal		

Warmup The Warmup is designed to simply prepare the children for the lessons that follow. Use any previous Warmup you prefer or have the children warm up with one of the following activities.

- Have the children review with the tapping game. Each child should say three letters in a row before tapping the next person on the shoulder.
- Encourage the children to choose a Warmup activity.

The Sound of *l*

Reviewing *l* Take the children through a review of *l,* using the Alphabet Card and the short poem for /l/:

Look! It's Leon the Lion.
Leon loves to lap water from lakes.
This is the lapping sound Leon makes:
/l/ /l/ /l/ /l/ /l/ /l/.

Listening for Final /l/ Give each child an *Ll* Uppercase and Lowercase Letter Card. Tell the children that you are going to say some words and that you want them to listen carefully for the ending sound. Have the children hold up their cards every time they hear /l/ at the end of a word. Use the following words:

call	card	**spool**	cool
tune	**tool**	rude	**rule**
balloon	**stool**	**forgetful**	**valuable**

Silly Sentences Game Play the Silly Sentences game by making a silly sentence that is full of words that begin with /l/. Try: *Leon the Lion loves to eat lilies.*

Pickled Peppers Poster Tell the children to find and point out on the poster the letter (capital or small) that makes the sound /l/. Take the children through a review of other letters they have learned by asking individuals to find them on the poster.

Linking the Sound to the Letter

Grab Bag of Letters and Words Use this activity as a way to review the consonants already covered while also concentrating on words with final /l/.

- Using the Pocket Chart Letter Cards, put the letters, *a l l,* in the Pocket Chart or on the chalkboard and say *all.* Have in a bag, the letters: *b, c, f, h, m.*
- Have individual children choose letters from the bag and add them to the beginning of *all.* Lead children in saying each word.

❯ **Exploring Sounds and Letters** Have the children open Exploring Sounds and Letters to pages 80–81. Explain that the crocodile in the picture will eat anything whose name ends with /l/. Name all the objects on page 80 and ask the children to listen for /l/ at the end. Tell them to circle all the things that the crocodile can eat. Repeat the procedure for the pictures on page 81. Encourage the children to write *Ff*'s or *f* words at the bottom of each page, but allow them to write whatever they wish.

- Have children add *Ll* to their **Letter Books.**
- Add *Ll* to the **Letters in a Row** game (See page 253 for directions).
- Add the Picture Cards for words that start with /l/ to **What Sound Is It?** for children to sort by sounds.
- Make the games **Hop Along, Bus Stop, Roller Ride, Race Track,** and **Make Tracks** available.
- Let children use designated areas of the room to practice **making their letters.**

Exploring Sounds and Letters, page 80

Exploring Sounds and Letters, page 81

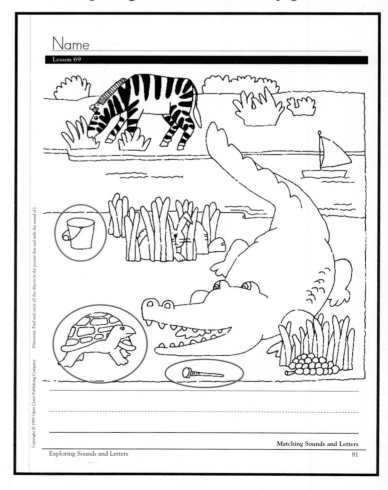

LESSON 70

••• Lesson Overview

New Learning

- *Mm*
- Initial /m/

Materials

- "If You Should Meet a Crocodile," page 38 of *Pickled Peppers*
- Picture Cards: *meat, milk, mittens, monkey, moon, mouse*
- Exploring Sounds and Letters, pages 82–83
- For each child, Letter Card: *Mm* or *Ff*
- Classroom Support Teacher Tool Card 3

Prepare Ahead

- A ball of yarn
- Uppercase and Lowercase Letter Cards in a bag: *Aa–Mm*

✳ **READING THE BIG BOOK**

"If You Should Meet a Crocodile"
page 38 of *Pickled Peppers*

- Open *Pickled Peppers* to "If You Should Meet a Crocodile." Point to and say the title and the name of the illustrator. Remind the children of the meaning of "Anonymous." Read through the poem again.
- Teach the children the following actions, and then recite the poem as they act it out together as a group:

If you should meet a crocodile, (Bow or curtsy as in greeting.)
Don't take a stick and poke him; (Make poking motions.)
Ignore the welcome in his smile, (Draw a wide smile across your face.)
Be careful not to stroke him. (Make stroking motions.)
For as he sleeps upon the Nile, (Fold hands under head.)
He thinner gets and thinner; (Stretch out tall and thin.)
And whene'er you meet a crocodile (Shake a finger in warning.)
He's ready for his dinner. (Rub tummy and lick lips.)

TIP FOR ENGLISH LANGUAGE LEARNERS

You may wish to read this poem to English Language Learners a day or so in advance of when it is read to the larger group. During the initial reading, the children have the opportunity to learn the movements associated with the poem and to clarify any confusion. When you read the poem again with the larger group, they may feel freer to participate.

✳ Oral Blending

Initial Consonant Replacement Continue to have children blend single-syllable words. Include some that begin with stop consonants.

Try the following word changes:

/h/ . . . op	/t /. . . op	/p/ . . . op
/s/ . . . oak	/p/ . . . oke	
/b/ . . . old	/k/. . . old	/t /. . . old
/w/. . . aste	/t/ . . . aste	/p/ . . . aste

Segmentation

Initial Consonants If you feel the children understand segmentation, then try it as circle game, the Spider's Web. Have children sit in a circle. Tell them that sometimes a new word can be created by taking away the first sound of some other word. Do a short review of some of the words used in Lessons 61-69, such as *seat, soil, bus,* and *rice.*

- Say a word, for example, *rice.* Then say /r/ /r/ /r/ . . . *ice.* Repeat *ice.*
- Repeat and have the children say the sound along with you.
- Holding the loose end of the ball of yarn, roll the ball to one child (unrolling the yarn), and ask, "What sound did I take away?"
- Help the child who catches the yarn to say /r/.
- Say a new word for the children to repeat. Tell the child with the ball of yarn to hold on to the piece of yarn and then roll the ball to a new child. That child says the word and the sound. Continue until a web forms in the circle. Although it is impressive if the whole class is part of the web, this takes a long time. For this reason, you might want to include only five or six children in the web at a time until everyone has had a chance to play the game.

Warmup Have the children warm up by playing the Sing Your Way to _____ game. Place a set of Uppercase and Lowercase Letter Cards *Aa–Mm* in a bag. Ask a child to draw one out and hold it up, but do not name it. Tell the children to sing their way to that letter as a group. If the letter chosen is one the children know the sound of, ask them to say it.

The Sound of *m*

Reviewing *m* The children have worked with the letter *m* before, so encourage them to give you as much information about the letter and its sound as they can on their own.

Display the Alphabet Card for *Mm* and say /m/. Recite the short poem for the /m/:

For Muzzy the Monkey, bananas are yummy.
She munches so many, they fill up her tummy.
When she munches, she mumbles
/m/ /m/ /m/ /m/ /m.

Listening for Initial /m/ and /f/ Hold up and name each of these
Picture Cards: *meat, milk, mittens, monkey, moon, mouse.* Ask children
to listen for /m/ at the beginning of the words. Follow the established
procedure.

- Give half the children an *Mm* Uppercase and Lowercase Letter Card
  and the other half an *Ff* Letter Card. Tell the children that you are
  going to say some words and you want them to listen carefully for
  the beginning sound.
- If the word starts with /m/ and they have an *Mm* card, they should
  hold it up and say /m/. If a word starts with /f/, and they have an *Ff*
  card, they should hold the card up and say /f/. Use these words:

fall	make	fire	map
marble	fine	fairy	mistletoe
marry	fence	festival	motion

Catching the Letter Train Play Catching the Letter Train game again,
but this time tell the children that you are the engine of the M train.
Instead of /ch/ /ch/ /ch/, this train says /m/ /m/ /m/. Remind the children that the ticket to the M train is a word that begins with the sound
/m/. Then continue as in Lesson 68.

***Pickled Peppers* Poster** Tell the children to find and point out on the
poster the letter (capital or small) that makes the sound /m/. You might
want to recite the *m* poem. Conduct a brief review, asking children to
find the letter that makes the sound /f/.

Linking the Sound to the Letter

Word Pairs Write two rhyming words, one beginning with /m/ and
one not, on the board. Say the word beginning with /m/, and then ask
the children to find that word.

- Write *make* and *take* on the board. Ask the children "Which word
  says *make*?"
  Point to *take* and say, "What do you think this word says?"
  Always say the word beginning with /m/. Continue with other words:

fate	mate	find	mind
mug	bug	meet	seat

Writing *Mm* Demonstrate how to form a capital *M,* using the established procedure.

- Have children open Exploring Sounds and Letters and turn to page
  82. Work with them as they write a line of capital *M*'s as in past
  lessons.
- Repeat for small *m*.

❯ **Exploring Sounds and Letters** Have the children focus on the pictures on pages 82–83 in Exploring Sounds and Letters. Ask the children to write the letter *m* under the pictures whose names begin with /m/.

✳ **WORKSHOP**

- Have several **activities or centers** available to the children. During Workshop, meet with individuals or small groups of children to have them share their work. See **Classroom Support Teacher Tool Card 3** for more details about Teacher Conferencing.
- Work with children who need extra help or extra challenges.

Exploring Sounds and letters, page 82

Exploring Sounds and letters, page 83

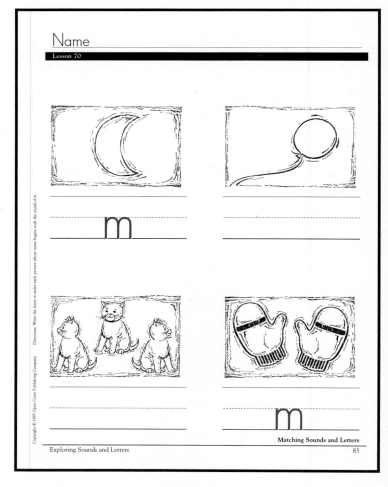

LESSON
71

●●●● Lesson Overview

New Learning

- *Nn*
- /n/

Materials

- "If You Should Meet a Crocodile," page 38 of *Pickled Peppers*
- Word Cards for the first four lines of "If You Should Meet a Crocodile"
- Picture Cards: *nails, needle, nest, newspaper, nine, noodle*
- Exploring Sounds and Letters, pages 84–85
- For each child, Uppercase and Lowercase Letter Cards: *Nn* or *Mm*
- Reproducible Master 14

Prepare Ahead

- Make a copy of Reproducible Master 14 for each child. In Workshop, label two containers, one *m* and the other *n*
- Two sets of small cards to use during Warm up: one set of capital letters and one set of small letters

---

✴ READING THE BIG BOOK

"If You Should Meet A Crocodile"
page 38 of *Pickled Peppers*

- Open *Pickled Peppers* to "If You Should Meet a Crocodile" and review the poem.
- Using the Word Cards, place the following four lines in the Pocket Chart:

If you should meet a crocodile,
Don't take a stick and poke him;
Ignore the welcome in his smile,
Be careful not to stroke him.

- Remember to say each word as you place it in the chart.
- Tell the children to close their eyes. Go through each line and reorder two words (for example, *you* and *crocodile*). Tell the children you are going to read the poem again and that they should stop you if they hear anything that sounds strange to them. Read the poem through again exactly as you have it and wait for the children to stop you. Have them tell you where each mistake is.

✳ PHONEMIC AWARENESS

Segmentation

Initial Consonants Have the children play the Spider's Web game as described in Lesson 70, or work with the puppet to segment the following words. Have the children identify the initial consonant that is dropped: *nice, ice,* /n/. It is not necessary to form a real word when the consonant is dropped.

/n/ . . . ice	/j/ . . . et	/m/ . . . ust	/d/ . . . ump
/p/ . . . et	/d/ . . . ust	/f/ . . . ill	/p/ . . . ill
/m/ . . . ist	/l/ . . . ist	/l/ . . . ast	/f/ . . . ast
/k/ . . . ast	/k/ . . . are		

✳ Oral Blending

Final Consonant Replacement At this time, you can begin to replace final consonants while working at the chalkboard. Working at the chalkboard and allowing children to see that a letter change creates a sound change will help prepare them for the phonics work that starts in Lesson 96. Continue to give the children the parts of the word to blend. But after they have successfully blended one word, change the final consonant, ask for its sound, and have the children blend the new word.

- Begin with the word *fort.* Say the first part of the word, *for,* then write it on the chalkboard. Say the final consonant /t/ and write it on the board. Ask the children to put the parts of the word together and say it back to you.

Teacher: for
Teacher: /t/. What's the word?
Everyone: fort

- Now erase the *t,* and write an *m.* Say, "Now the word ends with the letter *m,* so it doesn't end with the sound /t/ anymore. What sound does it end with? What is the new word?"
- Because you are using as replacements only letter sounds that the children are familiar with, they should be able to identify the new sounds and then blend the new word. Try the following word changes:

for . . . t	for . . . m	for . . . k
cur . . . l	cur . . . b	
moo . . . d	moo . . . n	

LETTER NAMES, SHAPES, AND SOUNDS

Warmup Divide the children evenly into two groups. Give one group of children a small letter, and the other group the matching capital letters that you prepared ahead. Tell the children that, at the signal, they must go about the room, looking at others' letters until they find their partner. Explain that they should hold up their hands when they have found their partners. Ask one of each pair of partners to say their letter's name and its sound.

The Sound of *n*

Introducing *n* Display the *Nn* Alphabet Card and say the sound /n/. Show the picture and recite the poem for /n/:

> Norman Newsome has a cold.
> His nose is noisy all through the night.
> He tries to sleep, but it just won't do.
> 'Cuz this is what his nose will do: /n/ /n/ /n/ /n/ /n/.

Recite the poem again, emphasizing the initial /n/ sounds, and asking the children to pinch their noses and join in on /n/ /n/ /n/ /n/ /n/.

Listening for Initial /n/ and /m/ Hold up and name these Picture Cards for the letter *n*: *nails, needle, nest, newspaper, noodle, nine*. Ask the children to listen for the sound /n/ at the beginning of each word.

Give each child an *Nn* or *Mm* Uppercase and Lowercase Letter Card. Ask the children to listen to the word you say. Explain that if it starts with /n/, and they have an *Nn* card, they should hold it up and say /n/. If the first sound of the word is /m/, and they have a *Mm* card, they should hold it up and say /m/. Use these words:

need	net	met	nut	
note	mice	nice	nine	
mine	nothing	now	nap	map

***Pickled Peppers* Poster** Ask the children to find the letter that makes the /n/ sound on the poster. Ask a child to go to the poster and point it out. You might want to recite the /n/ poem again. For review, ask a child to go to the poster and find the letter that comes before *n* in the alphabet.

Silly Sentences Play the of Silly Sentences game by making a sentence that is full of words with beginning /n/ sounds.

Linking the Sound to the Letter

Writing *Nn* Demonstrate how to form a capital *N*, using the oral descriptions from the earlier lesson. Have the children imitate your strokes in the air.

- Have the children open Exploring Sounds and Letters to page 84. Work with them as they complete several capital *N*'s.
- Repeat for small *n*.

❯ **Exploring Sounds and Letters** Focus the children's attention on the pictures on pages 84–85 of Exploring Sounds and Letters. Explain that some of the pictures show things whose names start with the sound /n/, and some with the sound /m/. Ask them to write the letter *n* under a picture if its name begins with the sound /n/, and an *m* under a picture if its name begins with the sound /m/.

✳ WORKSHOP

- Give each child a set of the pictures from **Reproducible Master 14**. Show the pictures and name each one before children go on to independent work. Label two containers *m* and *n*. Tell children that they can sort through the pictures and write an *m* or an *n* on each for the initial sound. Then they can place the pictures in the correct container.
- Have other activities available for children during Workshop such as **Game Corner**, **Creating Letters**, **Letter Books**, **writing folders**, and activities to reinforce letter recognition and sounds.

Exploring Sounds and Letters, page 84

Exploring Sounds and Letters, page 85

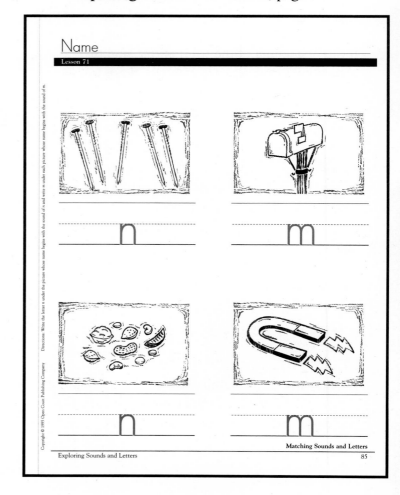

LESSON
72

••• Lesson Overview

New Learning

- *Nn*
- /n/

Materials

- "If You Should Meet a Crocodile," page 38 of *Pickled Peppers*
- Exploring Sounds and Letters, pages 86–87
- Alphabet Flash Cards
- For each child, Uppercase and Lowercase Letter Card: *Nn*
- Reproducible Master 15

Prepare Ahead

- Make a copy of **Reproducible Master 15** for each child. Cut out the pictures. In Workshop, label two containers with ____*l* and ____*n*.

✱ READING THE BIG BOOK

"If You Should Meet A Crocodile"
page 38 of *Pickled Peppers*

- Open *Pickled Peppers* to "If You Should Meet a Crocodile" and review the poem with the children.
- Go to the chalkboard or set up an easel, or use chart paper or an overhead. Tell the children they are going to help you write a story about another animal. Ask what animal they want to write about.
- Once the children have selected an animal, draw a picture of it and write its name next to the picture.
- Ask a child to start the story. Write the sentence and put the child's name next to it.
- Have another child add the next sentence. Write a story of about five to seven sentences.
- When you are done with the story, reread it. Have each child who contributed a sentence say it after you.

TEACHING TIP

This activity may be difficult for the children. Help them by picking an animal in advance and having a picture of it to show the children. Have individual children tell you something they know about the animal. Write each contribution down.

TIP FOR ENGLISH LANGUAGE LEARNERS

Maximize the potential to build language skills by pairing native English speakers with English Language Learners who share an interest in the same animal. Encourage them to work together to generate ideas for their stories.

Segmentation

Dropping Final Consonants This activity reinforces children's aware-ness of sounds in words by having them delete final consonants. Bring out the puppet and tell the children it is leaving off the ending sound of words today.

> *Teacher:* beet
> *Puppet:* bee
> *Teacher:* seen
> *Puppet:* see

Repeat and have children join the puppet on *see.*

moon	broom	beep
seed	feel	bait

✳ Oral Blending

Final Consonant Replacement Continue oral blending activities that involve some written work. Give the children the initial part of a word and then the final consonant to blend. Then change the final consonant, ask for its sound, and ask the children to blend the new word.

- Begin with the word *keep.* Say the first part of the word, *kee* and write it on the chalkboard. Say the final consonant of the word, /p/ and write it on the chalkboard. Ask the children to put the parts of the word together and say it back to you.

> *Teacher:* kee
> *Teacher:* /p/. What's the word?
> *Everyone:* keep

- Erase the *p* and write *n.* Say, "Now the word ends with the letter *n,* so it doesn't end with /p/ anymore. What sound does it end with? What's the new word?"
- Try the following word changes:

kee . . . /p/	kee . . . /n/	
hea . . . /t/	hea . . . /l/	hea . . . /p/
stea . . . /m/	stea . . . /l/	

Warmup Review the alphabet by using the Alphabet Flash Cards. When you come to a letter that the children have learned the sound of, ask them to say the sound. Point to the picture on the Alphabet Card as a reminder of its sound.

The Sound of *n*

• Review the short poem for /n/:

Norman Newsome has a cold.
His nose is noisy all the night.
He tries to sleep, but it just won't do.
'Cuz this is what his nose will do: /n/ /n/ /n/ /n/ /n/.

• Recite the poem again, emphasizing the initial /n/ and asking the children to join in on /n/ /n/ /n/ /n/ /n/.

Listening for Final /n/ Give each child an *Nn* Uppercase and Lowercase Letter Card. Tell the children that you are going to say words and that you want them to hold up their cards and say /n/ when they hear you say a word ending with /n/. Model an example for the children, then try the following words:

seen	lion	bean	beat
lean	train	track	rat
rain	green	great	spoon

Catching the Letter Train Have everyone sit in a circle and explain that the N train is getting ready to leave. Have the children make the /n/ /n/ /n/ sound. Next, remind them that to get on the train, they have to give you a ticket. Say that for this trip, the ticket is a word that starts with the /n/ sound. Walk around the circle and ask for tickets. When a child gives a word, he or she gets on the train and follows you around the room, making the /n/ sound.

Linking the Sound to the Letter

❯ **Exploring Sounds and Letters** Tell the children to open Exploring Sounds and Letters to pages 86–87. On the pages, the children will find shopping carts filled with many objects. Explain that some of the objects have names that end with /n/ and some do not. Name all the objects. Tell the children to circle the objects whose names end with /n/. On page 86 the objects are a lamp, a doll, a pan, a fan, a pen, a can, keys, and jam. On page 87 the objects are a moon, a spoon, a balloon, a chicken, a fox, and a mitt. Let children practice forming letters or writing their names on the writing line on the bottom of the page.

TEACHING TIP
You may want to have the children generate some *n* words before starting the game.

- Help children write stories about an animal.
- Give each child a set of pictures from **Reproducible Master 15.** Show the pictures and name each one before children go on to independent work. Label two containers ____*l* and ____*n.* Tell children that they can sort through the pictures and label them with an *l* or an *n* for the ending sound. Then they can place them in the appropriate container.
- Have children add *Nn* to their **Letter Books.**
- Add the Picture Cards for words that begin with /n/ to **What Sound Is It?** and let children sort them.
- Make the games **Hop Along, Bus Stop, Roller Ride, Race Track,** and **Make Tracks** available.
- Let children use the designated areas of the room to practice making their letters.
- During Workshop, hold conferences with individual children about a book from the classroom library or about a Read-Aloud selection from one of the Discovery Modules. Have the children show you what they know about how print works. Record your observations on **Observation Log 2,** Reproducible Master 29.

Exploring Sounds and Letters, page 86

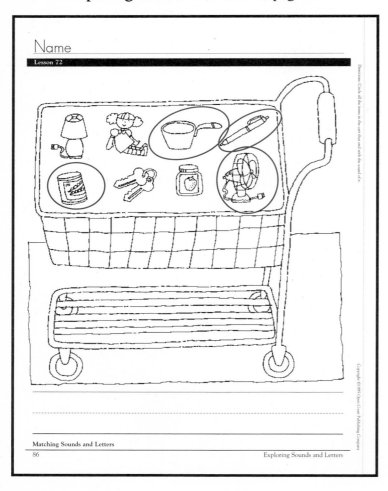

Exploring Sounds and Letters, page 87

LESSON 73

••• Lesson Overview

New Learning

- *Oo*
- Long *o* and short *o*

Materials

- "Higglety, Pigglety, Pop!" page 39 of *Pickled Peppers*
- Pocket Chart Letter Cards: *b, c, d, g, h, o, t*
- Picture Cards: *oatmeal, ocean, octopus, otter, overalls, ox*
- Exploring Sounds and Letters, pages 88–89
- For each child, Uppercase and Lowercase Letter Card: *Oo*
- Listening Collections Audiocassette
- Learning Framework Card 7
- Songs Teacher Tool Cards 4, 10
- Reproducible Masters 16 and 17

Prepare Ahead

- Make a copy of Reproducible Masters 16 and 17 for each child. Cut out the pictures. In Workshop, label three containers with *A, E,* and *O.*

✳ READING THE BIG BOOK

"Higglety, Pigglety, Pop!"
page 39 of *Pickled Peppers*

- Open *Pickled Peppers* to "Higglety, Pigglety, Pop!" Review the song with the children, then introduce the music provided on the Listening Collections Audiocassette, or use Songs Teacher Tool Card 10.
- Have the children sing the song several times with the tape. Encourage them to move around as they sing, jumping up on the word *pop.*

TIP FOR ENGLISH LANGUAGE LEARNERS

Use the Listening Collections Audiocassette to reinforce children's understanding of the song. Work in a small group with English Language Learners. Listen to the tape together, pausing frequently to practice the actions associated with the song. Children may also enjoy listening to the tape on their own.

Segmentation

Dropping Final Consonants This activity reinforces children's awareness of sounds in words by having them delete final consonants. Make
the puppet a part of this activity.

Teacher: soon
Puppet: soo
Teacher: grab
Puppet: gra

Repeat and have children join the puppet on *gra*
Have the children join the puppet on this list of words:

ba . . . ke	ma . . . ke	loo . . . p	sou . . . p
see . . . d	nee . . . d	rai . . . n	pai . . . n

✳ Oral Blending

Final Consonant Replacement In this activity, the children will make
final consonant changes with single-syllable short *o* words. Begin with
the word *mom.* Say the initial part of the word, *mo,* and write it on the
chalkboard. Say the final consonant, /m/, and write it on the chalkboard. Ask the children to put the parts of the word together and say it
back to you.

Teacher :   mo
Teacher: /m/. What's the word?
Everyone: mom.

- Now erase the *m* and write *p.* Say, "Now the word ends with the letter *p,* so it doesn't end with the sound /m/ anymore. What sound
  does it end with? What's the new word?"
- Try the following word changes:

mo . . . /m/	mo . . . /p/	mo . . . /b/
to . . . /t/	to . . . /p/	
co . . . /b/	co . . . /t/	

Warmup Review the Vowel Song; see **Songs Teacher Tool Card 4**.

The Sound of *o*

Introducing Long *o* Point to the Long *o* Alphabet Card. Encourage
children to name the letter *o* and its long *o* sound. Remind them that
the letter on the card is red because it is a vowel and that vowels are
special because they can say their names.

- Show the children these Picture Cards: *oatmeal, ocean, overalls.* Say
  the word on each card and ask children to listen for the long *o* sound
  at the beginning of the word. Have them repeat the words.

Introducing Short *o* Now point to the Short *o* Alphabet Card. Remind children that a vowel can make a sound other than its name. Say the short o sound, and recite the poem:

> Bob the Frog did not feel well at all.
> He hopped to the doctor's office.
> "Say /o/ Mr. Frog. /o/ /o/ /o/."
> "My head is hot, and my throat hurts a lot."
> "Say /o/ Mr. Frog. /o/ /o/ /o/."

- Show the children these Picture Cards: *octopus, otter, ox.* Say the word on each card and ask children to listen for the short *o* sound at the beginning of the word. Have them repeat the words.
- Say some single-syllable words. Ask children to listen carefully for the short *o* in the middle of the word. Ask children to repeat the word, and then say the short *o* sound. Try: *pot, pod, dock, rock, sock, top.*

Listening for Long and Short *o* Display the Long *o* and Short *o* Alphabet Cards. Point to the Long *o* card and say, "Sometimes the letter *o* says /ō/. Then point to the Short *o* card and say, "And sometimes it says /o/."

- Give each child an *Oo* Uppercase and Lowercase Letter Card and tell the children you are going to say some words that begin with the letter *o*. Ask them if they remember what to do when they hear a vowel say its name. If necessary, hold an *Oo* card high over your head and say the long *o* sound as a reminder. Next, ask if they remember what to do when the vowel says another sound. Scrunch down and say the sound of short *o* as a reminder. Try the following words:

oak	oasis	octopus	ox
otter	oats	oboe	overalls

- Remind the children that the vowel sound can come in the middle or end of a word, as well as the beginning. Ask the children to listen closely as you say the following words that have either the long *o* sound or the short *o* sound in the middle or at the end.

toe	top	so	no
not	got	go	know
knot	doe	dot	

Pickled Peppers Poster Ask the children to look for and point out the letter *o* (capital or small) on the poster. Next, ask for the short *o* sound.

Linking the Sound to the Letter

Grab Bag of Letters You will work with short *o* words, but this time you will change both the beginning and ending consonant to make new words.

Have in a bag Pocket Chart Letter Cards for *b, d, g,* and *h.* Put the Pocket Chart Letter Cards *ot* on the Pocket Chart. Say /o/ /t/. Then add the letter *c* to the beginning, making *cot.* Have the children say the word, then pick a letter form the bag and replace the *c* with another letter, such as *d,* and have them say *dot.* Continue with other words: *dog, hog,* and *bog.*

Writing *Oo* Review with the children how to form a capital *O.* Help them form a line of capital *O*'s on the writing line of page 88 of Exploring Sounds and Letters.

Review small o and have children write several small *o*'s on page 88 of Exploring Sounds and Letters.

❯ **Exploring Sounds and Letters** Focus the children's attention on the pictures on pages 88–89 of Exploring Sounds and Letters. Ask the children to write the letter *o* under each picture whose name contains the long *o* sound.

Exploring Sounds and Letters, page 88

Exploring Sounds and Letters, page 89

✳ WORKSHOP

- Give each child a set of pictures from **Reproducible Masters 16 and 17.** Show the pictures and name each picture before children go on to independent work. Label three containers *A, E,* and *O.* Tell the children that they can sort through their set of pictures and label them with an *A, E,* or *O* to show what vowel sound they hear in the word. Then they can place them in the appropriate container. (This may be difficult some for children but should challenge others.)

- Have other activities available for children during Workshop such as **Game Corner**, **Creating Letters**, **Letter Books**, **Writing Folders,** and activities to reinforce letter recognition and sounds.

- During Workshop, hold conferences with individual children about a book from the classroom library or about a Read-Aloud selection from one of the Discovery Modules. Have the children show you what they know about how print works. Record your observations on **Observation Log 2**, Reproducible Master 29.

LESSON
74

●●● Lesson Overview

New Learning

- *Oo*
- Short *o*

Materials

- "Higglety, Pigglety, Pop!" page 39 of *Pickled Peppers*
- Alphabet Card: Short *o*
- For each child, Uppercase and Lowercase Letter Card: *Oo*
- Listening Collections Audiocassette
- Classroom Support Teacher Tool Card 3
- Songs Teacher Tool Card 6
- Activity Sheet 14

✱ READING THE BIG BOOK

"Higglety, Pigglety, Pop!"
page 39 of *Pickled Peppers*

- Open *Pickled Peppers* to "Higglety, Pigglety, Pop!" Review the song with the children.
- Lead the children in singing the song several times with the Listening Collections Audiocassette. Encourage the children to move and stretch, jumping up on the word *pop*.
- Sit on the floor and place a ball in front of you. Invite the children to sit with you in a circle. Explain that you are going the change "Higglety, Pigglety, Pop!" to end with a new word. Tell them that when you roll the ball to someone he or she should say a word to rhyme with the changed word. Model the response by rolling the ball to a child and saying, "Higglety, pigglety *pap*! The dog has eaten the_____!" Encourage the child to answer *map*. Let the children know they can use nonsense words. Continue the game using *higglety, pigglety, poof; higglety, pigglety, pan;* or *higglety, pigglety, peep*.

* PHONEMIC AWARENESS

Segmentation

Restoring Final Consonants Have the children continue working with final consonants. This time ask them to correct the puppet by saying the whole word.

Teacher: seed
Puppet: see
Everyone: Not, see! Seed! /d/

Use the following words:

cloud	lane	steam	seem
rain	brain	train	treat
beat	feat	meet	

* Oral Blending

Final Consonant Replacement Continue the oral blending at the chalkboard, first blending one word and then changing the final consonant to make a new word. Try the following word changes:

ro . . . b	ro . . . t	ro . . . d
ho . . . p	ho . . . g	ho . . . t
no . . . t	no . . . d	
jo . . . t	jo . . . b	

LETTER NAMES, SHAPES, AND SOUNDS

Warmup Have the children sing "Apples and Bananas" as a review of vowels. See **Songs Teacher Tool Card 6** for the words and music.

The Sound of *o*

Reviewing Long *o* Review Long *o*. Point to the Long *o* Alphabet Card and ask a volunteer to say the letter and tell what sound it makes. Have the children volunteer words that start with the long *o* sound.

Reviewing Short *o* Review the poem for Short *o*:

Bob the Frog did not feel well at all.
He hopped to the doctor's office.
"Say /o/ Mr. Frog. /o/ /o/ /o/."
"My head is hot, and my throat hurts a lot."
"Say /o/ Mr. Frog. /o/ /o/ /o/."

Listening for Long and Short *o* Give each child an *Oo* Uppercase and Lowercase Letter Card and lead the children in listening for long *o* and short *o* sounds. Remind the children to stretch up high when they hear the long sound of *o* and scrunch down low if they hear the short sound of *o*. Use these words:

sob	soap	wrote	rob
top	tone	note	not
bought	boat	low	lot

Make Mine an _o_ Tell the children to listen for the sound of short _o_ in the words you are going to say. Say that you will go around the circle and say each child's name and then a single syllable word with a short vowel sound in the middle. If that child hears a short _o,_ he or she should repeat the sound, /o/. Otherwise, he or she should remain silent. Pause, and then move on to the next child. Try the following list:

| tip | **pot** | pet | pit | **dot** |
| **not** | **cot** | mitt | **hot** | **lot** |

Linking the Sound to the Letter

Word Pairs Write _top_ and _tap_ on the chalkboard. Ask the children "Which word says _top_?"

Point to _tap_ and ask a child, "What do you think the other word says?"

Write other word pairs on the chalkboard, one with the short _o_ sound and one without. Have the children identify the short _o_ words. Always repeat the word with the short _o_ sound after the children identify the correct words. Continue with these words:

| **not** | net | | pet | **pot** |
| **sock** | sack | | **hop** | hip |

✳ WORKSHOP

- Children can review the short _o_ and long _o_ vowel sounds with **Activity Sheet 14**. Be sure to name the pictures on the sheet before the children begin. Frog is ready for a trip. Frog is taking with him only the objects with short _o_ in their names. Children should circle the pictures whose names have the short _o_ sound. To challenge children, have them write the names of some of the objects Frog is taking with him on the back of the sheet. Encourage them to use what they know about the sounds of letters as they write. Explain that, if they like, they can draw pictures of the objects.
- Have several activities or centers available to the children.
- During Workshop, **hold conference** with children individually about a book or Read-Aloud. Have them show you what they know about how print works. Record your observations on **Observation Log 2**. For information about teacher conferencing, see **Classroom Support Teacher Tool Card 3**.

TIP FOR ENGLISH LANGUAGE LEARNERS

Encourage English Language Learners to feel free to question what they want to know about, to explain problems they are having, and to share and evaluate their own ideas for solving those problems. You might want to pair English Language Learners with native English-speaking children and have them review one of the songs or poems in Pickled Peppers. Encourage them to share what they know about the song or poem and what they notice in the illustrations.

LESSON
75

●●● Lesson Overview

New Learning

- *Pp*
- /p/

Materials

- "Sing a Song of Sixpence," pages 20–21 of *Pickled Peppers*
- Picture Cards: *pail, peas, pie, pig, post, pot, potatoes*
- Exploring Sounds and Letters, pages 90–91
- Alphabet Flash Cards
- For each child, Uppercase and Lowercase Letter Card: *Pp*
- Listening Collections Audiocassette
- Songs Teacher Tool Card 11
- Reproducible Master 18
- Home/School Connection 13

Prepare Ahead

- Make a copy of **Reproducible Master 18** for each child. Cut out the pictures. Label two containers *p* _____ and _____ *p*.
- Ball for The Ship is Loaded with _____ game

✳ READING THE BIG BOOK

"Sing a Song of Sixpence"
pages 20–21 of *Pickled Peppers*

- Open *Pickled Peppers* to the table of contents and locate "Sing a Song of Sixpence." Ask a child to help locate the page number, then turn to it. Point out the title of the song and the name of the illustrator.
- Read the song through two or three times, pointing to the words as you read. Ask the children to find pictures of the queen, the king, and the maid on pages 20–21.
- Play the song on the Listening Collections Audiocassette or sing it for the children. See **Songs Teacher Tool Card 11.**

✳ PHONEMIC AWARENESS

Segmentation

Restoring Final Consonants Continue to have the children restore final consonants. Tell them to correct the puppet by making the whole word.

Teacher: gap
Puppet: ga
Everyone: No, *gap*! /p/

Use the following words:

had	heat	mean
line	soon	rode
sun	run	make

✳ Oral Blending

Final Consonant Replacement Continue to change the final consonants of words. Write *park* on the chalkboard.

Teacher: par
Teacher: /k/. What's the word?
Everyone: park

Erase the *k* and write *t*. Say, "Now the word ends with the letter *t*. It doesn't end with /k/ anymore. What's the new word?"
Try the following word changes:

par . . . k	par . . . t	
lea . . . k	lea . . . f	lea . . . n
mea . . . t	mea . . . n	mea . . . l

LETTER NAMES, SHAPES, AND SOUNDS

Warmup Take the children through a review of the alphabet by using the Alphabet Flash Cards. When you come to a letter the children have learned the sound of, ask them to say the sound. Point to the picture on the letter's Alphabet Card as a reminder of its sound.

The Sound of *p*

Reviewing *p* Remember that the children have worked with *p* before, so encourage them to give you as much information as they can on their own about the letter and its sound.

• Review the short poem for the letter *p*:

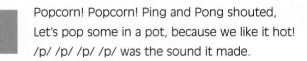

Popcorn! Popcorn! Ping and Pong shouted,
Let's pop some in a pot, because we like it hot!
/p/ /p/ /p/ /p/ was the sound it made.

Recite the poem again, emphasizing the initial /p/ sounds and asking the children to hop up and down like corn popping as they say /p/ /p/ /p/ /p/.

Listening for Initial and Final /p/ Hold up and name each of these Picture Cards: *pail, peas, pie, pig, post, pot, potatoes.* Ask the children to listen for /p/ at the beginning of each word.

- Give each child a *Pp* Uppercase and Lowercase Letter Card. Tell the children you are going to say words and you want them to hold up the card when they hear a word beginning with /p/. Use these words:

pan	pot	lot	lake	pack
proud	loud	pile	pill	pirate

- Remind the children that words can also end with /p/. Repeat the activity with these words:

sleep	deep	den	pup	cup
can	cap	trap	top	ton

***Pickled Peppers* Poster** Ask the children to look on the poster for the letter that makes the /p/ sound. Ask a child to go to the poster and point out the letter. For review, ask a child to find the letter *a* (capital or small).

The Ship is Loaded with _____ Game Play the Ship is Loaded with _____ game, asking the children to name words beginning with the sound /p/. Sit in a circle with the children and roll a ball to a child to start the game. Say, "The ship is loaded with peanuts." Tell that child to load the ship with another /p/ word and roll the ball to another child.

Linking the Sound to the Letter

Word Changes Write *ip* on the chalkboard, and say the letters. Then say, "Let's change *ip* into *lip*. If we want to change *ip* into /l/ /i/ /p/, we have to put the /l/ sound at the beginning. What letter do we need?" After the children give the correct answer, have them change *lip* to *hip* and then to *dip*. Continue with these word sets: *pe* to *pet, pep, pen, peg*.

Writing *Pp* Review how to form a capital *P*.

- Have children write capital *P*'s on the writing line on page 90 in Exploring Sounds and Letters.
- Review with the children how to write small *p*'s.

❯ **Exploring Sounds and Letters** Focus the children's attention on the pictures on pages 90–91 of Exploring Sounds and Letters. Say each picture name. Ask the children to write the letter *p* under the picture only if the word that names the picture starts with /p/.

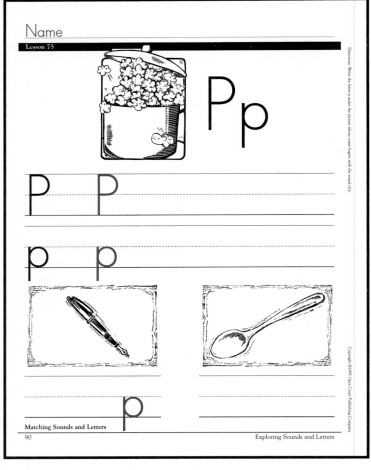

Exploring Sounds and Letters, page 90

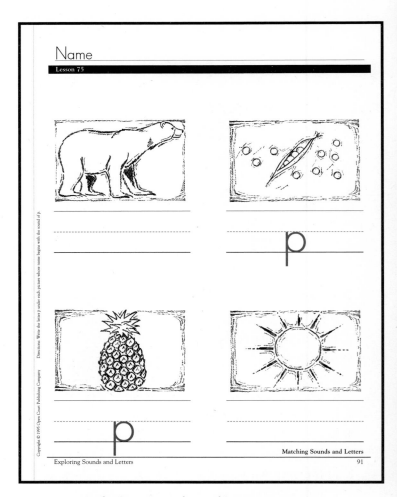

Exploring Sounds and Letters, page 91

✱ WORKSHOP

- Give each child a set of pictures cut from **Reproducible Master 18**. Show the pictures and name each one before children go on to independent work. Tell the children to sort through the pictures and then place them in the appropriate container that you prepared ahead, according to whether the words begin or end with the /p/ sound.
- Have children add *Pp* to their **Letter Book**.
- Add Picture Cards for words that begin with /p/ to **What Sound Is It?** and let children sort them.
- Make the following games available to the children, **Hop Along, Bus Stop, Roller Ride, Race Track,** and **Make Tracks**.

Home/School Connection Hand out **Home/School Connection 13** and send it home with the children. It suggests games families can play together to reinforce learning letter sounds.

LESSON 76

● ● ● Lesson Overview

New Learning

- *Qq*
- /kw/

Materials

- "Sing a Song of Sixpence," pages 20–21 of *Pickled Peppers*
- Picture Cards: *quail, queen, quilt*
- Exploring Sounds and Letters, pages 92–93
- Alphabet Flash Cards
- Individual Alphabet-Sound Card
- For each child, one Uppercase and Lowercase Letter Card: *Qq*
- One set of Uppercase and Lowercase Letter Cards: *Hh–Qq*
- Listening Collections Audiocassette
- Game Mats

✳ READING THE BIG BOOK

"Sing a Song of Sixpence"
pages 20–21 of *Pickled Peppers*

- Turn to "Sing a Song of Sixpence" and read the song through twice.
- Play the song on the Listening Collections Audiocassette or sing it for the children. Then sing it with the children and have them clap on the rhyming words in each verse: *rye/pie*; *money/honey*; *clothes/nose*; *sing/king*.
- Point to the words *four and twenty* and say them. Explain that *four and twenty* is just another way of saying the number *twenty-four.* As a group, count all the birds in the picture on pages 20–21 and try to find all twenty-four.

Segmentation

Final Consonants   Have the children repeat the final consonant sounds of words along with the puppet.

Teacher: pat
Puppet and class: /t/ /t/ /t/ /t/

Use the following words:

pot	pet	put	pit
pan	pane	pen	pun
peal	pail	pull	pill

✳ Oral Blending

Final Consonant Replacement   In this exercise the children will be replacing the final consonant sounds of words that end in silent *e.* Tell the children that sometimes the letter *e* appears at the end of a word as a silent helper who reminds another vowel to say its name. Then give them some examples of long vowel words ending in a consonant and a silent *e.* For the replacement exercise, give the children the first part of the word and then the final consonant sound. Help them with the replacement consonant and ask them to blend the new word.

- Write the examples on the chalkboard and point to the vowels and the silent *e*'s. Start with the word *mate.* Say /m/ /ā/ and write *ma.* Leave a space, and then write *e.* Say /t/ and write *t* in the space. Say *mate.*
- Erase *t* and write *k.* Ask, "What happens when I change the *t* to a *k*? Remember, the *e* is still there helping."
  Teacher: ma
  Teacher: /k/; make

Try the following word changes:

la . . . ke	la . . . te		la . . . me	la . . . ce
ra . . . ke	ra . . . te		sa . . . ke	sa . . . me
sa . . . fe	sa . . . ne			

Have the children repeat each word.

Warmup   Take the children through a quick review of the alphabet by using the Alphabet Flash Cards. When you come to a letter that the children have learned the sound of, ask them to say the sound. Point to the picture on the letter's Alphabet Card as a reminder of its sound.

The Sound of *q*

Introducing *q* Display the *Qq* Alphabet Card and say its sound, /kw/. Show the picture for the /kw/ sound and recite the short poem for the letter *q*:

Quincy the duck couldn't quite quack,
He said /kw/ /kw/ /kw/,
But he left off the ack!
Quincy kept trying, but all he could say was:
/kw/ /kw/ /kw/ /kw/ /kw/!

Recite the poem again, emphasizing the initial /kw/ sounds. Explain that the letter *q* needs a *u* after it in order to say /kw/. Tell them that *q* is always followed by a *u* in real words in English.

Listening for Initial /kw/ Hold up and say the word on each of these Picture Cards: *quail, queen, quilt.* Ask children to listen for the /kw/ sound at the beginning of each word.

Give each child a *Qq* Uppercase and Lowercase Letter Card. Have the children hold up their cards and say the /kw/ sound when they hear you say a word that begins with the /kw/ sound. Try these words:

quite	write	quail	quaint
paint	queer	quick	quiet
quest	pest	quote	

***Pickled Peppers* Poster** Tell the children to look for and point to the letter *q* (capital or small) on the poster. Ask what Quincy the Duck says.

Catching the Letter Train Use the **Catching the Letter Train** game as a way to review the letter sounds *Hh–Qq*. This time give everyone one Uppercase and Lowercase Letter Card from the group, *Hh–Qq,* and tell them to line up behind you. Tell the children that the train is going to stop at several towns, and that when you call out the name of the town, everyone with a card with the letter that makes the first sound in the name should get off the train. Then, tell the children to make train sounds and lead them around the room to different points. At each, stop and call out the name of the "station," for example, "Now approaching Hollister. Anyone holding the *H* card must get off here." Continue around the room, until all children have left the train.

Linking the Sound to the Letter

Writing *Qq* Demonstrate how to form a capital *Q* and help the children to write capital *Q*'s on page 92 of Exploring Sounds and Letters.

Do the same with small *q*.

➤ **Exploring Sounds and Letters** Focus the children's attention on the pictures on pages 92–93 of Exploring Sounds and Letters. Explain that some of the pictures show things whose names have the /kw/ sound in them. Name each picture. Ask the children to write the letter *q* under a picture if its name begins with a /kw/ sound.

✶ WORKSHOP

- Introduce the **Zoo** game to the **Game Corner**. Use the Zoo Game Mat and the Individual Alphabet-Sound Cards. In this game, players spin or roll the cubes and move the marker the correct number of spaces. They then draw a card unless they land on a "lose turn" space. Players draw an Individual Alphabet-Sound Card, name the letter, the sound of the letter, and a word that begins with the sound. Use the letters and sounds already introduced in class.

- Have other activities available for children during Workshop, such as the **Game Corner**, **Creating Letters**, **Letter Books**, and other activities to reinforce letter recognition and sounds.

Exploring Sounds and Letters, page 92

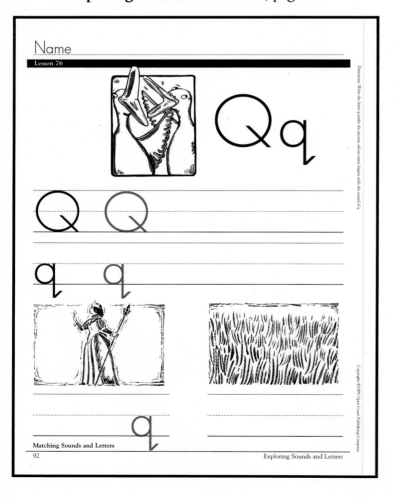

Exploring Sounds and Letters, page 93

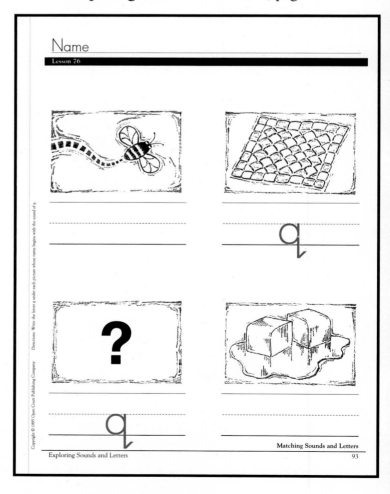

LESSON
77

● ● ● Lesson Overview

New Learning

- *Rr*
- /r/

Materials

- "Sing a Song of Sixpence," pages 20–21 of *Pickled Peppers*
- Picture Cards: *raccoon, radio, red, rice, rock, rug, ruler*
- Exploring Sounds and Letters, pages 94–95
- For each child, Uppercase and Lowercase Letter Card: *Rr*
- Listening Collections Audiocassette
- Songs Teacher Tool Card 11

Prepare Ahead

- A set of Uppercase and Lowercase Letter Cards in a bag

✳ READING THE BIG BOOK

"Sing a Song of Sixpence"
pages 20–21 of *Pickled Peppers*

- Play the song on the Listening Collections Audiocassette or sing it for the children. (See **Songs Teacher Tool Card 11**.)
- Look at the line "Four and twenty blackbirds, baked in a pie." Ask the children to think of all the kinds of pie they have had. Have a child name a kind of pie, change the line, and then have everyone repeat the changed line:

Four and twenty *apples,* baked in a pie.

Four and twenty *blueberries* baked in a pie, etc.

Segmentation

Final Consonants Have the children repeat the final consonant sound of each word with the puppet.

Teacher: leaf
Puppet and class: /f/

Use the following words:

sat	job	attic	read
leaf	twig	but	poke
seal	cream	seen	

✳ Oral Blending

Final Consonant Replacement Continue to have the children do oral blending with long vowel words ending in a consonant and a silent *e*. Remember to give the children the first part of the word and then the final consonant sound. Help them with the replacement consonant and ask them to blend the new word.

- Tell the children you are going to say words that have the silent *e* at the end. Remind them that the final *e* is telling the vowel to say its name. Start with *cope.* Say /k/ /ō/, and write *co   e* on the chalkboard. Say /p/ and write *p* on the chalkboard to complete the word.

Teacher: co
Teacher: /p/; cope

- Erase the *p* and write *n.* Ask, "What happens when I change the *p* to *n?* Remember, the *e* is still there helping."
- Try the following word changes:

co . . . pe	co . . . ne	co . . . de	
ba . . . se	ba . . . ke		
fa . . . ke	fa . . . de	fa . . . te	fa . . . me

Warmup Conduct a quick warmup by playing the Sing Your Way to ____ game. Use the Uppercase and Lowercase Letter Cards in a bag that you prepared ahead. Ask a child to draw one and hold it up, but not name it. Then have the class sing its way to that letter. If the letter selected is one the children know the sound of, ask them to say it.

The Sound of *r*

Introducing *r* Display the *Rr* Alphabet Card and say the letter's sound, /r/.

- Show the picture for the /r/ sound and recite the short poem for /r/:

Rosie the Robot just runs and runs /r/ /r/ /r/,
Racing around to get her chores done /r/ /r/ /r/.
Running here, running there /r/ /r/ /r/.
Running almost everywhere /r/ /r/ /r/.

- Repeat the poem, emphasizing the initial /r/ sounds, and asking the children to make the sound of the robot: /r/ /r/ /r/, /r/ /r/ /r/.

Listening for Initial /r/ Hold up and name each of these Picture Cards: *raccoon, radio, red, rice, rock, rug, ruler.*
- Ask the children to listen for the /r/ sound at the beginning of the words: Have them repeat each word and the sound /r/.
- Give each child an *Rr* Uppercase and Lowercase Letter Card. Tell the children you are going to say words and that you want them to hold up the card and say /r/ when they hear a word beginning with the /r/ sound. Use the following words:

rake	take	**raft**	**rat**
rain	pain	**rent**	**reel**
run	**roof**	pool	**rise**

***Pickled Peppers* Poster** Ask the children to look on the poster and point out the letter (capital or small) that makes the /r/ sound. Review by asking a child to find the letter *d* (capital or small) and name its picture. Say, "What sound is Dinah making with her feet?"

Words, Words Have children list words that begin with the /r/ sound. Write the words on the chalkboard. Add words to the list as the children think of them during the day.

Linking the Sound to the Letter
Word Pairs Write *roast* and *coast* on the board. Ask, "Which word says *roast?*" Ask a child to come to the board and point to the word. Say, "That's right. /r/ . . . oast has an /r/ at the beginning." Point to *coast* and ask another child, "What do you think this word says?" Try the following pairs of words:

roll	toll	sound	round
rip	sip	rocket	socket

Writing *Rr* Demonstrate how to form a capital *R* and help children write capital *R*'s on page 94 of Exploring Sounds and Letters.
Do the same with small *r.*

➤ Exploring Sounds and Letters Have the children focus on the pictures on pages 94–95 of Exploring Sounds and Letters. Explain that some of the pictures show things whose names begin with the /r/ sound. Name each picture. Ask the children to write the letter *r* under

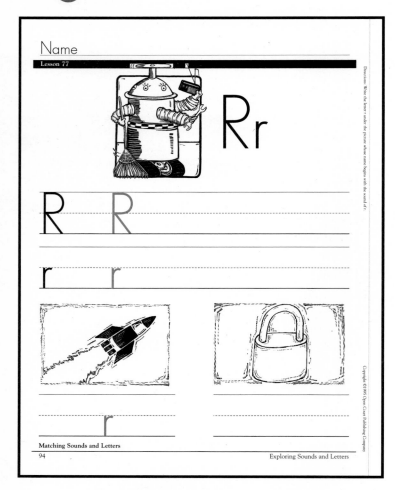

Exploring Sounds and Letters, page 94

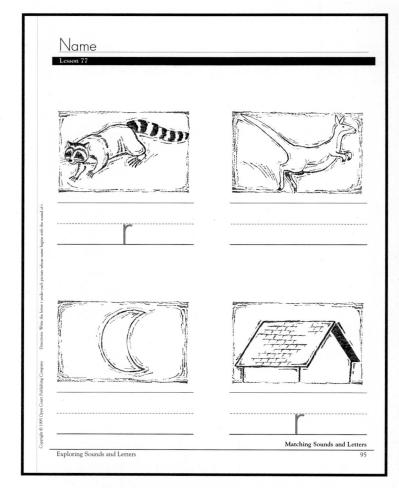

Exploring Sounds and Letters, page 95

the picture whose name begins with the /r/ sound. When everyone has
finished, go back and review the other words, identify the initial
sounds, and have children write the initial letters under each. Help them
as needed.

✳ **WORKSHOP**

- Have children add *Rr* to their **Letter Books**.
- Encourage the children to play the **Ordering Letters** game.
- Add the Picture Cards for words that begin with /r/ to **What Sound Is It?** and have the children sort the cards by sound.
- Make the games **Hop Along, Bus Stop, Roller Ride, Race Track, Make Tracks,** and **Zoo** available.

LESSON 78

●●● Lesson Overview

New Learning

- *Rr*
- /r/

Materials

- "Sing a Song of Sixpence," pages 20–21 of *Pickled Peppers*
- Alphabet Flash Cards
- For each child, Uppercase and Lowercase Letter Card: *Rr*
- Listening Collections Audiocassette
- Activity Sheet 15

✳ READING THE BIG BOOK

"Sing a Song of Sixpence"
pages 20–21 of *Pickled Peppers*

- Read the poem through again. Pause each time you come to the second half of the rhyming pairs, *rye/pie*, *money/honey*, etc., and let the children fill in the word.
- Ask children to point out the clothes, the honey, and the bread, etc. in the picture.
- Say *rye/pie* and then encourage the children to generate more rhymes for these words. Call on them one by one to offer a rhyme. Help them out by giving them an initial sound if necessary.
- End the session by having everyone sing the song along with the Listening Collections Audiocassette.

Segmentation

Dropping Final Consonants This segmentation activity is a variation of the previous ones, in which the puppet left out the final consonant sounds. Ask the children to listen to what the puppet says and to tell to you what it wants to sing about. Tell them to repeat the sound the puppet has left out.

Puppet: I want to sing about ice crea . . .
Everyone: ice cream, /m/ /m/ /m/ /m/
Puppet: I want to sing about the sunshi...
Everyone: sunshine, /n/ /n/ /n/ /n/

Try the following words:
the stars, so bri . . . /t/
a big glass of mil . . . /k/
lot of money in my pocke . . . /t/
moon at ni . . . /t/
a long-necked gira . . . /f/
a monkey with a long tai . . . /l/
a little blackbir . . . /d/

✳ Oral Blending

Final Consonant Replacement In this activity the children will continue to replace final consonants, however, the next few lessons will also include sets of words that all begin with initial consonant blends. The use of these words is intended to help the children begin to hear these blends. In later lessons, they will look more closely at initial blends.

Try the following word changes:

gree . . . t	gree . . . n	gree . . . d
brai . . . d	brai . . . n	
spoo . . . n	spoo . . . l	spoo . . . f
tri . . . p	tri . . . m	
fla . . . t	fla . . . g	

Warmup Lead the children through a review of the alphabet by using the Alphabet Flash Cards. When you come to a letter that the children have learned the sound of, ask them to say the sound. Point to the picture on the letter's Alphabet Card as a reminder of its sound.

The Sound of *r*

Reviewing *r* Because the children worked with *r* in the previous lesson, encourage them to give you as much information about the letter and its sound as they can on their own.
• Review the short poem for the letter *r*:

Rosie the Robot just runs and runs /r/ /r/ /r/,
Racing around to get her chores done /r/ /r/ /r/.
Running here, running there /r/ /r/ /r/
Running almost everywhere /r/ /r/ /r/.

- Recite the poem again, emphasizing the initial /r/ sounds and asking the children to make the /r/ sound like a robot.

Listening for Final /r/ Give each child an *Rr* Uppercase and Lowercase Letter Card. Tell the children that you are going to say words and that you want them to hold up the card and say /r/ when they hear you say a word that ends with the /r/ sound. Try the following words:

clear	hear	head	tour	poor
fair	fate	flour	stir	her

Pickled Peppers **Poster** Ask a volunteer to go to the poster and find and name the letters in order from *a* to *e* (capital or small).

Silly Sentences Game Play the Silly Sentences game by making a sentence that is full of words with beginning with /r/.

Linking the Sound to the Letter

Word Pairs Write *care* and *cake* on the chalkboard and say *care*.

Say, "Which word says *care*?" Ask a child to come to the board and point to *care*.

"That's right /k/ /ā/ /r/. *Care* has /r/ at the end." Point to *cake* and ask another child, "What do you think the other word says?"

Try the following pairs of words:

deer	deep	store	stone
cheep	cheer	steep	steer

✳ WORKSHOP

- Children can review the final /r/ sound with **Activity Sheet 15.** Remember to name each picture first. Tell children to write an *r* in the blank if the picture name ends with the /r/ sound.
- Have other activities available for children during Workshop, such as **Game Corner, Creating Letters,** and **Letter Books.**

LESSON 79

● ● ● ● ## Lesson Overview

New Learning

- *Ss*
- /s/

Materials

- "Sing a Song of Sixpence," pages 20–21 of *Pickled Peppers*
- Picture Cards: *sack, sandals, seal, seven, six, sock*
- Exploring Sounds and Letters, pages 96–97
- Alphabet Flash Cards
- For each child, Uppercase and Lowercase Letter Card: *Ss* or *Rr*

Prepare Ahead

- Materials for a play based on the song, such as a pile of flour, a pie pan, towels to use as robes for the king and queen, a crown for the king and queen, a baker's hat, an apron for the maid, coins, bread, paper birds (optional), string

✴ READING THE BIG BOOK

"Sing a Song of Sixpence"
page 20–21 of *Pickled Peppers*

- Read the song through once. By now, the children should know the song very well, so they will enjoy performing a little play to go along with its verses. You can give the children simple roles and read the song as they act it out.
- You might want to have the characters for each verse set up in different corners of the room. As you read a verse, walk or gesture toward the appropriate corner.

TIP FOR ENGLISH LANGUAGE LEARNERS

Before the whole class acts out the song, work with English Language Learners to practice the different roles in the song—king, queen, baker, and maid. As you read the song, have the children perform the actions. Observing children as they act out the roles is a good way to assess their understanding of the song. Acting out the song in small groups will give children the confidence they need to participate with the whole class.

Characters:

King: (wearing crown and robe)

Queen: (wearing crown and robe)

Baker: (Wearing baker's hat or white clothing)

Maid: (Wearing an apron)

Blackbirds: (Any number of children who sing and flap their arms about)

Sing a song of sixpence, a pocketful of rye,

Four and twenty blackbirds, baked in a pie. (Baker sifts flour through his
fingers and tosses it into the pie pan.)

When the pie was opened, the birds began to sing.

Wasn't that a dainty dish to set before the king? (The blackbirds come out
from hiding and flutter about the room.)

The king was in his counting house, counting out the money.

The queen was in the parlor, eating bread and honey. (The king sits at the
table stacking his coins while the queen is munching on bread.)

The maid was in the garden, hanging out the clothes,

When down came a blackbird, and pecked at her nose. (The maid is hanging
clothes over a string line, when a blackbird character flies by and
pretends to pinch her nose.)

✳ PHONEMIC AWARENESS

Segmentation

Dropping Final Consonants This segmentation activity is a variation
of the previous ones, in which the puppet left out the final consonant
sounds. Ask the children to listen to what the puppet says and to tell
you what they hear. Tell them to repeat the sound the puppet has left
out.

Puppet: I hear the horn of a tru . . .

Everyone: I hear the horn of a truck, /k/ /k/ /k/ /k/

Do the following words:

pitter patter of rai . . . /n/

beat of a dru . . . /m/

the roar of the lio . . . /n/

a croaking fro . . . /g/

the ring of a telepho . . . /n/

the siren of an ambulan . . . /s/

✳ Oral Blending

Final Consonant Replacement In this activity the children will continue to concentrate on the final consonant sound of words ending in
silent *e*. As before, say the first part of the word and write the word on
the chalkboard, leaving a space for the missing consonant. Then say the
consonant sound and fill in the blank with the letter. The sample words
in this exercise will start with consonant blends simply to give the children more experience with hearing the blends.

Remind the children that the silent *e* is helping the vowel to say its name. Use the following words:

fla . . . ke   fla . . . me

stri . . . pe   stri . . . ke   stri . . . de

LETTER NAMES, SHAPES, AND SOUNDS

Warmup Review the alphabet by using the Alphabet Flash Cards. If you come to a consonant or vowel that the children have learned the sound of, ask them the sound. Point to the picture on the Alphabet Card as a reminder of the sound.

The Sound of *s*

Reviewing *s* Because the children have worked with *s* before, encourage them to give you as much information about the letter and its sound as they can on their own.

Show the Alphabet Card and review the poem for /s/:

Sue buys sausages on Saturday.

Sam cooks sausages on Sunday.

The sausages sizzle /s/ /s/ /s/ /s/ /s/ /s/ when hot.

Sam eats sausages, but Sue does not.

Listening for Initial /s/ and /r/ Hold up and name each of these Picture Cards: *sack, sandals, seal, seven, six, sock.*

- Ask children to listen for the /s/ sound at the beginning of each word.
- Give each child an *Ss* or an *Rr* Uppercase and Lowercase Letter Card. Using the following words, follow the established procedure:

sent   rent   red   said

sand   sight   right   rag

rail   sail   set

***Pickled Peppers* Poster** Ask the children to look for and point to the letter *s* (capital or small) on the poster. Conduct a quick review by asking another child to find the letter *f* (capital or small) and name its picture and sound.

Catching the Letter Train Have the children say /s/ /s/ /s/ as you lead the S train around the room. Explain that a ticket is a word beginning with the sound /s/.

Linking the Sound to the Letter

Grab Bag of Letters and Words Put the letters *ad* on the chalkboard and say /a/ /d/. Then add the letter *s* to the beginning, making *sad*.

- Write the word again directly beneath. Erase the *d* and replace it with *m*, making *Sam*. Capitalize the *s* in *sam* and remind the children that names begin with a capital letter.

- Write *Sam* again, then erase the *m* and write *t,* making *sat.* Continue with other substitutions.
- Repeat the process starting with the letters *am* and making the words *ham, tam, tap,* etc.
- When you are finished, your lists may look like this:

sad	ham
Sam	tam
sat	tap
pat	rap
hat	ran

Have the children say each word when you make the change.
- Then make a sentence on the chalkboard: *Sad Sam sat on a hat.* Replace *hat* with *cat, bat,* and *mat.* Read the new sentence each time.

Writing Ss Review with the children how to make the capital *S.* Work with them as they practice capital *S*'s on the writing lines on page 96 of Exploring Sounds and Letters.

Do the same for small *s.*

❯ **Exploring Sounds and Letters** Focus the children's attention on the pictures on pages 96–97 of Exploring Sounds and Letters. Explain that some of the pictures show things whose names start with /s/. Ask them to write the letter *s* under a picture only if its name starts with /s/.

✳ WORKSHOP

- Tell the children they can play **The Ship is Loaded with _____** game together in small groups as described in Lesson 75. Explain that they can roll the ball back and forth, taking turns saying words that begin with /s/.
- Have other activities available for children during Workshop, such as **Game Corner, Creating Letters, and Letter Books**.

Exploring Sounds and Letters, page 96

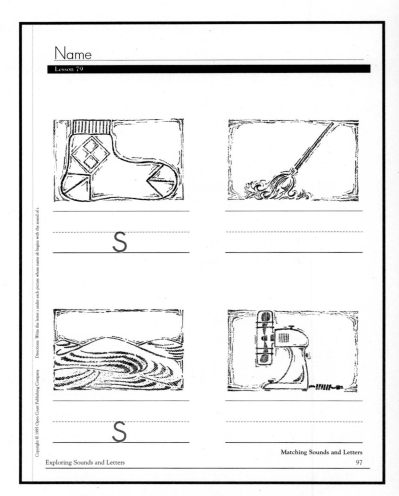

Exploring Sounds and Letters, page 97

LESSON

80

••• Lesson Overview

New Learning

- *Tt*
- /t/

Materials

- "Rhyme," page 27 of *Pickled Peppers*
- Picture Cards: *table, tail, telephone, tie, toast, tomatoes, turtle*
- Exploring Sounds and Letters, pages 98–99
- For each child, one Uppercase and Lowercase Letter Card: *Tt* or *Nn*
- Reproducible Master 19

Prepare Ahead

- Make a copy of Reproducible Master 19 for each child and cut out the pictures. Label one container ___*p*, and another one ___*t*.
- A set of Uppercase and Lowercase Letter Cards in a bag

✳ READING THE BIG BOOK

"Rhyme"
page 27 of *Pickled Peppers*

- Open *Pickled Peppers* to the table of contents and find "Rhyme." Have a child help you find the page number, then turn to that page.
- Point to and read the title, the author's name, and the illustrator's name. Read the poem, then talk about the simplicity of the title. Ask the children what they would name this poem.
- Read the poem through again, with as much expression as possible. Let your voice get louder and louder as you describe the storm.
- Help the children to learn the first three lines of each verse, so they can join in.
- Ask the children to identify all the rhymes for *thunder*: *dunder, blunder, plunder, wonder.*

Segmentation

Dropping Final Consonants Continue to have the children help the puppet say what it sees. Ask them to repeat the sound that the puppet leaves off.

Puppet: I see...

Puppet: I see a pair of mitten.

Everyone: I see a pair of mitten, /z/ /z/ /z/ /z/

Puppet: I see . . .

Do the following words:

a huge dinosau . . . /r/

a delicious mushroo . . . /m/

a small ladybu . . . /g/

a knife and a for . . . /k/

a prickly cactu . . . /s/

✳ Oral Blending

Blending Consonant-Vowel-Consonant in Story Contexts In this activity, you will return to purely oral work. Here, you will begin orally to blend words, sound by sound. Working with single-syllable words, you will make a string of separate sounds that the children will then blend together. Placing this activity within a story context will hold children's attention, as well as give them clues to the words to be blended. The clue will not be too strong, however as you want the children to process the sounds on their own. Remember, this is purely oral work. Children will be listening for the separate sounds and then blending them together.

Teacher: I found a shiny red /b/ /ē/ /n/
And I planted it in a pot.
What did I find?

Class: a bean!

Teacher: I gave it water
when it was /h/ /o/ /t/.
When it was what?

Class: hot!

Teacher: It grew and grew
into a big red /v/ /ī/ /n/.
It grew into a what?

Class: a vine!

Teacher: It's a pretty red plant
and it suits me /f/ /ī/ /n/.
How does it suit me?

Class: fine!

LETTER NAMES, SHAPES, AND SOUNDS

Warmup Have the children warm up by playing the Sing Your Way to _____ game. Use the set of Uppercase and Lowercase Letter Cards in a bag that you have prepared ahead. Ask a child to draw one out, hold it up, and say its sound. Then have the children sing their way to that letter as a group.

The Sound of *t*

Reviewing *t* Because the children have worked with *t* before, encourage them to give you as much information about the letter and its sound as they can on their own. Review the short poem for /t/:

> Tom Tuttle's timer ticks like this: /t/ /t/ /t/ /t/ /t/ /t/.
> Tonight Tom Tuttle wants tomatoes on toast.
> He sets his timer. Listen carefully /t/ /t/ /t/ /t/ /t/ /t/.
> What sound would the timer make if you set it? /t/ /t/ /t/ /t/ /t/.

Listening for Initial and Final /t/ Hold up and name each of these Picture Cards: *table, tail, telephone, tie, toast, tomatoes, turtle.* Ask children to listen for the /t/ sound at the beginning of each word.

- Give each child a *Tt* or an *Nn* Uppercase and Lowercase Letter Card. Tell the children you are going to say words, and that if they have a *Tt* card, you want them to hold up the card and say /t/ when they hear you say a word beginning with the /t/ sound. If they have an *Nn* card, you want them to hold up the *Nn* card and say /n/ when you say a word that begins with the /n/ sound.

tip	nip	nail	tail
toad	take	never	tooth
twist	tough	name	

- Repeat the activity using words that end with /t/ or /n/.

lion	lit	gate	boat	burn
learn	meet	seat	beat	bean

***Pickled Peppers* Poster** After the children have looked for and pointed out the letter *t* (capital or small), ask two individuals to find the *s* and the *g*.

Word Braids Have the children stand in a close circle. Explain that you want them to think of words that start with the sound /t/. Tell them that everyone who says a /t/ word gets "braided" into the circle.

- Show them that they can make a braid by crossing their arms and taking the hands of the child on either side of them.

    Teacher: Now we will make a T braid.
               Kathy, tell me a word that will help make the T braid?
    Kathy: Tail!

- Kathy then crosses her arms in front of her and takes the hands of the two children on either side of her.

- Ask the question again and name another child. When everyone has been braided in, say:

> Now we have made a T braid,
> and now we can unbraid it!

- Then have everyone twist around, going under the upper arm to uncross, or unbraid, all of the arms.

Linking the Sound to the Letter

Grab Bag of Letters and Words   Put the letters *a t* on the chalkboard. Say /a/ /t/. Then add a capital letter *P* to the beginning, making *Pat.* Write the word again directly beneath.

- Erase the *P,* and replace it with an *s*, making *sat.* Continue, adding the repeat word to the list and then changing it into a new one. When done, your list may look like this:

Pat

sat

cat

rat

fat

- Use the words to make a sentence on the board: *Pat sat on a fat cat.*
- Replace *cat* with *rat,* and then *bat.* Read the new sentence each time. Have the children say the sentence after you.

Writing *Tt*   Review with the children how to make a capital *T* and help children write capital *T*'s on the writing lines on page 98 of Exploring Sounds and Letters.

Do the same with small *t.*

❯ **Exploring Sounds and Letters**   Focus the children's attention on the pictures on pages 98–99 of Exploring Sounds and Letters. Explain that some of the pictures show things whose names start with the /t/ sound. Ask the children to write a capital *T* under those pictures. Review the pictures again. Tell the children that one of the pictures shows something that ends with the /t/ sound. Ask them to write a small *t* under it.

✱ WORKSHOP

- Give each child a set of pictures from **Reproducible Master 19.** Show the pictures and name each one before children go on to independent work. Tell the children they can sort through the pictures and label them with a *p* or a *t* for the ending sound. Then they can place them in the appropriate container that you have prepared ahead.
- Have other activities available for children during Workshop such as **Game Corner, Creating Letters,** and **Letter Books**.

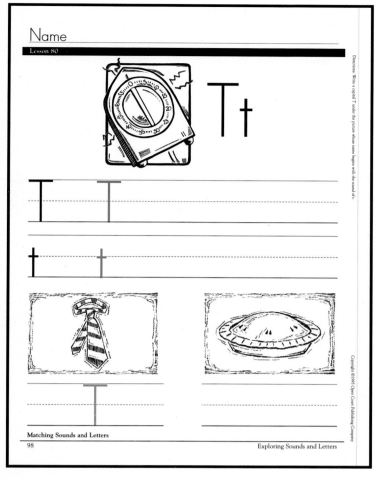

Exploring Sounds and Letters, page 98

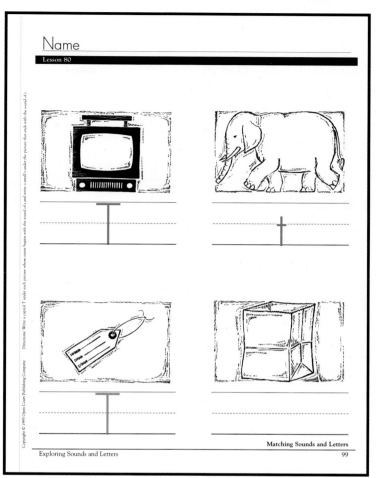

Exploring Sounds and Letters, page 99

LESSON
81

Lesson Overview

New Learning

- *Uu*
- Long *u* and short *u*

Materials

- "Rhyme," page 27 of *Pickled Peppers*
- Pocket Chart Letter Cards: *b, d, g, r, t, u*
- Picture Cards: *bee, dog, eel, hog, pig, seal, tree, ukulele, umbrella, umpire, unicorn, uniform, usher, wig*
- Word Cards: *I* (2), *like* (2), *to* (2), *see, hear, a* (2)
- Exploring Sounds and Letters, pages 100–101
- Alphabet Cards: Short *u* and Long *u*
- For each child, one Uppercase and Lowercase Letter Card: *Uu*
- Reproducible Masters 20–21
- Home/School Connection 14

Prepare Ahead

- Make a copy of Reproducible Masters 20 and 21 for each child and cut out the pictures. Label three containers, one with *U*, one with *O*, and one with *E*.
- One set each of capital and lowercase letter cards from Lesson 71 to use for Warmup.

✳ READING THE BIG BOOK

"Rhyme"
page 27 of *Pickled Peppers*

- Open *Pickled Peppers* to "Rhyme" and reread the poem. Talk about the way the author describes things that she saw and heard. Ask the children to give their own descriptions of thunderstorms.
- Have the following Picture Cards on hand: *pig, wig, tree, bee, seal, eel, hog, dog.* Put the following Word Cards on the Pocket Chart:

I   like   to   see   a
I   like   to   hear   a

- Read each line, emphasizing the words *see* and *hear*. Display the *pig* and the *wig* Picture Cards. Ask a child to come forward and place the Picture Cards in the Pocket Chart to complete each line. It does not matter which order the child chooses for the cards, but you might encourage the child to use *pig* with *hear* by saying, "What sound does a pig make?"
- Continue with the remaining picture pairs.

✳ PHONEMIC AWARENESS

Rhyming Ask children to think of words that rhyme with the following short *a* words. Keep a list of children's suggestions on the board.

rat   back   pan

If the children get stuck on a word, allow them to make a few non-sense rhymes, then go on to the next word.

Oral Blending
Blending Consonant-Vowel-Consonant Words in Story Contexts
Continue with purely oral work, blending sound by sound. Children will be listening for the separate sounds and then blending them together.

Teacher:	There once was a giant dragon.
	She had a very long /t/ /ā/ /l/.
	A long what?
Everyone:	tail
Teacher:	Her tail was lumpy and bumpy
	and as green as the /s/ /ē/.
	As green as the what?
Everyone:	sea
Teacher:	She was proud of her spikes;
	they were sharp as a /n/ /ā/ /l/.
	Sharp as a what?
Everyone:	nail
Teacher:	She was proud of her tail;
	just as green as a /p/ /ē/.
	As green as a what?
Everyone:	pea
Teacher:	Oh, her tail was pretty,
	but heavy as heck!
	So she threw it over her arm
	and around her /n/ /e/ /k/!
	Around her what?
Everyone:	neck

LETTER NAMES, SHAPES, AND SOUNDS

Warmup Divide the children into two groups. Give one group small letters, and the other group the matching capital letters that you prepared ahead. Explain that on your signal, they should find the person with the letter that matches their letter. Tell them that they should hold their hands up when they have found their partners. Call on pairs and have them say their letters and their letters' sounds.

The Sound of *u*

Introducing Long *u* Point to the Long *u* Alphabet Card.

- Encourage children to tell you what they know about the letter *u*.
- Show the children these Picture Cards: *ukulele, unicorn, uniform*. Say the name of each picture and ask children to listen for the /ū/ at the beginning of the word. If necessary explain what a *ukulele* and a *unicorn* are. Have the children repeat the words.

Introducing Short *u* Now point to the Short *u* Alphabet Card.

- Remind children that sometimes a vowel makes sounds other than its name. Say that *u*'s short sound is /u/. Recite the poem for /u/.

Tubby the Tugboat can huff and puff
And push and pull to move big stuff.
/u/ /u/ /u/ /u/ /u/ /u/
That's the sound of Tubby the Tug;
He works all day from dawn till dusk.
/u/ /u/ /u/ /u/ /u/ /u/

- Show the children these Picture Cards: *usher, umpire, umbrella*. Say the name of each picture and ask children to listen for /u/ at the beginning of the word. Have them repeat the words.
- Say some single–syllable words that have /u/ in the middle of the word. Ask children to repeat the word and then say /u/. Try these words:

| but | bug | bun |
| pun | punt | hut |

Listening for Long and Short *u* Give each child a *Uu* Uppercase and Lowercase Letter Card.

- Remind the children that the letter *u* sometimes says its name (pause and hold up the Long *u* Alphabet Card) and sometimes has the sound /u/ (pause and hold up the Short *u* card).
- Ask the children to hold their *Uu* cards up high and say /ū/ when they hear the long *u* sound and to scrunch down and say /u/ when they hear the sound of short *u*.
  Use the following words:

United States	umpire	underwear
uncle	uncut	under
union	undo	unit

- Once again, explain that vowel sounds can come at the middle or end of a word as well as at the beginning. Here are some words with the long *u* sound or short *u* sound in the middle:

but	dust	must	fun
cute	cube	lunch	

***Pickled Peppers* Poster** Have all children look for long *u* and short *u* on the poster. Ask one child to point out the picture for short *u* and another to point out long *u*. Have each child name the letter and then make its long or short sound.

Linking the Sound to the Letter

Grab Bag of Letters and Words This version of the Grab Bag of Letters is slightly different from the earlier versions. Place the selected Pocket Chart Letter Cards on a low table so that the children can choose the correct letter to make the change you call for. Work with short *u* words.

- Put the letters *ub* on the Pocket Chart. Say /u/ /b/. On the table place these Pocket Chart Letter Cards: *t, d, r, g*. Say, "How can we make the word *rub?*" Ask a child to come and find the letter that will make *rub* and to place it in the Pocket Chart.
- Continue, asking other children to make the following words: *tub, tug, rug, dug*.

Writing *Uu* Review with the children how to form a capital *U* and have them write capital *U*'s on page 100 of Exploring Sounds and Letters. Repeat for small *u*.

❯ **Exploring Sounds and Letters** Focus the children's attention on the pictures on pages 100–101 of Exploring Sounds and Letters. Explain that some of the pictures show things whose names have the short *u* sound in them. Ask the children to write the letter *u* under the picture only if the word that names the picture has the short *u* sound.

Exploring Sounds and Letters, page 100

Exploring Sounds and Letters, page 101

✱ WORKSHOP

- Give each child a picture set from **Reproducible Masters 20** and **21.**
  Show the pictures and name each one before children go on to independent work. Display the containers labeled *U, O,* and *E.* Tell the
  children that they can sort through the pictures and either label them
  with the letter that represents the vowel sound they hear in the word
  or, if they can, write the word. Then they can place the pictures in the
  appropriate container.
- Encourage children to draw pictures of, or write about, thunderstorms.
- Have other activities available for children during Workshop such as
  Game Corner, Creating Letters, Letter Books, Writing Folders, and
  other activities to reinforce letter recognition and sounds.

Home/School Connection Give the children **Home/School
Connection 14** to take home. It suggests ideas for developing oral language skills

LESSON 82

● ● ● Lesson Overview

Materials

- "Old MacDonald," pages 14–15 of *Pickled Peppers*
- Picture Cards: *ukulele, umbrella, umpire, unicorn, uniform, usher*
- Alphabet Cards: vowels
- Alphabet Flash Cards
- Classroom Support Teacher Tool Card 3
- Activity Sheet 16

Prepare Ahead

- Ball for The Ship is Loaded with ____ game

✽ READING THE BIG BOOK

"Old MacDonald"
pages 14–15 of *Pickled Peppers*

- Open *Pickled Peppers* to "Old MacDonald." Review the song, allowing children to take the lead. Then, sing for them the version that emphasizes the long vowels:

Old MacDonald had a farm, A-E-I-O-U
And on his farm, he had a _____(Hold up the Long *u* Alphabet card), A-E-I-O-U
With a /ū/ /ū/ here, and a /ū/ /ū/ there.
Here a /ū/, there a /ū /, everywhere a /ū/ /ū/
Old MacDonald had a farm, A-E-I-O-U

Do the same with long *a*, long *i*, long *e*, and long *o*, holding up the Alphabet Cards and waiting for the children to say the vowel name.

✳ **PHONEMIC AWARENESS**

Rhyming

Ask children to think of words that rhyme with the following short *u* words. Write the children's suggestions on the chalkboard.

fun

tug

sunk

If the children get stuck on a word, allow them to make a few non-sense rhymes, then go on to the next word.

Oral Blending

Blending Consonant-Vowel-Consonant Words in Story Contexts

The children are familiar with this format now and should enjoy the silly rhymes.

Teacher:	Bud liked to play in the /m/ /u/ /d/.
	He played in the what?
Everyone:	mud!
Teacher:	He put mud on his nose,
	and mud on his /t/ /ō/ /z/!
	Mud on his what?
Everyone:	toes!
Teacher:	Silly Jilly liked to play at the /s/ /ē/.
	Liked to play at the what?
Everyone:	sea!
Teacher:	She put sand in her lap,
	and threw sand in her /k/ /a/ /p/!
	Sand in her what?
Everyone:	cap!
Teacher:	Jake liked to fish in the /l/ /ā/ /k/.
	He fished in the what?
Everyone:	lake!
Teacher:	He put worms on his line,
	and thought worms worked just /f/ /ī/ /n/!
	Thought worms worked just how?
Everyone:	fine!

LETTER NAMES, SHAPES, AND SOUNDS

Warmup Review the alphabet by using the Alphabet Flash Cards. If you come to a letter that the children have learned the sound of, ask them to say the sound. If necessary, point to the picture as a reminder of its sound.

The Sound of *u*

Reviewing Long *u* Review long *u*. Hold up the Long *u* Alphabet Card and have the children tell you what they know about long *u*.

Hold up the Picture Cards for long *u*: *ukulele, unicorn, uniform,* and have the children name the words.

Reviewing Short *u* Hold up the Short *u* Alphabet Card and review the poem for short *u*.

> Tubby the Tugboat can huff and puff
> And push and pull to move big stuff.
> /u/ /u/ /u/ /u/ /u/ /u/
> That's the sound of Tubby the Tug;
> He works all day from dawn till dusk
> /u/ /u/ /u/ /u/ /u/ /u/

Repeat the poem again. Hold up the Picture Cards for short *u*: *usher, umpire, umbrella,* and have the children name the words.

Listening for Vowel Sounds Give the children the following verse:

> A bug in a rug with a mug went glug.

Have them repeat it several times. Ask them what vowel sound they hear in *bug, rug, mug, glug.* Ask them to listen to what happens when you change that sound to /a/:

> A bag in a rag with a mag went glag.

Change to other vowel sounds such as /i/ and /ī/, and let the children say the silly verses.

The Ship is Loaded with _____ Game Play the game by rhyming /u/ words. Start with a single-syllable word that is easy to rhyme, such as *sun.* Roll the ball to a child and say, "The ship is loaded with *sun.*" The child who has the ball must think of a word that rhymes with *sun.* If the child has difficulty, suggest possible rhymes: *bun, fun, done, run,* etc. Try other words with the sound of short *u.* Encourage the children to rhyme the short *u* any way they can, even if it is not a real word: *lun, vun, zun,* etc. You might also want to try *bum, gum, hum,* or *bug, dug, plug.*

Linking the Sound to the Letter

Word Pairs Write *cut* and *cat* on the chalkboard.

- Ask the children, "Which word says *cut*?" When the children give the correct answer, say, "Right! There's an /u/ in *cut."*
- Point to *cat* and ask, "What do you think the other word says?" Continue with the following words:

nut   net   luck   lock

rug   rag   tug   tag

✳ WORKSHOP

- Identify for the children the pictures on **Activity Sheet 16**. Tell the children they should circle the word that names each picture. Remind them that they can listen for the vowel sound in the word or the ending sound to help them choose the correct word.
- Have several activities or centers available to the children. At times, meet with individuals or small groups to have them share their work. (See **Classroom Support Teacher Tool Card 3** for more details.) Continue to work with children when they need extra help or extra challenges.

LESSON
83

●●● Lesson Overview

New Learning

- *Vv*
- /v/

Materials

- First-Step Story 4
- Pocket Chart Letter Cards: *v, i, n, e, d, f, l, m*
- Picture Cards: *van, vase, vegetables, vine, violin, volcano*
- Exploring Sounds and Letters, pages 102–103
- For each child, one Uppercase and Lowercase Letter Card: *Vv* or *Pp*
- Learning Framework Card 7

✷ USING FIRST-STEP STORIES

First-Step Story 4

- Give each child a copy of First-Step Story 4. Give the children a few minutes to flip through the book and look at the pictures. Explain to them that this story has no words, but that they can see what is happening by looking at the pictures.
- Go through the story page by page and call on individual children to explain what is happening on each page. For example, on the first page, the girl is using her head to bounce the ball away from the goal. What is happening on the next page? What happened to the sleepyhead on the third page? And finally, where does the ball end up on the last page?
- Have the children look at the first page again. Point to the dog. Ask the children if they can find anything in the picture that rhymes with *dog*? Point out that the words *dog* and *log* both end with /g/. Tell the children that you see two things in the picture that begin with the /g/ sound (girl, grass). Ask if anyone can name them.

> **TIP FOR ENGLISH LANGUAGE LEARNERS**
>
> Maximize the potential to build language skills by pairing native English speakers with English Language Learners to discuss the illustrations. Have the pairs share with each other the story they think the pictures are telling before you discuss the pictures with the whole class. Informally assess the children's speaking abilities by monitoring their conversations. Help them to identify unknown items in each picture.

Oral Blending

Initial Consonant Blends Blending initial consonants is one of the more difficult steps in oral blending. However, in this first step, the rest of the word following the initial consonant gives a strong clue as to the word's identity.

Tell the children that you are going to ask them to put some sounds together to make words. You will say just the beginning sound and then the rest of the word. Then you will ask them to tell you what the word is.

Teacher: /b/ . . . lackboard. What's the word?
Children: blackboard

Try the following words:

/p/...layground	/t/...rampoline
/b/...lueberry	/f/...lamingo
/g/...roundhog	/s/...pinach
/d/...rumstick	

LETTER NAMES, SHAPES, AND SOUNDS

The Sound of *v*

Introducing *v* Display the *Vv* Alphabet Card and say its sound, /v/. Show the picture for the sound and recite the poem for /v/:

Vinny the Vacuum is cleaning again.
Before visitors visit, he always begins.
This is the sound of his very loud voice:
/v/ /v/ /v/ /v/ /v/ /v/
As he vacuums and vacuums all over the place:
/v/ /v/ /v/ /v/ /v/ /v/

Listening for Initial /v/ and /p/ Hold up and name each of these Picture Cards: *violin, van, vase, vegetables, volcano, vine.*
- Ask children to listen for /v/ at the beginning of the words.
- Give each child a *Vv* or a *Pp* Uppercase and Lowercase Letter Card. Tell the children that you are going to say words and that those who have *Vv* cards should hold them up when they hear you say a word that begins with /v/. At your signal, they should say /v/. Tell the children with *Pp* cards to hold up their cards when they hear you say a word that begins with /p/. At your signal, they should say /p/. Try these words:

vane	pane	pan	van	vacuum
vast	past	verse	purse	vowel

***Pickled Peppers* Poster** Have the children try to find and point out a *v* on the poster. Ask a child to say the sound that Vinny the Vacuum makes.

Linking the Sound to the Letter

Grab Bag of Letters and Words Remember, this version of Grab Bag of Letters is slightly different from the earlier versions. Place the selected Pocket Chart Letter Cards on a low table so that the children can choose the correct letter to make the change you call for.

- Put the letters *ine* on the Pocket Chart or have three children line up in front of the class, each one holding a card: *i, n,* and *e.* Say *ine* and remind the children that they do not hear the *e* because it is a silent helper, helping the *i* to say its name. Place on the table the letters: *v, d, f, l, m.* Ask, "How can we make the word *vine*?" The children can put the letter in the Pocket Chart or take it and stand in front of the three children holding the *i, n,* and *e* letters. Ask a child to come and find the letter that will make *vine.*
- Continue, asking other children to make the following words: *dine, fine, line, mine.*

Writing Vv Demonstrate how to form a capital *V.* Lead children as they form capitals *V*'s on the writing line on page 102 of Exploring Sounds and Letters.

Have children write small *v*'s in their Exploring Sounds and Letters workbooks.

❯ **Exploring Sounds and Letters** Have the children focus on the pictures on pages 102–103 of Exploring Sounds and Letters. Say that some of the pictures show things that begin with /v/. Ask the children to write the letter *v* under the picture only if the word that names the picture begins with /v/.

TEACHING TIP

Whenever the children write, whether at the chalkboard or on paper, you should encourage them to proofread their work. Reflecting on their own work helps them develop the habit of revising and rewriting when necessary. Walk around the room and tell the children to look over their work and to circle anything they think they can make better. See **Learning Framework Card 7, Writing,** for more information.

✳ WORKSHOP

- Explain to the children that because their **First-Step Story** has no words, they will be the "authors." Today they will work on the first page of their stories. Tell them that they can do whatever they like: write whole words or sentences, label pictures with the beginning letters, add to the drawing, or simply practice their letters. Be sure to circulate during Workshop, offering help when needed.
- Have children add *v* to their **Letter Books.**
- Make the games **Hop Along, Bus Stop, Roller Ride, Race Track, Make Tracks,** and **Zoo** available.

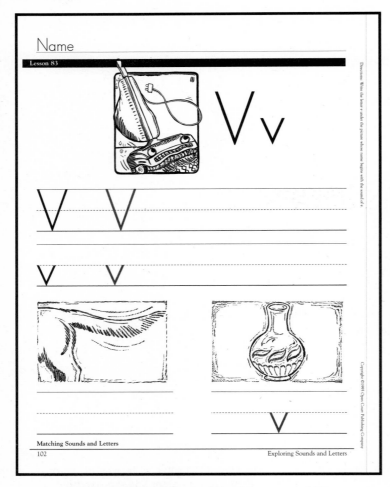

Exploring Sounds and Letters, page 102

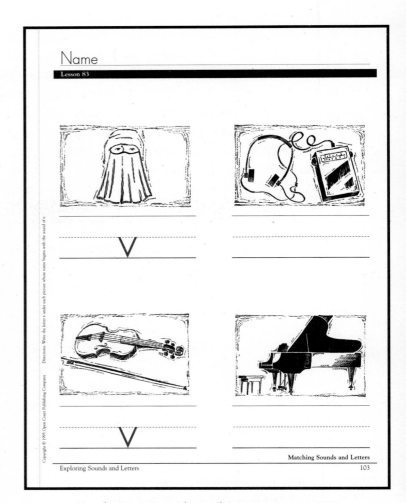

Exploring Sounds and Letters, page 103

LESSON

84

● ● ● Lesson Overview

New Learning

- *Vv*
- /v/

Materials

- First-Step Story 4
- Picture Cards: *bat, bug, cat, hat, house, mouse, rug, van, vase, vegetables, vine, violin, volcano*
- Word Cards: *bat, cat, hat,*
- Uppercase and Lowercase Letter Cards: *Pp–Vv*
- Classroom Support Teacher Tool Card 3
- Activity Sheet 17

✳ USING FIRST-STEP STORIES

First-Step Story 4

- Ask children to take out their First-Step Stories again and turn to page 2. Ask them to identify these rhyming words in the picture: *hat, cat, bat; mouse, house; bug,* and *rug.*
- Place the Word Cards *bat, hat,* and *cat* on a low table. Place the *bat* Picture Card in the Pocket Chart. Say *bat* and ask a child to find the Word Card *bat* and put it in the chart under the picture of the bat. Remind the child to think about what letter makes the /b/ sound, the first sound in *bat.*
- Continue by placing the pictures for *hat* and *cat* in the chart, and asking children to find and place the matching Word Card.
- Go over the rhyming words *bug, rug; house, mouse.* Write *rug* on the chalkboard and say the word. Erase the *r* and replace it with *b.* Then write *bug* beneath *rug* and ask the children to say the new word. Do the same with *mouse* and *house.* Leave the words on the chalkboard for the remainder of the class. From time to time, direct the children's attention to the words and review the activity.

TIP FOR ENGLISH LANGUAGE LEARNERS

The Picture Cards serve as valuable visual clues for English Language Learners and will help build their English vocabularies. Review the Picture Cards you will use in the activity with English Language Learners before using them with the whole class. Then, during the whole class activity, encourage English Language Learners to offer responses. Praise them for their speaking efforts.

✳ Oral Blending

Initial Consonant Blends Continue blending initial consonant words, using words in which the remainder of the word gives a strong clue as to the word's identity.

Tell the children that you are going to ask them to put some sounds together to make words. Say, "I'll give you the beginning sound and then the rest of the word. Then I want you to tell me what the word is."

Teacher: /f/ ...lorida. What's the word?

Children: Florida

Try the following words:

/F/...rankenstein	/s/...tampede	/s/...corpion
/b/...lackbird	/b/...lindfold	/b/...riefcase
/k/...ranberry	/k/...rayfish	

Reviewing *v* Display the Alphabet Card for *v* and say its sound, /v/. Review the poem:

Vinny the Vacuum is cleaning again.
Before visitors visit, he always begins.
This is the sound of his very loud voice:
/v/ /v/ /v/ /v/ /v/ /v/
As he vacuums and vacuums all over the place:
/v/ /v/ /v/ /v/ /v/ /v/.

Silly Sentences Game Play Silly Sentences by making a sentence that is full of beginning /v/ sounds. You might begin with this sentence:

Vinnie the Vacuum visited Velma.

Catching the Letter Train Review the sounds for the letters *Pp–Vv*. Then tell the children you are going to play the **Catching the Letter Train** game again. Give each child one Uppercase and Lowercase Letter Card, choosing from *Pp–Vv* as they board the train. Explain that when they get their card, they must say the sound of the letter. Then lead the children around the room to different points, calling out the name of a "town" every time you stop. Tell the children to listen for the first sound of the town's name and to hold up their cards if they have one with a letter that makes the sound. For example, say,"Now approaching Unionville." Tell the children that anyone holding the *Uu* card must get off the train because *Unionville* starts with the sound /ū/. Continue traveling around the room until all children have left the train.

Linking the Sound to the Letter

Word Pairs Write *vase* and *base* on the chalkboard. Ask the children, "Which one says *vase*?" When they respond correctly, say, "Right! There's a /v/ /v/ /v/ in *vase*." Point to *base* and say, "What do you think this word says?"

Always say the word with the *v* sound and have the children identify it. Then have them say the other word. Continue with other words:

vain   pain   very   berry   tan   van

✳ WORKSHOP

- Tell the children to work on the second page of **First-Step Story 4**. Again, tell them that they can write whole words or sentences, they can label pictures with the beginning letters, they can add to the drawing, or they can simply practice making their letters. Suggest that they may want to label their books with some of the words they used in other activities earlier in the day. Be sure to circulate during Workshop, offering help when needed.

- Identify for the children the pictures on **Activity Sheet 17** before they go on to independent work. Tell them that they will cut out the pots at the bottom of the page. They should say the name of each picture. If they hear /v/ at the end of the word, they should paste that pot on the stove at the top of the page.

- Have several activities or centers available to the children. At times during Workshop, meet with individuals or small groups to have them share their work (See **Classroom Support Teacher Tool Card** 3 for more details.) Continue to work with children who may need extra help or extra challenges.

- During Workshop, observe children's ability to use phonetic spelling and construct sentences with capitals and periods while writing their First-Step Story. Record your observations on **Observation Log 2, Reproducible Master 29.**

LESSON
85

••• Lesson Overview

New Learning

- *Ww*
- /w/

Materials

- First-Step Story 4
- Picture Cards: *wagon, wallet, walrus, wig, wing*
- Exploring Sounds and Letters, pages 104–105
- Alphabet Flash Cards

✳ USING FIRST-STEP STORIES

First-Step Story 4

- Have children take out their First-Step Stories and turn to page 3. Point out all the *b* words on the page: *bed, ball, bounce, blanket.* Ask what sound the bouncing ball makes: /b/ /b/ /b/ /b/.
- Ask if anyone can see something in the picture that rhymes with *bed.* Say, "What did the ball bounce on?" Ask if anyone can see anything that rhymes with *clock.*
- Finish the session by pointing to each number on the clock and having the children count to ten with you.

✳ PHONEMIC AWARENESS

Oral Blending

Initial Consonant Blends Continue with initial consonant blends. This time, use words in which the remainder of the word does not give a strong clue as to the word's identity. Encourage the children to listen carefully.

- Tell the children that you are going to ask them to put some sounds together to make words. Explain that you will say just the beginning sound and then the rest of the word. Say that you will ask them to tell you what the word is.

Teacher: /b/ . . . low. What's the word?
Children: blow

- Try the following words:

  /f/. . . lap   /g/. . . love   /d/. . . rag   /d/. . . rip
  /s/. . . care   /s/. . . tick   /s/. . . tone

Segmentation

Initial Consonant Blends   This activity helps children distinguish the sounds in initial consonant blends. You will say a word and the puppet will repeat the word, dropping the initial sound. Ask the children to listen to what the puppet says. Say *sly* and have the puppet say /lī/. Then say *sty* and have the puppet say /tī/. Tell the children to say /tī/ with the puppet. Continue, using the following words:

spy	py	scab	cab
stab	tab	slab	lab
stub	tub	score	core
store	tore	scope	cope
slope	lope		

LETTER NAMES, SHAPES, AND SOUNDS

Warmup   Review the alphabet with the children by using the Alphabet Flash Cards. When you come to a letter that the children have learned the sound of, ask them to say the sound. Point to the picture on the letter's Alphabet Card as a reminder of its sound.

The Sound of *w*

Introducing *W*   Display the *Ww* Alphabet Card. Say its sound and show the picture for /w/. Recite the poem for /w/:

Willie the Washer washed white clothes all week.
When he washed he went: /w/ /w/ /w/ /w/ /w/ /w/
Willie the Washer was tired; he sprang a leak.
He washed and he washed and he went: /w/ /w/ /w/ /w/

Listening for Initial /w/   Hold up and name each of these Picture Cards: *wagon, walrus, wallet, wing, wig.* Ask children to listen for the /w/ sound at the beginning of the words.

Make Mine a W   Remind the children that they should be listening for /w/.

Say each child's name and then a word beginning either with *w* or with another letter. For example, "Jamie, *wait.*" Tell the child that if he or she hears the letter *w,* he or she should repeat the sound, /w/. If he or she doesn't hear the letter *w,* he or she should remain silent. Try the following words:

west	pick	wet
met	wild	not
wart	war	wax
last	wish	

Pickled Peppers **Poster** Have the children look for and point out the *W* on the poster. Ask a child to come forward and point out the picture for *W* and say its sound.

Linking the Sound to the Letter

Word Pairs In this activity, write two words on the chalkboard that begin with consonant blends.

- Write *snug* and *slug* on the board. Ask the children, "Which word says *snug*?" When they give the correct answer, say, "Right! /s/ /n/ /u/ /g/." Point to *slug* and say, "What do you think the other word says?"
- Continue with these words:

swam	slam		snap	slap
cram	clam		swim	slim

Writing Ww Take the children through a review of how to form a capital *W* and have them write capital *W*'s on the writing line on page 104 of Exploring Sounds and Letters.

Review and have the children write small *w*'s.

❯ **Exploring Sounds and Letters** Focus the children's attention on the pictures on pages 104–105 of Exploring Sounds and Letters. Name the pictures. Ask the children to write the letter *w* under a picture only if the word that names the picture starts with /w/.

✳ WORKSHOP

- Tell the children that they will be working on the third page of **First-Step Story 4**. Again, tell them that they can write whatever they like. Suggest that they might want to label everything in the picture with its beginning letter. Be sure to circulate during Workshop, offering help when needed.
- Tell the children that, with a partner, they can spend a few minutes at the *Pickled Peppers* **Poster**, challenging each other to find a letter and say its name.
- During Workshop, observe children's ability to use phonetic spellings and to construct sentences with capitals and periods while writing their First-Step Stories. Record your observations on **Observation Log 2**, Reproducible Master 29.

Exploring Sounds and Letters, page 104

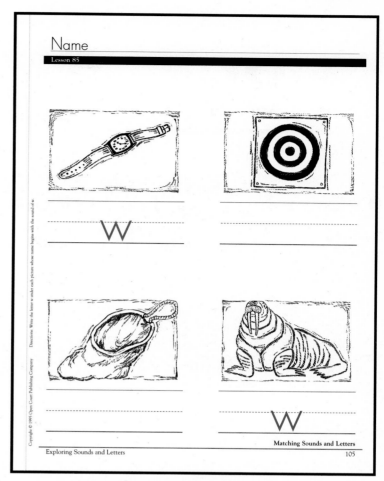

Exploring Sounds and Letters, page 105

LESSON
86

Lesson Overview

New Learning

- *Ww*
- /w/

Materials

- First-Step Story 4
- Picture Cards: *baseball, basketball, bowling ball, football, soccer ball*
- For each child, one Uppercase and Lowercase Letter Card: *Ww* or *Dd*
- Activity Sheet 18

✱ USING FIRST-STEP STORIES

First-Step Story 4

- Tell the children to take out their First-Step Stories. Remind them that this story has only pictures and they will continue to write their own stories to go with the pictures.
- Ask whether anyone has ever played soccer. If anyone has, allow those children to tell the class about the game. You might ask the children to name every kind of ball game that they can think of. Show them these Picture Cards: *soccer ball, basketball, football, baseball, bowling ball* and ask them to name what is on each card.
- Hold up the Picture Card *soccer ball* and ask the children to think of words that show actions that might involve the soccer ball, such as *kick*. Write this sentence on the chalkboard: *Kick the ball.* As children name more words, list them on the chalkboard. After they say a word, make a sentence out of it, for example: *throw. Throw the ball.* Invite everyone to join in when you recite the sentences.
- Leave all the words on the chalkboard so that the children can refer to them during the day. Some suggestions include: *pass, bump, shoot, bounce, catch, fling, toss, punt, drop, hit, pitch, roll.*

TIP FOR ENGLISH LANGUAGE LEARNERS

Invite English Language Learners to share their experiences and provide new knowledge to other children. Encourage English Language Learners to talk about any sport that they are familiar with. Have them say the name of the sport and tell how it is played.

✳ Oral Blending

Initial Consonant Continue blending initial consonants, using words that do not provide an immediate clue as to the word's identity. Encourage the children to listen carefully.

- Tell the children that you are going to ask them to put some sounds together to make words. Explain that you will say just the beginning sound and then the rest of the word. Then you will ask them to tell you what the word is.

  Teacher: /b/ . . . right. What's the word?

  Children: bright

- Try the following words:

/b/ . . . rilliant	/f/ . . . lute	/f/ . . . low
/g/ . . . rade	/p/ . . . rince	/s/ . . . nack
/s/ . . . tamp	/s/ . . . nake	/s/ . . . quirt
/s/ . . . quare		

Segmentation

Initial Consonant Blends This activity will help children distinguish the sounds in initial consonant blends. Again, you will say a word and this time the puppet will repeat it, leaving off the initial consonant sound.

- Ask the children to listen to what the puppet says. Say *fled* and have the puppet say *led.*
- Say *skin* and have the puppet say *kin.* Have the children repeat what the puppet says.

  Use the following words:

snow	nōw	stone	tone
crane	rane	blimp	limp
blow	low	price	rice
crow	row	crust	rust

Warmup Do a quick warmup by having the children recite the alphabet while standing in a circle. Say *a* and tap the shoulder of the child next to you. That child should say *b* and tap the child next to him or her. Continue around the circle until you reach *z.*

The Sound of *w*

Reviewing *w* Encourage the children to tell you what they know about *w.* Review the poem for /w/:

Willie the Washer washed white clothes all week.
When he washed he went: /w/ /w/ /w/ /w/ /w/
Willie the Washer was tired; he sprang a leak.
He washed and he washed and he went: /w/ /w/ /w/ /w/ /w/

Repeat the poem, emphasizing the initial /w/

Listening for Initial /w/ and /d/ Give each child a *Ww* or *Dd*
Uppercase and Lowercase Letter Card. Follow the procedure established
in earlier lessons, using these words:

warm	done	dent	went
water	day	way	wire
weak	wig	dig	

Silly Sentences Game Play the Silly Sentences game by making a silly
sentence that is full of /w/ words. Make sure the children add words to
the beginning and middle of the sentences as well as to the end.

Linking the Sound to the Letter

Word Pairs Write *waste* and *paste* on the chalkboard. Ask for a
volunteer to come to the chalkboard and point to *waste.*
Point to *paste* and say, "What do you think this other word says?"
Continue with other words:

tear	wear	weak	peak
pay	way	will	mill

✱ WORKSHOP

- Today, the children will work on the last page of **First-Step Story 4**.
  Suggest that they label the rhyming words in the picture or try to
  write a sentence, modeling their work on the sentence you wrote on
  the chalkboard: *Kick the ball*. Be sure to circulate during Workshop,
  offering help when needed. Allow children time to share their stories
  with each other. Then encourage the children to turn to page 1 and
  "write" a title for their stories on the line at the top of the page.
- Identify the pictures on **Activity Sheet 18**. Have the children listen
  for the beginning sound of each picture name. Say that if a picture
  name begins with /w/, they should write in the *w* to complete the
  word. Suggest that they go back to the other pictures and try to fill in
  their beginning sounds, too. Children are familiar with these letters
  (*b*, *p*, *s*), so they should be able to complete these words as well.
- During Workshop, finish observing all children for their ability to use
  phonetic spellings and to construct sentences with capitals and periods while writing the First-Step Story. Record your observations on
  Observation Log 2, Reproducible Master 29.

LESSON 87

Lesson Overview

New Learning

- *Xx*
- /ks/

Materials

- "Jennifer Juniper," First-Step Story 5
- Pocket Chart Letter Cards: *b, t, g, d, r, s, u*
- Picture Cards: *ax, box, fox, ox*
- Exploring Sounds and Letters, pages 106–107
- For each child, one Uppercase and Lowercase Letter Card: *Xx*

✳ USING THE FIRST-STEP STORIES

"Jennifer Juniper"
First-Step Story 5

- Hand out First-Step Story 5. Have the children follow along as you read through the entire story. Cue them on when to turn the pages.
- Ask children to tell you the first two words on every page (*Jennifer Juniper*). Ask who remembers why the *J*'s are capitalized.
- Talk about Jennifer Juniper and her world. Ask, "How big do you think Jennifer is?" Let them tell you what gives them a clue that Jennifer Juniper must be very, very small.

✳ PHONEMIC AWARENESS

Segmentation

Initial Consonant Blends In this lesson you will once again say a word that the puppet repeats, dropping the initial consonant. In addition, you will write the word on the chalkboard and erase the initial consonant to show the children what the written words look like.

- Ask the children to listen to what the puppet says. Say *clay,* and write it on the board.
- Have the puppet say *lay,* and erase the *c* from the board.
- Say *smash.* Have the puppet and everyone say *mash.* Erase the *s.*

- Use the following words:

smart	mart	broom	room
tray	ray	brag	rag
scare	care	gray	ray
stop	top		

The Sound of x

Introducing x Point to the Alphabet Card for *x* and say its sound, /ks/. Show the picture for the sound and review the poem for /ks/:

Rex is called the Exiting X;
He runs to guard the door.
To get past Rex,
Make the sound of the X:
/ks/ /ks/ /ks/ /ks/ /ks/.

Listening for /ks/ Hold up and name each of these Picture Cards: *ox, ax, box, fox.* Ask children to listen for the /ks/ sound in the words.

Give each child an *Xx* Uppercase and Lowercase Letter Card. Tell the children that you are going to say words and that you want them to hold up the card and say /ks/ when they hear a word ending with /ks/.

flax	flip	**six**	**relax**	**box**	**ax**
fix	fly	**wax**	wait	mate	**mix**

***Pickled Peppers* Poster** Ask a child to find the picture for *x* on the poster and then make its sound. Ask if anyone has ever seen an EXIT sign in buildings. If you have such a sign in your school, point it out during the day.

Linking the Sound to the Letter

Grab Bag of Letters and Words Work with consonant blends today.
- Put the Pocket Chart Letter Cards *u b* in the Pocket Chart, or have children hold the cards. Say /u/ /b/. Place on a table these Pocket Chart Letter Cards: *t, g, d, r, s.* Ask, "How can we make the word *rub*?" Ask a child to come and find the letter that will make *rub* and to place it in the Pocket Chart or to hold up the letter and stand in line with the other children holding letters to spell out *rub*. Ask, "How can I change *rub* to *grub*?"
- Continue, asking other children to make the following words: *rug, drug, tub, stub.*

Writing Xx Demonstrate how to form a capital *X* and help the children write capital *X*'s on page 106 of Exploring Sounds and Letters.
Do the same with small *x*.

❯ **Exploring Sounds and Letters** Have the children focus on the pictures on pages 106–107 in Exploring Sounds and Letters. Explain that

Exploring Sounds and Letters, page 106

Exploring Sounds and Letters, page 107

some of the pictures show things whose names end with /ks/. Ask the children to write the letter *x* under the pictures whose names end with /ks/.

- Have the children write their names on the covers of **First-Step Story 5 "Jennifer Juniper."** Say that today they will be illustrating the first page. Remind them that they can make Jennifer Juniper look any way they wish.
- A shallow pan of sand makes a great erasable writing surface. Children can work in pairs, taking turns writing a letter or a word and having the other child name its sound. Point out to the children that they can quickly smooth over the the letter or word and start again if they make a mistake.

TIP FOR ENGLISH LANGUAGE LEARNERS

Before English Language Learners complete the pages, work with them in small groups to identify the animals and objects pictured. Encourage them to share how to say the names of these animals and objects in their primary languages.

LESSON 88

●●● Lesson Overview

New Learning

- *Yy*
- /y/

Materials

- "Jennifer Juniper," First-Step Story 5
- Pocket Chart Letter Cards: *a, b, c, f, m, n, t,*
- Picture Cards: **yam, yard, yarn, yellow, yo-yo**
- Exploring Sounds and Letters, page 108–109
- For each child, one Uppercase and Lowercase Letter Card: *Yy* or *Ll*
- Activity Sheet 19

✳ USING FIRST-STEP STORIES

"Jennifer Juniper"
First-Step Story 5

- Read "Jennifer Juniper" through once for the children. Then read it again, and, as you begin each new page, point to a child. The child you point to says, "Jennifer Juniper." Allow the child to continue reading with you if she or he is able to do so.
- Go through the poem page by page. Ask individual children to give the rhyming words on each page: *walk/stalk*; *see/me*; *sing/wing*; *rest/nest*.

✳ PHONEMIC AWARENESS

Segmentation

Initial Consonant Blends This activity will help children distinguish the sounds in initial consonant blends. Ask the children to listen to what the puppet says. Say *bring.* Have the puppet say *ring.* Say *brave.* Have the the puppet and the children say *rave.*

Use the following words:

bread	read	stub	tub	branch	ranch
crash	rash	blast	last	bride	ride

TIP FOR ENGLISH LANGUAGE LEARNERS

Return to this activity often to provide opportunities for English Language Learners to feel comfortable with it. Encourage them to participate when the whole class is engaged in the activity. Watch for children who are not responding and work with them in small groups during Workshop.

The Sound of *y*

Introducing *y* Introduce the *Yy* Alphabet Card and say /y/. Recite the poem for /y/:

> Yolanda and Yoshiko are yaks.
> They don't yell.
> They just yak: /y/ /y/ /y/ /y/ /y/
> Yakety-yak! Yakety-yak!
> What is the sound of the curious yaks?
> /y/ /y/ /y/ /y/ /y/

Recite the poem again, emphasizing the initial /y/ sounds.

Listening for Initial /y/ and Initial /l/ Have children look at the Picture Cards for *y*: *yard*, *yarn*, *yo-yo*, *yam*, *yellow*, and try to name each picture.

- Give each child a *Yy* or *Ll* Uppercase and Lowercase Letter Card. Tell the children you are going to say words beginning with one of these sounds.
- Explain that if the word begins with the sound of the letter on their card, they should hold the card up and say the sound. Say these words:

yucky	lucky	lawn	yawn	year	lend
yell	yes	less	young	you	

Pickled Peppers Poster Have the class try to locate the letter *y* on the poster. Ask a volunteer to come to the poster, point to the *y* picture, and say /y/. Ask who can remember the animal name beginning with /y/.

Linking the Sound to the Letter

Grab Bag of Letters and Words This version of Grab Bag of Letters and Words is slightly different from the earlier versions.

- Place on a table the Pocket Chart Letter Cards: *b, c, f, m, a, t, n*. Tell the children that you want to make the word *cat*. Analyze the sounds in *cat*: /k/ /a/ /t/. Ask children what makes a /k/ sound. Have a child identify the *c* card from the table. Do the same for /a/ and /t/.
- Create the words: *bat, mat, fat, man, fan*.

Writing Yy Review with the children how to make a capital *Y*. Have children write capital *Y*'s on the writing lines on page 108 of Exploring Sounds and Letters.

Do the same with small *y*.

> Exploring Sounds and Letters Focus the children's attention on the pictures on pages 108–109 of Exploring Sounds and Letters. Explain that some of the names of the pictures start with /y/. Ask the children to write the letter *y* under those pictures. The children may also identify the starting sounds of the other picture names and write those letters.

TEACHING TIP

If you have not done so yet, you may want to have the children hold up the Pocket Chart Letter Cards rather than use the Pocket Chart.

Exploring Sounds and Letters, page 108

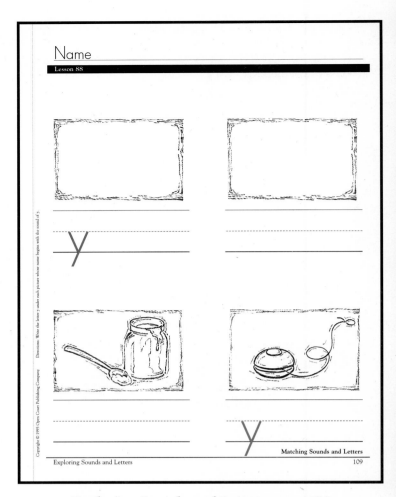

Exploring Sounds and Letters, page 109

✳ WORKSHOP

- Tell the children that they can illustrate the second page of their **First-Step Story 5,** "Jennifer Juniper." Encourage the children to draw insects.
- Name all of the pictures on **Activity Sheet 19** (ham, yam, yarn, barn, bell, yell). Have the children listen for the beginning sound of each picture name. Tell them that if a picture name begins with /y/, they should write in the *y* to complete the word under the picture. Suggest that they go back to the other pictures and try to fill in their beginning sounds, too. Children are familiar with these letters (*b, h*), so they should be able to complete these words.
- Have other activities available for children during Workshop, such as **Game Corner, Creating Letters, Letter Books, Writing Folders,** and other activities to reinforce letter recognition and sounds.

LESSON
89

●●● Lesson Overview

New Learning

- **Zz**
- /z/

Materials

- "Jennifer Juniper," First-Step Story 5
- Pocket Chart Letter Cards: **b, f, p, i, t, n**
- Picture Cards: **zebra, zero, zoo**
- Exploring Sounds and Letters, pages 110–111
- For each child, one Uppercase and Lowercase Letter Card: **Zz**

✳ USING FIRST-STEP STORIES

"Jennifer Juniper"
First-Step Story 5

- Invite the children to read through the First-Step Story "Jennifer Juniper." Call for volunteer "readers" to recite each page.
- Ask a few children to come forward and show the class their illustrations of the first two pages of their books.
- Look at the first page and say the rhyming words: *walk/stalk.* Ask the children to think of and say more words that rhyme with *walk.* Give them a beginning consonant if necessary. Do the same with the second page.

✳ PHONEMIC AWARENESS

Segmentation

Initial Consonant Blends Ask the children to listen to what the puppet says. Say *blow* and write the word on the chalkboard. Remove the *b.* Have the puppet and the children say *low.*

Say and write *stool.* Have the puppet and the children say *tool.*
Use the following words:

cream	ream	play	lay
gruff	ruff	gripe	ripe
grid	rid		

The Sound of *z*

Introducing *z* Display the *Zz* Alphabet Card and say its sound. Recite the poem for /z/:

> Zack's jacket has a zipper.
> Zack zips it up and it makes this sound:
> /z/ /z/ /z/ /z/ /z/ /z/
> Zack zips it down and it makes this sound:
> /z/ /z/ /z/ /z/ /z/ /z/

Listening for Initial /z/ Hold up and name each of these Picture Cards: *zoo, zero, zebra.* Ask children to listen for /z/ at the beginning of the words.

- Give each child a *Zz* Uppercase and Lowercase Letter Card. Tell the children that you are going to say words and that you want them to hold up the card and say /z/ when they hear you say a word beginning with /z/.
- Try the following words:

zip	hip	**zipper**	**zap**
lap	land	**zany**	**zigzag**
broom	**zoom**	**zone**	

***Pickled Peppers* Poster** The children now have just one letter left to find on the poster. Ask someone to point out the *z* and say its sound.

Z Braid Have children stand in a close circle. Lead them in calling out nonsense words beginning in /z/.

> *Teacher:* Now we will make a Z braid.
> Alyssa, how can we make *top* into a word for the *Z* braid?
> *Alyssa:* zop!

Alyssa then crosses her arms in front of her and takes the hands of the two children on either side of her. Say the poem again and name a new child. Always give the child a word to change. The child must change the word by making it begin with /z/. When everyone has been braided in, say:

> Now we have made a **Z** braid,
> And now we will unbraid it!

Then have everyone twist around, going under the upper arm, uncrossing or unbraiding their arms.

TIP FOR ENGLISH LANGUAGE LEARNERS

Some English Language Learners will have particular difficulty with /z/ as it may not exist in their primary languages. Have children practice this sound by moving around the room buzzing like a bee or imitating a zoom sound as they pretend to be a fast car.

Linking the Sound to the Letter

Grab Bag of Letters and Words Place on the table the Pocket Chart
Letter Cards: *b, f, p, i, t, n.*

- Tell children that you want to make the word *pin.* Analyze the
  sounds in *pin:* /p/ /i/ /n/. Ask the children what letter makes the
  sound /p/. Have a child identify the *p* card from the table. Do the
  same for /i/ and /n/.
- Create the words: *bin, tin, fin, bit, pit.*

Writing Zz Review with the children capital *Z,* and help them practice
making capital *Z*'s on the writing line on page 110 of Exploring Sounds
and Letters.

Do the same for small *z.*

❯ **Exploring Sounds and Letters** Focus the children's attention on
the pictures on pages 110–111 of Exploring Sounds and Letters. Explain
that some of the names of the pictures start with /z/. Ask the children
to write the letter *z* under a picture only if the word that names the picture starts with /z/.

✳ WORKSHOP

- Tell the children to illustrate the third page of their **First-Step Story**
  "Jennifer Juniper." Say that they can draw as many butterflies or
  other animals in the scene as they choose.
- Tell the children to find a partner and spend a few minutes at the
  ***Pickled Peppers* Poster**, challenging each other to find a letter and
  say its name.
- Have other activities available for children during Workshop, such as
  Game Corner, Creating Letters, Letter Books, Writing Folders, and
  other activities to reinforce letter recognition and sounds.

Exploring Sounds and Letters, page 110

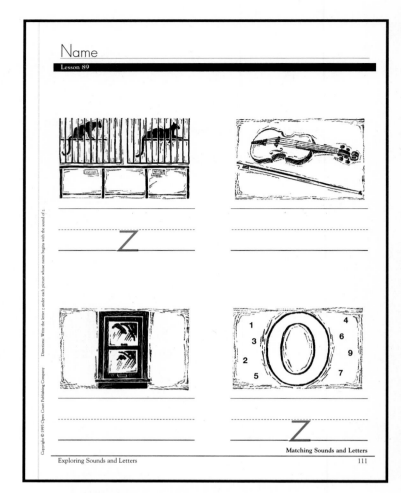

Exploring Sounds and Letters, page 111

LESSON 90

• • • Lesson Overview

Materials

- "Jennifer Juniper," First-Step Story 5
- For each child, one set of Uppercase and Lowercase Letter Cards: *Vv, Ww,* and *Yy*
- One set of Letter Cards: *Aa–Zz*

Prepare Ahead

- Have a sheet of construction paper for a placemat and a paper cup for each child. Mark each set of cup and paper with the same letter, a different letter for each child.
- Have large sheets of butcher paper cut for each child, each about as long as the child's height.
- Healthful snacks and juice for the Letter Party

✳ USING FIRST-STEP STORIES

"Jennifer Juniper"
First-Step Story 5

- Read through the First-Step Story "Jennifer Juniper" for review. Ask for more volunteer "readers" to recite a page.
- Ask a few other children to come forward and show the class their illustrations of the first three pages of their books.
- Look at the third page of the First-Step Story and say the rhyming words: *sing/wing.* Ask the children to think up and say more rhymes. Give them a beginning consonant if necessary. Do the same for the fourth page.
- Ask the children if they think Jennifer Juniper's bed would be comfortable. You might want to display pictures of nests of many types of birds.

Listening for /v/, /w/, and /y/ Give each child a *Vv, Ww,* and *Yy* Uppercase and Lowercase Letter Card.

- Have them place the cards in front of them. Tell the children that you are going to say words and that you want them to listen for the beginning sounds.
- Tell them they should hold up the letter that tells the beginning sound they hear. Give them plenty of time to hear the word and to choose their cards. Repeat the word several times if necessary. Use these words:

vine	wine	yell	well
waist	vase	yes	west
vest	yarn	warm	

Linking the Sound to the Letter

Letter Party Celebrate the fact that the children have learned all the letters of the alphabet. Set out the letter placemats and cups that you prepared ahead on a low table. Place an Uppercase and Lowercase Letter Card in a bag matching each letter you have used for the cups and placemats. Call on each child to take a Letter Card from the bag. The child should name the letter, say its sound, and then go sit by the cup and placemat marked with that letter. When everyone is seated, serve the children juice and a healthy snack. Go around the room and ask every child to say a word beginning with her or his letter. When children are done snacking, ask them to draw or write on their placemats, drawing pictures of things or writing words that start with their letter.

✳ WORKSHOP

- Tell the children that today they will complete the final page of their **First-Step Story,** "Jennifer Juniper." They can picture Jennifer Juniper in her nest bed or wherever else they choose. Ask them to think about where they might sleep if they were spending the night outdoors. Remind them of First-Step Story 1, "Sleeping Outdoors."
- Children can continue their celebration of all that they have learned by making giant posters of themselves and having an **A–Z Celebration of Me.** Give each child a body-sized piece of butcher paper that you prepared ahead. Let them work with a partner, each tracing around the other's body. Then, each child can draw in the details to finish off their life-sized self-portraits, adding clothes, hair, and facial features. To complete the work, tell the children they can write the letters from *Aa–Zz* all around the edges of the poster. Allow at least two days to complete this project.

MONITORING TIP Use the Monitor Log, **Reproducible Master 26–27,** to record notes about the children's work on the **First-Step Stories 3 and 4.**

TIP FOR ENGLISH LANGUAGE LEARNERS

Pair English Language Learners with native English-speaking children who are at, or slightly above, the same reading level. Have the pairs take turns reading their First-Step Stories. Ask one child to read a page, or describe what is happening on the page, while the other child listens. Then have them switch roles. Informally monitor the children's responses to their partner's speaking and reading and to their own speaking and listening.

LESSON 91

●●● Lesson Overview

Materials

- *One Hungry Monster*, pages 28–37 of *Pickled Peppers*
- Pocket Chart Letter Cards: *l, p, b, n, e, t*
- Picture Cards: *alligator, apple, astronaut, bat, beans, bed, bee, bow, bowl, can, cap, cat, coat, cook, core, corn, cup, deer, dish, dog, dollar, door, duck, eagle, easel, eel, elephant, elk, envelope, feet, fern, fish, fork, four, fur, gate, glue, goat, guitar, hat, hen, hive, hook, horse, house*
- Individual Alphabet-Sound Cards: *Aa–Hh*
- Exploring Sounds and Letters, page 112
- Reproducible Masters 26–27
- Activity Sheet 20
- Home/School Connection 15

✳ READING THE BIG BOOK

One Hungry Monster
pages 28–37 of *Pickled Peppers*

Open *Pickled Peppers* to the table of contents. Ask a child to help you find the page number for *One Hungry Monster* and turn to it. Read each page, running your finger under the words as you do. Ask children to identify the rhyming words in each four-line verse.

✳ PHONEMIC AWARENESS

Rhyme

Consonant Riddle Game This activity helps children focus on initial consonants and provides practice in rhyming. Children will do this for several lessons, and they will start rhyming with blends. Write the word *rat* on the board, and then ask:

What rhymes with *rat* but starts with /m/?
What rhymes with *mart* but starts with /p/?
What rhymes with *fan* but starts with /t/?

Continue the activity using the following words:
fast - /l/   late - /d/   lime - /t/   sunk - /d/

✷ Oral Blending

Blending Consonant-Vowel-Consonant Words in Story Contexts
Using single-syllable words, say each sound of the word and have the children blend the sounds and say the word. Placing the activity within a story context will hold the children's attention and show them the purpose of their hard work. Say each sound clearly, pausing between sounds:

Teacher: I see a /m/ /a/ /n/.
         What do I see?
Children: a man!
Teacher: He is in a /v/ /a/ /n/.
         What is he in?
Children: a van!
Teacher: The man is /n/ /e/ /d/.
         Who is the man?
Children: Ned!
Teacher: His van is /r/ /e/ /d/.
         The van is what?
Children: red!

Review of Sounds for Letters *a–h*

Warmup Shuffle the Individual Alphabet-Sound Cards for *Aa–Hh.* Hold up each card, call on individual children to name each picture, and give the sound for the letter. If children remember the poem for the letter's sound, encourage them to say it.

Making Words with *a–h* Lay out the Individual Alphabet-Sound Cards for *Aa–Hh.* Tell children that you want them to help you make words, using the cards. Say the sound /b/. Have a child come and select the *Bb* card and hold it up. Say the sounds /a/ and /g/ and continue in the same manner. When the children holding the cards are lined up in front of the class, have everyone say the word: *bag.* Make other words by combining sounds.
   Try these words:
   bed   cab   bad   fed   dad

Listening for Initial /a/–/h/ Randomly hold up Picture Cards listed below for the sound of letters *a–h.* Ask children to name the picture, and then say the sound of the starting letter. You can have children do this exercise as whole class, in groups (such as everyone wearing red), or as individuals. Use a subset of the Picture Cards for *a–h*: *alligator, apple, astronaut, bat, beans, bed, bee, bow, bowl, can, cap, cat, coat, cook, core, corn, cup, deer, dish, dog, dollar, door, duck, eagle, easel, eel, elephant, elk, envelope, feet, fern, fish, fork, four, fur, gate, glue, goat, guitar, hat, hen, hive, hook, horse, house*

Catching the Letter Train Play the Catching the Letter Train game. This time, tell the children that a ticket can be any word starting with /a/ through /h/. Explain that when someone says a word such as *bat*, then the train goes /b/ /b/ /b/ /b/ /b/ until someone else says a word. Then the train will mimic the beginning sound of the new word.

Linking the Sound to the Letter

Making New Words Put the Pocket Chart Letter Cards *l, p, b, n,* on a low table near the Pocket Chart. Place the letters *et* in the Pocket Chart and say /e/ /t/. Ask the children if anyone knows how to change *et* into *let*. Say, "If we want to change this into /l/ /e/ /t/, we have to put the /l/ sound at the beginning. What letter do we need?" Ask a child to choose the correct letter from the cards on the table and place it in the chart to make the word *let*. Ask other children to make the following changes:

let > pet > bet > net

❯ **Exploring Sounds and Letters** Have the children open Exploring Sounds and Letters to page 112. Tell them that they get to choose what to write on this page. Have them look at the border of letters and choose the letters they would most like to write. These may be the letters they feel they can write the best, or perhaps the letters they think they need to practice. They might even be letters that the children think are fun to look at or fun to write. Have the children share with one another why they chose the letters they did.

✳ WORKSHOP

- Identify for the children the pictures on **Activity Sheet 20** before they begin independent work: *ball, fox, seal, bee, hat, pail.* Tell the children to look at each picture, think about the beginning sound, and then circle the word that names the picture.
- Encourage the children to continue the **A–Z Celebration of Me** by adding details to their self-portraits.

Home/School Connection Give the children Home/School Connection 15 to take home, along with their First-Step Stories 4 and 5.

Exploring Sounds and Letters, page 112

LESSON 92

● ● ● Lesson Overview

Materials

- *One Hungry Monster*, pages 28–37 of *Pickled Peppers*
- Pocket Chart Letter Cards: *c, p (2), n, f, b, u, p*
- Picture Cards: *apple juice, bowls of spaghetti, bread, eggplants, ice, ice cream, inch, infant, insect, iron, jam, jar, jeans, jellyfish, judge, juice, kangaroo, keys, kitchen, kite, kittens, koala, ladybug, lamp, lion, lock, lockers, meat, milk, mittens, monkey, moon, mouse, nails, needle, nest, newspaper, nine, noodle, oatmeal, ocean, octopus, otter, overalls, ox, peanut butter, pickled pears, pizza pies, pumpkins, turkeys, watermelons*
- Individual Alphabet-Sound Cards
- Exploring Sounds and Letters, page 112
- Reproducible Masters 22–25
- Activity Sheet 21

Prepare Ahead

- Make a copy of Reproducible Masters 22 through 25 for each child. Cut out the monsters and food pictures and place them in separate envelopes for each child. Children will use these pictures throughout the next four lessons.
- 4 sheets of colored construction paper for each child, glue

---

✳ READING THE BIG BOOK

One Hungry Monster
pages 28–37 of *Pickled Peppers*

- Open *Pickled Peppers* to *One Hungry Monster*. Point to and say the title and the names of the author and illustrator.

- Read the poem through again. When you read, pause and let the children shout out the rhymes: "Nine hungry monsters wearing roller skates, hunting through the kitchen for knives and forks and _____."
- When you get to the verse where the monsters are being fed, ask the children to look at the pictures and point out and count the different foods mentioned. Ask, "Are all the foods there?"
- Display the food Picture Cards and ask ten different children to come forward and choose a card. Then, going from child to child, ask each for the letter that makes the beginning sound for the following cards: 1, *juice;* 2, *bread;* 3, *bowls of spaghetti;* 4, *eggplants;* 5, *pickled pears;* 6, *pumpkins;* 7, *turkeys;* 8, *pizza pies;* 9, *watermelons;* and 10, *peanut butter.*

✱ PHONEMIC AWARENESS

Rhymes

Consonant Riddle Game This activity will help children focus on initial consonants and provide practice in rhyming. Write *lit* on the board and then ask:

What rhymes with *lit* but starts with /h/?
What rhymes with *rat* but starts with /p/?
What rhymes with *ray* but starts with /d/?

Continue using the following words:
man - /f/
lap - /t/
bite - /k/
tick - /p/

✱ Oral Blending

Blending Consonant-Vowel Consonant Words in Story Contexts
Say single-syllable words sound by sound and have the children blend them. Say each sound clearly, pausing between sounds:

Teacher: Pat has a /r/ /a/ /t/.
Pat has a what?
Class: a rat!
Teacher: She carries it in a /h/ /a/ /t/!
What does she carry it in?
Class: a hat!
Teacher: Imagine that!
Pat has a /f/ /o/ /ks/.
Pat has a what?
Class: a fox!
Teacher: She carries it in a /b/ /o/ /ks/!
What does she carry it in?
Class: a box!
Teacher: Oh, my gosh!

Review of Sounds for the Letters *i–o*

Warmup Shuffle the Individual Alphabet-Sound Cards for letters *i–o*. Hold up each card and call on individual children to name the picture and give the sound. After each letter, recite the sound poem for the letter with the children.

Blending Words with Long and Short *i* As in earlier lessons, make a few words by combining sounds. Have individual children select and hold up the appropriate Individual Alphabet-Sound Cards and blend the letters together. Start with:

/k/ /i/ /k/ – kick

Follow with:

/m/ /ī/ /k/ – Mike

/k/ /i/ /m/ – Kim

/n/ /i/ /k/ – Nick

Listening for Initial Sounds Using the picture cards listed below, randomly hold up Picture Cards for the letters and sounds *i–o*. Ask children to say what is in each picture and then to say the sound of its first letter. Have the children do this exercise as a whole class, in groups (for example, everyone wearing green), or as individuals. Picture Cards: *ice, ice cream, inch, infant, insect, iron, jam, jar, jeans, jellyfish, judge, juice, kangaroo, keys, kitchen, kite, kittens, koala, ladybug, lamp, lion, lock, lockers, meat, milk, mittens, monkey, moon, mouse, nails, needle, nest, newspaper, nine, noodle, oatmeal, ocean, octopus, otter, overalls, ox.*

Linking the Sound to the Letter

Making New Words Put the Pocket Chart Letter Cards *c, p, n, f,* and *b* on a low table near the Pocket Chart . Put the letters *up* on the board and say /u/ /p/. Ask the children to change *up* into *cup*. Ask, "What letter do we need?" Ask a child to choose the correct letter from those on the table and place it in the chart to make the word *cup*. Ask other children to make the following changes:

cup > pup > pun > bun > fun

❯ **Exploring Sounds and Letters** Have the children open Exploring Sounds and Letters to page 112. If the children have not finished writing their letters, have them do so now.

Name

Lesson 91–92

A a b c d e f g h i j k l m
n
o
p
q
r
s
t
u
v
w
x
y
z
O P Q R S T U V W X Y Z

Writing Letters
112   Exploring Sounds and Letters

Exploring Sounds and Letters, page 112

Copyright ©1995 Open Court Publishing Company

✳ WORKSHOP

- Give each child four pieces of construction paper and an envelope with pictures of monsters and food from **Reproducible Masters 22–25** that you prepared ahead. Tell the children that over the next four lessons, they will be making **Letter Monster Posters**. Explain that first they should label the envelopes with their names. Instruct them to glue a monster picture to each piece of construction paper, then sort through the food pictures and glue each food picture to the correct monster poster. Explain that the *T* monster will eat only foods starting with /t/, the *C* monster only eats foods starting with /k/, and so on.
- Name the pictures on **Activity Sheet** 21 before the children go on to independent work: *bell, bat, bag, bus, bud.* Tell the children to cut out the words and paste each one next to the picture it names.

LESSON 93

Lesson Overview

Materials

- *One Hungry Monster*, pages 28–37 of *Pickled Peppers*
- Picture Cards: *apple juice, bowls of spaghetti, bread, eggplants, pail, peanut butter, peas, pickled pears, pie, pig, pizza pies, post, pot, potatoes, pumpkins, quail, queen, quilt, raccoon, radio, red, rice, rock, rug, ruler, sandals, seal, sack, six, seven, sock, sun, table, tail, telephone, tie, toast, turkeys, turtle, ukulele, umbrella, umpire, unicorn, uniform, usher, van, vase, vegetables, vine, violin, volcano, wagon, wallet, walrus, watermelons, wig, wing, yard, yarn, yellow, yolk, yo-yo, zebra, zero, zoo*
- Individual Alphabet-Sound Cards: *Pp–Zz*
- Pocket Chart Letter Cards: *i, c, k, s, t, l, p, w*
- Activity Sheet 22

✻ READING THE BIG BOOK

One Hungry Monster
pages 28–37 of *Pickled Peppers*

Read through the story once more, emphasizing the rhyming words. As you read the section in which the monsters get fed, pause at each food mentioned and hold up the appropriate Picture Card to cue the children. Go over the section again, this time pausing to let the children shout out the rhymes.

TIP FOR ENGLISH LANGUAGE LEARNERS

To help English Language Learners remember the sequence in the story, write the numerals on self-sticking notes and place them on the story next to the word for each number. Then make simple drawings of objects named on each page on self-sticking notes and place them by the appropriate words in the story. Point to each self-sticking note and say aloud the word as English Language Learners repeat it. Repeat this until they feel comfortable with the story. These visual reminders will help children remember the story.

Rhyme

Consonant Riddle Game In this activity, the rhymes for the cue words now contain consonant blends. Write the words on the board then ask:

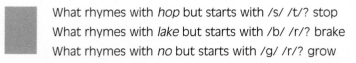

What rhymes with *hop* but starts with /s/ /t/? stop
What rhymes with *lake* but starts with /b/ /r/? brake
What rhymes with *no* but starts with /g/ /r/? grow

Continue using the following words:
gave - /b/ /r/-brave
cap - /t/ /r/-trap
hip - /s/ /k/-skip

✳ Oral Blending

Blending Words in Story Contexts Continue blending orally. Work with easy-to-pronounce, single-syllable words with consonant blends.

Give each individual sound, pausing between each:

Teacher: Down by the seashore,
             Mara found a /b/ /ō/ /t/.
             What did she find?

Children: a boat!

Teacher: But when she tried to sail it,
             it just wouldn't /f/ /l/ /ō/ /t/.
             It wouldn't what?

Children: float!

Teacher: Down by the seashore,
             Mara found a /k/ /ī/ /t/.
             What did she find?

Children: a kite!

Teacher: But when she tried to fly it,
             it wouldn't take /f/ /l/ /ī/ /t/.
             It wouldn't take what?

Children: flight!

Teacher: Down by the seashore,
             Mara met /s/ /a/ /m/.
             Whom did she meet?

Children: Sam!

Teacher: But when she tried to talk to him,
             he was quiet as a /k/ /l/ /a/ /m/.
             Quiet as what?

Children: a clam!

LETTER NAMES, SHAPES, AND SOUNDS

Review of Sounds for the Letters *p–z*

Warmup Shuffle Individual Alphabet-Sound Cards for letters *p–z*. Hold up each card and call on individual children to name the picture, and give its starting sound. Review the sound poem for each letter with the children.

Blending Words Make a few words by combining sounds. Have individual children hold Individual Alphabet-Sound Cards for each sound in a word and let everyone blend the sound. For ease in making words, include short *a* in your card set.

Use the following words:

rut	/r/ /u/ /t/	rat	/r/ /a/ /t/
sat	/s/ /a/ /t/	tuck	/t/ /u/ /k/

Listening for Initial /p/–/z/ Sounds In this activity use the Picture Cards listed below for the letters and sounds *p–z* with the exception of *x*. Hold up each card and ask individual children to name the picture, say the beginning sound, and tell which letter makes the sound. Picture Cards: *pail, peas, pie, pig, post, pot, potatoes, quail, queen, quilt, raccoon, radio, red, rice, rock, rug, ruler, sandals, seal, sack, six, seven, sock, sun, table, tail, telephone, tie, toast, turtle, ukulele, umbrella, umpire, unicorn, uniform, usher, van, vase, vegetables, vine, violin, volcano, wagon, wallet, walrus, watermelons, wig, wing, yard, yarn, yellow, yolk, yo-yo, zebra, zero, zoo.*

Catching the Letter Train Play the Catching the Letter Train game. Tell the children that this time, a ticket is any word starting with the sounds of letters *p–z*. Explain that when someone says a word such as *pepper,* the train goes /p/ /p/ /p/ /p/ /p/ until someone else says a different word. The train then makes the beginning sound of the new word.

Linking the Sound to the Letter

Grab Bag of Letters and Words Put the letters *ick* in the Pocket Chart and say /i/ /k/, *ick*. Have in a bag, Letter Cards for *s, t, l, p, w*. Add *s* to the beginning, making *sick*. Then have a child replace the *s* with one of the remaining letters. Continue until the children have made *tick, lick, pick,* and *wick.*

✳ WORKSHOP

- Tell the children to continue making their **Letter Monster Posters**.
- Name each picture on **Activity Sheet 22** before the children go on to independent work: *tiger, zebra, hippo, lion.* Tell the children to say the name of each animal, listen for the beginning sound, and then write in the beginning letter to complete the animal's name.

LESSON
94

●●● Lesson Overview

Materials

- *One Hungry Monster*, pages 28–37 of *Pickled Peppers*
- Picture Cards: *apple juice, bowls of spaghetti, bread, eggplants, peanut butter, pickled pears, pizza pies, pumpkins, turkeys, watermelons*
- Pocket Chart Letter Cards: *c*(2), *o, k, s, l, d, r*
- Activity Sheet 23

✱ READING THE BIG BOOK

One Hungry Monster
pages 28–37 of *Pickled Peppers*

- Read through the story again. By now, probably all you need to do is point to *One, Two,* or *Three,* and the children will shout *hungry monsters,* and finish the line for you.
- After reading, ask the children to help you order the food Picture Cards from one to ten. Lay them all out on a low table and ask for a volunteer to choose the card that shows a picture of one item. Have the children count the items together to make sure you are progressing from one to ten.
- Children especially love this poem because the monsters are so ill-mannered. Use this opportunity to talk with the children about how they are expected to behave at home. Ask them what kinds of things they are not allowed to do.

✱ PHONEMIC AWARENESS

Rhyme
Consonant Riddle Game In this activity, children focus on initial consonants and practice blending sounds.

Write *hive* on the board and ask: "What rhymes with *hive* but starts with /d/ /r/? *drive.*" Have the children repeat the word, then say, "What rhymes with *part* but starts with /s/ /m/? *smart.* What rhymes with *town* but starts with /k/ /r/? *crown.*"

Continue, using the following words:

lass - /g/ /r/ - grass
date - /p/ /l/ - plate
time - /s/ /l/ - slime

✻ Oral Blending

Blending Words in Story Contexts Continue blending orally, giving the children a very simple story context. Work with easy-to-pronounce, single-syllable words that contain short vowels.

Say each sound clearly, pausing between sounds:

Teacher: Look at /s/ /a/ /m/.
    Whom should we look at?
Children: Sam!
Teacher: He is eating a /y/ /a/ /m/.
    A what?
Children: a yam!
Teacher: Look at Sam.
    He is eating a /k/ /l/ /a/ /m/.
    A what?
Children: a clam!
Teacher: Look at Sam.
    He is eating a clam with /j/ /a/ /m/!
    A clam with what?
Children: jam!
Teacher: I'm surprised at Sam.
    I sure am!

LETTER NAMES, SHAPES, AND SOUNDS

The Ship is Loaded with _____ Because children have played this game several times, they are probably ready for a more difficult version. Roll the ball to a child in the circle and say, "The ship is loaded with _____ ," for instance, *clams.* Tell the children to say either a word with the beginning sound /k/ or a word that rhymes with *clams,* for example, "The ship is loaded with hams," as they roll the ball to a classmate. This child must then say a word that begins with /h/ or a word that rhymes with *hams.*

Linking the Sound to the Letter

Grab Bag of Letters Put the Pocket Chart Letter Cards *ock* in the Pocket Chart and say /o/ /k/. Have the cards *s, l, d, r, c* nearby. Choose the letter *l* and add it to the beginning, making *lock* . Then replace the *l* with *s* for *sock.* Then make *dock, rock,* and back to *lock.* Now add *c* to *lock* for *clock.*

- Encourage children to continue to work on their **Letter Monster Posters**. Suggest that they may want to add more foods by drawing their own pictures or by cutting pictures from magazines.
- Name each picture on **Activity Sheet 23** before the children go on to independent work: *elephant, alligator, ape, eagle.* Tell the children to say the name of each animal, listen for the beginning sound, and then write the beginning letter to complete each animal's name.

TIP FOR ENGLISH LANGUAGE LEARNERS

Encourage English Language Learners to share foods they enjoy. The sharing of personal experiences and different cultural heritages will show children the importance of their contributions to classroom discussions and help all children to learn more about the world.

LESSON

95

●●● Lesson Overview

Materials

- *One Hungry Monster*, pages 28–37 of *Pickled Peppers*
- Pocket Chart Letter Cards: *a, k, e, m, l, t, b, r*
- Uppercase and Lowercase Letter Cards: *Aa–Zz*
- Activity Sheet 24

✳ READING THE BIG BOOK

One Hungry Monster
pages 28–37 of *Pickled Peppers*

- Read through the story again, encouraging children to say the rhyming words with you.
- Write the numbers 1 to 10 on the board. Tell children that you want them to think of a new list of foods to feed these very hungry monsters. Start with 1 and go to 10, allowing different children to contribute their ideas. If they have difficulty, suggest foods such as pancakes, broccoli, or tacos. Ask the children to help you write the words on the board by naming letters for initial sounds.

✳ PHONEMIC AWARENESS

Rhyme

Consonant Riddle Game In this activity, children focus on initial consonants and practice blending sounds.

Write the word *pick* on the board and say:

"What rhymes with *pick* but starts with /s/ /t/? *stick*."

Continue, using the following words:

tap - /k/ /l/ - clap	pick - /t/ /r/ - trick
port - /s/ /p/ - sport	lip - /k/ /l/ - clip

✱ Oral Blending

Blending Words in Story Contexts Continue blending orally, as in previous lessons. As the children say the blended word, write it on the chalkboard.

Teacher: Matty's mother shook her head.
She said, "I can't even see the /b/ /e/ /d/."

Class: bed!

Teacher: With a frown on her face
she said, "Look at this /p/ /l/ /ā/ /s/."

Class: place!

Teacher: Well, Matty did not make another /p/ /ē/ /p/.

Class: peep!

Teacher: Instead, he just started to /s/ /w/ /ē/ /p/.

Class: sweep!

Teacher: After a while his room was /k/ /l/ /ē/ /n/.

Class: clean!

Teacher: The cleanest he'd ever /s/ /ē/ /n/.

Class: seen!

Teacher: When Matty's mother looked in,
she couldn't believe her eyes.
Every toy was put /b/ /a/ /k/.

Class: back!

Teacher: Even socks were in a neat /s/ /t/ /a/ /k /!

Class: stack!

Teacher: "Why, Matty, your room is so /n/ /ē/ /t/!"

Class: neat!

Teacher: "You deserve a special /t/ /r/ /ē/ /t/!"

Class: treat!

Teacher: So she gave him a great big hug!

LETTER NAMES, SHAPES, AND SOUNDS

Sounds

Silly Sentences Game Have the children create some silly sentences all about monsters using words that begin with /m/. An example would be, "Marty the monster munches mashed macaroni." Encourage the children to think of words beginning with /m/ and to make the sentences longer and longer.

Linking the Sound to the Letter

Object Matching Give each of the children an Uppercase and Lowercase Letter Card. Tell them to find something in the room, other than the Alphabet Cards, that begins with their letter's sound or that has the letter written on it as part of a word. Then have each child announce what letter he or she has and name and point to the matching object.

Grab Bag of Letters Put the Pocket Chart Letter Cards *a k e* on the Pocket Chart and say /ā/ /k/. In a bag nearby, have cards for *m, l, t, b, r.* Add a letter *m* to the Pocket Chart, making *make.* Then replace the *m* with an *l* for *lake.* Then have individual children pull letters from the bag to make *take, bake,* and *rake.*

✳ WORKSHOP

- Tell the children to complete their **Letter Monster Posters** today.
- Name all of the pictures on **Activity Sheet 24** before the children go on to independent work. Explain that each flower shows pictures whose names begin with one sound. The children should say the name of each picture and listen for its beginning sound. They will then cut out the letters at the bottom of the page and paste each letter on the correct flower.
- Have other activities available for children during Workshop such as **Game Corner, Creating Letters, Letter Books, Writing Folders,** and activities to reinforce letter recognition and sounds.

LESSON
96

●●●● Lesson Overview

New Learning

- Blending

Materials

- *One Hungry Monster,* pages 28–37 of *Pickled Peppers*
- Pocket Chart Letter Cards: *e* (2), *d, s, f, r, n*
- Picture Cards: *apple juice, bowls of spaghetti, bread, eggplants, pickled pears, pumpkins, turkeys, pizza pies, watermelons, peanut butter*
- Word Cards: *Pat, Sam, Dad, Peter, and, has, a, the, is*
- For each child, one Uppercase and Lowercase Letter Card
- Activity Sheet 25

✳ READING THE BIG BOOK

One Hungry Monster
pages 28–37 of *Pickled Peppers*

- Read through the story one last time, enjoying the illustrations and rhymes.
- Ask if there are any volunteers who would like to read along with you.
- Place the food Picture Cards on a low table, along with the Word Cards for *Pat, Sam, Dad, Peter, and, has, a,* and *the.* Ask the children to arrange the cards in the Pocket Chart to create different sentences: *Dad has the (2 loaves of bread); Sam has a (jug of apple juice),* and so on.

LETTER NAMES, SHAPES, AND SOUNDS

Sounds

Silly Sentences Game Help the children make silly sentences about some type of monster, for instance, a dragon. Choose words with the beginning sound of the name of the new monster.

Linking the Sound to the Letter

Object Matching Give every child an Uppercase and Lowercase Letter Card. Tell the children to look around the room and find something (other than the Alphabet Cards) that begins with the letter's sound or that has the letter written on it as part of a word. Then have each child tell the class what letter he or she has and name and point to the matching object.

Grab Bag of Letters Put the Pocket Chart Letter Cards *eed* in the Pocket Chart and say /ē/ /d/. Have cards for *s, f, n, r* nearby. Place the letter *s* in front of the letters on the chart, making *seed.* Replace the *s* with an *f* for *feed.*

Then make *reed* and *need.* Leave the word *need* in the Pocket Chart. Have the children say each word after you make it.

PHONICS

Blending

Identifying the sounds of letters to decode written words is fundamental to learning to read. The activities in **Oral Blending, Segmentation,** and **Linking the Sound to the Letter** have been leading children to this skill. The children will be learning blending in the *Phonics* sections of the next several lessons, but it will be different from the oral blending they have been practicing in previous lessons. In **Phonics,** the children use the written letter rather than the sounds given by the teacher as a guide to blending. Whereas in previous activities **you** linked sounds to written letters, from this lesson on, you will ask the children to do that linking on their own.

- Write the letter *a* on the chalkboard. Touch the letter and say /a/. Have children say the sound with you.
- Write the letter *t* on the chalkboard after the *a,* making *at.* Touch the *t* and say /t/. Have the children say it with you.
- Next, tell the children you will blend the sounds together to make a word. Move your hand under the letters and pronounce each sound slowly and smoothly, without stopping between sounds.

- Repeat this procedure, asking the children to say the sounds as you indicate them. Ask whether anyone can tell what the word is. Confirm the children's response by pronouncing the word *at* naturally.
- Continue with this procedure and make the word *hat*.
- Go to the Pocket Chart and point to the word *need*. Ask children if they remember what the word is. Use the word to write a sentence on the chalkboard:

    I need a hat.

    Ask children if they can say what you wrote.
- If the children are ready, challenge them to change the sentence to:

    I need a (bat, rat, mat, fat bat, fat rat).

✳ WORKSHOP

Identify for the children each picture on **Activity Sheet** 25 before they go on to independent work: *cat, can, cup, cut, ham, hug.* Instruct the children to write the letter whose sound they hear at the end of each picture name.

LESSON 97

●●● Lesson Overview

Materials

- First-Step Story 6
- Pocket Chart Letter Cards: *i, k, e, s, h, b, l*
- Activity Sheet 26

✳ USING FIRST-STEP STORIES

First-Step Story 6

- Give each child a copy of First-Step Story 6, which depicts the events of a birthday party. Have the children browse through the book page by page. When everyone has been through the book, ask them what they think the story is about.
- After they have identified that the general theme of the book is a birthday party, take a closer look at each page. Ask them to look at the first page—how does this scene compare to the scene on the last page?
- Ask individual children to describe what they think is happening or what is pictured on each page. Print their ideas on chart paper. Allow as many children as possible to contribute. Encourage children to use these ideas to think about a story that they would like to write.

> **TIP FOR ENGLISH LANGUAGE LEARNERS**
>
> Provide an opportunity for English Language Learners to practice using creative language in conversation. Pair English Language Learners with native English-speaking children. Have the children share their own birthday party experiences. Exchanging information reinforces what children are learning and helps to validate their ideas.

LETTER NAMES, SHAPES, AND SOUNDS

Sounds

The Ship is Loaded with _____ Game Play the more advanced version of the Ship is Loaded with _____ game, as described in Lesson 94, in which the children listen for either the beginning sound of a word or a rhyming word.

Linking the Sound to the Letter

Grab Bag of Letters   In this activity, you will place four letters in the Pocket Chart.

- Put the Pocket Chart Letter Cards *ikes* in the Pocket Chart and say /ī/ /k/ /s/. Have the Pocket Chart Letter Cards *h, b, l* nearby.
- Add *h* to the beginning, making *hikes.* Ask the children to say the word. Then replace the *h* with a *b,* making *bikes.* Then make *likes.* Leave the word *likes* in the Pocket Chart.

PHONICS

Blending

In these activities, you will ask the children to link sounds to written letters.

- Write the letter *a* on the chalkboard. Touch the letter and say /a/. Have the children say the sound with you.
- Write the letter *p* on the chalkboard after the *a,* making *ap.* Touch the *p* and say /p/. Have the children say the sound with you.
- Next, tell the children you will blend the sounds together. Move your hand under the letters and pronounce each sound slowly and smoothly, without stopping between sounds.
- Repeat this procedure, asking the children to say the sounds as you indicate them. Then add a *t* to the beginning of *ap.* Continue with the same procedure. Ask whether anyone can tell what the word is. Confirm the children's response by pronouncing the word *tap* naturally.
- Then change *tap* and make the word *nap.*
- Go to the Pocket Chart and point to the word *likes.* Ask children whether they remember what the word is. Write a sentence on the chalkboard using the word *likes:*

  > He likes to nap.

  Ask children if they can say what you wrote.
- If the children are ready, challenge them to change the sentence to:

  > He likes to (rap, tap, snap).
- Change the sentence to:

  > He likes the hat.

  Ask children if they can say what you wrote.

✳ WORKSHOP

- Tell the children that they can "write" the first two pages of **First-Step Story 6.** Encourage them to do as much as they can—they may want to label things in the scene or write a sentence about what is happening. Tell them to begin by labeling the books with their names.
- Name each picture on **Activity Sheet 26** before the children go on to independent work: *mat, cup, rug, hat, bat, bug.* Explain to the children that they should listen carefully for the vowel sound in the word and then write the letter that stands for that vowel sound.

LESSON
98

●●● Lesson Overview

Materials

- **First-Step Story** 6
- Activity Sheet 27

✳ **USING FIRST-STEP STORIES**

First-Step Story 6

- Tell the children to take out their First-Step Stories and turn to the second page. Ask, "How many bowls do you see?" Have them turn to the third page, then ask, "How many cooks are there?" For the fourth page, ask for the number of cakes, and for the fifth page, "How many candles are there? How many roses are there? How old will the birthday boy or girl be?" Have them look at the sixth page for the number of hats and the number of horns. Ask, "How many children do you think will be at the party?"

- Write the word *party* on the chalkboard and say it. Ask the children to look on the first page of their First-Step Stories and see what things on the page start with /b/: *balloon, box, bowl.* Ask what things they can find that start with /k/: *cat, cup*; that start with /h/: *hat, horn.* Ask what they can find that starts with /t/: *tape, table.* Write the words on the chalkboard under *party* as children say them. Leave the words on the chalkboard and add to them over the next two lessons. Include the word *cake* on the list, because children may want to use this word in their Workshop writing.

The Ship is Loaded with_____ Game Play the more advanced version of The Ship is Loaded with_____ game in which the children listen for the beginning sound of a word or for a rhyming word.

PHONICS

Blending

In this activity, the children will link sounds to letters.

- Write the capital letter *E* on the chalkboard. Touch the letter and say /e/. Have the children say the sound with you.
- Write the letter *d* on the chalkboard after the *e,* making *Ed.* Touch the *d* and say the sound /d/. Have the children say the sound with you.
- Tell the children you will blend the sounds together to make a word. Move your hand under the letters and pronounce each sound slowly and smoothly, without stopping between sounds.
- Repeat this procedure with the children. Ask if anyone can tell what the word is. Confirm the children's response by pronouncing the name *Ed* naturally.
- Continue with the same procedure and make the word *led.*
- Use the word in a sentence:

  I led Ed.

  Challenge the children by writing sentences such as:

  I led Ed (Ted, Ned, Fred).

  I led a sled (red sled).

  Ask the children if they can say what you wrote.

✳ WORKSHOP

- Tell the children that they can "write" the third and fourth pages of their **First-Step Story 6**. Encourage them to be creative. Suggest that they give names to the children or draw or write something to help describe the cake.
- Identify each picture on **Activity Sheet 27** before the children go on to independent work: *raccoon, seal, queen, turtle.* Explain to the children that they should say each picture name and listen for its beginning sound. Then they will cut out the letters at the bottom of the page and paste each letter with the correct picture.

LESSON
99

●●● Lesson Overview

Materials

- **First-Step Story** 6
- Pocket Chart Letter Cards: *a, c, e, k, n, o, p, t*
- Picture Cards: *beans, bread, fish, pie, pizza pies,*
- Word Cards: *I, bake, a, the*
- For each child, one Uppercase and Lowercase Letter Card: *Aa–Mm*
- Activity Sheet 28

✳ USING FIRST-STEP STORIES

First-Step Story 6

- Ask for volunteers to share some of their writing from their First-Step Story.
- Have the children open their books to page 3, to the two children about to bake a cake. Tell the children that you will create some sentences about baking.
- Place the Picture Cards for *pie, fish, pizza, beans, bread* on a low table.
- Tell the children that you are going to make some sentences in the Pocket Chart. Place the Word Card for *I* in the chart and say the word. Tell the children that this word says its name and so it is easy to remember. Use the word in a few sentences. Now place the word *bake* in the Pocket Chart and say the word. Tell children that the *e* is a silent helper, helping *a* to say its name. Place the word *a* and say it, telling the children that it says its name.
- Say, *I bake a pie.* Ask a child to place the Picture Card for *pie* in the Pocket Chart and then read the complete sentence, pointing to each word as you say it.
- Replace the word *pie* with *bread.* Ask the children, "If I want to say 'I bake bread,' what word should I take out of the sentence?" Let a

child remove the *a*. Then replace the card for *bread* with the one for *pizza* and read the sentence through.

Catching the Letter Train Review the letter sounds for *a–m*. This time give everyone an Uppercase and Lowercase Letter Card *Aa–Mm* as they board the train. Explain that as they get their card, they must say the sound of the letter. Then lead them around the room to different points. Tell the children to listen for the first sound of the towns that you call out. For example, if you announce, "Now approaching Mudville," anyone holding the *Mm* card must leave the train. Continue moving around the room, until all children have left the train.

Blending

In this activity, ask the children to link sounds to letters on their own.

- Write the letter *a* on the chalkboard. Touch the letter and say /a/. Have the children say the sound with you.
- Write the letter *m* on the chalkboard after the *a* making *am.* Touch the *m* and say /m/. Have the children say the sound with you.
- Tell the children you will blend the sounds together to make a word. Move your hand under the letters and pronounce each sound slowly and smoothly, without stopping between sounds.
- Repeat this procedure with the children. Ask whether anyone can say the word. Confirm the children's response by pronouncing the word *am* naturally.
- Continue with the same procedure and make the word *ram,* then *jam,* then *ham.*
- Write a sentence:

    I am a ham.

    Ask the children if they can say what you wrote.
- Change the sentences to:

    I am (a ram, jam, a clam, Sam, Pam).

    With each change, ask the children if they can say what you wrote.

- Tell the children that they can write on pages 5 and 6 of **First-Step Story 6.** Have them share their stories with a partner.
- Name the pictures on **Activity Sheet 28** before the children begin independent work. Tell the children to cut out the letters on the side of the page. They should say each picture name and listen for its ending sound. Then, next to each picture, they should paste the letter that stands for the ending sound.

TIP FOR ENGLISH LANGUAGE LEARNERS

Provide English Language Learners with additional practice identifying words that begin with the letters a–m. Hold up classroom objects whose names begin with these letters and have children take turns identifying the initial sound in each object's name.

MONITORING TIP Observe the children working on their First-Step Stories and write your observations on the Monitor Log, **Reproducible Masters 26–27.**

LESSON 100

●●● Lesson Overview

Materials

- First-Step Story 6
- Pocket Chart Letter Cards: *w, i, p, e, f*
- Picture Cards: *bowl, dish, kitchen, spoon*
- Word Cards: *I, the*
- For each child, one Uppercase and Lowercase Letter Card: *Nn–Zz*
- Activity Sheet 29

✳ USING FIRST-STEP STORIES

First-Step Story 6

- Have the children look at page 8 of First-Step Story 6. Point out that there is a big mess to clean up. Tell the children that you are going to make some sentences about cleaning up.
- Place the Picture Cards for *kitchen, dish, spoon,* and *bowl* on a table.
- Place the word *I* in the Pocket Chart and tell the children that this word says its name. Place the Pocket Chart Letter Cards to form the word *wipe* in the Pocket Chart and say the word. Then add the Word Card *the* and say the word.
- Say, *I wipe the dish.* Ask a child to place the Picture Card for *dish* in the Pocket Chart and then to read the complete sentence, pointing to each word as it is said. Ask another child to replace *dish* with *spoon* in the chart and to read the sentence in the same way.
- Call on another child to replace *spoon* with *bowl,* and *bowl* with *kitchen.* Ask the child to read each new sentence, pointing to each word.

LETTER NAMES, SHAPES, AND SOUNDS

Catching the Letter Train Have everyone sit in a circle and give them tickets to get on the train: Uppercase and Lowercase Letter Cards *Nn–Zz* (do not use *Xx*). Tell the children that they must create a word starting with the sound of their letter to board the train. Walk around the circle and ask for a ticket. When the child gives a word, he or she can get on the train. The train says that letter sound until the next child says a word.

Grab Bag of Letters Put the Pocket Chart Letter Cards *eed* in the Pocket Chart and say /ē/ /d/. Then add *f*, making *feed*. Replace *f* with *w* to make *weed*. Leave *weed* in the Pocket Chart.

PHONICS

Blending

In this activity, ask the children to link sounds to letters on their own.

- Write the letter *a* on the chalkboard. Touch the letter and say the sound /a/. Have children say the sound with you.
- Write the letter *n* on the chalkboard after the *a*, making *an*. Touch the *n* and say the sound /n/. Have the children say the sound with you.
- Tell the children you will blend the sounds together. Move your hand under the letters and pronounce each sound slowly and smoothly, without stopping between sounds.
- Repeat this procedure with the children. Ask whether anyone can say the word. Confirm the children's response by pronouncing the word *an* naturally.
- Continue with the same procedure and make the word *man*, then *tan*, *fan*, and *can*.
- Write a sentence:

    The man had a tan.

  Ask children if they can say what you wrote.
- Change the sentences to:

    The man had a (*fan, plan, pan, can*) or The man can (*fan, tan, plan*).

  Ask children if they can say what you wrote.
- Point to the word *weed* in the Pocket Chart. Ask the children whether they remember the word. Write the sentence on the chalkboard:

    I see a weed.

  Ask the children if they can say what you wrote.

  Tell everyone that they have done an excellent job. Applaud for them and then have them applaud and give a cheer for themselves.

✳ WORKSHOP

- Identify for the children the pictures on **Activity Sheet** 29 before they go on to independent work. Say each word sound by sound, for example, /k/ /u/ /p/. Tell the children to do the same and then write the word under each picture (cup, cap, cat, cot, pen, pan).
- Have the children write on the last two pages of First-Step Story 6.
- Again, congratulate them for doing good work and let them celebrate by sharing their writing with their classmates.

Appendix 1   Introduction of Letters and Sounds

	Introduction to Letter	Introduction to Written Letter	Introduction to Sound
A -long	1, 3	5	16
-short			45
B	1, 3	6	52
C	1, 3	7	54
D	1, 3	8, 37	37
E -long	1, 3	9	17
-short			57
F	1, 3	10	59
G	1, 3	11	61
H	1, 6	12	44
I -long	1, 6	13	18
-short			63
J	1, 6	14	65
K	1, 6	15	66
L	1, 6	16	68
M	1, 6	17, 34	34
N	1, 6	18	71
O -long	1, 10	19	19
-short			48
P	1, 10	20, 40	40
Q	1, 10	21	76
R	1, 10	22	77
S	1, 10	23, 31	31
T	1, 10	24, 42	42
U -long	1, 11	25	20
-short			81
V	1, 11	26	83
W	1, 11	27	85
X	1, 11	28	87
Y	1, 11	29	88
Z	1, 11	30	89

Appendix 2   Word List

The following word list can be used in a number of ways to extend the lessons. Words are listed by beginning sounds, ending sounds, and medial vowel sounds.

*Words represented on Picture Cards   **Words represented in Exploring Sounds and Letters

Beginning Sounds

Beginning /ā/
acorn *
ape
apron *

Beginning /a/
acrobat
alligator *
apple *
apple juice *
astronaut *

Beginning /b/
bag **
bait **
ball **
balloon **
banana **
baseball *
basketball *
bat *
beans *
bed *
bee *
bell **
bird **
boat **
book **
bow *
bowl *
bowling ball *
box *
bread *
broom **

bug **
bus **

Beginning /k/
cake **
can *
cane **
cap *
cat *
clam **
coat *
cook *
core *
cup *
cut **

Beginning /d/
dad **
deer *
dice *
dime
dish *
dog *
doll **
dollar *
donkey **
door *
dress *
drum **
duck *

Beginning /ē/
eagle *
ear
earphones
easel *
eel *

Beginning /e/
eggplant *
elephant *
elk *
envelope *

Beginning /f/
falcon **
fan **
feet *
fern *
fir *
fish *
five *
fly **
food
football *
fork *
four *
fox *
Frisbee *
frog **

Beginning /g/
game *
gate *
glue *
goat *
goose *
grass **
green *
guitar *

Beginning /h/
ham **
hand**
hat *

hawk **
heaven *
hen *
hive *
hog *
hole *
hook *
horse *
hot *
house *
hug **

Beginning /ī/
ice *
ice cream *
icicles *
iron *
island
ivy

Beginning /i/
igloo
ill
inch *
infant *
insect *

Beginning /j/
jam *
jar *
jeans *
jellybean **
jellyfish *
judge *
juice *

Beginning /k/
kangaroo *
kettle **
keys *
kitchen *
kittens *
koala *

Beginning /l/
ladybug *
lake **
lamp *
lion *
lock *
lockers *

Beginning /m/
magnet **
mailbox **
man **
map **
mask **
mat *
meal
meat *
milk *
mittens*
monkey *
moon *
moose
mop **
mouse *
mug **

Beginning /n/
nails *
necklace **

378

needle *
nest *
newspaper *
nickel **
nine *
noodle *
nurse**

Beginning /ō/
oak tree *
oasis
oatmeal *
oboe
ocean *
overalls*

Beginning /o/
octopus *
olive **
ostrich**
otter *
ox *

Beginning /p/
pail*
pan **
panda**
pants *
pear **
peas *
pen **
penny
pickle **
pickled pears *
pie *
pig *
pineapple **
pink *
pizza pies *
plum bun*
popcorn **
post *
pot *
potatoes *

pumpkins *
purple *

Beginning /kw/
quail *
quart
queen *
quill
quilt *

Beginning /r/
raccoon *
racer **
radio *
rake**
rat **
red *
rice *
road **
robot **
rock *
rocket **
rug *
ruler *

Beginning /s/
sack *
sad **
sail**
Sam
sand**
sandals *
seal *
seven *
silk **
six *
skate **
soccer ball *
sock *
spoon*
star **
stew *
sticks *
stir *
store *

storm **
sun *

Beginning /t/
table *
tail *
tap **
tape **
target **
tear **
telephone *
television **
ten *
tie *
toad
toast *
toe **
tomatoes *
top **
tree *
turkey *
turtle *
two *

Beginning /ū/
ukulele *
unicorn *
uniform *
United States
utensil

Beginning /u/
umbrella *
umpire *
uncle
under
usher *

Beginning /v/
van *
vase *
vegetables *
veil **
vine *

violin *
volcano *

Beginning /w/
wagon *
wallet *
walrus *
watch **
well**
wig *
wing *

Beginning /y/
yam *
yard *
yarn *
yell
yellow *
yo-yo *
yolk *

Beginning /z/
zebra *
zero *
zinnia
zither
zoo *

Ending Sounds

Ending /ā/
away
bay
day
gray
hay
Jay
may
Monday
play
ray
say
today

Ending /b/
Bob
cab
cob
cub
cube
jab
job
mob
rob
robe
rub
scrub
tab
tub
tube
web

Ending /d/
bad
bed *
bread *
did
feed
had
lid
mad
mud
red *
rid
sad
seed
weed
yard *

Ending /ē/
bee *
Frisbee *
he
key
knee *
me
monkey *
see
she

three*
tree *
turkey *
we

Ending /f/
calf
cough
cuff
deaf
elf
half
laugh
off
rough
stiff
stuff
tough

Ending /g/
bag**
big
dog *
egg
hog *
hug
jog
ladybug *
leg
log
pig *
rag
rug *
tag
twig
wig *

Ending /ī/
by
cry
die
dry
fly**
high
my

pie *
sigh
tie *
why

Ending /k/
bike
black *
clock *
cook *
dock
duck *
elk *
fork *
hook *
lake
like
lock *
milk *
pack
pink *
poke
rack
rake**
rock *
sock*
take

Ending /l/
basketball*
bell**
bill
eel *
feel
football*
oatmeal *
pail *
quail *
rail
seal *
snail
tail *

Ending /m/
broom**
dime
drum**
game *
hum
jam *
room
seem
uniform *
yam *

Ending /n/
can *
fern *
green *
hen *
kitchen *
lion *
moon *
ocean *
queen *
raccoon *
spoon *
sun *
ten *
unicorn *
van *
vine *
violin *
wagon *
yarn *

Ending /ō/
blow
bow *
doe
flow
go
low
mow
no
radio *
row
slow

so
toe
volcano *
yellow *
yo-yo
zero *

Ending /p/
cap *
cape**
cup *
deep
hip
hop
keep
lip
map *
pup
skip
sleep
tap
tip
top
trap

Ending /r/
alligator *
bar
car
core*
deer *
door *
fur *
four
guitar *
jar *
more
newspaper *
otter *
pour
roar
ruler *
stir *
usher *

Ending /s/
bus**
class
dress
goose *
grass
horse *
house *
miss
moss
mouse *
octopus *
pass
toss
walrus *
yes

Ending /t/
astronaut *
bat *
cat *
coat *
feet *
gate *
goat *
hat *
hot *
infant *
kite *
knot *
meat *
pot *
quilt *
wallet *
white *

Ending /ū/
cue
few
hue
menu
nephew
preview

rescue
review
view

Ending /v/
brave
cave**
dive
dove
eve
five *
gave
give
glove
have
hive *
live
love
save
shave**
stove**

Ending /ks/
ax *
box*
fix
flax
fox *
mix
ox*
relax
six
wax

Ending /z/
breeze
buzz
daze
fizz
freeze
fuzz
haze
jazz
maze
peas

quiz
size
sneeze *
squeeze
trees

Medial Sounds

Medial /ā/
date
face
fade
game *
gate *
gave
lake
lane
late
made
make
mate
race
rake**
table *
wave

Medial /a/
bat *
black *
can *
cap *
hat *
jam *
lamp *
pants *
sad *
van *
yam *

Medial /ē/
beam
bean
feet *

heap
keep
mean
meat *
neat
seal *
seed
seen
sneeze *
team
weed

Medial /e/
bed*
bet
head
hen *
let
men
met
nest *
net
pen
pet
red*
set
ten *

Medial /ī/
five *
hide
hive *
kite *
life
line
mine
nice
nine *
rice*
ride
right
side
sight
time
vine*

Medial /i/
bib
dish *
fib
fin
fish *
him
kittens **
lip
milk *
mittens **
pig *
pin
pink **
rip
tin
tip
wig*
win

Medial /ō/
boat
bowl *
coal
coat *
goat *
hole *
home
joke
mole
nose
poem
poke
post *
roll
rose
toes

Medial /o/
dot
hot *
knot
lock*
lot
mop

not
pot *
rock*
sock *
top

Medial /ū/
cube
cute
feud
fuel
fuse
huge
mule

Medial /u/
bug
bun
cup *
cut*
duck *
dust
fun
hug**
must
nut
rub
rug*
run
sun *
tub
tug

Index